AMONG YOU TAKING NOTES . . .

AMONG YOU TAKING NOTES . . .

The Wartime Diary of Naomi Mitchison

1939–1945

Edited by Dorothy Sheridan

LONDON
VICTOR GOLLANCZ LTD
1985

First published in Great Britain 1985
by Victor Gollancz Ltd,
14 Henrietta Street, London WC2E 8QJ

British Library Cataloguing in Publication Data
Mitchison, Naomi
    Among you taking notes–: the wartime diary
    of Naomi Mitchison 1939–1945.
    1. World War 1939–1945—Social aspects—
    Great Britain   2. Great Britain—Social life
    and customs—20th century
    I. Title   II. Sheridan, Dorothy
    941.084'.092'4   DA566.4

ISBN 0-575-03561-7

Photoset in Great Britain by
Rowland Phototypesetting Ltd, Bury St Edmunds, Suffolk
and printed by St Edmundsbury Press
Bury St Edmunds, Suffolk

"A chield's amang ye takin' notes
And faith he'll prent it"

> Robert Burns
> *On the late Captain Grose's Peregrinations*
> *Thro' Scotland*
> 1793

CONTENTS

ILLUSTRATIONS

FOREWORD

by Naomi Mitchison

THIS DIARY, WHICH I wrote for Mass-Observation, runs to a million words: who is going to read all that? Not me. So it was up to Mass-Observation who held the copy to try to make of it a picture of how one family and friends lived during this period of history, what changes they hoped for, and what actually happened.

Most of the time I was living in Carradale House. (How we came to be there will be clear to readers of my book *You May Well Ask*.) It is the Tigh Mor, the '"Big House" with all the advantages and disadvantages that go with that. To begin with we had inherited from the previous owners a large outdoor staff, which gradually diminished. We also inherited a considerable acreage of land, though the best fields of the old estate had been bought by neighbouring farmers, leaving us with the rough grazing and very little arable.

Basically Carradale is a fishing village. There were summer visitors, most of whom came, *en famille*, every summer. There were two or three boarding houses and a small hotel, but no tourism as we know it now. The tenants of the eight farms had bought in their land from the old estate; all had a good acreage of hill as well as the arable. Most of the rest belonged to the Forestry Commission which had a saw-mill; most of the timber went for pit props. There were two main shops, two post offices, but for some years no bar nearer than Campbeltown. There were two Presbyterian congregations in Carradale. Mr Mac-Kenzie, who lived at the Manse with his wife and sister, was the Free Church Minister. Mr Baker, a kindlier man, was the Minister of the Established Church of Scotland.

The boat from Campbeltown, either the *Davaar* or the *Dalriada*, arrived at the pier just after breakfast: when we saw it crossing the bay we knew it was time to go down to the harbour if we, or our guests, wanted to go comfortably back to Glasgow via Gourock and catch the one o'clock train to London. Around lunch time the other boat would bring visitors or family. The plane to and from Glasgow took off and arrived in a field west of Campbeltown, but the Laggan, where now there are huge hangars and silos for nuclear weapons, was still the best barley land in Kintyre.

So much for the setting. The house itself was rebuilt and enlarged from an older and smaller perhaps seventeenth-century house in 1870 by an architect called Bryce, who was well known in his day. All his houses are based on the same pattern of high-ceilinged large rooms (hard to keep warm) grouped round a central hall and staircase, with a landing which leads to bedrooms, a basement, and a back-stairs to attics. His models which he showed to clients had little turrets, round or square, which could be tastefully arranged here or there. All is slated, and baronial additions might be crows' steps or stone balustrades. The upkeep on this kind of house can be imagined. On the other hand it is extremely good for playing all versions of hide-and-seek.

This sort of house usually had a walled garden. When we moved in it was beautifully kept with clipped shelter hedges, small flower beds at either side of a central path, a double herbaceous border and several greenhouses. There were estate houses which, luckily, we improved before 1939, some cottages let, and Mains house. The land was in a bad state. Nobody had done anything about it. A few fields were let to a neighbouring farmer for such grazing as they had. But there were interesting rhododendrons, some probably from seed brought back by people on one of the Himalayan expeditions. None of the houses had electricity, but we put in an engine which did enough for house lighting, though liable to break down. We also put in some rather inefficient central heating, fuelled with anthracite. Cooking was on an Esse stove. And that was that.

I look at this account of my life so many years back. Some of this comes new to me, though I must have written it. It is odd that events or sights that I remember most vividly don't seem to have made it to the diary, or were not well enough expressed to go in. There was so much more, but the seasons repeat themselves, the branches break. Many people are dead or, like me, grown old. Was I as I appear in the diary? I rather hope not as I don't like myself much, but with any luck the book will be read less for the diarist than for what we at the time thought was happening and how we acted. It reads sadly, at least I think so, because it is full of hope for a new kind of world, for something different, happier, more honest, for a new relationship between people who had been cut off from one another by money, power and class structure. It was the same kind of vision that people have had all over the world, whenever they began to question the morality of the system they happen to live under. But the bright vision fades, always, always. I tried to begin the change with personal relations, but Dick, my husband, working with Beveridge and Cole on the political and economic foundations of the welfare state, got much further in the end.

Of course, there have been changes for the common good. There has been increased upward mobility. General health is vastly improved. Very few in this country have to go hungry. Knowledge increases. But realities have not kept up with expectations and personal relations are not changed that much. The welfare state is being eroded under our eyes.

I believe these kinds of hopes were common enough in the UK and probably to some extent in all the countries involved in the war, above all in the Soviet Union. With us the evidence is that the hope for drastic change was stronger in the Armed Forces. You can't go on with war unless you think you are fighting for something worthwhile. But you may be deceived by those who are controlling your lives and activities. Or your masters may be their own dupes. The 1945 General Election showed up the hopes. If only—

One other point, not unimportant. This diary will show how many of us in Scotland worked to get at least a measure of self-government and a recognition of nationhood. That too failed, though it seemed so near.

We wait for a new wave of hope.

NM

CARRADALE OCTOBER 1984

INTRODUCTION

NAOMI MITCHISON, POET, novelist and left-wing political writer, was one of the very first people to take part in the work of the social research organisation, Mass-Observation.[1]

In 1939, only two years after its inception, Mass-Observation was faced with the problem of how to continue its activities during wartime. It feared that the overwhelming impact of a world war would disrupt regular contact with the 500 people who were already participating in its work. In response to questionnaires or 'directives' these 500 people had recorded their reactions to some of the key events of 1938 and the early part of 1939 but the dispatch of the monthly or bi-monthly directives and the receipt of people's replies depended on the smooth running of the national postal and transportation systems. Determined not to miss the opportunity of documenting a period of unquestionable social significance, the Mass-Observers hit on the idea of asking for diaries: they began to recruit men and women from all parts of the British Isles who would be prepared to keep a continuous record of their everyday lives. Unlike the directive replies, a diary could be written without the need for regular prompting or guidance and it could be kept at home by the writer until such time as it was safe and feasible to post it off to Mass-Observation.

Naomi Mitchison was one of the 200 or so people who agreed to keep a wartime diary. She was a friend of two of the original founders of Mass-Observation, Charles Madge and Tom Harrisson, and she was eager to support their work. Both she and her brother, the scientist J. B. S. Haldane, who also took part in Mass-Observation's early projects, were committed to productive and socially useful applications of scientific method and this naturally led them (along with Julian Huxley, H. G. Wells, B. Malinowski and many others) to take a keen, if not entirely uncritical, interest in Mass-Observation's claim to be a 'science of ourselves'. It was Naomi, however, rather than her brother, who stayed with Mass-Observation beyond its initial phase and although she was never centrally involved in planning the research, she contributed a substantial diary from which this present volume is derived.

Naomi Mitchison was born on 1 November 1897, the daughter of John Scott Haldane and Kathleen Haldane, née Trotter. She grew up in Oxford (her father was a Fellow of New College) where she attended the Dragon School. Her brother Jack was sent to Eton and then, following in his father's footsteps, to New College. Naomi's formal education was not taken beyond the Dragon School but she continued her own self-education using the opportunities provided by her surroundings to pursue her interest in biology and genetics.

In 1916, at the age of 18, she married Gilbert Richard (Dick) Mitchison. Dick came from a well-to-do family and had been a contemporary of Jack's at Eton and New College. Even after her marriage, Naomi was expected to lead a fairly sheltered life. She was, however, a spirited and adventurous young woman and managed to escape temporarily from the constraints of an upper-class Edwardian background to serve as a volunteer nurse at St Thomas's Hospital in London. Her experience of nursing soldiers who had suffered horrifically in the 1914–18 war was a crucial one for her and it enabled her to cope more resourcefully when Dick, who had joined the Queen's Bays in 1914, sustained a severe head injury in France. Naomi crossed the Channel to help care for him. He was eventually moved back to England and it was during his long convalescence that he was able to study for his Bar exams. He qualified as a barrister in 1917.

The Mitchisons' first home was in London where Dick developed his legal practice, specialising chiefly in commercial cases. They lived in a small house in Chelsea until 1923 and it was there that Naomi began her prolific and illustrious career as a writer. Her first book, *The Conquered*, was published in 1923 and was a great success. Other publications quickly followed including her best known novel, *The Corn King and the Spring Queen* in 1931.[2] After the births of their first three sons, Geoff, Denny and Murdoch, the Mitchisons moved into a much larger house in Hammersmith, 'River Court', where they employed five household servants and a nurse. Naomi was therefore well provided with domestic help and was able to combine the upbringing of her children with her own development as a writer. She led a full and varied social life and hosted numerous gatherings of writers, artists and London intellectuals at River Court during the 1920s and 30s. This whole period has been very fully described in *You*

May Well Ask: A Memoir.[3] It was during these years too that Naomi became active as a socialist working mostly in the Labour Party and Fabian Society circles. Her progressive views on women and sexuality led to her involvement in the early birth control movement: she helped found the North Kensington Birth Control Clinic. Her three younger children, Lois, Avrion and Valentine, were born during this time at River Court. In the midst of all her successes, Naomi suffered one agonising tragedy: her eldest son Geoff contracted meningitis and died at the age of 9.

Naomi's ancestry on both sides of the family was Scottish. She was one of the aristocratic but progressively-minded Haldanes. Her father, J. S. Haldane, was a distinguished physiologist and philosopher; her Uncle Richard (Viscount Haldane) had been a Liberal Lord Chancellor and later led the first official Labour Opposition in the House of Lords in the 1920s. Her surviving uncle, Sir William Haldane, was an eminent Scottish lawyer. During the war he lived at Cloan, one of the two family Haldane homes in the Ochils, north of the Firth of Forth where Naomi had spent many of her holidays as a girl. Throughout the 20s and 30s, she kept up her contact with Scotland by taking Dick and the children back there for the summer holidays. When the Carradale estate in Kintyre came on the market—and was regarded as a bargain—it was a logical step for the Mitchisons to think of buying it. At first they had no intention of setting up a permanent family home in Carradale but, with the war imminent, the prospect of an alternative to River Court became increasingly attractive. By the time war was declared, in September 1939, Naomi had settled into Carradale House with the children. River Court was still used by various family members and friends as well as by visitors from abroad, many of them refugees from German-occupied Europe. Dick Mitchison remained in the south to continue with his legal work but instead of staying on at River Court, he moved in with G. D. H. (Douglas) and Margaret Cole, old friends of the Mitchisons who lived in Hendon. Both Dick and the Coles made frequent trips to Carradale and Margaret Cole has written warmly of the hospitality she received at Carradale House in her autobiography.[4]

Naomi's love of Carradale and her growing identification with Scotland were constant sources of inspiration in both her political work and her writing. The diary demonstrates the extent of her personal involvement in the Carradale community. One of her first ventures after she settled in Scotland was to help found the local branch of the Labour Party. Much of her earlier political activity had taken place within the Labour Party although she was catholic in her choice of comrades and described her guests at her pre-war London parties as ranging "from the Communist Party through to right-wing labour or Liberal left".

Both the Mitchisons had worked with Douglas and Margaret Cole, founders of the Society for Socialist Inquiry (of which Dick was treasurer), and Dick had collaborated with Margaret Cole at the New Fabian Research Bureau. Naomi's first visit to the Soviet Union in 1932 had been with a Fabian Society party; the funds she had carried to Vienna to help the socialists who had been tyrannised by the Dollfuss regime had been gathered by the Labour Party.[5] In 1931, when Douglas Cole's health failed (he suffered from diabetes and was never very strong), Dick Mitchison took his place as Labour candidate at the King's Norton bye-election. In 1935, Dick stood for the second time at King's Norton and although he was unsuccessful, it was a useful experience for the Mitchisons. Naomi worked whole-heartedly in support of her husband and many of her most longstanding friendships were forged during those election campaigns. There were times when she considered going into parliamentary politics herself. But the Mitchisons' affiliation with the Labour party was not without problems. Dick's name had been associated with that of left-wingers Aneurin Bevan and Sir Stafford Cripps at the time they were feuding with the Labour Party over a 'United Front' alliance with the Communist Party and Naomi was in many ways even more radical than Dick. She had a great respect for her brother Jack who was a prominent member of the Communist Party and from 1940 was Chairman of the editorial board of the *Daily Worker*. She privately shared many of his views but she was never seriously tempted to leave the Labour Party to become a Communist. All the same, her confidence in the Labour Party waned when the wartime political truce between the main parties effectively weakened the Labour Party at a local level. She was involved in the Argyll bye-election of 1940 which was contested by a Scottish National Party candidate. Thereafter her impatience with the Labour Party's lack of attention to Scottish affairs and its slowness in pushing for devolution led her to look more closely at Scottish nationalism, particularly the broad-based Scottish Convention founded by ex-SNP leader, John MacCormick. The Convention, together with her critical support for the wartime Secretary of State for Scotland, Tom Johnston, provided the framework for her political activities from 1942 until the war ended. Then, in the great optimism of the immediate postwar period, she once again campaigned on her husband's behalf in the 1945 General Election. Dick Mitchison was elected MP for the Kettering Division of Northants in the historic postwar Labour victory.

The diary which Naomi wrote for Mass-Observation was one of the most substantial pieces of writing which she produced during the war. It is unlikely that she considered it to be very significant at the time, at least at a literary level, and she seems to have written it in a perfunctory and spontaneous way, without revision or afterthoughts. In contrast, her poems about Carradale life (which included "The Alban Goes Out" and "The Knife") were continually refined in the light of her own critical judgement and the reactions of her local friends, especially the fishermen who advised her on the technicalities of fishing language and on Highland dialect and customs. The poems and her play *A Matter between the MacDonalds* were written for and about the people of Carradale. Even her major creative work of the war years *The Bull Calves* was inspired by the complexities of the Carradale relationships.[6]

The diary was first and foremost a social record written expressly for Mass-Observation to be used in purely anonymous forms as background information. It was never designed for public consumption. It lacks the coherent professionalism of the polemical articles which she wrote for various periodicals during the same period even though it covered many of the same themes: education and health, the Forestry Commission, farming and fishing and Scottish affairs in general and of course the progress of the war. Naomi had kept diaries before 1939 (although not on a regular basis) and only one directly autobiographical work had ever been published. This was *Vienna Diary*, an account of her visit to Austria in 1934. The main purpose of the book was to publicise the plight of the Viennese socialists. Because it was intended for immediate publication, *Vienna Diary* was necessarily a much less personally revealing document than Naomi's wartime diary. Mass-Observation's assurances of confidentiality and the absence of any specific instructions about keeping the diary left Naomi free to write according to her own inclinations as to length, subject matter, style and degree of candour. Not surprisingly, the diary quickly became much more than a purely functional and detached account of wartime life. Many years later, in a note to her friend Tom Harrisson of Mass-Observation, she reflected:

I wrote this diary every evening at my desk. It was not easy to do any real writing, though in 1940 I did a play for Carradale and later wrote *The Bull Calves*. But in general, ordinary professional writing wasn't on. A lot of it was about being tired; it was a kind of getting in touch with something outside, not that I wanted or asked for help, but maybe one needs to cry on an invisible shoulder.[7]

★   ★   ★

All the diaries which were written for Mass-Observation between 1939 and 1945 have been deposited at the University of Sussex together with the other papers generated by Mass-Observation's research. It has been my responsibility since 1974 to look after this unique and fascinating archive and to make it accessible to historians and others interested in the 1939–1950 period. As a consequence I have been aware of Naomi Mitchison's prodigious diary for several years. I met Naomi herself for the first time in 1975 at the Archive's official opening party organised by Tom Harrisson. Her interest in the ideas of Mass-Observation has carried over into support for the present archive and its work. In 1981, when Professor David Pocock launched a revival of Mass-Observation, she was ready to resume her role of 'note-taker' and observer of everyday life. Her contributions on a wide variety of contemporary themes—from the Falklands War to the Miners' Strike of 1984–5—are being accumulated at the archive together with reports and diaries from 1,000 other new volunteer observers across the country to form a portrait of the 1980s.

We had not considered the question of publishing any of the Mass-Observation diaries until we were approached by a producer from Thames Television who hoped to use a diary as the basis for a drama documentary. For various reasons, the documentary never materialised but a book did. The diary which we chose then was written by a housewife from Barrow-in-Furness called Nella Last.[8] The success of this book made me think more seriously about the possibility of publishing other diaries from the Archive, and Naomi's diary seemed a good candidate. I have always admired Naomi Mitchison and, as a feminist, I was intrigued by her diary not just because it was written by a woman but because she acknowledges—without overstating the case—the distinctiveness of being female in the context of a particularly contradictory set of social demands and constraints. Her personal and socialist standpoint provides us with a refreshingly less traditional perspective on the Second World War.

Naomi's diary is rich in social comment but it is the kind of diary in its original state which paradoxically presents the greatest problems for the historical researcher. Each month's instalment runs to 30 or 40 closely typed quarto pages and at first glance not one day seems to have been missed. The information is densely packed with a plethora of names and places; there are brief and often unexplained references to both world events and local events all of which make it difficult for readers with a specific research interest to discern themes and follow the narrative. It is much harder to pick up the threads of someone's life from a diary than from an autobiography where part of the author's job is to provide background information. This is especially true of a very detailed diary: to dip into it is to catch a glimpse of a life already in motion; the momentum has been gathered many years earlier and there are usually no reassuringly confidential asides to guide the reader.

In editing Naomi Mitchison's diary, I have tried to provide these asides in the form of an occasional commentary within the main body of the text. I have tried to avoid footnotes where possible as I felt they might be too intrusively academic and would interfere with a sense of continuity. I was reluctant to accumulate notes at the end of the diary for the same reason. In practice, it seemed useful to have one complete list of the most prominent people for quick reference at the start of the diary, and a more detailed alphabetical list at the end; but for the most part, I have incorporated explanatory notes about people and events into either the yearly introductions or into short pieces between the diary entries. These editorial interpolations are distinguishable by the smaller typeface.

Naomi produced two copies of her diary. The edited version is based on the fuller 'top' copy which Naomi very kindly loaned to me. The carbon copy which belongs to the Mass-Observation Archive contains a small number of gaps which usually correspond to more personal (or more potentially libellous!) passages in the top copy. Although I have tried, in consultation with Naomi herself, to be circumspect about matters which may hurt or offend people who are still living, it hasn't been necessary to exclude anything of substance from the final version for these reasons. Occasionally names have been changed or abbreviated to protect people's identities. My main concern has been to reduce the manuscript in size while still retaining as much of the original pace and flavour as possible. Approximately nine tenths of the whole diary have been cut out but I hope that by excluding detail and repetition, the inevitable losses will be offset by a gain in clarity and readability. Cuts have been indicated by a row of three dots at the beginning or end of a passage; occasionally this device appeared in the original diary, and it has of course been retained. When used editorially a small space is inserted on either side. The only major break in the original diary falls between November 1939 and March 1940. Otherwise the diary covers every day of the war. Some entries cover a group of days. Very few amendments to the actual text have been made apart from the correction of occasional typing and spelling errors; editorial insertions into the text are enclosed in square brackets.

One further aspect of the diary deserves a comment here: Naomi makes reference on at least two occasions to censorship. Just before war broke out in 1939, the Government announced that all postal and telegraphic services from Britain to overseas destinations were to be subject to censorship. It is difficult to ascertain the extent of internal censorship.[9] Letters from interned enemy aliens and from members of the armed forces stationed in Britain were certainly censored and trunk calls tapped. Kintyre was regarded as an area of military sensitivity and would therefore have been a prime target for Government surveillance. Official files on internal censorship are still not fully available but in June 1940 the Home Secretary signed a warrant for the censorship of internal communications. This facilitated not only checks on breaches of military security but also the monitoring of the contents of letters for intelligence purposes. There are no apparent cuts in Naomi's diary but it was almost certainly examined from time to time when it was sent through the post.

Although the selection of extracts and the writing of the commentary have been entirely my responsibility, I have been particularly fortunate in having had Naomi's advice and encouragement. There must have been times when my constant questions about things that happened over 40 years ago were tiresome and difficult to answer but Naomi has been unfailingly resourceful and kind. The greatest delight and privilege for me have been my visits to Carradale House where she still lives. There can hardly be a better way of researching the background than by absorbing first hand the atmosphere of the place itself. I would therefore like to thank Naomi Mitchison for her generosity and support and above all for entrusting me with this project in the first place.

There are a number of other people to whom I owe a debt of gratitude for their help and advice, in particular my friend Julia South who accompanied me to Carradale and with whom I shared many crucial discussions on the editing process; to Angus Calder whose book *The People's War* has been my constant companion, to my friends Kate Page and Sally Wyatt, and to Julie Helm, my friend and colleague at the Archive, who took on the immense task of typing the final version; I would also like to thank the Trustees of the Mass-Observation Archive, particularly Professor David Pocock, the Archive's Director. Last but not least, thanks to Barry, Tony and Luke who managed to live with me and Naomi's diary for over two years.

DOROTHY SHERIDAN

SUSSEX 1984

NOTES

1. Mass-Observation was set up in 1937 by Charles Madge, Tom Harrisson and Humphrey Jennings. The idea was to carry out a major investigation into the lives of ordinary British people. The peak of Mass-Observation's activities occurred during the 1939–45 war but it continued to operate until 1949 when it became a limited company. An introduction to the history of M.O. is included in *Speak for Yourself: a Mass-Observation Anthology 1937–49* edited by Angus Calder & Dorothy Sheridan, Jonathan Cape, 1984. To be published in paperback by Oxford University Press in 1985.
2. *The Corn King and the Spring Queen* has been republished by Virago, 1983.
3. During the 1970s, Naomi wrote three autobiographical books describing her life up to the beginning of the Second World War: *Small Talk. . . . Memoirs of an Edwardian Childhood*, Bodley Head, 1973; *All Change Here: Girlhood and Marriage*, Bodley Head, 1975; *You May Well Ask: A Memoir 1920–40*, Gollancz, 1979. A fourth autobiographical book, *Mucking Around*, was published by Gollancz in 1981.
4. *Growing up into Revolution* by Margaret Cole, Longmans, 1947.
5. This visit is very fully described in *Vienna Diary* published by Gollancz in 1934.
6. *The Bull Calves* was a historical novel set in seventeenth-century Perthshire and it required months of painstaking research. It was eventually published by Jonathan Cape in 1947, and was republished by Richard Drew in 1985. Naomi's wartime poetry is included in *The Cleansing of the Knife*, Canongate, 1978.
7. This was a private note to Tom Harrisson written at the Mass-Observation Archive in about 1972.

8. *Nella Last's War* was edited by Richard Broad (the Thames TV producer) and Susie Fleming and was first published in hardback by Falling Wall Press in 1981 and in paperback by Sphere in 1983.
9. My information on this subject has been taken from *Civil Liberties during the Second World War* by Neil Stammers, Croom Helm, 1984 (originally a Sussex University D.Phil. thesis).

PEOPLE IN THE DIARY

The people listed on this page are those appearing frequently in the main body of the diary.

Members of N.M.'s family
Dick Mitchison (husband)
Denny Mitchison (son)
Murdoch Mitchison (son)
Lois Mitchison (daughter)
Avrion Mitchison (son)
Valentine Mitchison (daughter)
Ruth (Denny's wife)
Maya (mother)
Jack or J. B. S. Haldane (brother)
Graeme Haldane ⎫ (first cousins)
Archie Haldane ⎭
Uncle Willie ⎫ Graeme and Archie's
Aunt Edith ⎭ parents

People staying at Carradale House
Eglè Pribram (Austrian refugee)
Betty Gibson (Glasgow evacuee)

Frequent guests at Carradale House
The Cole family: Margaret &
   Douglas with children: Jane,
   Anne & Humphrey
Joan & Jimmie Rendel
Eric Strauss
Tony Pirie

N.M.'s friends in the south
Elizabeth & Frank Pakenham
Christine & Michael Hope

Noel Brailsford
Margery Spring Rice
Zita & Lewis Gielgud
Margaret Lloyd
Agnes Maisky
Rudi Messel

People in Scotland
John MacCormick
Neil Gunn
Tom Johnston
Emrys Hughes

Landgirls and helpers on farm
Joy (vet Student)
Lena
Maisie

Free French at Carradale House after 1943
Paul   Georges
Guy   Albert
Pierre   Michel
Yves

Household & estate
Rosemary (Secretary/farm worker)
Lachie (Farm worker)
Hugh (gardener)
Bella (cook)

Eddie } (estate keepers and later in
Taggie } armed forces)
Angus (estate joiner)
Sarah }
Maggie } (domestic staff)

Teachers
Dorothy Melville } Evacuated to
Anna Simpson } Carradale from
Eda Muego } Glasgow
Miss Park
Donald Jackson (local Headmaster)

Fishermen
Denny M
Young Dick
Sandy
Willie
Red Rob
Alec
Archie
Johnnie

Other local people/neighbours
Jean & Duncan Semple
The Omans
Peter & Ellen MacKinven
Dougie & Chrissie Campbell
Baillie Ramsay
Duncan Munro
The MacLeans: Peter, Jemima etc.
Bob & Nora Leys (in
 Campbeltown)
Jennie
Lilla MacIntosh (Denny's wife)
Mr Stewart (Fiscal)
Ian MacLaren (plumber)
Mr MacKenzie (Minister)
Mr Baker (Minister)
Dr Cameron

Fishing Boats
The Alban
The Cluaran
The Amy Harris

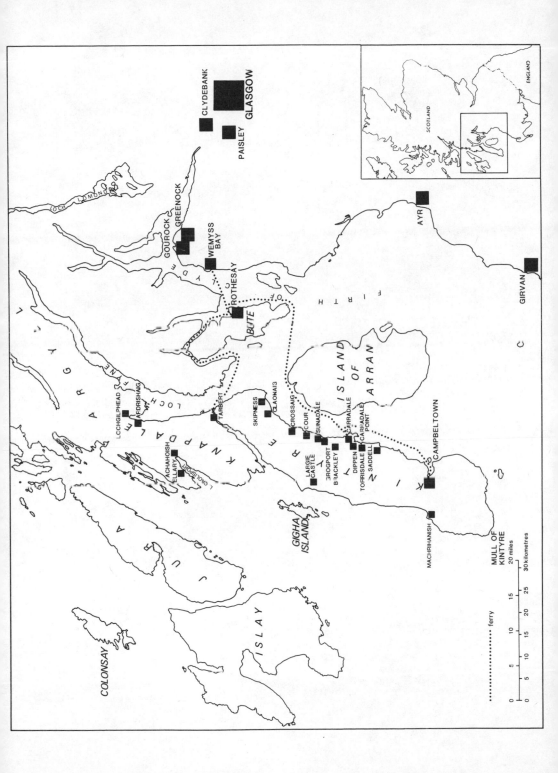

THE DIARY

1939

GERMAN TROOPS MARCHED into Poland on Friday 1st September 1939. Only a week before, Britain had signed a treaty of alliance with Poland and, despite the vacillations of Neville Chamberlain, the British Prime Minister, most people realised that war with Germany was inevitable. The official evacuation of mothers and children from city centres had commenced; the black-out restrictions came into effect, and soon after war was finally declared on Sunday 3rd September, the first air raid sirens were heard in London.

Carradale had been designated a reception area for evacuees from Glasgow and Clydeside. Four hundred children were expected (though many fewer actually arrived): beds had to be prepared, food organised, teachers billeted, advice and encouragement dispensed. Carradale House with its four storeys and turreted bedrooms had plenty of room to offer even if it was only floor space. Mains, the farmhouse on the Carradale estate, and all the estate cottages were expected to take as many children as possible. This influx of urban refugees promised to impose an unusual strain on the small fishing community which had never been very prosperous and depended on the herring industry and the Forestry Commission for its economic survival. Electricity supplies had not yet reached Carradale and the provision of heating and lighting and the storage and cooking of food without electrical appliances considerably added to the domestic burden. Only Carradale House had a small generator which enabled the Mitchisons to have electric lights in some of the rooms; but for heating and cooking, they relied on a system fuelled by anthracite.

When Naomi Mitchison began writing her diary on 1 September, one of her chief preoccupations was the problem of the evacuees. Carradale House was already well-filled with family and guests. All five Mitchison children, as well as their father Dick, were at home. Denny was on vacation from Cambridge where he was studying medicine; the others were back for their summer holidays from school. Murdoch was soon to finish at Winchester and go on to Cambridge. Lois was attending Badminton School. Plans for the education of the youngest two, Avrion and Valentine, were still uncertain. The guests included Murdoch's friends, Hank and Stewart, and Denny's friend, Robin. Two of Naomi's close women friends were also staying: Joan Rendel, a fellow novelist and poet, who was accompanied by her husband Jimmie, and Tony Pirie, who was engaged in research in ophthalmology at Oxford had come up to Carradale for the summer with her small son, John. Tony's husband, Bill, was stranded in America where he had been attending a scientific conference. Naomi was also taking care of a young Jewish refugee from Austria, Eglè Pribram, who was about the same age as Lois. Later in the year, she also accepted responsibility for three Glasgow children, Betty, Matthew (Mat) and Ina Gibson. She grew especially fond of Betty, the eldest, who stayed at Carradale House for a large part of the war.

The household and estate workers at this time included, of course, Lachie (Lachlan MacLean), Bella, the cook, and three maids including Annie; Hugh and Willie, the gardeners; Eddie and Taggie, the estate keepers; and James Downie, one of the estate workers. Jean had been engaged at Mains to cook for the evacuee children. Angus was the estate joiner.

The opening part of the diary (some of which has already been published in the last chapter of *You May Well Ask*) has a disjointed and confusing feel to it.

1 September 1939

Woke from nightmare to realise that at least it hadn't happened yet: so until after breakfast. Got the news at 10.30. Two of the boys had been out all night herring fishing so were asleep still; the others came in and listened. At the end Dick said That's torn it. Thought I had better at once return the cups and saucers borrowed from the W.R.I. [Women's Rural Institute] and the school urn, and see what news there was of the children to be evacuated. Felt a bit sick. Went into the garden, and saw Willie, very white; he had been listening to Hitler "working them up"—Willie himself conducts a choir. Talked a little to him and James Downie, all felt it had got to come now. We talked of the ordinary people in Germany and tried to hope this would mean the end of privilege everywhere. So to the stables; Lachie was filling up the car, so I waited talking to Eddie and Taggie, both of them curiously without enmity towards Germany; we discussed ploughing up the fields for potatoes, and they argued as to whether they would bear two crops in succession and I said I hoped they wouldn't have to. Taggie talked about his young brother who is a C.O. said They'll shoot him before he goes, and then It's no free country where they can do that. I said I thought it important that there should be some real pacifists in any community, and they agreed; I said I would do what I could for the boy. Both agree that the ordinary people in Germany don't want this. Lachie brought the car back; I said Bad news, and he soberly said, Aye.

I took it round to the house and went to the kitchen to tell Bella who said, My goodness, they'll be taking all the young men. She began to tell me about her folk on the croft at Baleshare. Stewart and I went round to the school with the things; I found Mrs Jackson and Mrs Cameron (schoolmaster's and doctor's wife—the doctor is in Glasgow recovering from appendicitis). They talked about the way the billeting arrangements had broken down, and of what had to be done. I offered to do anything I could; we agreed there must be central catering etc if possible. Mrs J. said the church ought to take the children; they could sit there comfortably and be fed, and what was the good of the church anyhow. The minister wanted his holiday; let him go over to Warsaw and see what sort of a Christian he calls himself! I talked to Mrs Cameron about a child in one of the cottages who was ill, said I would go and see that it wasn't measles.

Back to Mains, to collect some furniture in case we have to furnish the bothy for children or others. Found Jean in tears and saying she must go home to see her parents who are in a mining district in Dumfries: calmed her down with some trouble, and told her how much use she would be cooking for the children. Dick came over to try and hurry the men who are working at the new cottage, as we very much want to get it finished. The question is whether they will go on with the much needed housing estate . . .

. . . Realise at the end of the news that there is to be a complete black out, and that only one or two rooms will be habitable. Leave Denny to paste up brown paper, and drive over to school. Find Jackson and helpers with forms. Jackson says The very man we want! Tells us to expect over 400 children and has only been able to billet 120. Some people have relatives or still have visitors with them. We say we will try and put up the surplus. Dick is asked to drive some of the billeting officers down to the village, which he does. One of them asks me to look in on Angus and ask him if he will take a child. I drop off at Mains and ask Annie (Angus' wife). She says at once she will take 2, not in her spare room, as a relation is coming, but in the sitting room; she has been very ill, and I say she must take care—they can be fed at Mains. I am talking to her about how much we all value Angus when he comes in. I go to Mains and talk to Jean, who has, as I told her, laid in flour, cereals, prunes, sugar, etc. I ask her to get a hot meal for 2 o'ck. Pinkie (her husband) is there, very serious, says his two young brothers are called up already in the Air Force reserve; he doesn't want to go. We decide we can take two more children than I had thought at Mains.

Angus has offered me a chair bed, and his old bedstead which is in the bothy.

Back in falling dusk to look for tacks; Denny is dealing with windows etc. I find a billeting officer and tell him Angus will take 2 and we will take 12 more somehow. The others are having supper —the birds we shot last week. Denny still dealing with windows. I go and get the littles, my two and Tony's one—to bed; Val is rather upset and clings to me saying Will there be a war? She is afraid of her old nurse in Edinburgh being bombed. John rather upset too and clings to Tony. Joan tells them stories. I tell Bella and Annie there will be children coming; they seem quite pleased. Find the bathroom shutters won't work after all.

The 9 o'ck news. Dick looks desperately unhappy. The boys quiet and horrified. Joan cries at her husband's feet; I go over to her. The girls seem all right. Tony hopes Bill won't try to come back from America; she has only one moment of looking like tears. Chamberlain's speech. Horribly like Asquith in '14. Greenwood—the die is cast! Oh a lovely leader for our Party! We take notes of a few regulations; I write some cards. It seems impossible. The gladiolus on the shelf shine and ramp at us . . .

We go out to look at lights, see if they are obscured in the two usable rooms. Murdoch and I unpack some things, sent from London. I go to see that the girls are all right. Dick and I walk down to the sea, talking about chances and what he ought to do, and about the boys, and about how incredible and lunatic it is, and how miserable we feel about Russia . . .

Denny had heard earlier that he was not certainly a medical student as he hadn't done enough anatomy; the question was whether he could be, especially in view of his First and Scholarship. Dick talks to the other boys, urging them to stay on here till they know what to do . . .

Stewart says his brother is called up and Robin says so must his be but can he get out as he speaks several foreign languages? I kiss them all, and they go down to the sea. Everyone writing letters. I say I will write my diary and keep sane . . .

2 September 1939
. . . At breakfast discussion about the children who are to come. The girls and the small children say their divans are perfectly all right without mattresses, and bring the latter down, also blankets, with a vision of winter and an unheated house. All run about fetching things.

Complicated housekeeping, Bella cross! Tuned in at 10, but no news, however Angus has listened in earlier, and told us, while putting up a blind. One was in a way glad that it hadn't happened yet. Italy out, as one had supposed it would be. I said, We shall be able to get olive oil and lemons after all! But Russia . . .

3 September 1939
I listened to the 9 o'ck news, realising fairly clearly what the next was to be. The others were mostly not down, but I had not slept well. Valentine went off to Mains to look after the Glasgow children; Dick and I discussed what was to be done about the education of Avrion and Valentine; the latter can go to school here for a term, but the former would learn nothing. Tony said I'll start this war clean and went to wash her hair; a little later I did the same; it wasn't quite dry by 11.15. As we listened to Chamberlain speaking, sounding like a very old man, I kept wondering what the old Kaiser was thinking, whether he was old enough to see it all fully. The boys looked pale and worried, though Robin was laughing a little. At the end Joan said How could he ask God to bless us? . . . As God Save the King started Denny turned it off and someone said Thank you.

The maids hadn't wanted to come through; I told Annie, who was wonderfully cheerful and said she remembered the Boer War, and Bella who said Isn't that heartbreaking. After a bit she began to cry, a saucepan in her hands, said Think of all our men going, then to me Of course you've got boys too. Dick said Think of the women in Germany all saying that too, but there was no response. Then she asked When will they send our men over? But none of us had much idea.

In the drawing room the big boys were writing and reading; I think perhaps writing poetry. I was feeling sick, and so were Stewart and Hank and I went over to Mains, but the teachers had just left—we followed them. Valentine had brought the Glasgow children over; they were talking happily but looked very white and thin and small. The village was empty; most people at church. It began to rain hard and we took shelter at the Galbraiths. Young Dick [Galbraith, one of the Carradale fishermen] said So it's come. Then he began asking Hank what are *you* going to do? He seemed less enthusiastic than he'd been the night before when he thought "appeasement" was possible, said he didn't think he'd ever be able to shoot anyone and he would rather do mine-sweeping. He explained his position, that he wouldn't fight, but would do work of national importance—he was too much attached to things and people to be able to be a clear pacifist. They talked about the possibility of dropping leaflets instead of bombs on German towns, and then we talked about these Words people use —National Honour and Justice and all that. Dick said Russia was going to be neutral; we kept on thinking how little there had been on the wireless about Russia. . . . Young Dick said that already some of the young fishermen were saying what they'd do to Germans if they got hold of them—not just Hitler. That worried Dick; it was all in fun now, but might get serious. His father was being very patriotic.

We looked in at Mains and found the children very cheerfully having dinner but the teachers were worried because some of the mothers were saying it was so quiet and lonely that they couldn't stand it and were going back, if they paid their own fares. I said I would come round in the afternoon and help with them.

At lunch Joan said she was on a small island of sand with everything cut off before and behind. I said I had been feeling the future cut off for some time. We all agreed it was queer to feel the past so cut-off, everything had a different meaning now. The 2 o'ck news and Greenwood's speech which somehow made the official Labour people feel rather sick.

From then until 4.30 I went round with Miss Simpson the teacher (who said her colleague was getting rattled), the superintendent, a very nice and efficient Miss Knight and James MacKinven who is one of the billeting officers. I told them not to worry because one child had swallowed a prune stone; they said what about a doctor; I explained that our doctor was only just back from an appendicitis, we had no district nurse though we had been hoping to get one, but the doctor's wife was a nurse and I had trained during the last war.

. . . I got back to the house, changed and dried my hair, while the boys talked, taking in this gulf we have stepped over. Robin said All my tastes are pre-war! And they all began saying things were pre-war; there was a certain amount of genuine laughter: *pourvu que ça dure*. Denny went on with his anatomy. Then Denny and I took the groceries round to the woman at Portrigh and I talked to her soothingly. She and the others are Glasgow slum prolet; one of the other mothers had a boy of sixteen in a territorial pipe band; I said I was sure he wouldn't be taken overseas. Another had a daughter unemployed.

The Mains children had been having a grand time dressing up and were very cheerful. After tea we had the 6 o'ck news; three of the maids came for the King's speech. I talked to the boys and to Dick, whose application to the Treasury Solicitor has been refused. I advise him not to rush off for the moment. The storm has broken a lot of the beautiful gladiolus and brought down some apples; at least it is a natural thing. . . .

. . . After supper and the 9 o'ck news—and we've made up our minds not to listen too much, as this constant dripping of the wireless gets on our nerves badly—Joan read her poem. Later the boys and Dick discussed the same kind of things again. One feels curiously out of it here; in fact there is no war yet here, only marvellous moonlight over the trees. It is odd not having heard yet from anyone in London about coming up with children.

We all kept on noticing how these last two days have been a parody of all the Auden-Isherwood stuff; we might have been *On The Frontier*. I suppose the announcers just can't help parodying themselves.

Although both Dick and Naomi Mitchison were members of the Labour Party, they were doubtful about the pro-war stance taken by the Party leadership. They had both survived one war and were not eager to endure another. Naomi was deeply distressed by the Nazi-Soviet non-aggression pact, signed only a few weeks earlier. In common with many other socialists of her generation, Naomi had strong sympathies for the Soviet Union and she was concerned about the prospect of Britain and the Soviet Union being on opposing sides in the war.

The question of support for the war was debated fiercely by socialists everywhere including those in the Carradale Labour Party branch of which Naomi was a founder member. Her friend Denny MacIntosh (referred to as 'Denny M' throughout the diary to avoid confusion with Naomi's eldest son, Denny) and his wife, Lilla, were also members. It was chaired by a young fisherman, 'Young Dick' Galbraith who was Denny M's nephew. The membership also included estate workers (Hugh and Angus) and other fishermen (Alec and Sandy).

7 September 1939

. . . Found Denny M at home and listened to his radio. "Bad, bad times," he said, but also "Don't you be worrying your heads about it, boys." He says there are no herring; the submarine may have frightened them, but anyhow there usually aren't many round harvest. He thinks there is a submarine north of Arran or maybe two. They came back early last night and are not going out tonight. Hardly any of the boats are.

Lilla came back from the shop and said that she was doubtful about our having a [Labour Party] meeting on Saturday; it might split the party; some people thought we oughtn't to have any politics just now. I said I thought now was the time for comrades to get together, and Angus and Hugh had agreed—so of course had Alec, who wants his accounts out before the party. However I obviously knew less about people's feelings than she did. Denny M said he thought very few would come—he would, of course. We decided to ask young Dick and went across to the house. Sandy said We can't have a meeting now; we must all stick together. I said I was damned if I'd stick to Chamberlain and we had to keep in mind that we must get rid of him and his like or the war would only land us like the last one had. He just smiled and shook his head, and showed me a ship going by. The big ships usually go east of Arran, but now: Denny M says they look fearsome in the night without lights; they frighten him. Sandy in any case wouldn't come to the meeting; I couldn't find out what he would do except stay at home listening to the wireless and feeling united! We chased young Dick in the rain and finally found him talking to a couple of other lads in a shop door and sucking black ba's; he said he would like to see a big meeting and it certainly wouldn't be that. Finally we decided not to have it. A pity, but I can't impose my views in a democratic movement. Of course Chamberlain is being superbly put across by the BBC. Sandy, and one or two others I saw today, thought it would be a short war . . .

9 September 1939
As we are not wanted yet on the harvest—the corn is still soaked after this week's rain—and as the boats had not gone out on Friday night, we did a morning's shoot, with Denny M and Sandy; they presumably don't have game licences but I should think the police were too busy to bother! Hank, Stewart and Robin were fitting up the barn for the children, and Murdoch had a bad cough, but the rest of us walked across the face between Kilmichael and Brackley, rough and lovely, crossed every here and there by small burns half lost in a tangle of rowan and birch and fern. I have never seen the rowans so bright as they are this year, or so many. Denny and Sandy both enjoyed themselves a lot—Sandy had never been out before and Denny M only once before with us, that is legally! So did I in spite of everything. So did the keepers, they kept on laughing and making jokes. I think one sees things more vividly, storing them up, insisting on the moment, at

these times. If one is wise. During the last war, when I was a girl, I felt all the time that it was wrong ever to be happy; now I think one should be when possible. It was the kind of day one could carry into the trench or a concentration camp, in one's mind. I shot a blackcock; I don't believe in the sanctity of life, as such—though for years after the last war neither Dick nor I did any shooting—only of intelligent life, fore-knowing life and sensitive life. The birds have sensitivities, but not much else that matters except beauty. We took care not to shoot the pheasants; it seems odd, when men are shooting one another in Europe, and when we may be much more directly involved in that ourselves, yet I think it is probably a good idea to be punctilious at the moment about small and silly rules which are *not* part of this totalitarian plan which is eating us now. We may yet all meet again at New Year and shoot the beautiful pheasants then.

And all the time there was the marvellous smell of gunpowder and bog myrtle, and I found staghorn moss, and right at the end Denny found a lovely little snake—a blindworm—which he picked up and played with; but neither of the fishermen would touch it; at last we persuaded Denny M to but he hated it. I wrote a few more lines of my poem, and got Sandy to read it—it is about his boat.

At this time, Naomi was working on her poem about one of the Carradale fishing boats, the *Alban*. The poem was published the same year by the Raven Press illustrated with wood engravings by Gertrude Hermes. It was later included with other poems from this period in a collection entitled *The Cleansing of the Knife* (Canongate, 1978).

Dick and Denny depart for London together with Hank, Stewart and the Rendels. New visitors take their place; 'P' arrives with her two small children from London. P was a former secretary of Naomi.

13 September 1939

. . . P tells me about things in London. Her Labour Party is all going "underground", with secret passwords (and ARP of course making it all look much darker). At a tremendously thrilled meeting they discussed secret business . . . whether they could dare to hold their annual bazaar. They decided not to. She herself is a bit jumpy, but not so much so as the last crisis; I think she finds all this security rather irritating, as perhaps anyone from the real world is likely to—unless they can accept it as something apart. I think it may be very important at the end of all this to have some place which has not been cowed by totalitarian war, which will still feel reasonably anarchist or liberal or whatever it is one wants. Of course they would have to go out into the other world, and not become in any way precious or protected. I wonder what one will think in three years . . .

16 September 1939
. . . I feel like hell deep down because of the Russian news; it is certain to prolong the war, at the least. And it is knocking the bottom out of what one has been working for all these years: not that I was ever orthodoxly anti-Trotskyite—one couldn't help knowing that it wasn't all jam. And it's understandable enough that they want to come out of this the boss-country. We've done that ourselves often enough. But . . .

In the meantime, I don't want to talk politics all the time; I've done that since 1931 and I'm bored with it. It is useless to look possible death and defeat in the face. One can't do anything. Or not at the moment.

Anyhow we turned the wireless on and tried to listen to an American broadcast. And then most of them went and P went to bed. And then Robin and young Dick, who was still here, and I put away the chairs and Murdoch did things to the cinema projector and young Dick asked me to read the poem; he found one place where it had gone wrong, which I will alter. Robin says it is getting too technical for most people; I don't think that matters. It is not written for them, but for these people, to make something for them, to be with them.

Despite the considerable distance and the wartime transport difficulties, Dick made frequent visits back to Carradale from London. The train took him as far as Glasgow from where he either made use of the small passenger plane service to the airfield at Machrihanish, near Campbeltown, or sailed from Wemyss Bay by ferry boat to Tarbert.

19 September 1939
. . . Dick and I went for a walk after tea, and Clym [the dog], so happy to have his master back, sprang like a bird in the bracken. We made provisional plans of one kind and another . . .

There was a good deal of packing, marking Lois' school clothes etc. After dinner we listened to the news, I played halma with Lois, and the boys and P played records in the library; the London ones which were brought back sound much better on this gramophone. We played the Fifth which was grand; I wish we could get more of that kind of thing from the BBC. Murdoch and Robin and I discussed one another and young Dick. Outside there were Northern Lights, like sky spears, like still search lights. There seemed to be cracks between the shutters in our windows, but the policeman always touches his cap to us . . .

21 September 1939
. . . It was so nice at Lilla's, being welcomed by her and Denny M and talking about all sorts of things, with tea and biscuits and a fire in the kitchen grate and this feeling of togetherness that makes the mind dive into tenderness; they had liked Greenwood too. Lilla had been listening to Hamburg [German Radio] and said the man said so many of the things that we on the left can't help thinking, and it was hard just to catch where he went wrong. Denny M is going as our delegate to the Glasgow [Labour Party] conference; I wish I could go too, but I'm afraid the proprieties wouldn't stand it. The weaker brethren again. Lilla said she would teach me to sing. Denny M says that he has a tune coming for the Carradale Fleet; it is lovely to have set somebody on to creation like that. They told me about Mackerson, the ploughman, who writes as he ploughs, and then we talked about parties we'd have in winter, and what we'd do at Hallowe'en. There should be plenty of new ghosts by then. And they talked about the summer they had been on Luing netting salmon. Then we heard the 6 o'ck news with the odd romantic bit about the Russians disarming and freeing the Polish soldiers. Denny M said, it will all be over soon. I read them the poem, and got good praise from both; Denny M said I was out there while you were reading: how was that?—meaning that I had really taken him out to the fishing in the poem. He said people will be remembering this long long after we are all dead; he said nothing like this was ever written. I think the poem is getting so technical that ordinary readers won't like it. Then he touched my shoulders and said Naomi Mitchison, this is the best you have done yet. He saw with extraordinary sensitiveness why I had changed the metres here and there and what I was after. They both did, really, but he, being a man, has to be most important to me as inspiration or whatever it is. Then he began to talk about a poem which I identified as *The Ancient Mariner*, about the man who shot the albatross: "He should never have done that; we never hurt the gannets." He talked about the gannets and how once he had got one in the net and it had been awful cross, and then about how a man at Tarbert had lied about where he had caught his herring, and none of the Carradale men would have done that. And at last he picked me a red rose out of his garden and I put it in my hair . . .

26 September 1939

. . . I am beginning to wonder whether the point of a place like this may not be that it will keep alive certain ideas of freedom which might easily be destroyed in the course of this totalitarian war. There are increasing signs of totalitarianism in this country (for instance, decisions by local councils not to hold committees but to delegate things to chairmen) and democracy may most easily be kept alive in small communities. Meetings will not be possible in towns, but they will still be able to be held in the country. And again, here people will not be terrorised by darkness and regulations and this departure of the men, into accepting anything.

29 September 1939

. . . Came down, to finish my poem and write letters. Heard the 12 o'ck news with the new Russo-German treaty. In a way one had been expecting it, but not quite as definite. Of course one needn't make too much of protestations of friendship; and treaties are made to be broken. But it looks like a long, long war, involving even Avrion. And all the other children. Dick and I discussed it, I feeling rather strongly that it wasn't much good going on with it; it would mean ten years' war; we would not bring the Polish dead back to life—nor give the Polish landlords control over their minorities . . . There might be revolution in Germany—but would the present Russia help it? We might end Hitler, but only by becoming more and more like him. If we leave him, the Nazi rule is likely to end within a hundred years. Perhaps earlier; that is very little, historically speaking. We would have to become a second or third class power, but we should do that anyhow. And the alternative appears to mean a very long and increasingly horrible war, effectively smashing all that we care for, all that we mean by Athens . . . The ending of a civilisation, and above all the killing of people, the extermination of a generation. I don't see how that is to be avoided as the war goes on. Not to speak of famine and pestilence, and all that. Dick said that if we made peace now, with a win for Hitler, that would mean that Germany and perhaps Russia might go on to eat the Scandinavian countries, and the present neutrals. And end their civilisation if they fought, and perhaps if they didn't fight. If it was to be a genuine peace one could afford not to fuss about Poland, considering that the Russian share, at least, is tolerably fair. But could it be? Apparently there is no remotely hopeful way out of this dilemma.

I set down, for future reading, that I think now that, in three years, or five, I and mine will wish very deeply that we had made peace now; and this will be true of many millions. I only hope I am wrong.

In any case, none of us can do anything about it. Perhaps it is easier to be powerless.

The nightmare quality grows; one thinks one will wake up.

There has been occasional gun-fire all morning: where and what for?* . . .

7 October 1939
. . . Lilla had asked me to go back to tea with them and write down Denny M's conference report; but after lunch Munro [the head forester] turned up, and I spent all the afternoon with him, going round, looking at all the woods, deciding what trees to cut, what to prune, where to re-plant and what to re-plant. We found a lot of things neither of us had noticed alone, including a curious number of walnuts. We kept on trying to find ripe beech nuts, but it was only the infertile ones which had shed. We walked for nearly three hours and never once mentioned the war. Occasionally Munro climbed a tree. We talked almost wholly about trees; he loves them; he likes conifers best, because he works with them and knows them, and because he likes their shape. He is extremely sensitive to them, indeed to most trees; I don't think he ever mentioned a tree as value, only as to whether it was really bonny.

. . . I took him down to the wild garden to get his advice on the blue cedars and the macrocarpas;† he was so pleased with them, gasped with pleasure. And then we smelt a lovely smell, which neither of us could trace to any one plant or bush, but something balmy but pungent; the sun had been out then for a bit, and brought it to the surface. We both wandered about smelling and touching; we found a lot of macrocarpa seedlings I hadn't known about in front of the house; and we ate brambles.

Naomi's Haldane cousins, Graeme and Archie, were frequent guests at Carradale. They came particularly for the salmon fishing in the nearby river. The MacLean family were close neighbours of the Mitchisons and ran a farm at Brackley. The young daughter, Jemima, had become a friend of Naomi.

* It must have been practice gun-fire from the Navy which went on almost all the time from 1939 until the opening of the Second Front. It often disturbed the farm animals; I wondered sometimes about the wild ones. N.M.
† The Monterey Cypress tree.

12 October 1939

. . . After lunch Graeme and Archie, so happy to be here again, went off up the river; I took Archie and Lachie to Brackley and myself called at the farm to ask Jemima whether she minded being in the poem. I had tea with her and her mother and read it to them; they laughed and moved about while I read it—one of the boys is fishing—and then said it was "just great", and I must have been out all a season to have written it, and Jemima said it was a compliment to be in it herself. So that was all right . . .

In the field Father MacLean was digging potatoes; he called to me, showed me his potatoes, and said he thought it was great the way that Stalin had held up that Hitler on the East; he seemed to think I was somehow responsible for it, and gave me as many potatoes as I could carry, then said I could have a line if I would come and get them; so I said that Lachie and I would and put the other potatoes into the car.

Then I went over to Mains to find Isobel Park, one of the other teachers and the new helper in the sitting room, the helper sitting on the edge of a chair looking obstinate, saying she was going back. We all tried to persuade her to stay, saying it was very hard to leave us with eight children, the two mothers going and only Jean to look after things. She would only say it wasn't what she had expected and she was "disappointed". I took little May down to be weighed; she clung to my hand, saying she didn't want to go back, when could she come again? And she talked about all the nice things she had been doing. She doesn't seem to have put on weight, though she looks as if she had, but the weighing is not very accurate; the others seem to have gained two to four lbs each. May's idiotic mother said Oh she would be back on Monday, and poor May brightened up. I wish she wasn't going. The teachers were still busy with the "helper" and I weighed in and told her that this wasn't the way to help the country and all that . . .

Then I came back and wrote to the Corporation saying I thought we'd need another helper, though at that time Mrs Rodgers had said she would "think it over". Then Jessie [the Mitchisons' cook from London] came to ask my advice; her young man had written asking her to come south and marry him on his last leave before going out. I said Go on, marry him, if you feel it's for keeps and that you'd like to marry him anyhow, and we had rather an *intime* little talk about birth control. He is a Catholic, by the way. She was rather worried about not having a wedding dress and all the doings; said she'd wanted "a white wedding": asked me about my war wedding. Then I said what about having it here? You could have a dance and all that. She brightened up a lot so I rang up Stewart the lawyer and found out the legal position, then drafted an enormous telegram asking him to come up. She was frightfully thrilled and pleased and we discussed what clothes of mine she could borrow and so on. I said I would if she liked take her into Tarbert the next day to get the Glasgow boat, and generally petted her a bit.

Graeme and Archie came back with a salmon and various other fish. Then as usual we talked politics for the evening. Graeme feels that already there have been such changes in the way of eliminating the private employer and business that things will never go back to any kind of *laissez faire*; there would be "socialism". I said it would be a totalitarian state with you as Hitler! He began to talk about planning and how the obstacle to socialism in this country had been the conservatism of the private employer; but perhaps we mean two very different aspects of the same thing.

16 October 1939

A golden morning, frost on the ground and brilliant sun, Valentine in a cotton frock again. I'd had bad dreams, invaded by Denny M as liar and poacher. But when Graeme said they were going to shoot Rhonadale I said Could I bring my boy-friend, and went bouncing off down the road to get Denny M; he was in bed, asked if Willie could come; I went to find Willie [Galbraith, another fisherman] but he was trying to mend his car. I waited for Denny M to get up and we walked up to the house together, he telling me about his childhood in one of the condemned cottages at Airds, eight people in a but-and-ben, with loft, short of food and afraid of being put out if they took a rabbit: how he'd come up to the Big House once to ask for another cottage, but hadn't got it; there's a good deal to make up, but it must be made up to everyone, not to one person. I keep on telling myself that. The beech tree at Mains was one mass of orange and gold.

I drove them all up to Rhonadale; it was clear and brilliant, hot in the sun; it looked no distance to the end of the glen. "The hills are looking wee" Denny M said, and added that there would be a change of weather; we walked the two sides of Rhonadale, in this blinding, low, hot sunlight or patches of shade where a touch of frost still held; I was too happy to shoot, but no-one minded; Graeme doesn't like shooting rabbits either; but Denny M shot them in a business-like way,

approaching them for food; he kept on saying This is the life; he and
Taggie talked.

. . . When we got back I went to the cellar and drew beer for the
men; I hate the smell of it but it was pretty, like the river itself, where
Taggie had carried me over; I drove Denny M back with two rabbits
which Lilla will give to her Glasgow children. He liked it so much! He
and Graeme got on well, too. I think Graeme finds this atmosphere
very refreshing; he likes being first-named as much as I do, and hopes
Eddie will start it soon. Eddie is just a little more formal than the
others, being from Dumfries, and farming not fishing stock . . . They
all liked the look of things today so much, and the lovely feathers on
the new pheasants.

Workers on neighbouring farms often helped each other out when the
demand for labour was heavy. On this occasion, Naomi and Lachie had gone
over to Brackley to assist the MacLeans with potato lifting.

17 October 1939
. . . I washed at the tap outside that can't be turned off because the
water runs so strongly; it tasted good, but ironish, and Mrs MacLean
said that was why the children's teeth were all so bad—the water. I
thought it could have been counteracted by lime of some kind, or
calcium tablets; perhaps this soft water is always bad and I ought to
give [lime] to the children here. Jemima has just had a new plate and
looks all the better for it but is afraid it may effect her singing. We had
dinner at the table in the living room, with the dark walls and the two
little windows, one golden and streaming with soft sunlight: boiled
sausages and mashed potatoes, tea and scones and jelly. I sat on Father
MacLean's left with Lachie opposite me; we talked about all sorts of
things; I told them about English pubs, where people can go in and
have a drink and don't feel they've got to get drunk as quick as possible
so as to get over the stage in which they still feel shame. The country
pub is the best thing England could give Scotland. We talked about
distilling and I reminded Lachie of the stills on Pabbay. We were all
hungry; again, they petted Lachie, who ate lots of scones and lots of
bramble jelly and smiled and said Oh Yiss. I kept on wondering
whether I was double-crossing myself, whether this meal at which I
was so happy, was really in some way bogus, whether I was just
taking refuge among these people out of a romantic or sentimental
feeling and possibly out of pique at being criticised by the London

46

highbrows or of being the intellectual inferior of various people. Yet I couldn't make out at what point the sacrament was not genuine; I couldn't see myself not loving these people or not being at ease with them. By and bye Jemima went off to get the post; she delivers letters to the three farms. She came back with the letters and newspaper, which her father looked at first, then me, then Lachie. We talked a bit about the *Royal Oak*, then about taxation; he said that the taxes were hard on the rich, who really made industry; I tried to explain that putting up the standard of living in the lower income groups would be better for that, taking homely illustrations.

Then the men went out to work again and I was going but Mrs MacLean stopped me and took me into the other room where there was a photo of the boy who had died, the youngest, the sixteen year old, the flower of the flock, who had made a song about Jemima and all the folk had come to the door to listen to him singing it and his touch on the melodeon had been so light and he had been so fine and kindly, and she had never really had the heart for anything since he died four years ago. And we talked of children and death and illness and the mistakes of doctors, and the old doctor MacKay whom she loved and who was always so drunk, but yet he cured people. And she told me about her father the piper, and his brother who was always making up songs about people and places, with the tunes to them, as he was ploughing; she told me one of the songs, about his collie who had won plenty of prizes but got to be no use at the sheep; but it was in Gaelic and I couldn't follow at all; and she had not sung at all herself since the boy died, and these tunes were never written down. And she told me about her other children, and how she had been dairy maid and hen maid at a big house, and all the things they had done with the hens; she said we should keep second cross Rhode Islands.

There was a picture in the big room, not at all incompetent, of a sailing boat at the south end of Arran; it was by MacDonald of Airds, a fisherman, father of the boy in my poem, the one who is coming to work for us. I knew there was music enough but never that there was painting too. He makes his children's Hallowe'en lanterns and they always win the prize.

I went up to the field, with a large and startling pain in my back already. Graeme and Eddie had gone shooting over the hills and out towards Grianan, and had left me the car. I worked with Jemima mostly; she told me about her childhood, how much she had liked school and hated the hard work on the farm in the holidays, how her schoolmaster wanted her to take a bursary at the secondary school but her parents wanted her to work and wouldn't let her go, and how now the one thing she was sure about was that people shouldn't try to own one another, and if she had a family she would never force them against their wills, not even over religion. She said that she remembered young Dick too, and how he had been another who liked school; she asked me about his writing; I think they are very fond of one another, in fact I think they are really friends, in a way that is rare for people of the opposite sexes here. I told her about my plan for a play and she was enthusiastic; she loves acting and anything gay; she is hoping I will have more parties; I said I must go carefully as there were plenty of people watching to catch me out, and she said You don't need to bother yourself about them! But I do . . .

21 October 1939

. . . Valentine and I drove into Campbeltown to meet Dick at the aerodrome. However we waited and waited and after about an hour discovered that he and someone else had missed the plane. I did some shopping, saw Nora Leys, who was pretty gloomy about the Party, and very much taking the peace line, on more or less CP grounds, saw Weir about concrete, and had lunch at the hotel, which recognised me (as indeed all the shops had done—and I was frightfully untidy, dressed in shooting clothes as I had arranged for Dick to come straight back and shoot) and was very friendly. Valentine was being very interesting about school. Her theory was that the children started all right, were interested in school and liked it, but about 7 or 8 they began to see that what they were being taught had nothing to do with them, that there was no connection with their own lives, they became bored and at the same time began to be punished for faults due largely to inattention; they got frightened and began to dislike school and to shut their minds down deliberately. Some of them would recover from that at a later stage, but many did not. She also said that they were treated so much as objects of ownership by the parents (that was not her phrase of course) that they longed to be grown-up and expressed this by the boys smoking and the girls varnishing their nails; she said they were never "proud of being children". She is rather shocked by the smoking etc. Some of the older children ask her if I like my job and how much I make and some of the girls say they want to be writers! I urged on her the duty of collaboration with Mr Jackson, and of getting them to see that there was some point in school; she said that some of them competed with her in things she beat them over, but that when she tried to talk about education they shied away; I said that she wouldn't be able to see results yet.

We went over to the airfield again later; Mr MacGeachy told me how the bigwigs of Campbeltown had opposed the aeroplanes getting the letter contract but were now extremely pleased with the quick service. Dick arrived; he had had various adventures, largely owing to getting the wrong train at Euston; it seems to be rather easy to get wrong trains just now.

26 October 1939

. . . I found young Dick's article in the *Manchester Guardian*★ and couldn't resist taking it round to show everybody and making them guess who R.G. [Robin Gandy] was. They were all awfully pleased but Angus says there is a mistake; you don't bother about the wind when shooting the net, only about the tide. That's different from what Sandy told me. Angus also said that when he was fishing they hit with the anchor, not with a mallet on the gunwhale. Angus thought I wrote it, but I swore I hadn't, and he was really proud of young Dick. I felt, myself, like a hen who's hatched out a pheasant. And I did type it all for him! I don't suppose he has seen it himself yet. I wonder how shy he'll be.

Again, a good many letters to write. I'm beginning to get some fan mail for the *Blood of The Martyrs*, [her most recently published novel] which is a comfort after the nasty reviews I've had. There are some rather nasty crab apples on the *Pyrus floribunda*. But better than no apples . . .

28 October 1939

. . . I had tried to read the *New Statesman* at intervals all day to see if there was anything for our meeting, but never really had time. Young Dick turned up and we had supper—roast grouse and jam tarts and cream. Val brought cider for the two men. Young Dick looked tired and had a cold. He hadn't seen his article, and said Oh my goodness and made a face. I don't know what he really thinks. Alec and Anna

★ An article called 'After the Herring' appeared in the *Manchester Guardian* on Thursday 26 October 1939. It was signed RG but was the joint effort of Robin and Young Dick. It described a night out on a Carradale fishing boat and although the names have all been changed, it obviously came directly from Young Dick's own experience as a fisherman.

read it, and thought it good; so had Bella, who liked the conversations.

We talked about our resolutions at supper, and then Lilla came and we drew up the agenda. Then Hugh; Angus couldn't because his wife isn't well and in view of her heart trouble, he thought he ought to stay [at home]. Then a few others, and we moved to the library. But it was a very small meeting. The young people were mostly in Campbeltown, including Mairi who is on the Executive. We elected Mrs John Ritchie in lieu of Mrs MacQueen.

Alec spoke from the chair, about the seriousness of things. Denny M gave his delegate's report, reading it out; I avoided catching young Dick's eye as he was bound to know I had typed it, and would notice where the phraseology departed from Denny M's own; on the whole it wasn't bad. But even reading it, Denny M was frightfully nervous, and twisted his feet. Then I moved my resolutions on civil liberties, war aims etc. I spoke in some detail about them, trying to get into people's heads what they were about and why it mattered passing them, at the same time trying to show them that from now on it might be dangerous being a real socialist. Dick moved an anti-war, CP amendment to one of mine, which we transferred to Mrs Ley's resolution. The only people who really spoke were Alec, me and Dick, with a few remarks from Willie Buchanan, Willie Galbraith and Lilla, who were on the whole opposed, and Hugh seconding Dick's anti-war resolution. I tried to be devil's advocate and asked them if they really wanted a conference with Hitler and so on, hoping to make the opposition vocal, but it didn't work. I think the difficulty is that most of the meeting weren't anything like so conscious as the rest of us; the thing isn't really out of water. They are scarcely thinking politically, only vaguely feeling about things. A word like "working-class" doesn't really mean much, nor words like liberty and democracy. They are emotional counters, not representing sets of facts. God knows what was going on in Lachie's head; he is aware of people and animals, perhaps very deeply; I believe he gets a feeling that socialism means a new way of people being in relation with one another, which is perhaps right as an end, but is he aware of the means? I feel so much that these young men of military age must not be allowed to get involved by me in something which might be dangerous to them—in doing something which may be illegal, which may put their heads in the noose. Young Dick knows and the responsibility is his. But the others? I doubt if Denny M understands really, or Taggie. Perhaps Hugh does; perhaps Willie Buchanan. But they vote for these violent resolutions, and we have to have the meetings here in the big house because of ARP, and obviously they are to some extent following me, either out of love or out of habit.

At the end the Executive stayed on; we discussed where to send the resolutions. I was to type them. Not to the local press; I think this is wise. I said to young Dick Are you in a hurry to go? And he said No. So he stayed; Alec whispered Goodnight—Naomi, and dashed off. Young Dick and I sat in the drawing room on the floor by the fire and talked about all this problem of the unawareness of most people, also about Robin and the difficulty of communicating with him, how Robin is much more aware of class distinctions than Dick himself is. I think Dick would be at ease anywhere; he has a curious poise and sense of atmosphere; he is double-minded, which is such a pleasant change from the orthodox Marxists—he knows that this is half true but only half, that there are other ways of looking at the world beside the political, that one never speaks the real truth. That makes him a refreshing companion, because I, as a writer, know that too. We both know that you can die for a thing, but all the same that won't make it completely valid, at least for the double-minded, the fully conscious, who are perhaps the ones that matter in any generation. But can you be a good politician if you are like that? I don't know . . .

30 October 1939
. . . After tea the Mains children and MacGregors and the Barclays from Waterfoot came over and dropped forks into apples in a tub; Lachie came over in the middle to say that the horse had been lovely in the plough, and we made him try; he looks exactly like a propaganda film with his sweet smile and his blue overalls and his general un-grownupness, and always makes me feel ridiculously maternal. They all enjoyed themselves a lot; Cathie Law ordered everyone about. Then Val, Betty and Ina, John, and Ina Barclay dressed up and took their lanterns; the latter, mostly painted by Betty, are blue and white, with stripes and spots, looking very like something out of an anthropological museum; the house stinks of turnip. I drove them over to Waterfoot to Robert Campbell's; Ina dressed as a very skimpy fairy, did a music-hall turn with a spot of tap dancing; Val turned cartwheels, then took off her trousers (but she did have small knickers underneath!) and did a fling; Betty and our Ina sang a gloomy song "Down Mexico Way"; John as a policeman kept order. Mrs Campbell gave us all apples. I took them half-way back then left them to go on

with their show, bringing back John who suddenly said he was very sleepy! Then I hastily began to dress; half-way Willie and Mairi turned up. I fitted Mairi out with my red skirt and black velvet top, and Willie with the mediaeval tunic and hose, to which he added a chinese pigtail. They were very worried at not having "false faces",* as all had been sold out. So I fitted them up with black lace scarves, doubled, which looked very sinister, and are a perfect disguise.

. . . By and bye, while I was inducing poor Clym to go and sit in the car, two false faces were found, for Willie and Jennie—they are almost always *white* with a few dabs of colour, and this whiteness has a curiously ghostly effect. Added to this there is a good deal of exchanging of clothes between the sexes, so that it is very much of an apaturia: we *are* the returning ghosts. We went first to the MacDougalls, I very shy, not knowing the procedure, and almost blind in the rat mask. We sat down and were talked to; I squeaked, and Lilla (with the dog mask, Denny's trousers and a shirt with a cushion under it—she had one moment of hesitation: "Is it vulgar?") barked; Then all went into the living room and danced. We were offered tea, but of course declined it in various ways. Everyone tried to guess us . . .

We went to Lockpark and to Mrs Paterson's by the side; the refugee children in their flannel pyjamas came to look, half frightened. We were given red apples, and all sorts of attempts were made to guess us; Jennie was half guessed. Then I took them along in the car; Clym was in a state of distress, and very frightened of my mask. We stopped at the Mains to see Angus; I wasn't sure if his wife was well enough but he came to the door saying "Come in, come in!" I sat down beside Angus, who seized me round the middle and proceeded to tickle. In most of the houses Willie, and sometimes Lilla did a kind of dance. Lilla was being ragged about her cushion: "What hae ye there? Pups?" or she'd be said to be needing an operation.

I left Clym at the house and we stopped at Lachie's; all went into the wee kitchen and sat down, and Lachie stared at us in turn, like a big smiling child. Sometimes he'd make some remark in Gaelic. Then on, squashed into the little car. We tried to get into the manse but, though there were lights, it was locked against us. Willie was cross! Then to Alec's, where we had a good roughhouse; Willie had pulled me down on to his knee and was pretending to make love to me and Lilla was

* Dressing up or 'guising' is a traditional way of celebrating Hallowe'en. The 'false faces' were home-made masks worn to conceal the identities of the revellers as they romped from house to house.

doing a turn; Alec was determined to know who we were, especially the women; I'd been keeping my hands under the sleeves, but in the rough and tumble Anna spotted a ring, so that set Alec off and he began to pull my dress off. Then we all ran for it, but going blind up the steep path Willie and I tumbled over a stone, and rolled about in dumb giggles, while Alec chased us and tried to get our masks off.

Then to Dippen but they were in bed and so were [the others] at the smithy; we met another gang of maskers, and exchanged pinches and hugs; I've no idea who they were. I had the car half-way up the hill; they got in and I was afraid they'd let the brakes off. But finally they got out, shouting that they knew it was Lachie (he being the only other to drive the car!) and we went back. There was a light at Eddie's, but only Lilla and I still had our false faces, so we went in to the back door, and Eddie welcomed us. His brother was there; they said they'd guessed everyone else and they were going to know who we were; they said Give us a song, so we squeaked and barked; they put their hands down our necks, as soon as they had decided we were females, on the pretext that the dog and the wee mouse were wanting collars, and at first they decided I was Minnie someone. But they wanted to be sure, and Eddie put his back to the door so that we couldn't bolt. I had to take care not to blunder into the pram which was in the middle of the room with wee Helen asleep. Then someone came in, and proceeded to do a spot of investigating in the course of which my hair became visible; then I had an arm round my shoulders and a loud whisper—from Taggie—Cover your neck! The others didn't know me, though, and kept on trying to get hold of my hands; next time I shall take off my wedding ring! Then Taggie looked at Lilla and said: "You should know yon trousers, Eddie, you were carrying cartridges for them on Kilmichael's face!" Then there were a lot of jokes about trousers, and we were offered apples, to try and make us take the masks off. I managed to get my apple inside my mask and pretended to eat the sugar off the table and in the scuffle we got away. No one else was up, and we got to the house, where I found my coffee and biscuits that I usually have in the evening, waiting. We all had coffee and Willie and Mairi undressed; I took my mask and my top thing, but I was only in a petticoat and Denny's shirt when in came three more ghosts; I knew what to do now, welcomed them, tried to make them eat, and then proceeded to backchat, till they were all in fits of laughter. Willie helped, and soon got to know who they were—three girls from

Portrigh. It was near midnight before they left and I took the others back; it was a lovely moonlight night by now.

Describing it like that I lose the fun, the magic, the grand sense of being in the game, being part of what was going on, the apaturia that had turned into something else; I was so glad that there were no other people of my own social standing with whom I could be lumped and left; I *had* to be one of the gang. It was such fun going into the houses, and seeing them as they were, having this grand rag that was just a shade realer than any game. It was a de-tension, it was constant laughing and togetherness. I said to Willie I'm so glad you've taken to the name! And he said Aye, it comes easy now.

The diary stops temporarily on 2 November. While the war was in this 'phoney' stage, a war diary seemed irrelevant. Naomi decided to devote more of her time to the play she was writing for the people of Carradale.

1940

NAOMI MITCHISON RESUMED her full diary in May 1940 after short entries written during March. She later recalled that during this period she had been anxious and depressed. It had been a particularly harsh winter. War events felt remote and there hadn't seemed much point in keeping a war diary.

Nevertheless, military conflicts were still taking place, notably at sea. Several young men of Naomi's acquaintance had joined the Navy, including Hank Earle and young Dick Galbraith. The impact of German naval activities on merchant shipping together with the government's measures to gear the economy to war production were beginning to affect everyday life in small but irritating ways. Food rationing had been introduced in January and petrol rationing had been in operation since the previous September. In June 1940, the Home Office declared that Kintyre was no longer a safe reception area for evacuees but by then many of the mothers and children who had been billeted in Carradale had returned to their homes.

Apart from one visit south in February, Naomi was now firmly established in Carradale. She was, at the age of forty-two, once again pregnant and intended to be at Carradale House for the birth of her baby which was due in July. Meanwhile she was fully involved in local affairs, especially the building of the new village hall which she and Dick had helped to initiate. The three Gibson children, Betty, Mat and Ina were still in her care and she had taken responsibility for Betty's education. Her own four younger children were away at school and Denny, the eldest, was continuing his medical training at University College Hospital in London. Dick, who was working with Douglas on Beveridge's Manpower survey, was still lodging at the Coles' house, 'Freeland' at Hendon.

The offensive which Stalin had launched against Finland in order to consolidate his position against potential German aggression ended on 12 March. The Finns were compelled to accept Russian terms.

Thursday 14 March 1940
It seems appropriate to re-begin this diary on the day that the Finns accepted the Soviet peace terms, and the day that the boats came in after winter fishing.

I want to go on with it for a few weeks, anyhow. It seems doubtful whether anything very spectacular will happen within the next few weeks, but one may as well record the moods of this war while they are happening. It is now more than six months since the beginning. A year ago none of us would have imagined that after the six months of a modern war we should still be capable of normal existence, normal —pre-war—pleasures and disappointments and worries. But that is what is happening. At the end of January, I, at least, felt more doubtful; it looked like "a push in the Spring". When I went down to London early in February I thought I might possibly be there when the air raids started; I took my gas-mask and all; I felt the dark shutter of the future immediately ahead. Now even that seems doubtful.

We don't know what effect the ending of the Russo-Finnish war will have; my immediate feeling was one of great relief; I like wars to end. Also the last thing I wanted was our going to war with the Soviet Union; I thought that was one of the things I probably ought to be willing to go to prison about, and at the moment I don't want to have to go to prison. Also, I have become so counter-suggestible to capitalist newspapers, Government propaganda, the BBC and Transport House, that I found it hard to believe even the good of the Finns which I knew for certain existed. Yet I'm not sure how much this can be thought of in those sort of terms. Good and evil and all that. Nor do I now believe that this is victory for "the other side", that it is a victory for fascism.

. . . Lunch alone, reading Foster's *Lectures on the History of Physiology*, and Yeats' poems. I like meals by myself with a book. Then post came, with a letter from Jacobsen saying they'd taken my thing for *Lilliput*, and one from Nancy [agent] who has sold one of my shorts. The first things I've placed this year though. Also two days' papers, etc. It has been wet and gloomy but today was brilliant sunshine; I thought I'd go out, and perhaps should see old Campbell, so went down to the stepping stones, but it was high tide; Clym on the lead kept jerking me. Then I saw the boats were in at Waterfoot, and went on down; the *Alban* was just coming in, the last of them. I watched her berthing. Everyone was busy on the other boats; one or two waved to me; the *Cluaran* was there. I liked watching these men whom I now know so well doing their work, coiling ropes and jumping and handling the boats skilfully. It was like watching someone in a lab, or a sculptor, or whoever it might be. Some of them I had seen last at the wedding, all dressed up and fine; now they were in their working clothes, part of a community of which I believe that I know something. And the wind blew cold and sharp and the sun shone and everything was lively and bustling with movements and shouting.

Some of them were jumping off on a pole, and one fell in, others were ragging them; the tide was making all the time. Several of them talked to me. Then the *Cluaran*'s crew came off, and I walked up with them. Denny M and Archie and I branched off to walk back across the warren; I let Clym go and he bounced off through the bracken, jumping in arcs with the sunlight silvering his outline. We talked lightly of all sorts of things, Power standing for Argyll, Nationalism and all that; we sat down by the fence, then it got cold and I said I'd go on with them and see the cows.

. . . It was nice being with them; I would never have thought to be so much at ease across so thick a class barrier. Quite apart from any special feelings, it was this ease, this lightness, which was odd: the fact that one could speak or be silent, and the silences were not embarrassing.

The death of the incumbent Unionist MP for Argyll prompted the Argyll bye-election of 10th April 1940. As a result of the wartime electoral truce between the three main parties, neither the Liberals nor the Labour Party contested the seat. The Unionists put forward Major McCallum as the Government candidate. The Scottish Nationalists, who were not party to the truce, put forward William Power. Power's campaign attracted considerable support in Argyll because it gave priority to the immediate needs of the Highlanders, addressing the issues of rural depopulation and economic decline. Power was criticised by many for being 'unpatriotic' despite the fact that he was not campaigning on an anti-war platform.

Saturday 16 March 1940
The fates seem against this diary. My typewriter is behaving badly, and I can't see just how to put it right. Also, Alec has been here all evening, and it is late now. He and I are both very much bothered about the Labour Party here. While I was away, the study groups dropped off and the one meeting had about six people at it! Excuses are produced, but—it isn't a real Party at all, and how can we make it into one? How can we stop the Big House influence? I'd resign, but if I did it would just be a victory for the church. I met Mrs M twice today. It is such an effort to remain polite, when the smarmy old bitch oozes at me and I know she is doing all she can to smash my kind of life. I don't know whether she can be overcome by pacifist methods: not, I think,

until she attacks. I wish I could induce her to. But the church has a hellishly strong hold and all this Sunday business. I don't know if people are frightened of hell-fire or merely of breaking the conventions. People have joined the Party for the most inadequate motives.

. . . I feel pretty depressed about the whole thing; I'm willing to give them a good deal, of time and energy and thought and love. Take, eat. But what good is it going to do? Mightn't they be better let alone? Is it possible to do anything from above? I have to sacrifice a good deal in order to live here: above all the privacy that a big town gives, the privacy of the crowd in the Underground, in which one can think one's own thoughts and let one's eyes cloud with any kind of imagining. Here I have to be good. And it's difficult, especially with no supernatural sanction. Alec thinks I'm good; by now he would think almost anything I did was right. But all round there are men and women waiting to catch me out. Sometimes I could scream. How can a writer work in these conditions? . . .

The Unionists held Argyll in April but the Scottish Nationalists acquitted themselves more than honourably by getting 37 per cent of the vote, the largest vote against a Government candidate since the war began. The Unionist candidate was given a rough reception by the fishermen when he visited Carradale during his electioneering tour. At an open-air meeting on the pier, he was confronted with local grievances: the discontinuation of the passenger steamer service to Campbeltown, the closing of the pier, the requisitioning of fishing vessels for military use which deprived the fishermen of some of their income. The *Glasgow Herald* reported that Mrs Mitchison was "prominent among the questioners". When McCallum finished, she seized the platform to oppose his views and to expound her own. Many people, including Naomi herself, believed that the SNP would have done even better if people had not been frightened by the announcement only a day or so earlier that the Allies had decided to challenge Scandinavian neutrality by mining Norwegian waters and landing troops. On 9 April the Germans invaded Denmark and Norway. The 'phoney war' was finally over. In early May, Hitler's troops moved into Belgium, Luxembourg and Holland. Chamberlain resigned and Churchill formed the National Government.

Monday 20 May 1940
In the morning Dick went back to London; we would both have liked some assurance that we would be seeing one another again: and in at least tolerable circumstances. It was less dramatic, less moving perhaps, than when he went back to London from Glasgow Central

the Wednesday of Munich, or when he went back from Campbeltown by air last September. But it was more depressing. I am alone now for the first time for some weeks; the last time I was alone, in March, none of this had happened. One hardly listened in; one could forget for hours. I feel sick this evening; I have a kind of pressure at the back of my head, the same I used to get as a child after frightening nightmare. The rats are making a lot of noise under the drawing room floor: not that I mind them . . .

Thursday 23 May 1940
Nightmares. Almost inevitable. And the baby wriggling terrifically all night. I am thinking much less about this baby than I ever did about the others; I haven't made little she-plans about it as I did with the others; the future is black fogged ahead of one; all one can cultivate is acceptance.

I read Sitwell's *Gothick North* in bed: 1930, last year of the millenium. Foreseeing nothing. Exquisitely unconnected. Then, this morning, Calderwood's *Kirk of Scotland*, which *is* connected. People thinking of one another with the same hate they now put into the political ideologies. It makes one long for centuries of tolerance, the late 17th and 18th. Or must there be hate in order to be life? Is it that the western democracies lack enthusiasm, lack hate except of a private kind, that makes them weak? Can we also not love? When the French are commanded to die for their country, what does it say to them? Does it rouse anything now? It says nothing at all to me. All that was finished between 1914 and 1918. And surely it says nothing to the young.

George Wishart, Helene Stirk and the rest of the Scottish martyrs, they did at least believe simply and definitely in an immediate future life. Must we restore superstitions, heaven and hell, to make people brave? Or does my own cowardice simply reflect itself through my mind on to others? Are other people, stupider people perhaps, braver? I *did* hate during the Austrian counter-revolution; I hated Dollfuss and Fey and that lot; I hated Dollfuss enough to shock respectable folk on the *New Statesman*; but I was hating them through other people's eyes and minds. Would I hate if my immediate family were killed, if Dick and Denny were killed in London, as obviously they may be, without my seeing either of them again? I don't know. But I rather doubt it. I think I hated Ernie Bevin quite a lot at the Hastings Conference, when he spoke against G.L. [George Lansbury]. But it was an immediate, personal kind of thing; I don't really hate him. I hope he'll do a good job. But the people in the Reformation hated one another properly.

In the afternoon went over to Mains to see how things were there. Ian MacLaren putting in the drains and gutter for the Hall in a leisurely way. He says they are building a big new aerodrome at Machrihanish "for the aeroplanes from America, after all it's the nearest place". There has certainly been a lot of air activity lately. How I hate them. Some of them do practice diving at the house which is horrid.

The Glasgow children all look extremely well and gay (except Cathie who always looks grumpy); Mrs Ritchie says the boys are better about bed-wetting, though not right; Ina much better so long as someone gets her up twice a night; John hopeless. I don't see how I can park the bed-wetters out on anyone else, but Mrs Ritchie just must have a rest; in fact she wouldn't stay on after Miss Crawford leaves at the end of June. Unless there are actual air raids, the bed-wetters must go back to Glasgow. Apparently Mrs L, on leaving her Portrigh billet, had all the mattress covers washed or cleaned, and it wasn't till afterwards that Mrs Galbraith realised the state the beds themselves were in! I'd no idea of all this when I took them in. The house is in an awful mess, but most of it can be put right with distemper and paint.

. . . Everyone seems pleased to hear that Val is coming back; I am arranging for her to have lessons with Jackson after school; she could also learn carpentry from Angus and singing from Lilla. Betty had escaped this afternoon so I couldn't give her any French. I read a review book from the *Tribune*, Hitler Youth; it is obviously true, and rather moving. I am to do a long article on that, a small one on the minority report on abortion; it's nice having a job of writing to do, even if one isn't paid for it. It keeps one's mind and hand in.

The 6 o'ck news, with the fighting at Boulogne and capture of Abbeville, was a bit of a shock. I remember so well going through Abbeville when Dick was wounded and I went out as next of kin. I began to worry a lot about him and Denny in London and the others at school. Winchester is very near Southampton. I looked at the map, to see just how far all the children's schools were from Boulogne. They might easily drop parachutists in Surrey. Also worrying about possible suppressing of CP with all one's friends. I do hope Denny will be sensible and just work and not try to make "contacts" in London; he isn't old enough to know who's trustworthy, and he's pretty good at putting his foot in it from the highest motives.

Saturday May 25 1940

... Val turned up, dirty and charming, having done her journey most successfully, picking up the usual number of people on the way, including, finally, the Minister Johnson, who, she said, was much more like a journalist. We discussed what she was to learn here.

... After tea I read part of *Midsummer Night's Dream* to her and Betty. How lovely it is, how I should like to have written it. V curled up beside me ...

... Dick says in his letter "We might all have to bolt for Australia, if indeed we could get there. I wonder if any of the fishermen would risk an Atlantic crossing." Of course we've both got bad political records, if the Gestapo *did* come over—But it seems so fantastic. He half thinks so and half not. I should like just to have a taste of the London atmosphere; it is too safe here to understand. Funny, I suppose I would be in London but for this baby. I can't say I'd like an Atlantic crossing at the moment, in a herring boat; one wouldn't be able to take much, because most of the space would be needed for the diesel oil. Yet I feel guilty to have been so little involved. Dick, I think, has joined the anti-parachutists, both at Hendon and here; he says he has dissuaded Margy from laying in a barrel of doped beer for them—some might be teetotallers! ...

Thursday 30 May 1940

... Remains of the Carradale [Labour] Party turned up tonight, mostly the committee, except Mairi who had gone to the pictures. We decided to go on but only to meet once or twice a year. Most of the time we talked amateur strategy; several had heard Gram Swing's story that Italy was coming in. As this has officially been denied, it is probably true. Are we to bomb Florence and Venice? That will be a triumph of modern civilisation! All a little depressed by Moscow being so high-hat. Alec was very gloomy, Angus and Taggie sure we should win in the end. Both Angus and Alec, who were very ILP, had decided that this was after all a war for survival, not an Imperialist war, as they had thought at first.

Discussed rumours; several sinister people have been seen; one, who was deliberately mis-directed by our woodcutters, was the net-man from Campbeltown! He was later seen on the golf course, making notes—presumably about nets. Angus found a bit of an aeroplane on the warren and took it over to show MacKillop the joiner; they decided that whoever the tradesman who had worked on

it, it was grand work. The next day this had got round to Campbeltown and a Govt official came to see the bit of wood. The milkman is
one of the main rumour culprits. We also talked about the amount of
scrap iron lying about and the stupidity of the new rails they are
putting up round the housing estate.

We discussed German agents in disguise; Archie said he had often
noticed what big feet nuns had, and probably the half of them were
men; the conversation, as Scottish Presbyterian conversations do,
then became extremely ribald. We also tried to think what it would be
like *here* supposing the Nazis won; I have a nasty feeling that I should
get into a concentration camp; I wish this baby were due a month
sooner. It is a damned awkward time.

Then all came into the other room to hear the 9 o'ck news. All were
thinking in terms of the men, especially those who had been in the last
war. We wondered if there was any truth in the rumour that tanks had
been seen lying idle for lack of petrol, and discussed Rumania. All
these folk with fishing connections are particularly upset at naval
disasters, such as the loss of these destroyers.

I notice I have bitten my nails very badly, a thing I have not done for
months . . .

Sunday 2 June 1940
In the morning read *New Statesman*, *Tribune* and part of a pamphlet.
Very odd to see the *N.S.* going all militarist, blaming the Government
because it "postponed conscription to the last moment" etc. Cross-
man—? Kingsley Martin, in diary, sympathetically saying that imagination and education "make life more difficult". Undoubtedly
they do. Is it simply because I am living in a safe or practically safe
place, that I still feel so *minoritaire*, so unable to be whole-hearted about
all this, to lose myself in the herd feeling about the war. I do agree that
Hitler has to be stopped, but—by giving up everything? Isn't this the
trahison des clercs? Mustn't one try to keep some intellectual values,
some aesthetic values, even? On the other hand, if intellectual values
are represented by the *New Statesman* reviewers, to hell with them!

Food rationing had been introduced on January 8. Each adult person was
allowed 4 oz bacon or ham per week, 4 oz butter and 12 oz sugar. Later the
same month, the bacon ration was increased to 8 oz. In March, meat was
rationed to 1s. 10d worth per week (about 1–1½ lbs depending on quality).
The entry of Italy into the war affected the importation of many goods,
including foodstuffs. In July tea, margarine and cooking fats were reduced to

2 oz per person. The weekly cheese ration also fluctuated to between 2 and 8 oz per person. By May 1941, the cheese ration was cut down to 1 oz per person.

Monday 3 June 1940

Semple has started the ice-cream business; Val and I got some. They're as good as ever. Unfortunately all the rhubarb we'd been bottling is beginning to go. Everything seems to unless there is masses of sugar in it, which is so maddening. We have a certain amount of sugar saved, but of course it won't be easy after the present ration. The cut in butter will be no hardship, as nobody really knows the difference except me. I am trying to have cheese dishes etc, as much as possible. The meat isn't nearly as good as it used to be when Paterson killed and sold his own instead of having to take what he could get. We have bought about half a big jar full of eggs laid down in water-glass; I am getting smoked haddock once a week from Campbeltown which helps with that. The hens are not laying very well, and Eddie still hasn't cleaned out the hen house in the warren. Only I don't like to scold him too much when he's just going off. I have still a fair amount of last year's jam—or rather mostly jelly (red and white currant and gooseberry, all tasting exactly the same) but we use it fairly quickly between here and Mains. Few of us eat much sugar, but this week Jessie is making birthday cakes for both Lois and Murdoch. Have laid in some more soap, and coffee, which we can't get locally. Difficult to get Jessie to take the rationing seriously, though. She so enjoys cooking and longs for more material and more elaborate things to do! . . .

Friday 7 June 1940

Again very hot; we are cutting the long grass in the orchard, lovely as it is, and the shorter grass outside the house. Matthew helped the plumber with the pipe in the field, which is curiously eaten into—I hope only in one length!

This last broadcast of Reynaud [French Prime Minister]: talking of the time when the military virtues were under-estimated, but now they would come into their own. One thinks of people in whom the military virtues are encouraged; after the last war they became Black and Tans. And now? If this is to be a world of military virtues, then my side has lost. Be we not swift with swiftness of the tigress, Let us break ranks when nations trek from progress. We have *got* to have other virtues.

Letters: from poor Mrs Pribram: her husband (naturalised two generations and a skilled engineer) has been sacked from his position in the plane factory just because he was an Austrian. They are leaving and going to the Bahamas, as there is no job here. Goodness knows what there will be there. I should think Eglè would fall on her feet, but it is a wretched commentary on things now and on the anti-German (as opposed to anti-Nazi) propaganda which is being put across. The return of nationalism . . .

Monday 10 June 1940
. . . French with the children; could not find the book, used another. Ordered maths books for Val. Stopped to listen to the news; Italy in. One had expected it though.

While we were going on with French Jemima came in; walked round the garden with her; she says that her boyfriend who was wounded came back and was quite changed; she had expected they would come to a formal understanding, but, as she said, "I've been jilted". She said it had hurt a lot, but now she was beginning to be able to laugh and to see that he wasn't like he had been. She'd have liked to find out why he'd altered but she didn't want to see him now. I said it was no use trying to find out about people's motives unless one was going to write novels about them, and suggested she should write a poem. She said what was worrying was that everyone was laughing at her and talking about it, and she was feeling so restless and would like to go off after harvest and do nursing but she didn't know if she was up to standard, educationally. I said I would find out about nursing, and thought that anyhow she was bound to go away and have a life of her own some time; her parents couldn't keep her forever to farm work. She said she wished she'd gone on with the first aid class as she had found it interesting, but after she had missed two lessons—it was very bad weather—she had felt affronted, that she couldn't face the class again, they'd feel she'd shirked.

With the evacuation of the British Expeditionary Force from France at Dunkirk, the war took a serious turn. Mussolini declared war on the Allies on 10 June. There followed a wave of anti-Italian feeling which even reached Campbeltown. The government rounded up many Italians together with other 'enemy aliens' (mostly Germans and Austrians) and incarcerated them in internment camps. The plan was to deport them eventually to the Dominions.

Tuesday 11 June 1940

. . . In the afternoon to Mains. They are getting on well with the Hall; I had a talk to Ian MacLaren, the plumber, who said there had been bad anti-Italian riots in Campbeltown; the three Italian shops had been broken up. The old man had been rather rash, saying that England needed a totalitarian govt and so on, but the younger ones were all decent, good citizens who gave money in charity and paid their taxes; one had contributed £50 to the Provost's fund; one of the youngest generation was in a mine sweeper. Ian had passed there early in the evening, and had seen a crowd hanging about and laughing, and wondered what was going to happen; people were beginning to get drunk; but he went home, then heard crashes and came out again and found the shops being broken up. If the tide had been in they would have put the old man into the harbour; the worst were the Polish sailors. But mostly they were like "grown-up boys", out for a bit of fun, and could easily be made to go the other way. Half of them were no good, on public assistance and so on. Someone had said it was a shame, and had promptly been knocked down. He, Ian, had stood by; you couldn't help thinking it was funny. But he would be as friendly as he could to the Italians next time he saw them.

Thursday 13 June 1940

. . . Wrote several letters, one to Tony [Pirie]; there are a few people that I want desperately to see, mostly women, like Tony, Storm [Jameson] and one or two others.

I feel they're more likely to be sane than men, less certain of themselves, less arrogant, more able to see two sides to any question. Perhaps if they had men's power they'd become as destructive, though: the best argument for the subjection of women! . . .

German troops entered Paris on 14 June; on the 16th, Paul Reynaud, the French Prime Minister, resigned and was replaced by Marshal Pétain. In Britain the fear of invasion by Germany grew acute and a second spate of evacuations took place. Denny Mitchison returned to Carradale with his girlfriend, Ruth Gill, a fellow medical student.

Friday 14 June 1940

Everything overshadowed by Paris going. I suppose one had to expect it, but it was a bit of a bump. I've lived there enough for it to have got into my bones a bit. One can't help feeling a bit of the real war hate creeping into one. The feeling that one wants to do the same thing to Berlin and all that. Ruth says she feels the same. Says she thinks a lot of people have been trying to stop that feeling, but it's difficult now . . .

. . . A letter from Mrs Earle saying that Hank was in the *Glorious* and is missing. Extremely unlikely that he can be a prisoner. Especially as he was in a gun turret. I never knew he had left Greenock; I was expecting him to ring up any evening. Somehow I had counted on his coming through. He hated war so much, and the whole life. He had been going to be a C.O. and then decided to go into the Navy. He said in his last letter that it was hell being in a gun turret, not able to stand upright. And then you get shelled and probably scalded to death. I've done up cuts and things for him so often.

Last war, the first person I loved to be killed was Tom Gillespie; I remember hearing about that, in the front drive at Oxford, by the chestnut tree, which was smaller then. This leaves a duller pain and no excitement or dramatisation . . .

In mid-June, Dick Galbraith (Young Dick), returned to Carradale on leave from the Navy.

Saturday 15 June 1940
[Young Dick] . . . was looking well and brown, his odd-coloured blue eyes showing magnificently; but he was jumpy. He had been posted to a boat after two days at Lowestoft; after some hesitation he confessed that it was called *Our Bairns*! They were sent off to mine-sweeping in the Channel and told to go to Le Havre; they expected nothing, but arrived to find half the town in flames and evacuation going on; they were bombed from the air; he said it was terrible being dived at; the planes were in the eye of the sun and they couldn't see them properly till they were almost on them. There were no Allied planes. One bomb dropped close astern and cracked the condenser and did other damage—hence his leave. They all went ashore and looted the closed shops, as otherwise the Gerrys would have got the stuff; they got chocolate and wine "which was awfully nasty", cheap champagne it sounded like, but the mate, older and wiser, filled a sack with coats and hats. The Old Man asked him where the hell he'd been and gave them all a lecture on looting, but it doesn't sound like strict discipline. The minesweepers are Harry Tate's Navy—none of the fishermen take to discipline and all wear overalls on board. There is a crew of seven "two Scots forby me", the rest mostly from 'ull and Fleetwood; he imitated

66

Yorkshire dialect, thinking it very funny, but they used some Scots words.

This was the first time he had been south of the Border; he found the South English very hard to make out, with their quick, clipped talk. He had had an hour or two in London and had walked along the Embankment; he hadn't thought much of the Houses of Parliament. He liked the life all right, but there was no serious talk and coming north in the train he had dreamt of being bombed. He was still all shaken; it was afterwards you felt it. London had been hurried and full of war, but by Carlisle he felt he was getting out of things; Glasgow looked gloomy too, but by the time he got to Wemyss Bay and the steamer and the Argyll voices, he knew he was home. He walked along the terrace, looking at the flowers and the gap in the tree that he always said was like a door into another world: the garden where he'd been garden boy not so many years ago . . .

Tuesday 18 June 1940
. . . Ruth and the rest of us went down to the Mission Hall to the LDV★ meeting.

It was a real farce; by the end of it I couldn't possibly believe there was a real war on, in fact I was in fits of giggles. Mr Baker was in the Chair and made some strange remarks about the Empire; it was a fullish meeting, about two thirds men. The speaker was a sweet man called Watson, I think a farmer, who began to read to us out of a document called SECRET. He told us which were danger zones for sea-planes, and produced a special reason why Carradale should be guarded. Rifles might be issued soon. Campbeltown seems to be held by what appears to us a rather small force, but they managed to get from Campbeltown to —— in seven minutes, and "wounded two men while they were at it" by letting off a gun accidentally. Most of the arms are going to the towns at present, but country districts would have their turn. Watchers were important; when they saw something they were to ring up the police station and would then be asked "a series of questions in set form" by the policeman.

He read us some more bits and then asked for questions. As there were none to start with, I asked if women could be watchers, as several

★ The LDV (Local Defence Volunteers, later re-titled the Home Guard) had been formed in May. It was composed of men who, for one reason or another, were not eligible for military service. The LDV provided Britain's civilian defence organisation against invasion by Germany.

had asked me. He said that he thought it was what should be done but it couldn't be official. They could be runners too. I suggested it was a long run to Campbeltown. He said we should use cars if possible: "the most people have plenty petrol here." There was then an argument about the special reason, settled by Mrs Ritchie, who knew all about it. Alec said the best way to Campbeltown was by a speed boat if we had one. Cameron asked for duties and hours, which Watson was very vague about. He said that when we got the rifles (or even before!) we could have rifle instructions from one of the old soldiers here. Semple thought we had better get names, so it was decided to do that at once. So about seventeen men, probably about all who could go (they wouldn't take fishermen) went over to the table and had their names taken . . .

Saturday 22 June 1940

. . . Denny M came over in the evening, back from the north, much as ever. Wondering whether he'd be getting called up later on, if so he would like to go into the merchant service. Most of the boats would be taken and there would be no point in staying on. He obviously feels restless about the fishing. Walked round the garden, looking at the flowers: How can they have a war with everything so bonny? Had seen Mrs MacLeod, the Chief, at Dunvegan, talked about me: said she was "almost a socialist", as I suppose he feels that anyone who isn't as oppressive as his late lairds must be! Denny produced the *Daily Worker* for him, and he agreed, but he hasn't much political sense really. He said how sorry he was about Hank: there was something noble about that fellow, he was the best of the lot.

Got on very well with Ruth, asked were they engaged, he hadn't seen any ring, I said that's not the way they do things; they've never said to me they were engaged, only discussed how many children they were going to have! Added it was important that she should get qualified and start practising without being bothered; perhaps some day they might turn up married. He doesn't really see the point of equality of sexes, of course, though he pretends to, but says there must be "a hairsbreadth of difference" between them. . . .

In preparation for the arrival of the new baby, Naomi had engaged a young Australian woman, Rosemary Jones, to act as her secretary and to help with the running of the household. The birth itself was to be attended by a nurse and by Dr Hunter, an obstetrician from Glasgow. Of the Mitchison children, only Val and Denny (with Ruth) were to be at home for the birth. The other three returned later in the month from their schools in the south.

Saturday June 29 1940
... Avrion has had air-raids too; they were rather cold and frightened at first, but now sleep downstairs. I wish I knew how certain this place was to be safe. Ought he to come up? There is a queer kind of lull in the news; pleasing that Balbo★ is killed, though I'm afraid he is of little importance now. Last night there were planes over here, but presumably our own.

My nurse turned up this afternoon, and seems very nice, friendly and sensible, comes from far north, near Wick, Sinclair's land. She and Rosemary got things together. Have my carpet up and the floor washed etc. But still I don't quite believe in it. Took her round the garden.

Monday 1 July 1940
Start the day with hot bath, quinine and castor oil. Still feel a bit remote, even with the latter. Wish they'd tell us which towns had been bombed but suppose they can't. Wonder if we ought to have buckets of sand, etc . . . But so improbable here . . .

Seemed to start off after third go of pituitrin, but then died down. Forgot to listen to 1 o'ck news! Started pituitrin again in afternoon; some effect after two doses. Definite news from Mrs Earle that Hank is killed; she wants to know what she could give the money to; Stuart might know.

Another two doses of pituitrin—but I went to sleep and it stopped. Damned nuisance!

Eglè has turned up, having had air-raids almost every night where she is near Hull. But very full of life and conversation! They had their passages booked for the Bahamas, but their visas didn't arrive. She has also had offers of American hospitality, but the trouble is getting the passage. She seems very cheerful, though.

Started reading Agnes Mure MacKenzie's history of Scotland.

Wrote a letter to *Time* suggesting they should take more of our anti-Nazi refugees. One possible way of getting things across.

Dr Hunter turned up with a charming little dog; wandered round the garden with her. She doesn't want to start anything till tomorrow

★ Governor of Libya, Italy's North African colony.

morning. The baby in the meantime frightfully stirred up and wriggly.

Rang up Dick to tell him not to sit up for me! He was rather worried. But said he had been to Bristol to see Lois, was told the hotel and railway station were in ruins, but found a few windows broken in the hotel and the approach to the station about as much ruined as the Bristol Corporation could have done by taking it up! Is leaving them both.

Denny to an LDV meeting; mostly about who was to take what watches. He and Alec take Wednesday nights. Great discussion about caves . . . in case enemies were found in them. Val is making him an armlet. He and Ruth went out and chopped wood; I would so much like Ruth to stay on! I hate the idea of her going to Cambridge. They were cutting wood after supper and I went out and joined them. We played a great game of throwing the wood in through the shed door; I do like having someone to play with.

Thursday 4 July 1940
Slept all right, with Dial, a few contractions in the night but not many. Pretty nervous and worried by morning: also rather frightened, more for the baby than for myself. However Dr Hunter was extremely nice. Says it is perfectly o.k., that it does sometimes take days with an induction. We also talked about schools, housing etc, and about Ruth and Denny and the difficulties of a woman being able to work and also be married. But it is a nuisance to have these days with nothing to do in them, as I have everything tidied up; one is bound to concentrate more on oneself, which is so stupid, more than ever now.

4th to 7th
I had better get this over. The induction began to work about 1.30 on the 4th; by 3.15 I had vomited, etc, had a very severe shivering fit, and was beginning to have very adequate first stage pains. I was however very glad it had started. By 6 they were quite severe, and shortly afterwards I asked for some kind of dope. I had scopolamine★ and morphine, on the strict understanding that these would have no effect on the baby. After a quarter of an hour I got drowsy, had another injection, and all but the worst pains got clouded over. I think I had another later, but my time sense is uncertain, and I remember little

★ A relaxant drug.

70

until two or three violent pains, which appeared to me to be second stage; I said that the head was breaking through and I wanted some chloroform at once. I was right and the final stage was over in a few minutes, before Dr Cameron had arrived, even. I awoke to hear them say I had a lovely little girl; I said that was right, that was what I wanted. I asked several times, was she all right. They said yes, and I think I thought so, as they had worked on her for some time and thought she was breathing all right; I just saw her and kissed her. The rest of the night—it was then after 2 o'ck, I lay, uncomfortable but happy, mostly listening to her small noises, but thinking they were not very loud. In the morning I was still rather persistent to know what they thought of her; they said she was not very strong, but no more; I thought she was no worse than Val as a tiny. Then they said she should be bathed to get her to cry and fill her lungs, and brought her through. Ruth came in, and Val. Nurse bathed her close to me. I thought she looked cyanosed, but hoped it was a matter of establishing breathing properly. I watched her in the bath, and touched her soft hands; she had a pretty shaped head and a lot of dark hair, but seemed very weak and never opened her eyes. I was a little worried, but not much; I said to put up the flag, so they hoisted the Red Flag for her.

They said she should not come to me but must stay warm all day; I was rather sad about it, but began reading Agnes Mure MacKenzie's history of Scotland; my throat still a little sore from the chloroform. I was very thirsty. I had got to the chapter on the Bruce when the Nurse came in saying Baby's not so well. It sounded pretty ominous; she and Dr Hunter were in the other room. Rosemary came to me; I asked her to look in; she said She's not responding. I sat up, trying to make up my mind to something which still seemed not quite inevitable. By this time Denny and Val had started for Tarbert to meet Dick. Then Dr Hunter came in and I knew.

The septum of the heart had not closed properly. It would not have made any difference if she had been ten days later at full term. If she had lived it could not have been for more than a few months or years of a very wretched kind of existence. It was just one of those things which do happen. It was excessively hard to face. No one was to blame. Nothing could at any point have been done.

Dr Hunter was extremely nice to me. I did to some extent break down, although realising all sorts of logical things. It was a pretty complete crash at the moment and one could not fix on to anything else. I said to take the flag down, and asked Dr Hunter to tell Dick. I said I would like one of the boats to take her out to sea. It was no use my seeing her again, my poor sweet.

. . . On Saturday there were a number of things for Dick to do, about the estate, Hugh MacGregor, Willie, Semple, etc. He talked to me about them. I was not interested, but had to pay attention, as I shall have to deal with them. I began to realise how all this small scale life here would have been tolerable with the baby which was to have tied it all together, but now—? I envy Dick having this Ministry of Labour job; I wish I could immediately do something which would employ my mind. I dread going about again and facing people; they will be extremely sympathetic, but damn their sympathy. I feel I shall get landed with agricultural work which would have been tolerable and even delightful with a background of baby—of creation. But intolerable with one's mind empty and groping. To some extent, too, I had used this as an excuse to be out of the war, out of destruction, still on the side of creation; now that's over. I wish I could go to the south and get into an air-raid. But what's the good? The only thing I can do is write. And the only people who can write now are the real successful professionals like Priestley and co, or the equally whole-hearted antis, who can write against. Denny, no doubt, thinks I should do proper *Daily Worker* anti writing, but that's no good for a Liberal anarchist like me. Nor is it really writing.

I wish there was a chance of my making contact with any of my friends who are doing the same kind of thing as I am. If I could have a few hours with Storm [Jameson], or Margaret [Cole] or Stevie [Smith] or Joan [Rendel]—diverse enough people—or Tony [Pirie] who isn't a writer, but is my kind of woman—I might be able to work something out, stop this now ungeared engine in me from racing and battering me to destruction. But, much as I love the folk here, they can't help nor heal. Dick says I can do a great deal here; perhaps, but can one when the heart is out of one?

. . . The silly thing is that I realise perfectly that much worse things are happening at this moment to thousands of people (and indeed have done so for a long time), but one cannot generalise as simply as that. I at least cannot change pain into love. And all the little things hurt, hurt, hurt, and there is nothing to be done. Nor is it fair to speak about them to others; nor indeed, would the others understand one's minding so much. But she was part of me, and wanted, all these months, and warm, and one said what a nuisance, but lovingly, and now the whole thing is ended: the love has no object. I had dreamt so often of the sweet warmth and weight of a baby at my breasts and now my bound breasts ache. If I get at all drowsy I begin to expect someone to bring the baby in, and that's hell. One has to keep awake.

... All this was meant to be a kind of binding between me and Carradale, and now that's smashed. I envy Dick going to Yorkshire to see about Labour conditions, somewhere ugly and nasty, and slightly more dangerous. I can't think how I shall face starting again on ordinary things. I have written to my brother and to Crewe to ask if there is any correlation between this and maternal age; if there isn't and if there is a possible-looking war situation I should like to try again. But probably I shan't be able. I am immensely impressed with the progress of obstetrics in ten years. None of the old internal examination during labour, for instance. Equally I have had no temperature (or only tonight, slightly, because of the binding up of my breasts).

Monday 8 July 1940

... Dick has gone off to Yorkshire to do an interesting job for the Ministry of Labour, to see what is actually happening about work: whether both factories and man-power are being adequately utilised, whether refugees could be used, etc. He may get back here in a fortnight, if—Extraordinary to have to run one's life on ifs.

Dr Cameron says I should start writing a book. As though one could turn on the tap. But I think I must consider it, even if nothing comes of it. I might write a history of Kintyre: that is a very small-scale history, but with implications taking in outside political and economic movements. Ending, not with vague statements about evictions, but definite family histories; and so on. I think there is a lot of material. Finished Agnes Mure MacKenzie's book: it's lively stuff, but Nationalist-Liberal-Feminist. One has to discount that. Perhaps I'll write to her. Perhaps. If. If only I had my baby I wouldn't need to write a book that probably nobody wants to read.

Tuesday 9 July 1940

... Winchester [where Murdoch is at school] is now a special area and a notice has been sent out saying that boys can be sent back, but they intend to carry on till the end of the half. Murdoch says that about 30 per cent of College have gone back, but obviously he doesn't want to come, and, if it is a case of being cut off, he would sooner be cut off in south England, as it would be more interesting; he wants to see what he can of the war, and of course is in a position of some responsibility at Winchester. I wish he were up here, but quite see his point; it would be much duller. And he is old enough to settle for himself.

Denny had a letter from St Mary's, saying they could take him to do his brain dissection now or September; he has written to say could he start at once, enclosing a telegram. He asked me if I would be all right; I shall miss him horribly, but of course he's right to go, at least I suppose so. September—? It might be next century. I expect London is as safe as anywhere; he will go to River Court. There's no shelter there (because anything underground would be flooded at high tide if the river wall went), but it's the far side of London. We had a long talk, largely about Ruth; all this makes me passionately anxious that he and Ruth should pull things off. If only one could be the sacrifice for someone else; but one can't be accidentally: that's clear enough. He of course feels that there will be a future; he's full of hope underneath. I feel I must carry on, but the underneath hope isn't there; I see endurance, but no happiness. I try and tell people that it will be a world full of building and excitement and new things: but not for me . . .

Wednesday 17 July 1940

. . . Jemima came; she has got into the other Glasgow Hospital, with no difficulty, and will be off in the middle of August; she's very pleased to be getting away, and to somewhere nearer the centre of things; I think she'll be a very good nurse. She was awfully nice to me, as usual. And after she left Lilla came, also very nice, bringing me sweeties. There was a meeting at Ayr a day or two ago, about the fishing; they have been warned not to show too many lights, and told not to go to Ayr, as it was dangerous, drifting mines presumably. So now the market is to be at Tarbert. There was some talk, even, of stopping the fishing. Lilla didn't like the BBC broadcast of the air-fight,★ says she hates Gardner anyhow. Nor did Nurse like it; both of them had the idea that the German airmen were only human too . . . Nurse talking about the airmen up north at her home: coming to tea one day and dead the next, all drinkers, many going up with something to drink inside them, boys who'll be finished when it's over. I thought of the Black and Tans. I don't know a soul in the Air Force; they aren't the kind of boys I would know . . .

★ From early July until mid-September, British and German fighter planes engaged in protracted skirmishes over British soil in what later became known as the Battle of Britain. A BBC reporter, Charles Gardner, was so excited by the conflict that he abandoned his script and broadcast a simultaneous account almost as if he were covering a sporting event.

Tuesday 23 July 1940

. . . A letter from Storm Jameson encouraging me about my history book; and saying that none of the refugee writers in France have escaped—that nice little man, Koestler—and only a few of the French writers. Romains out, but Giraudoux, Gide, Malraux all disappeared. Maurois is out. Another from Archie, saying I should come and stay; he has any amount of pull with the libraries and can get me all my documents. And sweeties for all of us from Nurse. Val beginning to feel birthdayish, but I'm doing so little for her. She and Betty will have a joint party on Saturday and ask some of the boys. . . .

. . . I wrote a review of the two Evacuation books for the *Tribune*; longer than they like, but so difficult to put in all one wants to say, especially on the main one. I want to defend the middle-class hosts who get so many of the kicks: it is assumed that any woman who takes in the children must be prepared to be a whole-time (if necessary) foster-mother. That means that the middle-class woman with any kind of profession has to drop it or else to try and keep up two jobs with the resultant extreme nerve-strain, bad for children. And also that she must be prepared to fit in with the average working class family solidarity which is extremely emotional, based on kisses and pennies one moment, and slapping the next. That's what most of the children understand, unhappily. What would the psychiatrists say if I told them about John whose bed-wetting was only cured when he was told he'd get the strap if he went on: that was what he understood and subconsciously wanted; it meant family life to him . . .

Saturday 27 July 1940

Went on reading history and having some slow ideas about it, and about what kind of book I could write. I can't really see that there's any unifying principle in history or that things get done for one reason: that is, I can't see history from the point of view of historical materialism, or national patriotism, or religion of one kind or another; the psychological view-point is attractive, the difficulty being that it can be used to prove anything—given the disastrous family, child and even pre-natal (as with James I and James VI) life of the major characters. In fact, I think people do things for a variety of reasons. I suppose I think that, because I am against (or for) several things, not just one thing. It is more comfortable to be for or against one thing, to be able to put the blame somewhere definite. But I don't think I can be. It makes one a less efficient politician of course. Over Scottish 14th to

18th century politics one has been influenced by (*a*) anti-Scottish English historians. They didn't know they were distorting facts, at least the later ones didn't. Why did they do it? Partly from archaistic national motives, especially over Henry VIII and Elizabeth. This hooks on to protestant and anti-catholic motives: here one can get in historical materialism—the main historians were all protestant bourgeois, eager to uphold their own morality, which had been a part of their getting into power. (*b*) anti-Stewart Scottish historians. These were protestant again, partly for the same motives partly from wanting to blame someone for the miserable condition of Scotland, and not being able to blame their allies the English Whigs. I suppose Scotland at the time when most historians were writing, was very dependent on British capital. Again, during the 18th and 19th centuries, kings were the enemies for many intelligent people, combining in some people's minds with priests. But now we know only too well that strangling the last king in the guts of the last priest isn't going to do the trick. So we don't feel instinctively anti-royalist. Agnes Mure Mackenzie feels that John Knox was the villain of the piece, equating him with others who have led or tried to lead, a totalitarian state. But she, in turn, does this equating too easily. I wish I knew what my besetting sin as a historian is: probably liberalism. I feel a lot of sympathy with the Armenians! I don't see that extremists of either kind could have made a decent society. I'll have to think all this out very carefully. Wish I had someone to talk it out with.

. . . Denny says he and Ruth want to get married in September, just after his 21st birthday. I think it's a good idea, as it makes it so much easier for them to share a room and so on. I should also like to feel she was definitely part of the family. But I do hope it won't interfere with her getting qualified. I told Lachie who merely remarked "Good!"

. . . I am beginning to wonder whether the tangled affairs of the Scottish nobles in the middle ages and after, aren't perhaps equally explicable in terms of Carradale—in terms of Hugh and Bella and the kitchen balance of power, in terms of Mrs Cook telling one of the Labour Party collectors that Labour Party members should visit one another when they were ill, and that if Mrs Mitchison didn't come to see her brother she would resign from the Party (this was not passed on to me by Nora—the collector—but fortunately I did go down shortly after to see her and her brother! I got no hint of her being cross then). I also wonder whether perhaps the book should be written completely backwards: whether I should take the village first, take an

76

incident, and hunt back to what it was really about. I could make a fascinating book that way; I would call it *The Roots of the Present*. But could I go on living in the place after I had published it? . . .

Saturday 3 August 1940

. . . The butter ration is complicated. We are registered with Paterson, but he doesn't so far seem to have enough stuff to go round. We take our ration 4 oz in butter and 2 oz in marg, but Paterson this week had none of the latter so we had to get it from Campbell who had marg over. I don't know if this is legal or not; it's all a bit muddling. We have had to cut down on cooking fat; but at present we have hardly any puddings, other than jellies with our own fruit in them, water ice made with fruit pulp, occasional curds, and any amount of raw fruit. We don't have meat or (our own or gift) fish more than once a day, unless there are sausages for breakfast, when we may have it twice. Sometimes "diningroom" has only vegetables, usually with cheese sauce for meals, but "kitchen" doesn't like that. We get a few eggs every day from the hens, not always enough to go round. We have fewer scones, especially the nice drop-scones that need eggs; only gingerbread cake, made with treacle . . .

Sunday 4 August 1940

Trying to get some ideas clear. About the war. It looks possible that Hitler may not try invasion now. I should think it was rather unlikely to succeed. He might try to consolidate Europe, incidentally nibbling up Malta, Gibraltar, etc. If this were effectively done, he could then stop spending on armaments, and begin to spend for prosperity, at any rate for prosperity in Germany. We should then be left out, to become poorer and poorer, shorter in wind as in memory long, to collapse through our own contradictions, at any rate to lose all our civilisation and become just a military machine. We are already beginning to do this.

. . . it looks a little bit as if we were unlikely to be able to make a successful attack on Nazi Europe. It may be possible that, if the war goes on, there may be some kind of political collapse inside Germany, but I doubt if it is more than a possibility. On the other hand it seems equally unlikely that Totalitarianism can last for very long *except* in war or near-war conditions. Which would lead one to suppose that the best thing might be to make peace. Yet we could not possibly do that and go back to anything like a peace-time footing and it would probably have a very destructive moral effect on the inhabitants of this country. We would be left in a position of permanent defence, which, in practice, means that all energies and all money must go to that. If we are to have peace it must be genuine peace, *despoina choron, despoina gamon*;* and that would not be possible with a Nazi Europe, even if it were eventually to disintegrate.

Personally, I think we are in a complete dilemma of the worst possible sort. The difficulty is that we must change very rapidly and practically nobody really wants that. We like our neighbours to change so long as it is not us. I think it was Augustine who said Lord, make me good, but not yet. This is universal. We can all stand a little change, but not a big one. Quantity alters quality. I do not think that the ordinary person can stand the amount of change which appears to be necessary. Still less, can I suppose that they can want or will it to happen. One can usually stand greater changes than one can imagine.

I may be exaggerating this, because social changes of the kind indicated would considerably lower my own standard of living and comfort; yet on the other hand, I am more aware than most people of how unimportant a good deal of this comfort is, even to my own happiness, and in fact I think I can will change of a fundamental kind (i.e. in quality) rather more than most people, at any rate than most women.

. . . Let me get on to another point. I am beginning to wonder about nationalism. This is doubtless due to reading these history books. I am wondering whether nationalism is entirely a bad thing. We have been led to suppose so and I would call myself an internationalist. *But*, why were we led to suppose so and by whom? I think that nationalism was first attacked by the Imperialist traders (first free traders, then, when other countries began to make the same things as ourselves, "tariff-reformers"); these, of course were the descendants or the Whig bourgeoisie who came into power after the revolution in the seventeenth century (which incidentally smashed Scotland as a country). Now, I think we were rather taken in. The Imperialists pretended to be nationalists of a new kind, but in fact they were against all genuine nationalism, in Scotland, Ireland etc. (This may have been partly because England is so heterogeneous, has so many different cultures, that it is hard for it to feel nationalist, especially with London bossing it; but I am not sure about this—Scotland is heterogeneous too,

* Mistress (or queen) of dances, mistress of marriages.

though not so much.) Some of them were racialists, for instance Kipling, though not of a very modern kind.

. . . Imperialism cannot develop in an international frame-work. But nationalism can do so: it does not want to conquer other nations. It wants to develop its own. I rather think that this is at the bottom of what is happening in the USSR just now. There is a tendency among the international minded Left to hold up hands of horror at Russian "nationalism", but this is because they have equated it with imperialism. But I am almost sure that nationalism is on the whole good for people, that it corresponds with something they want, and that it is not incompatible with internationalism or with peace.

Monday 5 August 1940

. . . Denny is being very gay and un-grown-up about his wedding, in fact he kept on giggling. The question is how to get the maximum number of wedding presents. We think we might ask people and put how to get here on the back; they won't come but they may be encouraged to send something! I gather my mother would like to come, and some of the Gills. We'll have a Carradale party, though most of the young people will have gone. I do hope someone will have the courage to produce the traditional wedding presents! I don't think either of them want a "quiet wedding"—they want the maximum possible fun. They also seem to realise my point of view: that in order to keep going with what is, after all, the rather wearing job of family organisation, I have to have some pegs stuck into the future to climb along by; all the pegs I had at midsummer have been knocked out, leaving gaps, and they are providing me with one. After which no doubt I can start again on my own. (This is different from my life as a writer.) So Denny was discussing details with me and making it all sound great fun. Dick didn't join in, but I don't think he needed to, and of course he hardly knows Ruth; he was talking about settling shares on them, but I am very bad at thinking seriously about money. Only it would have been nice if he could have found it fun too.

Of course it all depends on what's happening . . . and the same with their future. Yet they must plan on the supposition that the world will go on, that, for instance, there will still be Cambridge much as ever and Denny will be able to do his Part II after the war and after hospital. He is not quite sure, but he has one more term to keep. He can't get much out of going up next term (though he must be up in October to take his Qualifying) as there will not be a pharmacology course then. So he may start at hospital. They will either have a couple of rooms somewhere or share with her elder sister who is teaching. They don't plan on the supposition of any revolution or new world, but presumably that would be vain.

. . . We rang up Stewart later in the evening to find out about weddings; to my horror, I find one cannot any longer be married in a sheriff's court or by a J.P. These bloody English have altered our laws completely. So the choice is church (which of course they don't want) or being married by the registrar here. We suggested that Blackwood might be asked in to marry them in the house, which would have the excellent effect of making both ministers furious . . . but I don't believe under this rotten English law you can be married in a house any longer.

The nearest good shopping centre was Glasgow and Naomi made occasional excursions on the boat from Tarbert to Wemyss Bay and then by train to Glasgow Central. By August, many signposts and station signs had been removed to confuse the enemy in the event of an invasion. The 'Mightier Yet' poster showed a huge destroyer and urged support for the British Navy.

Denny accompanied her on this trip which was to include shopping for the forthcoming wedding, a post natal examination at Dr Hunter's, a visit to the dentist and meetings with various Glasgow friends and contacts. John MacCormick had been William Power's agent at the Argyll bye-election and was well-known in his own right as a prominent Scottish Nationalist. The socialist publication *Forward* had been edited in Glasgow since it began in 1906. It had always had a strong ILP line. Its wartime editor, Emrys Hughes, became Labour MP for South Ayrshire in 1946.

Monday 12 August 1940
Came over to Wemyss Bay in the very crowded boat. All the mouth of the Clyde filled with mixed shipping. Submarines and things. On the line up the small, sad and nameless stations; one slept for a moment, and tried to guess where one was on waking, but no clues. Some oat fields cut already. Ours will be early too. Somewhere a new works with buried and isolated shops, presumably for explosive of some kind. The new "Mightier Yet" poster. The only nice things the strips of stuff on the windows of the waiting rooms at Paisley(?) making clean patterns. A bit unnecessary to take off the names at Glasgow Central?

In the streets, strange uniform, Polish mostly, and camouflaged cars and lorries. Odd and dizzy being in a crowd again. Few people take their gas-masks. We go to a flick and see half a Marx brothers: great fun. The newsreel with the horrible commentator making frightful jokes and encouraging morale I suppose: Pathé. How I hate it all. How I should like to see united effort for construction, for peace (but would the same man still do the newsreel propaganda?); how I should like to look out of a train some day, spotting new constructive things instead of new war things.

Wednesday 14 August 1940
Dentist first thing. He was very amiable, patted me on the head when I bit his finger, and gossipped, said that a liner had been sunk on her way out from the Clyde at the week-end; I was very worried as I thought it must be Gert's [Gert Hermes, a sculptor friend of N.M.]. He also said that he thought the Jews oughtn't to have left Germany, that they could have brought Hitler down if they'd stayed; he wasn't really anti-Semite, but he felt they'd been lazy. I suggested it was pretty difficult for them to stay, and added that a lot of refugees were only wanting to help; he said he thought it would be a good thing if they all made munitions instead of setting up as doctors and dentists(!). I said that country districts needed more medical and dental services; he said that there wasn't enough money in the country districts to pay the fees and that when all medicine was State Medicine it would all be bad; I said that in the mean time the Carradale children had bad teeth, even those who'd had plenty of milk to drink. He went off on to the wrongness of brushing teeth; he's a regular old Liberal, and reveres me as a Haldane!

Then I walked over to MacCormick's office and had a talk to him about the National Party, of which he is secretary. I liked him a good deal, and found him in effect completely left-wing; he said it was easy to work with communists and Liberals but the Labour Party kept to itself. I asked him about *Forward*, which he didn't think much of, said they wouldn't help, and added that it was in a bad way as a paper —everyone says this about their rivals, of course. I said I didn't think much of the *Scots Independent*, and he said it wasn't as bad as it had been, but it was difficult to fit in such contradictory opinions, but that, from month to month, the right wing and traditionalists were dropping out of the Party and it was forming into something; possibly in the inevitable break-up of Parties after the war, Scottish nationalism might come into its own. In the mean time, Nationalist feeling is strong among the common people, less strong in the professional classes and non-existent in the business circles. That corresponds to what I think. I talked to him about Alistair MacNeill Weir [the Labour Party candidate who stepped down from the Argyll bye-election because of the electoral truce]: it would be a pity for the Nationalists to complicate our election; he quite saw, and said he thought well of A. Said that nationalism was gaining ground among the dissident T.U. officials and so on. I talked about my book and he said he wished I'd write a school history. I said it was no good because I wasn't respectable enough: just as Agnes Mure MacKenzie would never get a book taken because she is episcopalian.

. . . Then to *Forward* to talk to Emrys Hughes, who thinks very ill of all Nationalists, says it is quite unreal, that it doesn't exist at all, has all been made out of a "pack of tuppenny-halfpenny books". The Party will have disappeared in a few years and so on. Trotsky will be proved to have been right, etc. A lot about people. The thing which both he and MacCormick agree on, is that the church is a Bad Thing. MacCormick said (he is a solicitor) that the new marriage laws were pushed through by the church, with the heavy backing of the C of E, who are all hot and bothered about marriage without sacraments, that all the lawyers in Scotland opposed the change, although they didn't make much out of the old laws.

I didn't tell Hughes that I'd been seeing MacCormick; he'd only think it was childish nonsense. Yet I like them both. But I'm inclined to think that Hughes is wilfully refusing to see the nationalist feeling in Scotland, just because it doesn't fit in—and because he's a Welshman. A pity the Left should always quarrel.

Friday 16 August 1940
. . . Jemima came in to say goodbye; she is off to hospital next week; her people are still against it, but she feels she must do something. I said how sorry I was she should miss the wedding; she said she would be jealous. I also said that I should miss her; she is the only girl here whom I've got know; the others are all frightened; she said, "I was frightened too at first, but then I got to like you and I wasn't." She said she would send me a photo that I could put on the mantelpiece. She brought back the books she'd borrowed and asked me what I thought of the war; I never know how to answer. She went on about the planes that had been brought down "and all those lives. But I suppose one ought to rejoice". I said I didn't think one ought ever to do that, but it was better than their dropping bombs. She had seen Donald Paterson

since he came back; he says the Straits of Dover are like a grave-yard, bits of ships and bodies. She then said that she'd heard that Eglè's mother was interned—I said no, it's just that her father has been turned out of his job for his alien connections. But it shows how things get round.

In 1940, Douglas Cole became a temporary civil servant at the Ministry of Labour assisting Sir William Beveridge on the Manpower Survey which was designed to examine the nation's manpower resources in relation to war production. Dick also took part in the research by providing legal expertise. From her base at the Fabian Society's offices, Margaret Cole contributed to the Survey by collecting information in the London area. The work was completed by the end of 1940 and while Margaret continued to put her energies into the Fabian Society for the rest of the war, Douglas moved on to become Chairman of the Reconstruction Committee at Nuffield College (Oxford) which had been commissioned by Ernest Bevin to report on postwar problems. Dick Mitchison became Douglas' lieutenant at Nuffield.

The Coles had two daughters and a son: Jane who in 1940 was preparing to go to Girton College and later became a house-property manager at the Housing Department, Chelsea Borough Council; Anne, who became a medical student and Humphrey, a contemporary of Avrion Mitchison, who was still at school.

Saturday 17 August 1940
. . . A good deal of discussion at tea time; the others all have interesting jobs, and jobs connected directly with winning the war (Margaret had, incidentally, been seized on as part of a propaganda film and had enjoyed it thoroughly, going all over the place, interviewing builders, iron-founders etc, with lovely backgrounds of cranes and docks) which makes them more eager to go on with it, to *win*. I find myself in the position that some of them or their friends may have been in during the last war, saying is it worth while? and, what is this government likely to make of peace and all that.

They were all talking about rather hush-hush arrangements to be made in the Ministry of Labour; it sounds as if a lot were being done in a small way, but affecting a number of people, revising of contracts, reserving certain classes of people, so that certain firms could carry on etc. But there seems to be a certain amount of difficulty with the civil service, who don't like people like Douglas walking in on them, and of course with some manufacturers. I asked Douglas if there were no chance of nationalising certain industries. He said yes, he was sending in memoranda about that every week. Bevin wanted to, but not Morrison.

Douglas charming to me, but I get jumpy with the extra people, with things not being quite right, with extra complications about food, general raising of the standard of living, having drinks and so on. When Margaret does a quite unintentional snap at me, it hurts. Also, having been intellectually on my own for so long, I long to talk to people about the sort of things that are in my mind, but I don't think they'd interest any of them, they are too vague at present, and I just couldn't bear being jumped on at the moment. They are all clear-cut and grown-up, at least I suppose they are, they have definite jobs; I'm *désoeuvrée*, at least nothing that I have to do counts, and I have these woolly Scottish ideas about the whole end of man. And I'm so out of the London political and departmental life that I don't understand what they're talking about, nor what the various committees and things are.

A good deal about refugees; their Paul [Rosenthal] has completely disappeared, and it is pretty wretched telling his wife every day that nothing could be done. What has happened is that those refugees who don't mind going to Australia, etc, have taken the names of those ordered to go, so it makes it even harder to trace them. . . . The only thing to do is to get some important body to demand them back, and everyone is trying to wangle that for their friends. Said that Mosley not coming up to trial as there is really not enough evidence to convict him on.

Ll.G. [Lloyd George] not in the War Cabinet because he gets aphasia, and when he comes out of it, the first thing he always does is to produce a stream of obscene abuse of Chamberlain! A pity, all the same . . .

Douglas, being unpaid, and knowing all the heads of departments, and so being able to threaten to write to them, is in a good position for certain minor things (though of course in practice he wouldn't be able to appeal to them except *in extremis*). For instance, he managed to stop them evacuating children to Slough which is full of munitions works —one of his investigators (on man power) and the chairman of the housing committee came howling to him about it and he sent telegrams. Of course it wasn't really his dept but the Ministry of Health. But they couldn't be got at!

Wednesday 21 August 1940

. . . Dick says he feels that talking to me is like being dive-bombed; I feel I'm being frustrated all the time. I can't take emotions for granted, as I suppose he does. We walked over to Dippen yesterday; we said nothing except a few remarks about the Hall, the cattle and the beauty of the woods which Dick was enjoying very much. I didn't want to interrupt that, but oh I did so want to talk and I couldn't get any of the things I wanted to say to the surface. I am still overlaid by this animal grief; I still feel, and the more so with all the children here, that the only thing that can heal me is to try again; I can't talk about this. I suppose that Dick has no such feeling himself, if I ever get near it, the conversation draws away. I suppose rationally he is right and if one waits till the war is over . . . and the peace. Well, it'll be too late for me. But I can't face the word never, and possibly he may be right to avoid saying it. If I even knew he felt like that about it—but what I can't bear is the idea that he mayn't have considered it at all. But he doesn't like taking the skin off the onion of the soul. And I've always made that mistake with people, trying to bring things into consciousness, into words, into something I can be sure of—though why should I feel more sure of words? Because of being a writer perhaps.

Dick says he doesn't talk to me about things I'm not interested in and so sometimes he doesn't talk at all. But what is it he wants to talk about that I'm not interested in? God knows we *do* talk enormously about the Hall which I confess to getting desperately bored by, especially the drains and the light fittings. I don't understand about large sums of money and when he talks about that (for instance transferring shares to Denny) I can't tackle it, but what else? Is it a difference of method of approach to the thing talked about? Or what? He now, of course, has things in common with the Coles, short cuts as it were, which I can't follow. But that doesn't matter. I don't think I'm jealous.

He asks me if I like Margaret; I say surely my actions are motivated by love? I don't quite know what's meant by "like"; surely I "like" the people who are young and pretty, attractive like animals or flowers? Is it an adult relationship?

What I think about Margaret is that she has been screwed up to constant overwork by constant hormonic over-production—pituitary, I suppose, primarily. Even when she has a chance of resting, this over-production goes on for a few days; the dope I have given her has begun to stop that, has forced her into a complete relaxation and forgetting of strain. For she has been half asleep, very dopey, almost as if she was drunk (and a little alcohol having a tremendous effect). I think this is a good thing and a prelude to building-up. Also, of course, like most women who have to look after children and a hard-working husband and others, she does a lot of petting and giving out, and doesn't get it back; when I give her some, she lets go; and that's good and a necessary thing for her too.

Friday 23 August 1940
Talked to Murdoch about my own problems. He is a queer, dispassionate and I think really scientific-minded creature; I was pretty sure that my images wouldn't hurt him, as they might hurt (but I don't know) Dick or Denny or Ruth. He talked about Hank's death calmly, saying that he would probably not have made much of his life, except by some accident: although Hank had been his best friend—I believe Hank's death upset me more than him. Equally I could talk to him about this baby and the possibility of another, and told him I couldn't tackle Dick. At which he went off and apparently did so, as Dick then talked to me about it as a possibility. Whether or not it is, it is curiously soothing not to have the rational "never" *said*. Odd position, though!

Wednesday 28 August 1940
... The children burst in from their Red Cross fête, with masses of things they had won or bought. Av had the second volume of an enormous history of England, middle of last century, highly illustrated which he had bought for sixpence: "And nobody's even looked at it!" He thought of perhaps reading it and anyhow cutting a square hole in the middle of the pages and using it as a box. ... They all had various cheap books, objects from dips and so on, as well as long-eaten penny bars. It was amazing how much they'd got!

There is a running blitz-krieg between Av, Humphrey [Cole] and Val, but tonight Denny, Murdoch and Ruth had one at the far end of the table; it was really a family row and they hit, spat and pulled one another about as though they had been in the same family all their lives! Ruth moved back from my room to the big spare room this morning; Denny was helping to carry her clothes, dropped some of them and started ragging her about her under-clothes; she promptly gave him a bundle of Kotex to carry—which he did with complete lack of embarrassment. How sensible the young are; I hid these things with immense care for years and years of marriage and still find them rather embarrassing to have about or to allow males to see; so much for taboos.

During the war, Naomi's brother, Jack (J. B. S. Haldane) was based at Rothamsted Experimental Station at Harpenden. He had been invited to investigate the disaster in the submarine *Thetis* by the Amalgamated Engineering Union and the Electrical Trades Union. As part of his research, he had simulated some of the hazardous conditions suffered by submarine crews and subjected himself to a number of experiments to the detriment of his own health. He later worked for the Admiralty on the physiological effects of gases at high temperatures. In the political arena, he continued to be a determined critic of the government's air raid shelter provision and was prominent in the campaign to improve ARP services for civilians.

Monday 2 September 1940
. . . Jack turned up in the afternoon, looking tired and much older; I haven't seen him for eighteen months or so. What is left of his hair is very grey, and he has slightly dislocated his pelvis having fits, in the course of his experimental work. I am trying to rest him. He seemed frightened at first, like all of us, very suspicious of Margaret, very easily discouraged, stops speaking if interrupted, even by a child (as of course he is constantly), but also arrogant, talking about himself, all of course the same thing inside out. Add to this, that he has the most astonishing memory, can talk about pretty well everything, gets on admirably with children when there are no grown-ups about to frighten him, and he makes me feel extremely uncomfortable, mostly, I take it because he is really a much bigger person than I am, all round, and I get jealous, as one only can be of one's own family. In the evening he and Margaret and Dick quoted Latin and Greek in enormous quantities, Margaret terribly worried about Douglas, who seems to be really ill again, and in consequence behaving in a nervously drunken way (not that this would stop her quoting Catullus). He was by then ceasing to think we were going to bite him and was extremely amiable, like a large performing animal. His views about the possible future are extremely messianic; he thinks things are going to be much, much worse before they're better . . .

Tuesday 3 September 1940
Today Jack and I walked over to the deer point and sat in the heather; he looked about him for cover as soon as he stopped, doing it almost instinctively now (but pointing it out all the same!) It was very nice

and we didn't quarrel at all. But we were each keeping our end up a bit with the other, and also each flattering the other a little. He can swim but mustn't take much other exercise. He has been doing Admiralty work, involving extreme cold, etc, had fits, loosened the joints between the pelvic bones, and is pretty uncomfortable. This will probably be his only holiday. I am at any rate giving him the food he likes, and Dick giving him the drinks . . .

Thursday 5 September 1940

. . . Most people who write from the south are well into the battle, doing things, and comparing notes about raids. Nobody seems much frightened. Zita's children have gone to America. A general dislocation of life, so far acquiesced in. Jack, of course, thinks things will get much worse, that probably most of the aerodromes in the south will be destroyed and that then they will go properly for London. And that people will get really fed up.

Cyril, Ruth's brother, who came yesterday, is a more or less practising Quaker and going into the Ambulance when he is twenty; in the mean time working in a factory.

People come and gaze at Jack, as at a monument; Denny MacIntosh came to tea, said afterwards "Ah, he's bright, bright, bright, that one!" Jack is still embarrassed; he has peculiar, formal manners; he stands up when someone comes into the room, comes forward and bows in a rather continental manner like a performing hippopotamus and about as awkwardly. He has many of the mannerisms of the great; but I suspect that underneath he doesn't feel at all completely at his ease or grown-up. At any moment, he feels, as I do, that someone may come and send him up to bed . . . At least, I think so.

There is said to have been a bad collision between two navy boats outside Campbeltown. A lot of submarines here. Jack wouldn't advise anyone to go in for them: too dangerous. He was saying how nasty it was to be in the escape chamber and the water rising, and not to be able to get the lid open. That the submarine crews had to develop a very one-sided kind of courage . . . My goodness, these bloody awful machines, all the human ingenuity, the monkey ingenuity perhaps, going to that. I am quite unable to be anything but anti-war . . .

The first heavy air-raids on London had begun. It was the start of the blitz. Meanwhile, preparations for Ruth and Denny's wedding were going ahead. As well as Jack and the Coles, Ruth's family, the Gills, arrived in Carradale.

Monday 9 September 1940

A rather hectic day, and all the time one was fussing slightly about the news from the south. All kinds of things to do in the morning. Bella and Morag cutting piles of sandwiches, the extra girls all running round and giggling, the squeezing out of the oatmeal for the Atholl Brose, a sudden wish for buttonhole flowers by the males, and a posy made by Murdoch for me to put in my hair. Ruth and I both wore stockings for the first time for weeks, but not hats. Mrs Gill and my mother looking more respectable, Dick in a grey suit—a slight contretemps, because there were only enough studs to go round one tidy male collar in the Mitchison family . . . Av had his new kilt which used to be Jack's, and a shirt, but he wouldn't go as far as a tie or stockings, saying (very justly) that nobody really minded so why should he be uncomfortable. Lois and Val in their new dresses, me in my old blue linen and embroidered coat, newly ironed.

Angus came in to say would he put up the flag, so I said he could and we pulled out the May-day red flag from the chest: I remembering how it had flown last when my baby was born and before she died, Angus probably remembering too. Then he and Jessie said could they have some ribbons, I said I hadn't any, then they suggested I might have paper streamers and balloons, so I found them, and Angus dressed the cars, especially the little one where Denny would be driving. I was a little unenthusiastic, but Angus said firmly that he wasn't going to get away free!

Ruth had a plain blue dress, close-fitting with a rather flaring skirt and the green brooch. Cyril and Murdoch arranged an electric booby trap that made the gramophone play Here comes the bride; we moved a lot of furniture to clear the library.

The wedding reception was held at a hotel in Campbeltown. Afterwards they returned to Carradale House for a party.

We drank their healths, and then all went bumbling into the [hotel] dining room where we failed to arrange ourselves properly, and I wondered if the Gills (whose lunch it was) would approve of what I was responsible for. There were three kinds of pudding, and I had all three; one always eats more when one is nervous. I sat between Mrs Gill and Baillie Ramsay. She talked about the difficulties of fitting children into a professional life, and I told her about the married women doctors I know—they are naturally very keen for Ruth to go on; Mrs Gill is sweet—he is rather domineering and a bit deaf, but finds I am a bit slippery to be proper game—I can't bear people to be firm with me, at any rate not men. The Professor is a lamb; we talked about history afterwards. Baillie Ramsay said his father was a spinner from Kilmarnock, had moved all about, put his sons to a trade, and one brother was consulting engineer now (the Scottish success story again) but he himself had been a bit old to learn; but he had been rabbit-catching in Kintyre in summers and at the ship-yards in the Clyde in winter, had been at work on the old *Lusitania*; then had got the garage and started hiring, and done well, especially on the lorries; he employs about a dozen men now.

Then the Fiscal made a speech, proposing the bride and bridegroom, and making jokes about medicine and science, and of course putting in a lot about Dick and me and not much about the Gills, which seemed rather a shame as it was their lunch. And Denny returned thanks very pleasantly and earnestly, and one felt he was doing credit to his training as a Leftist speaker at student conferences! Only the whole thing seemed a bit funny and Mrs Stewart is very deaf and it's so difficult to know what to say when people present one with a kind of telephone affair. And the lovely harbour was full of horrible war ships, and Murdoch was unhappy because of losing his brother, and the bobbles on Val's dress kept on coming off, and Av grinned silently and took it all in.

. . . We all went into the dining room and the children and I handed round glasses and we poured out champagne, but everyone started drinking it before we'd finished a round and before the healths were started at all, and as they thought it was practically a temperance drink, that was the start of the party. Most of them had never had it; Mrs Campbell asked Rosemary: Is this champagne? And when she said yes, did Mrs Campbell want some more, she said no, she only wanted to know she was drinking it. However finally, after much whispering and arranging by all of us, Alec proposed Denny and Ruth and Ruth and Denny again replied very well, and they all thought what a bonny young couple they were, and Peter MacKinven proposed Dick and me, and Baillie Ramsay proposed the Gills, and in both cases the fathers replied . . . And more people came in, and Ruth cut the cake with a scalpel, only it was really cut already, and Mr Paterson beamed at his cake, and I went round telling people it was a present, and indeed, it was a singularly good cake. And Duncan Semple came in, very thrilled at having a son at last—the baby was born on Friday

—and the doctor and Jackson and various more people brought presents. Denny M looked pretty good in his kilt and velvet jacket and lace and silver buckle, all out of the proceeds of fishing; he was M.C. and kept it up the whole evening. Sandy turned up in ordinary evening dress, because he couldn't find his kilt and nobody would find it for him and he was in a huff about it, but Rosemary and Denny M firmly turned him back to get the kilt and the pipes which he had also left behind.

Bob MacCallum came with his fiddle, and Peter Buchanan with his accordion, and young Jim MacKinven in kilt and shirt sleeves to play the piano. So we all went into the library and they struck up for the first Scotch Reel, the foursome that we always start with. As I began to dance I began to stop being cross; I was dancing with Alec and Donald Jackson. The older folk sat round the room looking on. We went on dancing, reels and valettas and hesitations and schottiches, and Pride of Erin and Dashing White Sergeant and three times Strip the Willow, and the more I danced the less rheumatic I got and the less the swollen tendon on my left foot hurt, and the more I forgot what was happening in the south.

Then it became apparent that Duncan Munro had his whisky bottle up the tree by the back door again, and indeed he came up to me and said solemnly "I have been three times up the macrocarpa". By that time we were all trying to get him to drink tea. There was tea and plenty of food, but also the Atholl Brose, which they took to; but some of the young ones were T.T. None of the women were the least bit affected, nor did many of them take any alcohol. The young maids were all dancing, and Jessie, looking very pretty; but Bella wouldn't come at first, though she did finally and enjoyed it, and Chrissie wouldn't come at all, but sat downstairs with Hugh; however Sandy and Willie and one or two others went down and sang to them specially.

Sarah had just had her teeth out so she wouldn't sing; Sandy kept on wanting to sing, but Denny M wouldn't let him, as he said he'd only make a fool of himself and "that woman" (his wife!) wouldn't like it. Indeed poor Mrs Galbraith got more and more worried as the evening wore on and Sandy got more and more cheerful and began calling me Naomi and suggesting that we should sing a duet or that he himself would play the pipes as he felt it in him to be a great player. She felt that Sandy was demeaning her at the Big House, but I don't think many of them felt class-conscious; they were out for a good time and they got it. Baillie Ramsay put a great paw on my shoulder and said My dear lassie, there was never anything like this before in Carradale House; they all love you. But what about the ones we didn't ask?

Thursday 12 September 1940

The Gills left today. Mrs Gill walked round the garden with me, asking me my views on sex—why had I put so much into my books? Some of her friends had been bothered at the idea of Ruth having a mother-in-law who didn't believe in God; but she added that as soon as she saw me she knew it was all right. I never quite know what to say, but explained that I thought sex was rather important, and so one should write about it, simply and straight: also that an attitude of non-attachment about the body was rather important. Not to own people. She asked if I would mind if my sons had sex experience before they were married; I said I thought it was none of my business, but so long as they stuck to kindness and freedom, I would not mind what they did. She said she couldn't think of it like that. But I wonder what Cyril feels. She's nice though, but I can't feel she is my own generation . . .

Saturday 21 September 1940

. . . In the evening we had our Labour Party annual meeting. Denny M turned up with the minute book to say that Lilla had been called suddenly to a sick relation. Then Alec turned up, then Mrs Paterson from the Shore; then Hugh, Angus, Lachie and Eddie—i.e. the Estate! And that was all. I was sure little Dick would have come, as he is really keen and several others had said they were coming. No doubt several Galbraiths had gone off to the death-bed, like Lilla, but surely not all. Alec had brought his boring CP friend, R and Anne [Cole] who is a member of the Fabian Society came. Eglè said she wanted to come but wasn't a member of anything. We weren't even a quorum. I felt so ashamed. We re-elected Alec as chairman; I refused to stand and nobody else was competent. I resigned as Treasurer and much to my surprise old Mrs Paterson took it on, which was sporting of her; Angus would have, but persuaded her to, as he was connected too much with Carradale House and we all agree that we want to get away from that. She is going to have the next meeting at her house, on my suggestion. Denny and Eddie audited my books, I showing them what to look at (actually they are all right, but I could have got away with anything!) and I handed them over. Hugh, very reluctantly, took over the Secretaryship—I hope if he has something to do it will stop him grousing afterwards. The point of being an office bearer is that it is educative. We all agreed that as soon as the young people come back after the war we will hand over to them. In the mean time Angus, Denny M and I, are the rest of the Executive. I put forward the suggestion that we should help the DLP to pay its contributions to Transport House (all on the supposition that the Labour Party goes on, which is a bit doubtful . . .) as we are the only remaining solvent Branch of the Argyll DLP.

My Denny suggested study groups as the only thing we could go on doing. Unlike other places, there is no special local grievance—like deep shelters—for the LP to take up. I suppose the fishermen's main grievance is that they have to pay taxes on rather high scales now. They never fill in their tax forms honestly, partly that their earnings are very irregular anyhow, and partly that they can't be caught out. So all the Party members can do is to learn about things. Alec said it was no good having monthly meetings but Mrs Paterson was all for keeping them on. R suggested studying the USSR, all that they had done for women, children, THE WORKERS . . . This was met with silence and I suggested that this would be excellent and we might at the same time study what had been done in Germany. However Alec thought it would be grand and Mrs Paterson said we might as well do that as anything. I thought it was rather stupid; the USSR is remote from here, and (as we know from previous experience) very controversial in a silly way. I said what about Scotland, suggested taking *The Real Rulers of Scotland*, of which we have several copies, and going over it. However Alec and Denny thought this a bad idea, not simple enough, and when Denny M suggested a discussion on nationalism, which Mrs Paterson liked the idea of, he was sat on. So we decided to investigate the USSR and Mr R suggested a number of pamphlets from CP sources. I produced the Webbs, also *The Socialist Sixth of the World*, which Alec looked at with much interest—he really always wants to discuss socialism and Christianity in some form. They decided to meet on the 19th, when I shall be lecturing at Tarbert, anyhow.

. . . Av said how much he disliked going back to school. Oh I do HATE these beastly prep schools and the whole system that takes children away from one for nine months in the year just when they're growing interesting. Reading Worsley's book on the public schools and agree with it; so does Margaret, yet her Humphrey and my

Avrion are going to Winchester. Perhaps some case for College at Winchester as a kind of forcing-place for the intelligent, more like a University really. But he does hate the lack of freedom at his prep schools, and the assumption of bourgeois values, king and country and all that. But I have to let him go so that he can learn Latin grammar. Christ, Latin grammar in 1940!

Monday 23 September 1940
. . . Ruth got a letter from a friend saying UCH [University College Hospital] is moving, the medical school shut. A string of bombs came down across it. They may go to Cardiff or to somewhere just outside London. In any case it is no use Denny and Ruth trying to keep their little flat. I am rather relieved that they are not going to be in London; so is Ruth, I think. But Denny is awfully worried and upset about the flat, which was, as it were, his main grown-up toy and which he'd thought about a lot, the electric cooker, the curtains and so on. They didn't know what to do about furniture etc which was already in the flat but finally decided to ask Dick to move them out if possible before the quarter day, so that they shouldn't have to pay rent for nothing to the Prudential. They'd so much enjoyed all the furnishing and hated the idea of Cardiff lodgings!—"Farewell to the sheets on the warm double bed"—but still they were quite business-like.

From September until November, London was bombed every night. Millions of homes were damaged and 30,000 people killed. The bombing reached its peak on 15 October when 538 tons of explosives were dropped. The antipathy towards the appeasers in the Cabinet, Chamberlain, Halifax, Wood and Margesson, labelled 'Guilty Men' in a pamphlet produced by three journalists (one of whom was Michael Foot), had been building up. Chamberlain resigned on 3 October. Anderson became Lord President in the Cabinet re-shuffle.

Thursday 3 October 1940
. . . Great cheers for the news about Chamberlain, rather subdued when the rest of the changes came through. It just seems to be even more Tories, and Anderson and Kingsley Wood and all the gang just moved on one. In the USSR at any rate they shoot people instead of making them peers.
    Letters include one from Mr Wilson at Bumpus [bookshop] in London, saying only this morning has the time bomb which has

pestered us for twelve days been removed by the Engineers. I think "pestered" is the *mot juste*! They seem to have had the shop rather badly smashed up. I wonder if River Court will survive; it sounds pretty shaky. Poor old house. I don't think I'm really properly imagining that all this is happening in London; it seems so ridiculous. Memory is solider than fact.

The new village hall was near to completion. Naomi made an expedition to Glasgow to buy crockery and equipment for it. She went on to Paisley to visit her friend Mrs Hodgart.

Thursday 10 October 1940
... Then we got on to the wholesalers, and discovered at once that it was going to be a job to get the Hall things; they could show us the stuff, but couldn't give us any as they had finished their quota. They didn't even try to sell us alternatives; the stuff didn't exist. No glass, china, polishers, etc. In one shop I got 6 dusters, that was all. No metal ware either. We then tried a frightful bazaar that Davie Oman had recommended; Mrs M liked it very much! We got a quotation there for some pretty nasty cups and saucers, and even nastier tumblers like jam jars. Then to Woolworths where we found some very nice yellow cups and saucers at 4d (there had been none at the Woolworth I went to first). They said they couldn't sell more than 5 dozen to anyone unless we were a canteen and had a permit.

I hastily constructed and wrote out a document about the Village Hall, signing myself on behalf of the Management Committee. To my surprise they took this and let us have 20 dozen. But they had no tumblers except 6d ones. An extremely competent woman took us round; we got jugs, trays, dusters and things, roller towel fittings etc, no drawing pins! I paid for them. Then to "The Poly"—now Lewis' where we got kettles—they have any amount of aluminium!—and enamel jugs. We were all extremely exhausted and I had missed my train to Paisley, however we rendezvoused again for the next day at the sale rooms to see a piano, and I went to Paisley. Had got a copy of the *Scots Independent* at MacLaren's with my article.

Mrs Hodgart talked about evacuated children, her sister's four who are still with her—real little keelies—their father has come to see them occasionally, their mother never, but sends occasional post cards; they are part of a family of nine. All their heads were dirty and it was a month before they smelt like other children—"the smell of the fish and chips wearing out". Now they are sweet and clean, devoted to her sister and not wanting to go back. Then about spies; she is rather suspicious herself, said she was thankful to get rid of her refugee who had been cooking (she is now in Glasgow, Paisley being some kind of "area"), but admitted it wasn't really because she thought she was a spy, but because she was such a bore and so possessive. She was a Jewish refugee. Mrs H also talked of a German woman, wife of a doctor—she *knew* she was a Nazi, she had shown her a family tree with a swastika on it. She sounded Prussian to me, but I said I thought she ought to be treated in a friendly way; it would do no harm and might do a lot of good, and the woman might be terribly unhappy.

I was very sleepy, though; before going to bed Mrs H showed me their charming little air raid shelter, just in case, all tucked into an old porch and built up, with books and cushions; she was helping with ARP but had to run a mile and a half to her post when there was a warning; her brother was something in the Home Guard.

Saturday 12 October 1940
Back on the Tarbert boat, on a lovely morning. It seems to have been drier all the year at Paisley; they were still quite short of water, and it tasted queer. Quite a crowd on the boat, mostly week-enders for Rothesay and the other ports.

Friday 18 October 1940
. . . finished and typed out the play; didn't know I had it in me to be so soppy. I think they'll like it, though. Intend Jackson to do Kingsburgh, Chrissie Mrs MacD, Denny to do Angus, Sarah to do Eilidh, Duncan the Prince, Jennie Flora, and Semple to do MacLeod, Willie to do MacKechan, the small parts to the girls and the small boy to Val. Hope Sarah is up to it; it's really Jemima's part, but she's away. She writes me from Glasgow, to say she has passed her exam—obviously rather well—and is enjoying the work. I'm so glad; she'll make a grand nurse. But she misses her singing . . .

Saturday 19 October 1940
Over to the Hall a bit before nine, to find tremendous chaos, the piano, still in its wrappings, blocking the door, matting strips in the hall itself, and various small boys about. We got the piano unwrapped and on to its legs, and Lachie began bringing over the rest of the chairs, which Matthew, Roy, Val and others unwrapped. Got the parcels

Naomi, Archie Haldane, Avrion (on the car roof), Dick (standing with pipe),
Denny (on his right) and friends.

The Mitchison family: left to right, Lois, Denny, Naomi, Dick,
Murdoch with Valentine and Avrion in front.

Joy, the vet student who worked on the Mitchisons' farm in 1944.
Lachlan on top of the load.

Naomi in the garden
at Carradale.

Naomi with Paul, one
of the Free French
soldiers staying at
Carradale House in
1943.

Naomi and Denny MacIntosh.

Naomi working on her typewriter.

Naomi (left) with Carradale fishermen on the old pier.

Evacuees on the steps of Carradale House. John Pirie is far right,
Betty Gibson second from the right.

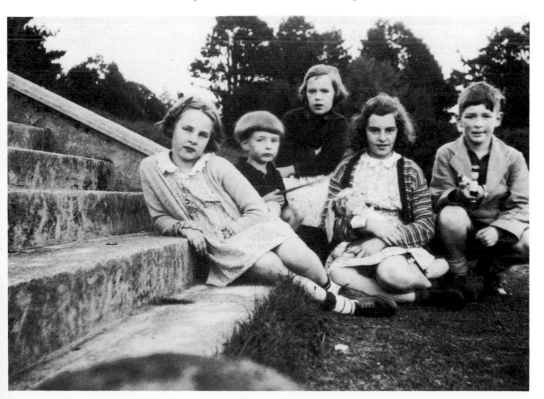

Douglas and Margaret Cole (front row) and Jack Haldane, Denny and
Ruth Mitchison (second row) at a performance of Naomi's play in
the village hall, Carradale, December 1940.

From left to right: Eglè, Valentine, Douglas Cole behind Naomi, Denny
and Margaret Cole.

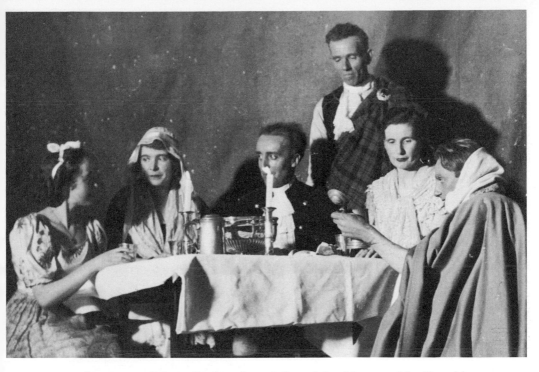

Performance of Naomi's play: from left to right, Margaret MacDonald, Chrissie Paterson, Donald Jackson, Willie Galbraith, Jennie Galbraith, and Duncan Munro (as the Prince in disguise).

Naomi driving the tractor.

Carradale port as it was.

undone: Lewis' all right, but the wretched Glasgow people had not sent the locks for the lavatory doors, etc! Most of the doors on; Ian MacLaren, though the plumbing was all finished, had turned up to give a hand, bringing his suit case so as to change into a kilt before the concert. Angus and MacKillop still working on the black-out. Left at 9.30 to meet Dick. Found small car wouldn't start, so took the big one. But by now Duncan Munro and Jackson had turned up.

Collected Dick from the Campbeltown plane, a bit tired after two night journeys, one to Crewe from London, the other to Glasgow from Crewe. Both should have been day journeys (he had to see some clients at Crewe) but were delayed by raids, blocked lines etc, into night ones. London sounds horrid, the Temple in a good mess, both Halls and the Library gone; Margaret thinks she must go to Oxford, as Douglas has gone with most of the books, and the New Fabian Bureau can't probably carry on much longer in London: the buildings opposite burnt out, etc.

Came back to find much energy round the Hall and still more children sitting inside on the new chairs, watching the grown-ups working. Rosemary dashing up and down steps, fixing curtains and greenery, etc. The piano tuner was just finishing, goodness knows he had managed to do his work in the general din; he said the piano would have been worth £120 new, the inside was in thoroughly good condition, and he really was impressed at our having got it for £20. Rosemary was having hell with the garlands, as all except those that she and I had made had come to pieces . . . They all looked grand, though, and the platform was wreathed round with green and orange and scarlet. It looked very nice, and people coming in wouldn't notice the absence of skirting boards, facings etc. I suggested that perhaps we would not need the heating but nobody paid any attention. Some of the windows, in the lavatories, and at the top (windows we depend on for ventilation!) were already blacked out. Dick went down to see Peter MacKinven, about appealing for money for the Hall, and I re-made some of the garlands; then Rosemary and Ian MacLaren and I hung them. At the end the place looked really lovely, with a warm, wild tone to it.

. . . Sir Hugh Roberton managed the show beautifully, with songs, community singing and funny stories. Sarah, Miss Crawford, Ian MacLaren—now in his braws!—and Mr Blackwood sang; finally Mr MacTaggart sang his Carradale song with new verses about the Hall, Dick appealed for funds, and was much cheered. There seemed to be quite a lot of money in the collection, and everyone seemed pleased with the Hall; Sarah said it was "just pairfect". It seems to be good acoustically too. Then we had high tea here, with all the guests I managed to catch.

Saturday 26 October 1940
. . . picked up Jackson and Miss MacFarlane the new teacher and drove them into Campbeltown to lecture to the Argyll teachers, or such of them as could be found, on Historical Evidence.

While they had a private meeting, I sat in a class-room, read some very bad compositions, and wrote some verses on the same subject on the black-board, also read a Senior History Reader, published in Edinburgh and apparently for Scotland, of such appalling badness that I brought it in and ragged about it for quite a bit; it mentioned Jenny Geddes, but not (except in a biographical note at the end) John Knox. It said that the Russian revolution was caused by German propaganda. And similar gems. The teachers said it was enforced by Dunoon but they didn't use it. I don't think this is a good enough excuse. Must try and do something about it.

I was introduced by a comic chairman who obviously deplored my political opinions and had read none of my books, but read aloud two ancient reviews. Then I talked to them for about an hour, showing them various ancient objects and explaining what historical evidence could be deduced from them: read them a bit out of the Lyon etc. I gave them a really good show anyway. They were all too shy to talk afterwards, especially the women, but I had a little talk with Clarke, who is intelligent. He has a friend who has worked a lot on Intelligence Tests: a teacher, but a C.O.: has been given exemption from military service on condition that he ceases teaching and does forestry. Things like that make one feel we don't deserve to win the war! Not that Clarke seemed to see its full implications; he said in an undertone that this chap was a Quaker, as much as to say he had B.O. The chairman of the Glasgow Tribunal is Bruce who was Editor of the *Glasgow Herald* a long time ago, and was a tick then.

We had a very good tea made by the cookery department and drove back in one of the loveliest evenings I've ever seen, the West Loch glassy grey-green and Jura and Gigha transparent mauve looking like Tir nan Og . . .

Wednesday 30 October 1940

... We had a very funny rehearsal in the evening. Got most of the cast together, except the fishermen and Sarah; Rosemary fetched most of them, because of the rain—the river is in a wild spate. They were all remarkably good, particularly the main people, Jackson as Kingsburgh, Munro as the Prince, Ellen as Flora and Chrissie as Mrs Kingsburgh. Lachie and Jackson retired and got the Gaelic straight. Lachie has a habit of whispering it so that it sounds like a conversation overheard down the telephone in Russian, only backwards. He enjoyed listening to the others and will be all right later.

As in all rehearsals, everyone laughed a lot, and there was fun about dressing up Chrissie in one of my grandmother's velvet dresses, and a mutch [linen cap] and lace scarf. I couldn't find one dress I wanted; I know it used to be in the acting box. We read it over first, then did some action. Like all amateurs they have a habit of standing in rows. I had no idea what should be done about the songs, but they fixed it up in no time, and will make a lovely job of it. Jennie was very good as Flora, just because she has this lovely voice full of musical tones; they all rose to the "poetic" passages. I feel I'd like so much to try them on Gordon Bottomley or Synge or Yeats. I think they all forgot about the real world; I didn't altogether—I kept on wondering what would happen by New Year, whether we'd have the heart to go on.

When it came to fixing up other rehearsals there was some difficulty; the fishermen only get back at weekends; there is usually something on for Saturdays and anyhow they often don't get here till the afternoon and want a bit of a rest. But Duncan Munro says he is a Wee Free and won't rehearse on Sunday ("there are enough sins on my conscience") and Jackson is bothered, I think, about public opinion. Chrissie had suggested rehearsing this Sunday; but Munro jibbed and then they remembered it was Communion Sunday anyhow, so they had better not. Chrissie said what about Friday if our men are at home? I, trying to consider feelings, said wasn't it a fast? They said, oh we don't keep it here. So we may rehearse then. I suggest that they can do a lot of learning their parts, and if we get the rehearsals for placing on the stage, at the end of November, that will be time enough.

Friday 1 November 1940

... My mother sent me a knife for my birthday—and I have sent her back a ½d stamp! I hope I shan't lose it. She says Oxford with a normal population of 90,000 has 150,000 and no new houses. "People simply won't stay in the country and drift back here, some of them back into the institutions they were drafted from, but others, with plenty of money, bribing people to take them in. There has been a good deal of that, lodgers turned out (people with work here) to make room for well-to-do East End Jews and it isn't good for anti-Semitic feeling to be allowed to spread. I never heard a murmur of it before down here." She says she isn't going to bother to open windows for the next raids, as it makes the house so cold. She has liked all the people who are billeted on her, mostly Army and families, very much, and sounds quite cheerful . . .

Thursday 7 November 1940

Bella said Campbeltown had been bombed; we all thought it was a rumour, of course, and Archie Paterson told Mrs MacMillan she was a silly bugger for saying she'd heard planes over Carradale. But by this evening it appears that it is true, that the Royal Hotel is smashed up, and that quite a lot of people were killed including Hunter, the West of Scotland Agricultural College expert, who was coming over to advise me about liming the fields. Damn silly. They were obviously going for the ships in the harbour. Mr MacKillop ran out to look for his son, but found the place was being machine gunned and had to run back . . .

Monday 11 November 1940

. . . Ian MacLaren was over about the damp patch, says it is the slaters, not himself; he is in the fire brigade and helped to put out the bomb fire; he hadn't liked the raid at all, said it gave him an awful funny feeling. Everyone in Campbeltown was nervous—also here; Mrs Mitchell says they watched last night's plane circling over our house! I have since heard that it is being said here that Lord Haw Haw [German radio propagandist] says that Carradale is to be bombed . . . I should suppose that someone deliberately invented this to see who would believe him.

Jessie talking about Chamberlain; I said he died a bit too late; she says that's just what Archie Downie was saying in the Hall last night, but she does feel a bit sorry for him all the same . . .

On 15 November, Naomi had a car accident at Grogport and sprained her wrist. She was unable to write her diary until mid-December.

Tuesday 10 December 1940

... *Hall and drink* At the Special Constables' dance the day I had the accident, a good deal of drunkenness both in and out of the Hall: perhaps exaggerated—? A good deal of scandal, some talk of connivance by the Big House, which came round to Angus who defended us and told Mouth that I'd said I would turn out the next drunk myself. Sermon on temperance the Sunday following, directed against Robbie Campbell and Sandy, who are pillars of the church, and now very angry.

At the next dance I *do* turn out a boy who has been drinking and is quite incapable of dancing properly; he goes quietly. At the next Management Committee Mrs Campbell is very angry, and says no lady would do such a thing. On Chrissie's suggestion I concocted a notice about smoking, to try and get people to use ash trays instead of stamping their ends into the floor and put it up "for the social committee". Wanted to do one about drink, but there were various opinions, and it fell through. Suppose we are going to print a rule about it? Agreed that alcohol may be consumed at weddings etc.

... The Campbeltown folks are very much shaken by the raid, there have been warnings since (though one of the wardens tells me they come from Newcastle). Quite a lot of them have bolted, and Reppke the kipperer asked if I could let his daughter have Mains when the MacMillans moved out; I said on the whole no—it is in an awful state of repairs and we must get it dealt with as soon as possible; and if I let anyone in, paying rent, I can never get them out again. The chemist told Rosemary: "If there is another bombing, Campbeltown will give in." But one bit of good news, Neil MacMillan and young MacGeachy, who were thought to have been killed at Abbeville, and who are both good left-wingers, are now thought to be prisoners.

... *Family* Dick has been down once from London, quite calm, though finding it a bore to work in the Temple behind shutters all the time; he has some calico windows, but another bomb tore them all. He has a lot of legal work. Denny and Ruth have both been given hospital appointments and will be looking after a certain number of beds ... The others are all right; Av saw a Blenheim chasing an Italian plane over the school. They say his Latin is not up to scholarship standard, though maths, history etc are very good. What balls!

... *Writing* Wrote two stories in Carradale dialect, both pretty good, one about the best thing I've written, I think—Five Men and a Swan. It came of Denny M clamouring to be told a story and saying wouldn't I write a love story, so I said yes, I'll write a swan story so I wrote this fairy tale about the swan woman and read it to Denny M on Sunday, having typed it with some pain; he was obviously completely caught by it and responded as I would have liked. It is pretty indecent; it would have passed all right a few years ago, but though the highbrows would take it, I'm doubtful about my present audience. The other is a historical story about two men fighting, blood and heather; I read it to Duncan today and he liked it, he thought he would act like that himself.

Exciting starting writing again; I did it in Glasgow and on the boat mostly: suppose the rest from the strain of here. But I write very easily in Highland speech.

Thursday 12 December 1940

. . . Various complications about Betty; she can't go on at Carradale, it is only a dead end; she shouldn't have been evacuated here anyway, but they didn't want to separate families at first. Question now, can she get to secondary school, for instance Campbeltown? I would help with expense if necessary. Miss Park is going to see the Education Officer at Glasgow—I wrote first to her old school, but she is out of their jurisdiction. Have written to the father, but he has rather tended to give the children up. It would be stupid if she had to stop, and half her trouble now is that the work is too easy, so she prefers boys.

Miss Park is very nice and very helpful about everything; she will come back after the holidays but I haven't room for her while everyone is here, though she fits in very well.

This Italian defeat; as Rosemary says one gets a sinking feeling, it seems so unlikely that anyone on our side should win! I've sent cards to various Greek friends with congratulations; one is tentatively thinking it possible that it may be a real defeat. I hope to goodness we shall encourage any kind of anti-fascist revolt in Italy, but feel it is rather unlikely, with the present lot of people running things.

Am not sending Christmas cards this year; we used always to get a design engraved by Gert Hermes, but she is in America, besides one couldn't anyway. Am sending a few picture post cards to people, presents to the usual twenty-five or so, as well as family and Rosemary, but just sending hankies to a few people to whom I used to send small presents.

Carradale House was full for Christmas. Dick and the children all returned; Jack and the Coles have also arrived for the celebrations. Murdoch has been unhappy studying medicine at Cambridge and was considering joining the Navy.

Tuesday—Christmas Eve 1940

. . . An awful lot of coming and going and swopping round of Christmas presents and the young rushing down to the shops for last minute things; at the moment there are quite a number of boxes of sweets, etc, here. Lachie Peterson is here, and says Taggie is coming. That's all very well here, but who are we bombing this Christmas Eve, Christmas Eve, who are we bombing on Christmas night, when the snow lies thick on the ground oh? This bloody silly war.

Christmas Day 1940

. . . stockings last night; Av and Val double-crossing us by pretending to have set a booby-trap, and so on. Found Ruth and Denny firmly in one bed so left their stockings on the other. Murdoch came in early with mine and the usual scrum unpacking, with everyone in pyjamas (Av in the top only . . .). Before they came Dick and I were discussing Murdoch, the probability of his being called up in summer, if, as one supposes from various rumours, the young are going to be. That will do in higher education nicely. Wondered what next Christmas would be like, what chance there could be of their all being here—and all that. Seldom felt more depressed.

They'd all got me all sorts of things, including the hat Val knitted, which is really very comfortable! And Margaret and Douglas got me the g'phone records of the *Beggar's Opera*, so I will be able to show these Scots what the English are really like. Rosemary gave me three pairs of scissors; I wonder how long they'll last! Jessie sent me a cake, which she must have made herself.

Then Dick and I went round giving pheasants to the various men, and to Annie Martindale, who says Eddie won't get leave for another month. Angus said he'd only tasted pheasant once before; it is ridiculous—and shows how exclusive the poachers were! Of course everyone here is working. No special church or anything. That would be Popish. Lachie can't borrow the other plough horse, so I am telling him to get on with harrowing the bit of the warren we were going to try with harrow and hay-sweepings.

Rather a relief at 1 o'ck to hear that neither we nor Germany had done any bombing of civil populations last night after all!

An enormous box of chocolates sent from Tarbert by Denny M, with a word or two of Gaelic: this oddly good language at expressing shades of affection. We ate our turkey and pudding, most of the males of all ages consuming a vast amount. I rather bothered by a letter from Miss Park who had seen the Glasgow authorities, who want Betty and Matty re-evacuated to Perth where she could go to the Perth Academy and Matty to the village school; it is thought that she'd get a better education there, because Campbeltown has been so much disrupted; but I wonder whether it isn't rather a bad thing to shift them now, considering that their mother is dead and all that? I'm afraid it might be a wrench for Betty. On the other hand if this is ultimately going to be bad for her—? I shan't say anything to them about it today.

Went down to Lilla with the woolly scarf I got for her, saw her, then went to the pier, where mostly all the boats were, saw Denny M, Willie and half the fishermen I know. Back to give Duncan the *Corn King*; sat in his office a bit and asked him to come over and see how bonny his little tree looked with the candles. Met the MacKenzies —the Minister, I mean—on the way back; she blithered as usual and I was polite and empty of charity.

Thursday 26 December 1940
. . . At lunch, Jack and Douglas were sparring, quite amiably, but you felt the deep cleavage between (virtual) communist and social demo-crat. Jack tended to lay down the law, Douglas to be eminent. I went dumb with discomfort. I went to the business room and cried; Rosemary came in and said They're only having a boasting match; I was scoring the points. It was dead true, and I felt better. Felt that I may be a coward and inaccurate but at least I'm not a man.

On 28 December, Naomi's play *A Matter Between MacDonalds, A Romantic Play* was presented for the first time by the Carradale Dramatic Club at the new village hall. The action of the play, according to the programme, took place in June 1746 on the Island of Skye. Approximately 30 people took part including Denny M, Duncan Munro, Lachie, Donald Jackson (the village headmaster), Jemima, Chrissie, Jennie and Naomi herself. There were two shows, matinee and an evening performance, followed by a party.

Saturday 28 December 1940
We began running up and down about the play pretty early, taking stuff across, etc. Anne helped a lot. Murdoch was fixing a couple of footlights, but only one of the engines was running; the crank-shaft of

the big one was gone and there was something wrong with the autovac of the Kohler! The electrician and Angus were working hard on it. Angus had a filthy cold and said he wouldn't do props, but explained to Jim MacKinven about the back-cloth and not letting the rope slip through at the top. We had asked people to come between 12.15 and 12.45 for make-up. But Denny and Willie had been fishing, the night before and weren't back. Jackson turned up, but I had to get Red Robert and some of the others to help me shift the piano and then the screens. No sign of Duncan. At last he and Sandy turned up, and he had been drinking. Rosemary was wild with them all. The women mostly made themselves up at Mairi's. Val did some of the make-up including odd arms and legs and things.

I was heaving props about, getting the screens up and so on. By and bye Denny M turned up; he has lost his sheep-skin strips so we had to cut more. I felt more and more cross and gloomy. The men were all being difficult. I kept on losing my bag.

. . . by 7.30 the audience were wanting to get in. Duncan was now sitting about in a fit of gloom, Denny M was furious with him and Sandy: The silly asses, he kept saying. I thought he'd be all right, knew Jackson would be. Knew the singers would be. Otherwise—! Rosemary was also furious, not un-naturally. I could get rid of some of my crossness by heaving large things about. Willie decided to play the pipes before the first scene . . . Once all the lights went out. Half-way through we found we had a bad overload on the engine and turned out all possible lights other than the stage.

The photographer did some of the audience, including Jack, hoped to get it into some paper.

We started almost on time. Denny M was grand; he'd had a bath between the shows, as he was so cold; he must have been tired too, after his night. Astonishingly, Willie went through his part in Scene I with no prompting; he was so happy, came prancing up afterwards: Did I please you? Duncan had taken a stiff glass of sal volatile and had bucked up more or less; I told him to drink nothing from the table in Scene III but of course he kept on doing it whenever he could, and the audience laughed. It was a difficult audience to play to; it kept on recognising its cousins and uncles and laughing wherever it possibly could. Chrissie was still nervous, but Margaret MacDougall acting better than I've ever known her. All the small parts were good. Sandy remembered his. Red Rob was good . . . Denny M and Eilidh had been nervous [in the last scene], and had never rehearsed enough, but they were on tiptoes; I felt it was queer how reliable my poacher and lecher was when it came to the bit. They got the knife scene all right, though I had my heart in my mouth every time Duncan paused, and so no doubt had Kingsburgh! . . .

He just got through the epilogue, but only just. Various people came up to shake hands. I said let's all go over to Tigh Mhor and dance. George Cadbury and Delia had come. I had an idea the cast had something up their sleeve and they all whispered, finally collected me, and Donald Jackson made one of those queer formal speeches and gave me a little knife, a sgian dhu. I said I thought they meant to trust me, they wouldn't give the sgian to someone who might use it against them. I said if I ever did that, might it turn on me. I said Might it cut the jealousies and quarrels and divisions in Carradale. I wished there had been more of the audience left. If there had been I might have said more. But anyway I was horribly tired.

Tuesday 31 December 1940
. . . We waited up late; Jack and I and Cyril and Lois played four-handed halma. I put out the Auchterarder cake and glasses. We listened to the midnight news—or didn't listen. Margaret was extremely gloomy; this place becomes less and less real to her every time she comes back now. I wonder what it will be like to me after I've been south. I propose going with Avrion and seeing the various children. I wonder whether I shall be as frightened of raids as I think I shall.

1941

THROUGHOUT THE EARLY months of 1941 the news from both the home front and the military front was unmitigatingly bleak. The heavy bombing of British cities continued; London was attacked repeatedly throughout January; in March, as part of a German offensive against British ports, it was the turn of Clydeside, bringing the reality of air raids much much closer to the people of Carradale. In North Africa, the army battled against the consummate skills of the German general, Rommel, who eventually succeeded in driving the British back to the Egyptian frontier in March. In April, the Germans invaded Greece and Yugoslavia mounting an air attack on Crete on 20 May which resulted in the evacuation of thousands of British and Dominion troops. The Navy fared little better and merchant shipping losses in the Atlantic were so great that Churchill ordered the Ministry of Information to stop publishing the weekly figures. In an atmosphere of increasing despondency, and faced with well-orchestrated opposition to British participation in an 'Imperial' War (by, for example, the supporters of the People's Convention), the Home Secretary, Herbert Morrison, banned both the *Daily Worker* and *The Week*, a privately circulated journal edited by Claud Cockburn. The ban remained in force from January 1941 until mid 1942.

There was some good news. Under the provisions of the Lend-lease Act, shipments of food from America began arriving in late May—dried eggs, cheese, lard, beans, canned meat, evaporated milk, and bacon. The nation's diet which had been rapidly deteriorating was now substantially improved. But the biggest break came with the news that Hitler had turned eastward. The worst of the bombing was over and fears of invasion subsided. On 22 June, German troops began a massive assault on the Soviet Union. At first, British commentators predicted that Russia would capitulate within a few weeks but it gradually became apparent that she was holding her own. The repercussions for the British political scene were immense; the Left mobilised behind the war effort and the Establishment (with some notable exceptions) embraced the new ally with opportunistic relief. Massive production drives (e.g. the 'Tanks for Russia' campaign) were launched. The first calls for the opening of a Second Front against Hitler from the west were beginning to be heard. The Russian front dominated the news until 7 December when the

Japanese attacked the US Navy at Pearl Harbor and America, at last, joined the Allies.

For Naomi Mitchison, the year began and ended with visits to the south. Both trips took the same form: a round of family and friends in London, Cardiff, Oxford and Cambridge. She used the journeys not only as a rest from the domestic and farming obligations of Carradale but also as opportunities to concentrate on her new book, the historical novel.

Wednesday 22 January 1941
Dealing with small last minute things, and packing things for a month (including a few heavy woollies) into a suit-case and rucksack. Take some apples and some of the chocolate left behind by Archie in 1939, in view of foodless journeys. No sign of little Dick getting leave. Take over a few letters that I want to avoid the censorship. Wet day. Lachie drove us in, gave him some instructions. Am hoping he won't get combed out.

Saw they had suppressed the *Worker* and *The Week*; however much of a nuisance I find them and however much I disagree with them, I think this is intolerable. Wonder what Jack will say or do; he doesn't like being squashed. Wonder if the Nazis are going to invade Africa . . .

Naomi, accompanied by Avrion on his way back to school, broke her journey south to have a meal in Glasgow with her friend Mrs Millar, a Glasgow doctor's wife.

. . . Had dinner with Mrs Millar and Jim; her husband a retired Indian civilian, a doctor; they have an enormous Min of Health hospital in their grounds, and the staff in their house, say it is very interesting but a bit grim being run by a matron who insists on absolute punctuality. She said her husband was so much interested in Jack and the *Thetis* [submarine] experiments. I told her a certain amount about his work, also that he was Chairman of the Board of the *Worker*! She found that a bit disconcerting, but not very, agreed that minority views should be allowed. Is ready for change, worried about education, wonders whether her boy ought to go to Winchester, whether Latin and Greek are *really* useful, whether there should be differences between "public" and "secondary" schools. Has a kind of respect for Eton and Winchester that I find lots of nice women have, on no real grounds. Tried to shake her faith. In the meantime we had a posh dinner, in that hotel dining room I know so well, five courses, all made up of bits and pieces of course, but still, one asks oneself how long—it seems a little unreal. This life one has been used to. First class sleepers, mostly officers and other parents taking children down to school. Also how long? In the meantime one pays for them through the nose, no doubt rightly. I'm afraid I like luxury, not dinner at the Central, god knows, but a sleeper (though I'd just as soon have a Pullman berth) and soft pillows and the possibility of typewriting. I do think civil war would be bloody, always was.

Mrs Millar very indignant about one of the Italians shipped on the *Arandora Star*★: her husband had been his wife's doctor, and they had always come up to Scotland and taken a cottage near them—he was one of the cooks at the Café Royal, had always cooked them a wonderful meal. He wasn't drowned, but the whole thing had been fantastic; he was no more a fascist than she was.

Thursday 23 January 1941
The train only an hour and a half late. Av and I both peered out, looking for damage. Little to be seen, nor in any way different from my dreams. Had breakfast at Euston, rang up Margaret [Cole], went with the boys to get Av another school shirt. Then on to River Court. It was a bit dingy, with odd leaks here and there; I made a bundle of blankets and towels that Margaret wanted, and a few odd things, but couldn't find everything as Dick had the keys. There were snowdrops out in the garden. Water and light cut off, of course. Wonder what to take back.

So far the damage doesn't look shocking; I catch myself wishing that this or that ugly building could be abolished. But of course it is all more or less tidied up. There was an alarm while we were shopping, but I didn't recognise it, only thought this is a noise like the saw-mill at home, I suppose someone is practising for something. Nobody paid any attention.

Lunched at the Isola Bella—extremely well: minestrone and fried chicken and chestnut pudding (the boys both at the age when they like fruit salad!). I lunched here first with Aldous Huxley about 1920. Bits of Soho rather smashed but again, not having seen flames nor heard shrieks or bangs, my reaction was to think it was a good thing to get these houses down.

★ The *Arandora Star* was a British ship carrying 1,500 German and Italian internees to Canada. It had been torpedoed and sunk in July 1940.

Saw the boys off, a bit gloomy, went on from Paddington to tea with Noel Brailsford [socialist journalist and old friend of Naomi] extremely depressed. Has been in London through everything and his area bad. Says Nehru is not getting rigorous imprisonment, will be able to write. On to the Coles, Tony [Pirie] there too; all talked a lot. Dick very worried about Churchill's "unity for three years after the war". Margaret says it doesn't mean a thing, but Dick on chance writes to Tom Baxter asking what will be his position as a Parliamentary candidate. I think it is likely enough and consider with profound annoyance that we mayn't be able to shift the Argyll County Council. Am still angry about the *Worker* and *The Week*: feel that Jack is my brother and Cockburn my cousin, and, however much I disagree with them, I shall want to fight on their side.

Obviously to the others there is something not quite real about this evening without an air raid—coffee upstairs and so on. To me, it is like return to pre-war. Only everyone bothers much more about the blackout. As things are so calm, I have the spare room, instead of our all being down.

Both Denny and Ruth Mitchison had been evacuated to Cardiff to continue their medical training with University College Hospital. Naomi's visit occurred at the height of Cardiff's blitz.

Saturday 25 January 1941
Early to Paddington, but find enormous queues. Waited in one for twenty minutes, which I fortunately had. Just caught the train, but no seats, except possibly one or two in Firsts—not even sure of that. Stood in corridor and sat on suitcase for some time. Not good at shoving around and finding seats. When I did it was in a very crowded compartment, all smoking.

Train in goodish time at Cardiff. Found the flat. Denny and Ruth charmingly as ever, like large puppies. D with a boil and various abrasions result of walking into a motor bike. Very fed-up because they are getting so few patients and so little teaching. Their hospital has been turned into a casualty clearing station so most beds are empty. The other hospitals won't take on the students. Talked a lot about their blitz, took me out to look at bomb craters; here, as in London, the thing strikes me as more untidy than dreadful, bits and pieces off everywhere, ornamental ridge tiles and so on. Often just looks like a place demolished on purpose. Sooner or later everyone in the south seems to talk about bombs.

They are very short of coal, although of course this is coal country. Also of meat, vegetables, fish and fruit. Other things patchy. Now rather better than they were. Went with them to the Co-op, which looks nicer than most Co-ops: much fuller of food than it was a week ago. There had been a sudden influx of lemons a month ago, none now . . .

Both very much upset about the *Worker*, on grounds it was the only paper that gave real news of what was wrong, often got them put right or initiated local action, on food, shelters, evacuation etc. They say Cardiff students too poor and frightened of the authorities to stand up for themselves at all . . .

Monday 27 January 1941
. . . A wild day travelling. All trains fantastically late and crowded. When the train came in at Cardiff, there were Firsts opposite where I was and we all scrambled away from them, one man saying: Bloody Firsts. Shouldn't be no bloody Firsts. A long and cold wait at Bath; only a very few buns. Cups of tea, but nothing much else. Later in a train with two Canadians, one very fed up with the rain, wanting to go home, saying why did anyone want to come to this country? He'd had pneumonia with the weather. We tried to persuade him that it could be nice in Spring. In a corner a London woman coming back from Devon, saying she couldn't live anywhere except in London: It's my home, see? The Canadian said he's been to London, there wasn't anything like as much damage as there seemed to be from the Canadian papers. The woman and another man sprang to London's defence, saying You ought to see the Docks. They wouldn't bomb the West End, not likely! Come over regular as buses they did, something wicked. The Canadian had a burst boil on his hand; I suggested he should tie it up with the bandage out of his first aid case, but a young airman reproved us, saying that could only be used in an emergency.

At Oxford, found Lewis and Zita [Gielgud], Lewis with some kind of Staff job; he was pretty gloomy, with the feeling that it was the same idiotic "They're running this war, just as they'd run last." Also two people billeted on my mother, one, I think a naval officer, another girl doing some job, also a young cousin on leave. Difficult to feed them all, as meat is very scarce. I read Lewis the play, and we had a long talk.

Of course I am seeing the south in this curious non-blitz period, but it doesn't strike me as particularly united or anything. Lewis and I agree that it may be just as well to put off any statement of war aims until such time as we feel that at any rate we shan't be hopelessly beaten; once war aims are stated, it will be realised that we are very far from united on that.

Wednesday 29 January 1941
. . . Talking to Christine [Hope] and others I realise that by no means the whole population are engaged in "war effort" as one tended to think from the papers. Nor even wanting to. Quite a bit of normal life, quarrels and intrigue going on. Michael [Hope] stationed in Ireland, leading a childish kind of life, with no intellectual interests and a lot of drinking—nothing else to do.

. . . Elizabeth [Pakenham] says that a pacifist will anyhow be standing at King's Norton, so the Labour Party have even less chance; all they can do is to put out a dignified pronouncement saying A plague o' both your houses. Says that one of the refugee dons arrested and now released from the Isle of Man has kept a diary, showing exactly how all the internees quarrelled with one another, and the various grades; the Jews took it for granted that others were Jews too; this don may or mayn't be but he took a copy of Homer with him and read it whenever possible—even so, one ringleted old boy came up and said: What a lovely Talmud! Quite a bit of anti-semite feeling here, mostly against the middle-class refugees, partly from the south coast. None against the working-class ones from Coventry etc.

In the evening, a long political wrangle, in which I lost my temper rather, as I always do here. My mother saying "When we have thrashed the Germans we shall have to police Europe", Capt A, who is Irish, wondering if we would really do it tactfully . . . She feeling that we've got to WIN, any other suggestion defeatism. Lewis and I feeling that the alternatives were a Sovietised or Americanised Europe, with the latter alternative much nastier; doubtful if we, exhausted, could have a pinkish Scandinavian fashion state, between upper and nether mill-stones. Capt A saying Is there any reason to suppose Russia will be communist by the end of the war, I and Lewis (oddly!) defending the USSR, saying what the Moscow group wanted was not power but responsibility, and that, anyway, it was quite different from capitalism. Wish I knew what was really happening there. A lot of this started because I couldn't help giving an exclamation of pleasure at hearing that Metaxas★ was dead, thinking, in my innocent way, that this was

★ Greek Dictator.

one dictator the less, and weren't we supposed to be the side of democracy and all that . . .

Friday 31 January 1941
To London. As always, felt guilty when leaving, at not having been nicer to my mother. But can't manage it. For instance, she thinks that I influenced Murdoch to go on with the medical course so as to keep out of the army; actually I suggested he should do zoology and take the chance of the call-up, and it was Eric [Strauss] who urged the other course. But can't tell her so!

Straight to River Court where Murdoch met me; sirens went, Murdoch and I looked out but could see nothing. Went on sorting things either for him or for me to take to Scotland. A whole lot of stores below: had laid them in during early 1939 when we were told to. Sent some to Denny, gave Mrs Gibson a couple of tins of condensed milk, put some olive oil and mince meat with bath towels, for Margaret. Rescued various MSS, children's things, etc. Took pictures down from my room, as they are all getting so damp. The window badly broken there and damp coming through walls . . .

. . . Margy [Spring Rice] turned up in great form. No word from Stephen, however his ship is probably off S. Africa. Charles probably going to India; she was very anti-war, but doesn't see what can be done now. In the mean time doing a lot with WVS etc. Very keen on all communal things, thinks they are the beginning of the change. Thinks they may be isolated in E. Anglia, but probably won't be over-run where she is.

Warning still going on, and some banging, but we go to meet Dick and lunch near Victoria. More bangings there, nobody appears to notice. Dick says he volunteered for fire watching but hasn't heard any more, nor Margaret. Has a lot of legal work. We discuss arrangements . . .

To Cambridge

Sunday 2 February 1941
. . . Murdoch and I go to supper at the K.P. cafe—very good. For a change I talk a bit about this book I had planned in Scotland, but here it seems impossible to think seriously of writing any non-immediate book. No chance of publishing of course. Most people I know seem to have lost books in the Paternoster Row fire. The poor Webbs. The quality of life here is different; one can't think long except in terms of

war, nor take any long view at all. Somehow my life is coloured by long-term questions about whether I shall keep next year's quey calves for two years more, whether the bull I am getting should be Galloway or Aberdeen-Angus, what the rotation should be for the year after next. But in the eastern counties the farmer can't be sure of what will happen to this year's wheat. There is not fear, but acute apprehension. In face of that one must be ashamed to do anything or think anything outside it; one cannot break the solidarity. Or will all that seem nonsense in ten years? Or should one just be planning for the future? But that seems impossible too; too little data.

Murdoch keeps on asking what do such and such people think about—classes of people, miners, etc. I can sometimes answer a little. But I keep on saying one can't be getting conscious happiness all the time—unconscious ease and gaiety perhaps, but once one gets conscious, gets a lot of the ice-berg above water, one must have a lot of unhappiness too. Nor can one help wasting some time; one can't live at the pace where each quarter of an hour is valuable. The unoccupied time, if one doesn't use it up in worrying, doesn't really add to one's age. As one grows up one has also to learn the technique of acceptance of events. Saying Yes to life: sound on pragmatic grounds, not to break oneself against the stream; he says he can't see how I can bear a life so full of petty arrangements, letters, tidying up after people etc. I say it's like an engineer's job, an awful lot of oiling wheels. The bore is that any "New Order" will mean that I have to do much more washing up and mending and shall then have *no* time to write! We listen to Priestley's broadcast about communal cooking. I think how much I would like it at Carradale, but fear we are still much too prosperous for that; also consider that Dick and the Coles would simply hate it—Douglas always shrinks from public things. An early dream of mine was people eating together in a hall—like the Carradale village hall—after harvest perhaps . . .

Tuesday 4 February 1941
. . . Cambridge must be very artificial, though; it seems much more prosperous than Oxford, perhaps more compact. The big bombers swoop low over Trinity, perhaps in scorn and anger, perhaps thinking if our education is interrupted why the hell shouldn't yours be. I wonder. Shall I come back here again? Ever in summer? I didn't think a year ago that now I would be eating macaroons in Cambridge and comfort. Will that all go in the next twelve months?

Took the train back to London. As it was dead on time I sat in Liverpool Street for some time with the blinds down thinking it was Bishop's Stortford! Back by tube, and a long walk at Euston to the mended part, through queer grey tunnels. All so like the Russian stations in 1932, with the families camped in them. I think the *indigènes* are a slightly different race, a shade darker and smaller; the many travelling soldiers and sailors gaze out at them, and whisper. They hardly gaze back, but go on reading the papers, drinking tea from mugs, knitting, doing their nails, gossiping. We don't exist for one another. They have curious luggage; even when they are on the move they are obvious; my own luggage, rucksack, suit-case, typewriter, Dick's wretched umbrella which he left behind, that's foreign . . . The canteens appear to be functioning. There are bundles on most of the bunks but the ticket holders are not in yet.

 . . . There is an air raid on, but we only hear a few bumps like distant shovelling of coal; the All Clear goes late in the evening. We stay in the ground floor room, play the gramophone; I darn some stockings and my jersey, read letters. Half the girls in Lois' school have been sick, Val is in quarantine for chicken-pox. I'm not in the list of new JPs for Argyll . . . politics, no doubt . . .

Thursday 6 February 1941
 . . . Dick worried as to whether to take the whole-time man-power job which would mean chucking all other work (but he would have to go on paying his clerk in the Temple) and living at Leeds, or Douglas' job, which would mean half-time work in London, where of course he prefers living, might develop into something under Greenwood, or might die out. With him to the Temple and walked through; I find the destruction rather shocking there; I knew it much better, of course. But a lot of the houses weren't really that good as architecture.

Lunch with Stevie Smith; her original room made unsafe after bombing, so she has a cubby-hole, with some peculiarly revolting presentation plate and pictures which her employer used to have in his room, also unsafe! We had sausage rolls and burgundy and gossiped; she hasn't been out of London except for four days since the beginning of the war, is quite un-shaken. "Never had such quiet nights—no dogs, no motor cars, no babies crying." She really doesn't seem to worry at all; office people popping in and out, some with steel hats. Went over with Stevie to *Country Life* Office; two tough old ladies, very nice to me, half commissioned an article on my Carradale play, with photos. Said "Nobody goes to the Office shelter now; in September we used to run like wet cats".

Tried to go north by Charing Cross, which gave me a ticket but told me to go by bus; sight-seeing tour through wrecked areas . . . but one gets more and more to think Now, there's a building they *ought* to have got! The many nasty buildings stand out like rotten teeth. But everything is so dirty. Back to Hendon, and Tony drove me down (through a warning but nobody paid any attention) to Harpenden. We talked, and occasionally picked people up. At the lab went to Jack's room; he greeted me with grunts, was working out figures; the whole room filled in round the walls with drosophila★ bottles. Spurway and Jermyn working. By and bye went to see Bill [Pirie], amiably distilling chlorophyll, hoping to enable us all to eat grass . . . also working on viruses: quite unchanged. Back with Jack, affairé and farouche and yet moving gently.

J. B. S. Haldane shared his Harpenden household with his colleagues Jimmy Rendel and Mr Kalmus (a distinguished Jewish scientist who had escaped from Austria) and two young biologists, Helen Spurway and Elizabeth Jermyn. The two other adults were Jimmy's wife Joan, a writer friend of Naomi, who had recently had a baby, and Mrs Kalmus.

The house is a piggery: a villa meant to be run by two maids, and with a nasty little kitchen and only one bathroom, inhabited by seven adults, two children and a baby, with no domestic help—partly shortage of labour partly, no doubt, ideology. Joan and Mrs Kalmus take turns on catering and cooking. I admire Joan; here is a poet, moony, elegant, precise in words, a girl who used to wear green silk gloves and very smooth hair, who could spend a week on three lines, now coping with this household, also feeding and looking after the most contented and jolly baby I have ever seen. She doesn't take naturally to domestic service, but she feels it *is* service, to some extent personal to Jack, who has the gift of making his workers love him, as our father had. She couldn't, though, face doing it for more than a year or two: after all she's at a period of marriage when young people do normally want their own home—they'd had it for a bit, even. It isn't really communal living, just a set of people heaped together by accident in an unsuitable building. I doubt if they will be able to remain

★ Fruit-fly, commonly used in genetic research.

friends indefinitely. There is no privacy, not even for Jack, except in extremely over-crowded bedrooms.

. . . I wanted to help with washing up, he [Jack] wouldn't let me, reserving it, as it were, as a painful privilege. Also masochist about beds; it would have been only sensible, as I am six inches shorter than he, for me to sleep on the comfortable sofa with a nice clean soft pillow, offered by Joan, but he wouldn't have it, raged that "he could doss down on a chair"—I raged too, said that even in the Labour Party we sometimes slept in sitting rooms! But finally had to have his bed: feeling masochist myself, refused the clean pillow and had his hard and grubby one—the laundry doesn't turn up regularly either! Will after-the-war mean this amount of grubby, mild but very discouraging, discomfort for everyone, and especially the women?

Friday 7 February 1941
I think Jack gets some kick out of cleaning his own shoes too. His attic with a bit of cheese on the mantelpiece, much gnawed, and Corvo's *Desire and Pursuit of the Whole*, and some ancient braces and my father's old hair brush. I wonder if he has any aesthetic perceptions, or if he crushes them: standing there saying that mankind should be judged by algebra as their highest achievement or reading a piece from Engels, giving on the whole sound advice to the more orthodox and batty political young, the white cat, Mitsi, in his arms.

Sunday 9 February 1941
To Newbury, by train and hired car, to see Av and take him to look at Leighton Park, where we think of sending him if he doesn't get a Winchester schol. His school looks pretty awful, and he rather more inside himself than usual. Says he would like to go to a school different from Horris Hill—"less socially biased." . . . Says they all say they are Conservatives, whatever they may think. He, on Nehru's imprisonment, had suggested that India might be free, and had been sat on by everyone.

We had lunch at a rather horrid respectable hotel, a "residential" hotel, full of rather aged middle-class. Went on to Leighton Park, which we both liked the look of: I disliked the headmaster at first sight, which usually means I like a person ultimately. It is very Quaker, but I think that's a possible kind of background to life; very good workshops, quite a high standard in work. A lot of Quaker manufacturers' children, no doubt, but is that worse than country gents at Winchester or aristoc at Eton or highbrows at Dartington? Will introduce him to a new lot . . .

Back to London, to stay with Dick and the Coles at Hendon.

. . . Douglas here, cheerfully desperate about the future, says he thinks there will be modified capitalism after the war in which we shall be "impoverished but not ruined" and another war in less than twenty years, or perhaps a series of less and less efficient wars. But I don't know how much he really means that. Churchill on the wireless; Douglas and I, disliking his voice, washed up instead, while a very mild rain went on in the distance. Shall we ever get him out before the peace? Douglas suggests he may die; it is hard work. And then—? Whenever one hears a speech or a piece of news, one doesn't think: this is what has happened, or is going to happen, but simply: what are they after now? what do they want us to think and do? The double-crossing of propaganda. Douglas thinks on the whole there probably won't be an invasion, Dick that there probably will.

Tuesday 11 February 1941
. . . Tea with [Noel] Brailsford. Discuss all sorts of things: why Churchill said he didn't want an American army. Was it just to appease the Americans at the moment? Or didn't he think he would? If he thinks he can win this war without, he must have an alternative: the only alternative seems to be revolution on the continent—can he, the Conservative leader, possibly envisage that? Brailsford anxious in case there is a patched up peace after the failure of an invasion, say. I keep on wondering if fascism really can be broken by war . . .

Wednesday 12 February 1941
. . . To the London Library; asked them which of the Scots history books I want they've got, borrowed one to read in the train, they are sending the others. Met E. M. Forster in his old school muffler at the corner of St James Square. I said should one write novels? He said yes, if there was anything one wanted to write, but he didn't. Was kind and woolly as usual.

On 13 February, Naomi travelled to Huddersfield in Yorkshire with Dick to open a Labour Party bazaar and meet some of the people with whom Dick had been working on the manpower survey. The Mitchisons were guests of the Ws. Mr W was a factory manager; his son Jack was a Communist Party member. They returned to London on 15 February to make plans for the future of their old London home, River Court.

. . . Taken up to the platform; Councillor Greenwood in the Chair, a Quaker, speaks so slow that one thinks he's forgotten what to say, flanked by Councillor Cobb, like a Low cartoon of Beaverbrook but fatter. . . . Some fifty people there, including one or two young who are going on to a CP meeting in Huddersfield. I opened the Bazaar, laying stress on the need to think, not to believe and obey first thing, the "war on two fronts", on one of which at least things are going badly; i.e. suppression of the *Worker*. Went into that bit, trying to be reasonable, especially as there was a reporter there.

Afterwards . . . one or two mention the illegal *Worker*, which seems to be about quite a bit though I haven't seen it. Otherwise everyone talking about food difficulties though they don't strike me as having been great here. Nor have there been any raids. A London woman came here after being bombed out, but couldn't stand it, went back to London, I rather sympathise. Of course, quite a lot have sons in the Army, who mostly seem to enjoy it; again I don't wonder. They all seem to get their full ration of everything including meat, but say the butter ration goes no way if you're making sandwiches. A lot of the men have them. They say tea's all right now, but won't be if it's cut. W. is very keen on communal meals, has one centre started and hopes to get some more; I talk about that a bit but meet with little sympathy from these kitchen-proud women. They don't want to do other things instead. The only chance of communal feeding seems to be in the factories. W.'s kitchen will send out meals in containers, either to factories or homes, but he has little hopes of the latter.

W. back, we had an extremely interesting talk, partly about his works, govt inspection, lack of co-operation between departments (though this was not put so politely), inspectors not knowing their job. Instancing a man who had turned down a number of metal parts, which were not accurate to quarter thousandth; this would have mattered in aeroplane parts, but did not, for what they were. When he explained exactly what they were and their degree of essentialness, the idiocy of the thing became clear. Various other things. He is violently against academics of any kind and "scientists" as opposed to "engineers". Wonder what Jack would make of him. Also violently opposed to govt officials of all kinds. Thinks revolution inevitable and necessary; is quite prepared, I think. I ask him if he thinks the future will be in small works like his, if they aren't more interesting to work in for the skilled man? He says no, have nothing but big works; however skilled a man is, he won't mind doing repetition work—he'll go to the place that offers him a bob an hour more or less hours of work, however dull the job is. In his own works he has gone for shorter hours, but now had a small night shift as well. He has a real scorn for the ordinary stupid man, and yet he passionately wants to give him everything. It's a queer mix-up.

Friday 14 February 1941
. . . I asked what he [Jack W] thought of communal meals, he said he didn't hold with them, the only kind he wanted were big kitchens for a street, where women could go and cook; I said that wouldn't release the women. He said what for? to work in factories? I said to do all [or] anything they want to. He said If she has a nice home and a good wage and plenty to eat that's what a woman wants. We then went for one another, and his girl sat silently eating and looking blank. God knows, she wouldn't want anything else. His theory is that you can't alter human nature, not love and family life. I said what about birth control? He said Surely you don't hold with that, Mrs Mitchison? I very nearly savaged them both, but kept my temper sufficiently to suggest that part of Communism was to get people out of the enclosing walls of the home, to get them to see things, not individually but socially, to get them not to compete, but to co-operate. I said that it was possible for people to regard even their own families as respect-worthy individuals, not as objects of ownership. But of course it was no good. He just thinks I'm balmy, and that of course no real woman would believe any of that nonsense. He says of course if you'd ever been a working class wife . . . Very odd, it's really this kind of thing that makes me furious. The common working class attitude, when the girls are expected to do the domestic chores, the women must even spend their evenings sewing and mending while the men have a paper or a game. It makes me feel murderous. And it can't be changed in a generation. Mrs W agrees with me, says Yorkshire men are all like that. They all really treat their women as dirt, they don't understand that you don't want to be cooking and washing all day. But it's bothering when the younger generation are worse than the old.

Saturday 15 February 1941

... When we got to Euston the sirens were just going. We got into the Underground; people in bed all along the corridors; one felt an intruder, bed-fulls of bairns palely asleep under the hard light. In the stations they were sleeping on the bunks, and some had put coats across the lower ones to screen the light, or lashings between them to stop the children falling out. At Golders Green no more 240 buses running. We got one as far as somewhere in Hendon and walked. I wouldn't have minded in a normal state, but had started rather violent menstruation, a week too early. Kept on thinking of all the other women in Undergrounds etc. Dick carried the heavy luggage, but this (always a bit depressing) combined with [the] air raid to make me feel pretty uncomfortable. One heard planes vaguely wuzzing about, and, though they might well have been our own, one felt a bit naked; the moon was rising magnificently, and then there was a queer black streak at an angle of ten o'ck down the sky across the moon; I thought I smelt burning ...

Sunday 16 February 1941

... We both felt very sentimental about the house [River Court]; it had been our home for seventeen years; we'd had some good parties there. I'd had three children born there. Dick was thinking of all the times he had dressed and shaved in his room, all the people who'd been up and down the stairs. I was thinking of some beautiful summer flowers, tulips and things, that Winnie sent me the day before Val was born and they had been in a great jar on the dressing table and I had lain in bed, trying to keep my mind off the pain by fixing it on the flowers. And now there are no more flowers or babies, and the ship in the nursery collecting dust ...

The Mitchisons were invited to a wedding party to celebrate the marriage of their friend Judy who had worked at the Ministry of Information.

Wednesday 19 February 1941

I talked mostly to Mary, and a little to Judy. She says that the censor's dept got parts of my letters and diary, which were copied (with dashes in places—but I don't think I ever said worse than bloody!) and came to her; what I had said about not getting the anti-dip serum was passed on to the Min of Health, so let's hope our MO gets a kick in the pants. Judy says she has had a certain amount of struggle about getting war diaries through. I think Mass-Obs ought to get on to this and make their position clear with the censor's office: *please note*. In the mean time I shall try as far as possible to send my diary by people returning or boat. Shall remember that anything I say may be noted. I may be able to do a certain amount that way.

While Naomi had been away, a new teacher, Dorothy Melville, had been posted to Carradale. Dorothy stayed at Carradale House for several months and, despite the difference in ages, became good friends with Naomi.

A heavy air raid on Campbeltown during February had killed the well-loved Procurator Fiscal, Mr Stewart.

Saturday 22 February 1941
A peaceful and lovely journey across, sun and blue sea and snow on the hills, brilliant or shadowed. Waiting at Tarbert, talking to some men from Lancashire who were going to Port Ellen, I'm not quite sure on what job; one doesn't want to question too much. They found everything strange, the accent and the way of looking that the people had. I found it familiar and pillow-soft; there had ceased to be any urgency about anything; the war was not here.

Rosemary and Miss Melville came in the small car. And, as I asked about one thing and another, so it became apparent that there were a number of complications which would have to be dealt with.

It snowed hard in the afternoon, Rosemary slept, later I walked round the garden with Miss Melville; she is 23, earnest, charming, rather pretty in a snub-nosed way, very friendly, takes the dogs out for walks. At any rate we've had luck with our billetees! She is trying to get the juniors whom she takes, to do little plays. But she wants to be a missionary.

They are all talking about the raid on Campbeltown and Stewart's death; apparently it was a land mine. He wasn't killed outright but died of wounds. Rosemary said she had never seen so many men crying as there were at his funeral. Trust a Highlander to do that. They'd mean it too.

Naomi was invited to Ellary, a big Victorian house on an estate on the western side of Loch Caolisport. She drove via Tarbert and Achahoish and spent two nights with her hostess, Mrs Rodgers, a Christian Socialist, who organised the regular fortnightly ceilidhs. Naomi was the first outsider to speak to the gathering which consisted partly of singing and dancing and partly of discussion.

Wednesday 26 February 1941

. . . After tea the big room was cleared, I changed and wrote out some notes feeling very nervous. It might really matter what one said here. At a meeting one is little more than a sounding-board . . .

Between twenty and thirty people came, mostly women, including the school mistress, the minister's wife, a "private evacuee" from the mainland and the woman at the Post Office who is very full of life. . . . Also Mona, Margaret MacGregor's sister, and another woman who is sister of Mrs Lynn at Grogport, and the wife of a keeper on a Lithgow estate near here. At first there was singing, and then one of the men played the pipes, including a piece he had just composed called Loch Caolisport. Then there was coffee, cake and paste sandwiches, and I spoke. I talked about People's ways of working determining their social structure and ways of thought, but didn't say that was Marxist history. About monopoly capitalism with special reference to the Clyde monopolists and MacBraynes, about democracy, about Scottish and Russian history, about a Five Year Plan for peace and Planning for Scotland. I talked for about three quarters of an hour, and when I stopped they all began talking at once. It was very lively, fairly practical and very hopeful for the future. The keeper's wife seems to know all about the Lithgow-Bilsland-Nimmo★ group, and to be strong Labour and all that, but she hadn't been able to express it—her husband works on a Colville estate! She says the Co-op would have no chance to start at Lochgilphead or Ardrishaig, as nobody would sell them a site and all the shop-keepers are related. Somebody asked me if I was in favour of home rule for Scotland, and several said that Westminster was no good, men went there and forgot all about their constituencies. The schoolmistress and the Minister's wife both said there were not enough women running things, someone asked me why I didn't stand for Argyll.

Then they settled down, Douna [Mrs Rodgers] and I leading the discussion, to solid suggestions; it was decided to write a joint letter from everyone to complain that there was no w.c. either in the schoolhouse or the school; then that there was no telephone kiosk, though they agreed that the post-mistress was very nice about it and didn't charge them disturbance money after seven. Then the badness of the bus service (I had instanced MacBrayne's as monopoly capitalism and they were all delighted). Then the fact that they had no district

★ Sir James Lithgow, Sir Adam Nimmo and Sir S. Bilsland were major Scottish industrialists. MacBraynes operated the Highlands and Islands ferry service.

nurse. The women did most of the talking but the men were listening . . .

During early 1941, Mass-Observation was fully occupied monitoring the impact of the blitz on the lives of civilians. Tom Harrisson, the driving force behind Mass-Observation's operations at this time, was continually travelling about the country, usually accompanied by other members of the team. In March he and Humphrey Pease arrived in Carradale to investigate a wartime fishing community. They produced a report (FR616 *The Mull of Kintyre*) describing how the fears of air raids in the area were aggravated by the proximity of potential German targets, the airfield at Machrihanish and the naval anchorage and submarine depot nearby. The report also covered the tragic death of Mr Stewart, the influx of Glasgow evacuees and the boom in the fishing industry.

The local ring net fishing fleet operated from five main centres including Campbeltown which had 30 boats and Carradale which, until the Admiralty took over half of them, had 22 boats. The new price control introduced by the Ministry of Food had increased the price per basket of fish so that, in 1941, the minimum price was almost double the 1937 level.

Sunday 2 March 1941
Walked to the point with Tom, but Clym began chasing the deer; we ran after him, and finally he cut his foot and came back and I beat him till I was completely exhausted. Found Tom extremely refreshing, though fully as likely as ever to do something quite mad.

Tom, to my great pleasure, had very much liked my Swan story, which I gave him, thought I should send it to *Horizon*, but then, if I did, would the people I mean it for, read it? Rob Ruadh told me at the dance he had read it twice and wanted to read it three times "to get the point behind it all"—! I also read Tom my *Alban goes Out* poem; I like reading it, but never know if it is a bore. He wanted all information about fishing, though. I also gave him little Dick's stuff. He gets the smell of Nationalism very strongly here, thinks it is partly Hitler propaganda; no doubt in a way it is, but Hitler must to some extent represent the *Zeitgeist**—he wouldn't have any success otherwise. Nobody can be a power in their age unless they are part of its voice. I suppose the Nationalist thing is partly the D. H. Lawrence influence and all that, too: the same thing in other clothes.

The fishermen had said they would come at 7 and Tom even thought they would, having got used to government offices, but they

* "Spirit of the time or age".

wandered up about 8. Denny M said we would be needing to sit down to our dinner, and I said no, we were just having teas these days, and he was terribly pleased, grinned all over, said "Like ordinary folks!" Which shows that these little things do matter. I then reft him and Sandy away, leaving Humphrey for Dorothy and Rosemary; by and bye Willie joined us in the library.

They began on curing herring, the way it was possible to salt them and eat them raw, the badness of most kippering, went on to the grievance about the small Tarbert boats and some of the East Coast boats catching the wee herring in Loch Fyne, which would make it bad for next year, and selling at Control; it would stop it if they were only offered five shillings a basket for them. But they are mostly poor people, at least the Tarbert ones are, and Sandy doesn't want to get them into trouble. But the East Coast men are taking the sprat nets to them. Then we got on to the commandeering of the boats and unsatisfactory position about the allowance for them; I couldn't resist reminding Sandy of how the Carradale Labour Party had taken that up and been jumped on by the Fishermen's Association! At present they are getting an interim payment of about £10 a month per boat. If the *Amy* is taken, Sandy would like fine to go as skipper "and take a wee net and fish for the Admiralty". He then explained that "the Admiralty are awful stupid on a lot of things", smashed up boats, put a wrong crew "of cabinet makers" on to one of them, who couldn't handle her; his own Alec was skipper of the *Amy*, and the cruiser she was with as liberty boat would have nobody but him. At present they are under the Shipping Board, getting between £4 and £8 a week, but will soon be put on to the Admiralty, working rather shorter hours and with all food found, but for about a third of the pay, and above all under naval discipline which they won't like.

Then we got on to present selling conditions: the buyers have a quota or "ration" according to what they bought the year before the war, and must take it from each boat (or more or less as each boat has to guess the amount of baskets she has, and tends to put a few extra in on pressure, and all that: "The ration officer has plenty to say if he likes to say it" but is bound to know what goes on). It would be much more sensible if all the fish caught were put into one pool, and the quotas taken; as it is, a lot of time is wasted, giving ten baskets here and twenty there, waiting for the lorries to back up, and so on. They can sell to the Glasgow market steamers, but only two are allowed out, and for some reason one firm, Davison, can't get their steamer loaded except at a quay. If herring is bought under control price the buyer can take it all, but that seldom happens. Once, at Mallaig in warm weather, Sandy came in late and only sold his catch—good herring —at 5/- a basket, to MacRae there; that was for the limited kippering market; but the ration officer should have bought them at the govt knock-down price of 7/6. A tinning factory has got most of the Alban's boxes; they were mostly tinned at Dundee; that is a thing that ought to be started here.

As it is, the fishermen get 24/6 a basket, the wholesalers 38/- and the price of kippers is 10d a lb (7½ stone to a basket).

We discussed selling before the war, dumping, the Russian market before the last war, and the German market since; they all spoke with a certain esteem and even affection of the Klondykers, the German ships that bought the herring and saved them in the bad years, remembering feats of seamanship. Before the last war the Russian fish were mostly salted, but few people eat them now. Few of them had eaten tinned herrings or roes (mostly they don't eat the roes of fresh herring) but Sandy thought they were nasty with tomatoes and should be done in oil "like they wee fish, aye sardines". I said olive oil was hard to get, he said why not our own shark oil?

. . . Then they talked about the harbour they want, a wee place to keep our boats, the price of two torpedoes. They could have got a good harbour for £10,000. As it is they spend £600 a year among them on transport alone between Tarbert and here, let alone having to sleep in the boats instead of their houses. It should have been done. Tom suggested that the buyers would be against it, as it would be harder for them to get round here with their lorries, and that they were influential, could get at the people in the Govt who came to decisions and so on. This slipped away from Sandy and Willie but Denny M saw all right.

It's all just part of this bloody planning business that has got at everything, the sacrifice of the individual and the small community. It has got at socialists too. And of course there is no reason to suppose that the wholesalers will be abolished by the war; they may get a kind of govt sanction, even become part of the govt—have a Commissar over them, one of themselves. But I see no sign of the fishermen getting out of their grip. This kind of thing makes me feel completely anarchist. I just want to kill, as god knows, I have never wanted to kill Germans.

The three musketeers kept on disagreeing, reminiscing, yet somehow achieving a "sense of the meeting". Tom got on with them awfully well. Afterwards I played them songs on the gramophone; I gave them coffee, but NO WHISKY.

Tom got hold of a map after they left, decided to walk over to Glen Barr or indeed to walk over the sea to Gigha, to take a parachute. . . . He did this rapid, violent and yet (now!) extremely amiable, ragging. . . . I remembered him so well ten years ago. We talked a lot about all that; Humphrey is charming too, but looks such a gentleman, I get quite shy. Dorothy very taken up with them both . . . and she went to church twice, why on earth anyone can bear to do that.

In Glasgow visiting Anna Simpson, a teacher who had been evacuated to Carradale in 1939, and Jemima, the Carradale girl training to be a nurse. Jemima's family wanted her to return to the farm.

Wednesday 5 March 1941
[Anna] is working at a canteen at the Central Station on Saturday nights; says there are always up to fifty boys who can't find anywhere to stay, asleep with their heads on the tables. One day thirty ship-wrecked seamen came from Greenock in the small hours, but the Central Hotel wouldn't take them in, not even to the lounge to sit down or have a wash—they were too dirty. At last the Beresford took them. She is furious, says there oughtn't to be two luxury hotels in Glasgow, either Central or St Enoch's, not both.

She is worried about education, says there is a fearful shortage of teachers, all men under thirty called up, more to go soon, new teachers were not trained at the beginning but now they are needed. She has to take a big class, and has taken two Qualifying classes running (this means a great strain—the qualifying children have to be heavily pressed on arithmetic and spelling; literature, history and geography have to be cut out—it was bad enough before, but now most of them missed two or three terms' work and it is harder than ever). She expects to qualify 80 to 90 per cent, but not all of them go on with school after they've gone on to the secondary. From 14 on, they drop out and go into jobs. It's hard to get enough for the third-year classes. She has just qualified some children including Robert MacClure, a sweet small boy, a miner's son, who was with me for a bit; they have found out his musical talents in the higher school. Apparently there was an awful scene of weeping the last day of the class, and they gave her a bottle of scent with spray, a pair of silk stockings, some hankies and some toffee. She told them never to come and tell her they'd taken a job until after they were sixteen. But of course whatever they feel now, pressure comes later to become a wage-earner, make ten shillings a week, stay out at night and be treated as a grown-up . . .

Thursday 6 March 1941

. . . Jemima . . . was on night-duty now, in a mental ward; she didn't feel she was learning much; it was dull hard work. Ordinarily they had a sister, a staff nurse and a pro to a ward of thirty patients; it was too much. Lately several of the nurses had got into a row; they went on to a ship with some boys, and the boys wouldn't let them come back; wasn't that a dirty trick; one of them was a Sister, one of the nice ones, too. They'd been had up before the Medical Superintendent. I said I was sorry she wasn't going on with her training; she said she just couldn't, it would be selfish, but she didn't like the idea of going home.

. . . I also went to see MacCormick, the sec of the Nationalist Party, and MacDonald, the editor of the *Scots Independent*. He says its circulation has doubled recently, but the wholesalers still try to make things as difficult as possible, . . . But he has started sale or return in about 150 Glasgow shops, and that has worked well. Afterwards I asked a shop in Sauchiehall Street, which didn't have it, and a much poorer one in Cowcaddens, which did. MacCormick is hoping to have a plebiscite after the war, for or against self-government. I said I thought plebiscites sounded a bit old fashioned; he wasn't very hopeful, said the Scottish office of the Labour Party had been quite amiable, but now they'd had word from the English Office which had discouraged them. The SNP would like to work for Labour, but if Labour just put in their old trade union bosses, they would oppose them in Scottish seats. He had also seen some remains of Liberals who had been very friendly and he was usually on good terms with the CP. He got on well with most of the SCWS, though here there was a minority who wanted it and CWS to amalgamate, not realising that the advantages of that would be offset by corresponding advantages for the English. Neither of them, of course, were the least anti-English. But they were a little less occupied in war urgencies than people of the English parties. They hadn't a good word for Bilsland, who is, of course, very anti-Nationalist: from the Scottish point of view he's an "international capitalist" and a bit of a Quisling.

Jemima was much interested in Nationalism; I gave her a copy of the *Scots Independent*. Anna not much, said she didn't care what party it was, so long as it would do things for the poor people. She is really much angrier than anyone I have seen for some time about what is happening at this moment to the under-dog in this country. I think there is quite a lot of sympathy for the Clyde apprentices.*

There were two Presbyterian congregations in Carradale. Mr MacKenzie, who lived at the Manse with his wife and sister, was the Free Church Minister. Mr Baker, a kindlier man, was the Minister of the Established Church of Scotland.

Wednesday 12 March 1941
. . . Just as I had turned on the 6 news, Dorothy came in, in her riding breeches, with a face that made me think she'd either broken a bone or been raped. I jumped up, and took her to the sofa. She sobbed out that she'd been to the MacKenzies and Mrs MacKenzie and her sister had just torn her to pieces. She had come to tell them about her [Bible] study class, and the two old bitches had gone for her; of course they are jealous, and they want power. But they had accused her of being no Christian, of going to dances, wearing riding breeches, and generally being tarred with my brush. The poor kid, who has felt a genuine call to do this, was frightfully upset; it really was a kind of spiritual rape—MacKenzie himself had gone out and left her to it. They had of course succeeded in shattering her self confidence which I had to build up again, while she sobbed; the elder sister who is a head-mistress talked to her about "refugee teachers" how their business was not to interfere with a community which was getting perfect spiritual guidance, and how she hadn't yet got her diploma, and she would write in to the authorities. I was pretty furious; of course I knew I could stop this by writing to Allardyce. But I was determined to see these women myself.
. . . I was announced [at the Manse], found them finishing their tea; I said I had come to find out what they had done to Dorothy Melville. Their smiles went cold on them and they said what do you mean. I said

* During March, and immediately before the Glasgow blitz, there had been several industrial disputes on Clydeside. One of the bitterest was the strike by over 11,000 shipbuilding apprentices which affected between 40 and 50 local firms. The apprentices objected to having to give rapid training to new war-workers (many of them women) who earned more than an apprentice who had been in training several years and whose pay and conditions were pretty unsatisfactory.

you are bullies and cowards. Then the storm broke. They got into a wild state, called in MacKenzie, who said every now and then that he could not have his wife insulted. That was usually after she had insulted me. She lost control considerably, began talking about being a lady, her "war service" (she was a nurse in the last war and has all a Sister's worst points). She began to explain how she had only given Dorothy Melville good advice, how she had explained how *she* went about it "in my quiet way", how she was "Christ's Ambassador", how Carradale had plenty of spiritual guidance. If any young people didn't attend services it was at the other church. I said that I thought the other church averaged 40 to 50 at morning service, and they rather less; she exclaimed that they had a "lovely" congregation; I said that it was the quantity rather than the quality which interested me. She said that of course I was not interested in spiritual things: I said that I was primarily interested in statistics. She said I couldn't approach it in that spirit! . . . Her sister "whose name is known far, far beyond yours" knew all about these evacuee teachers; they should be kept to teaching evacuee children. I said Supposing a girl has a call to do some Christian act, is she not to do it? No! screamed the sister. I said Do you mean that? MacKenzie slightly interrupted, but they merely qualified it to She should ask guidance of her betters. Then they said Why did you come and accuse two ladies in their home? "Even if you are the lady of Carradale House—" began MacKenzie heavily, but Mrs burst in; "Don't call her a lady!" When they gave me a moment to speak, which was not immediately, I said "Here is a girl living under my roof, for whom I have a certain responsibility. You have made her unhappy—" "That's a good thing!" shrieked Mrs M. I was really rather surprised, and she enlarged on it. "She *ought* to be unhappy, she will think seriously now!" I said I thought that was an awful thing to say, and above all that older people should never treat a younger one like this. Then they went back to my accusations, asked me if I denied saying them. I said Certainly not and repeated them, and told them to think it over. They then threatened to "take proceedings", and Mrs M said she had a weak heart! I can't remember what the final thing was, but it was refreshing to hear them lamming into me after their usual soft soap. At last I got up and said This is a nice Christian household, I am going. They went on maledicting as I got to the door, first said Dorothy must come herself and hear what they had to say, then no, she was never to cross their threshold again. I made the hell of an effort and for a moment I really *was* sorry for them. I said I forgive you for what you've said, and tried to touch the arm of one of them; she jumped away brushing at my hand as though it had been a wasp, and screamed "Forgive!" Then I walked out of the room and out of the house . . .

Despite the fact that, according to Tom Harrisson, very few Clydesiders really expected air raids, the distress relief agencies in Glasgow and the surrounding areas were distinctly better prepared than their equivalents in the south. The first severe raids occurred on the night of 13 and 14 March affecting mostly Clydebank and the outlying industrial areas of Glasgow: 439 planes came over; 528 Clydebankers were killed, 617 were badly injured and huge numbers of people sought refuge at night in the neighbouring countryside. The news quickly reached Carradale.

Friday 14 March 1941
. . . someone told me that young Jim MacKinven was missing. Peter and Ellen [Jim's parents] had gone to Glasgow in Sandy's car. The house he stayed in had had a direct hit, his landlady's body had been found, but not his; his aunts were going all round the hospitals, looking for him. He meant everything to Peter and Ellen. I thought I'd go down to see Lilla and find out how things were—I'd hoped to get her to Glasgow next week to see Dr Hunter, but suppose this may stop such plans. For months we have said Why was Glasgow not bombed? Have heard all sorts of stories, air currents over the mountains, and so on. Now these appear to be disproved. Dorothy had heard that Partick and Clydebank were "razed to the ground" and was very worried. I said I thought this was highly unlikely and one could do no good by worrying.
  Odd getting no newspapers. There was no post from the mainland today; that was how we first got the news of the raid. Duncan says there were no trains to Arrochar (where the forestry lorries go). That looks like Queen Street.

Naomi decided to go to Glasgow to support Peter and Ellen MacKinven while the search for their son's body was under way. Lilla, Denny M, Sandy and James MacKinven had arrived already and the men had taken up the search the demolition squad had given up.

Wednesday 19 to Friday 21 March 1941
These days have been extremely moving, and I find it hard to write about them; it was impossible to do so at the time.
  I went by bus and plane, via Campbeltown, intending to come back

by plane on Friday afternoon. I remembered in the bus that I had forgotten both my gas-mask and my identity card (for the first time); periodically this worried me; I had a very light rucksack and despatch case with me. I had also forgotten the notebook with the Wilkiesons' address, but found it in a post office. There was little damage to be seen on the way in from Renfrew.

. . . Ellen was in the kitchen and Peter sitting beside me, looking utterly done, when the door opened and Denny M and Sandy came in; they were wearing blue overalls, half undone at the neck, but the overalls and their hands and faces were grimed with plaster; their hands were cut; Sandy was looking wild, his hair on end and eyes bloodshot; my poor Denny's face was blotched with black shadows round eyes and mouth and grey with plaster. Sandy said We got him, we got Jim, we got poor Jim, I told you we would get him. I heard James MacKinven in the passage say something about the body, and then a cry from Ellen. Peter turned in my arms; I held him for a moment. Then Sandy began wildly: I have been drinking, she says I am a black sheep, I had to drink after getting poor Jim. I stood up and put my arms round his neck and kissed him, and my mouth was full of grit and my nostrils full of the smell of plaster. Denny M stood behind saying nothing, only looking unutterably tired.

I found afterwards that the demolition squad had given it up, the next house was likely to fall in on them, pieces of plaster were always falling off it. But the fishermen had just gone on digging. Angus had told them that if the next house started to fall, to run *into* it—it would fall their way.

. . . From what Sandy had said it seemed to me extremely probable that Jim had been knocked down and broken his neck at once. I said so to Ellen, explaining that he would be excited and full of a sense of adventure and then there would be a bang like an explosion of light inside his eyes and then he would be free of pain and free of the body, able to be in the hills that he loved again, and with her, part of the life of the eager young Highlanders—his ancestors, who had been drowned at the fishing and killed in wars, boys like himself who had been sensitive and gay and full of deep thoughts, but had not had his luck to be able to write any of it down. She said Are you sure he was not hurt? I said I am sure. She said We were three in one, now we are two. I said You are still three.

. . . They all kept on holding me and calling me Naomi, with the accent on the middle syllable; I felt I was bound to them for ever with blood and tears; I felt that this perhaps was being a laird. If so, I must be it well. Ellen wanted a blue hat with a white ribbon; we went out and got it.

... We got a car* out from the Botanical Gardens, damaged here and there, but not much till Dumbarton Road. Then things began to look bad. I had seen it a bit coming back from Balloch, houses down, pouring over the road, and still smoking. The car went no further; we got out and walked; there were crowds streaming the opposite way, men from the docks mostly—it looks to me as though the obvious Clydeside objectives had not been hit mostly. But they all looked incredibly strained and tired, grey-faced. I asked where to find out about people and was told Kilbowie Road; we walked on, every now and then glass dropped out, or a tile or chimney pot dropped into the road; I told the other two to keep out a bit—they were horrified. A lot of buildings were burnt out, others badly cracked and unsafe, some completely smashed. Off the main road it was worse; here and there houses were being demolished, blasting going on sometimes, traffic being cleared, here a railway bridge propped up, there a loudspeaker van telling people where to go for money or food. All windows gone everywhere. At the church hall I queued up, asked about MacVicars, was told that the father and mother and one boy were evacuated to Lenzie, they didn't know about the other boy. We went back to the main road; everywhere was the smell of plaster and burning, everywhere this incredible mess, everywhere people trailing about with a mattress or a bundle or a few pots and pans.

Tremendous queues for the cars back. After a time we got one that took us some way, then another, but Chrissie was getting awfully tired. All the faces everywhere were of people who were tired and *shocked*, naturally gentle people, taking this badly, not joking like the Londoners. The bits of conversation one overheard never seemed to be jokes, always stories of something bad.

... [They] asked me to go down and persuade Ellen not to come to the funeral service, just to go on; he told me the custom here was for men only to go (later my Angus said how surprised he had been at Paisley going to a funeral and finding women) and all the men wanted Ellen out of it. I asked if they thought Peter would be all right; they said yes. I said if she isn't to go, we'd best get her straight off the boat so she doesn't see the coffin. They agreed, and I went down and told

* A tram-car, usually painted green.

her I thought she should do this. She consented, and it was decided that all the women in the party should go straight on. We all sat in the ladies' wash-place, where we were finally joined by Peter and Sandy and Angus, rather to the embarrassment of any other women who wanted to come in. Sandy's tie was crooked. Peter and Ellen adjured one another to be brave, and embraced across me. It was all horribly moving, this raw business of a middle aged couple in love with one another, swept violently together by mutual tragedy. I said to them that when they married they had only thought of making a good job out of their marriage, and they had done that. Aye, a good job, Peter said, we've done that, haven't we?

At Tarbert we got off and found a car, driven by their cousin Alastair, and he took us off, driving fast. Sometimes Ellen said: I am being brave, aren't I? This is how Jim would like me to be? I said yes, and when we got in sight of Arran I quoted to her "I to the hills will lift mine eyes" and she liked that and said He's there, isn't he? And I said yes, and here; time and place don't count for the free spirit. And she pointed out the wee cottage where her mother had been born; they were all crofters. At Grogport old MacAlister came to the door to see us by. She only glanced at the cemetery. As we came to the village her face was set; I came behind her into Ardcarroch, and at once a wailing crowd of sisters in mourning burst into the passage and all over her. She began to cry, they were all crying; Jenny, in black, brought us a filthy drink, fizzy lemonade and gin—none of us had much to eat on the boat and it went slightly to my head and more to Ellen's. They all began to cry over me too, especially Mima; Mary began saying the most frightful things about poor wee Jim being too good for this world, he's happier where he is—all the *personal* things which I'd managed to get her away from in my concept of immortality. And Mima saying how we are all going to die and it might be any day at all, and the old mother crying. . . . I took Jennie out and told her to take off that dress and put on a coloured one; I went to Ellen and held her hands hard and spoke loud and calmly to her . . . whenever I stopped for a moment one of the other sisters began. But I managed to get Ellen steady before Peter came back. He came straight to me and said I nearly broke down but not quite; I was brave. I said I knew he would be. Then I went into the kitchen; there was a meat meal for the men and I sat with them—I was very hungry. Sandy began telling funny stories, mostly traditional stories about his boyhood. Peter smiled a bit. Then I helped to wash up, and they were all calling me Naomi; I had said to Ellen that now we were sisters; everyone was running round, and I got a dry dish-cloth and wiped the cups and plates and brought them in again for the women. We had mutton and girdle scones and butter and cookies, and lots of tea! I left some more dial for the two and kissed them, and Willie drove me over and said I must learn to call you Naomi too; sometimes I am forgetting; I kissed him too.

For Easter 1941, all the Mitchison family were together. Their guests included Av's friend Francis, the Coles and the Coles' lodger, Bernice Holt Smith who worked with Douglas at the LSE, the psychoanalyst, Eric Strauss, Jack and his two assistants, Helen Spurway and Elizabeth Jermyn. The main war news was the German invasion of Greece and Yugoslavia and the signing of a non-aggression pact between the USSR and Japan.

Sunday 6 April 1941
A lovely day at last. In the morning we all walked to the point —Dorothy cutting church, saying it was better for the soul out here—and scrambled about the rocks and got whelks (winkles). It was quite lovely, and everyone was friendly; at one point we all sang hymns; the various young scrapped a bit and Av went down and found a pool full of corallines and came back very excited saying it was the most beautiful thing he had ever seen. Everything was remote and bright, Arran half snow-covered, and brilliant orange lichens under one's hands. On the way back Murdoch, much more cheerful, lit heather and grass, Francis helping. He was lighting it on one of the big rocks, where it roared up like a waterfall upside-down and suddenly a mallard flew out. We all shouted to him and he found a nest and beat out the flames with some difficulty before they got to it. We came back—found three of Hugh's hens in the sown field!—to some disapproval from old Miss Blue who didn't like collecting whelks on the Sabbath.

We missed the news and it wasn't till Peter MacLean turned up that I heard "he" had declared war on Jugo-Slavia and Greece; it all sounds horrid, except for the Russian declaration.

Sunday 13 April 1941
... I had some small chocolate eggs over from last year; I gave everyone one egg round the table, and presents, but I hadn't enough cardboard shells from other years, and one can't get them—which

made it easier, as I could give things like pencils, which don't go into eggs! I shall keep the rest of the eggs for next year, when they will be even more valuable. Easter isn't much kept up here. I had one Easter card—from a German woman who had been released from internment on health grounds. I gave Avrion one of these war-games with a board (in this one Germany always moves first and is the only side allowed to invade neutrals!) and the family played it on and off most of the day.

Everyone quite likes my final arrangement of high tea or supper at 7; it means one meal less to wash up, and one less pudding (needing sugar) to be made, and less vegetables—we can have salad. It lessens the consumption of alcohol quite a bit, too!

All of us feeling a bit gloomy about the news; one realises how much the earlier African news had cheered us up! Bernice particularly gloomy. We try to say cheerfully that soon the troops will be back from Abyssinia and Eritrea, and make jokes about letting loose the patriots. Rosemary gloomy about the Australians being defeated. We ask ourselves what the USSR is after—in the evening the Japanese pact.

Tuesday 15 April 1941
. . . Lachie was taking over Jo [the horse] and the harrow, to go over the field wherever the cultivator had passed. Duncan had done about half [with his tractor]; I went over and he showed me how to work it, and went round with me a couple of times. Then said he must be going, asked if I thought I could take it on. Of course I said I would, though I was doubtful really; but I felt a nasty kind of pleasure because Anne, anyhow, wasn't able! But the first round had jolted me about, so that I almost pitched out; my skirt kept on working up past my knees, and I was always bruising the inside of my knees on the steering wheel; it was like nothing so much as steering a ship in rough weather. The hints were supposed to be filled in, but they were awfully rough to cross. At first I was rather frightened of the slope at the bottom but soon found that the tractor didn't run away. It was a job to turn, one had to make a wide circle usually over the cultivated part. It rocked, and sometimes gathered clods; then I had to back, to get them out of the teeth of the cultivator. Once I stopped the engine accidentally, by not accelerating enough on the slope up. Lachie had to come and turn it over—it was all he could do. He was going over it with Jo, after us, slowly; I told him it was rotten ploughing; he said it was the first he

had done. I think we should have ploughed this in autumn, instead of our leys.

It was grand, though, after a bit, when I had decided I wasn't going to fall out after all, and had got reconciled to the bruises, and used to the feel of the engine. The tractor was so powerful, and it was fun making a new break, judging how to turn and so on. I got it all turned over, and then undid the cultivator and turned the tractor, which now bounded along, down the grass edge of the field . . . Lachie picked up my notebook which I had dropped and was about to run over and gave it me, grinning. Gingerly I got out of the gate and turned down the drive. There was no horn, but I was making a lot of noise. I got on to the road and into the top; one is much higher up than in a car, able to look over hedges. I pulled my skirt down and chugged along and wished people could see me, I was so pleased. Several did—the doctor shook his fist at me, he always thinks I'm doing rash things.

Thursday 24 April 1941
. . . In the lovely late afternoon with Eric to the plane (and found that Dick after all hadn't got a return, so I had to pay for a single ticket, which annoyed me). He said it was like going back from leave. The marvellously casual, chatty, friendly and unpunctual office presided over by MacGeachy, so like Russia—or something in a Rex Warner story, with the caricature flying-men drifting in and out, talking shop—how annoying to an American or German! But not to Eric or me. In Glasgow, Rogano's full up so we dined at the Grosvenor, quite well, any amount of cream, probably made from pigs' fat treated, but who cares? Odd to have a proper dinner in Glasgow, after so many high teas there with my prolet and semi-prolet friends; one gets out of the habit. I begin to know Glasgow, to have emotional content about one place or another, as I had once for London. A nice, nice city, so friendly—so warm in its personal relations, so damned ugly.

Back by green car to Anna's, found Mamie and one of the others, sitting round the fire, drinking tea, eating biscuits, talking about the blitz, their own experiences, and food—Mamie, going to the greengrocer's, had found two oranges "you could have knocked me down with a stick of rhubarb". She had been doing the food racket for her paper, but it wouldn't publish most of the stuff; she says the fish is worst (I would have brought some back, but the prices were fantastic —lemon sole 6/- a lb, cod 3/-, no real kippers), and that speculators bought up fields of onions and leeks—how did they know so well beforehand? Very angry with the big hotels. Shortage of cigarettes in Glasgow at the ends of the months and the Glasgow week-enders take them from country places. From what Mamie said, and from over-heard remarks etc, I think the morale in Glasgow is very bad; they had all said "We won't be bombed", so when they were they just couldn't take it at all, and are now glooming about, feeling thoroughly defeatist. Anna says that a lot of children from her school have gone (and her Qualifying class filled up with non-qualifiers, who have failed three times, a bit depressing to teach!) but some are back already. They were evacuated to Moffat which didn't want them a bit; two thirds had to be compulsorily billeted; all had passed their medical but the Moffat doctors turned back sixteen, Glasgow say they are perfectly all right and are furious. One boy said by one doctor to have ringworm, by another not: same with impetigo: same with dirty heads. Still a wild lot of Poles about, all wanting to sleep with anyone, all pretending they came from noble families. A bit of a dust-up at Tighnabruaich.

After the others went Anna produced a half pound of Clarnico sweets someone had sent her; I wouldn't have looked at them pre-war, but they seemed marvellous. We feel about sweets just like we used to say the Germans—or Russians—did! But all the same, it's no great deprivation, in fact I think it's rather fun, and my teeth are never aching like they used. If this is the worst we needn't worry.

Denny M had been unwell; Naomi invited him to convalesce at Carradale House so that she could nurse him. Meanwhile, rehearsals were going ahead in preparation for a new showing of the play on 2 May at Tarbert.

Saturday 26 April 1941
. . . Denny M now seems quite reluctant to get up, unlike most of the men I know, who hate being in bed; I don't think he has ever had a rest in bed before, he keeps on speaking of it, being curiously grateful. I feel now that I ought to take Carradale one by one and keep it in bed for a few days and pet it a little; almost all these hard workers could do with it. He is a lot thinner and rather weak, but has no pain and I'm sure the ulcer is better; the shadows are almost gone from his eyes. By and by he got up and we walked round the garden, looking at the daffs and he was pretty gloomy about the war, saying that, whatever happened, things would be the same, the rich always rich and the poor remaining poor, that any levelling up now would be undone after-wards, and what would happen when all the men were demobilised

and thrown on the markets again? I said that would be the time for a revolution and he, having become nearly a capitalist by that time, like all the fishermen, would be caught between the millstones. He said with some passion: I'll never be a capitalist, no! . . .

Monday 28 April 1941
. . . Douglas [Cole] very jumpy, goes on writing verse; we talk about poetry, about ideas . . . I feel that everyone is a bit strung-up and I must be all out to give the right response, *a.* to Douglas and *b.* to my brother. I tried on Sunday to write something; I stopped my thing on Scottish nationalism in the middle, as I was so interrupted, now can't take it up, had the idea of a shorter thing on language, the moment I started that got interrupted. Douglas wants to read his poems, Jack wants to talk about himself in some form. Bella just won't deal intelligently with coupons. One keeps on fidgeting about the news, but at the same time I try to keep off it, because I should have the Marxist morals being drawn all the time, and that is such a bore. It is like having very religious people in the house. Worse. Jack and Douglas respect one another, but each is determined to keep his end up.

Thursday 1 May 1941
I slept late, didn't remember it was May Day till 10 in the morning, then dashed up to the roof with the red flag, to find the halyard broken. Got the ladder from the stables, Rosemary climbed it and with great difficulty caught the end as the wind blew it—and a plane came down to practice on us just as she was doing it. Got the flag fixed. Sowed the cricket field with all the remaining ammonium sulphate. Lachie has been rolling it. I wish we could get some rain. But it is lovely for sitting out; some of them are sitting out; some of them are sitting out and reading. I begin to think I'm not reading, not for lack of time, as because I can't bear doing anything so passive at the moment.

The Post Office rang up to say they had an express letter for me, but they hadn't given it to the postman—I think because they were so excited about it—so they would send it up by the bus; it would be only about three hours later than the ordinary post!

I don't think there has been any period in my life in which I have read so few books; I can't concentrate, and don't want to read light stuff unless I am definitely ill. Actually I'm pretty well, but already quite a bit thinner, which is all to the good! But I feel very inferior with

Jack and Douglas. Douglas is reading the old testament and finds it unpleasant.

. . . Everyone came for the rehearsal, Duncan a bit nervous after benzedrine, but dead sober. I was cross, as I'd just had a note from Effie saying she couldn't come as she couldn't get off work early enough. Denny M turned up; when I asked him how he was and said I was cross with Effie he promptly picked me up and then stuck me head-first into a chair, which shows he is still not too weighed down by a milk diet—any more than the Scythians were. One of the other girls got Effie on the phone and persuaded her to come. But Willie didn't turn up till 9.30 (for an 8 o'ck rehearsal) un-changed, saying he had to go over his books that evening. Of course he had completely forgotten his part . . .

Denny M and Betty were extremely good, throwing themselves into the part. I think Denny M moves like a ski-er, with his knees bent (or perhaps that's from the ship) which gives him a half-shy look, the disguised and resentful slave-king whose royalty is behind the eyes and the rope-scarred hands. Duncan was much better, Sandy excellent, Donald of course as good as ever, making up things to say in the gaps, including an introduction for Rob's English song—Rob, though, says it's no good, the girls won't know the chorus, it's too difficult. I said he was to find another, and hope it won't be "Speed Bonny Boat". I only hope they'll all have their own kilts, shoes, stockings, etc, when it comes to Friday.

. . . Afternoon, walked with Jack and the two girls—always rather torn about walking with Jack or Douglas: both seem to want to be walked with. Jack seems to want to come to the play! Wonder how he'll stick the dance. The girls much interested in the dubs by the shore: Helen is a good zoologist, found various sticklebacks. Jack took off his shoes and went paddling for them and enjoyed it. It was nice watching the wee barnacles opening as the tide reached them, and sweeping about in it. It was hot, and I would like to have stayed, but had to get back for the Junior games—then only two children came! I got some winkles, though. Found a letter from Mass-Obs (the Express one) asking for introductions in B'ham, so wrote a number hastily.

Friday 2 May 1941
. . . Walked a bit with Douglas [Cole] who is profoundly gloomy; says nothing can be done with the present govt for various reasons.

His own show being sabotaged from above. Gave me a lot of low-down on people. We wondered what end there could be; if it is over within eighteen months or so, as the USA will no doubt want, that probably means a compromise, leaving Europe under Hitler more or less. Otherwise—? If only the USSR hadn't proved itself so weak, as afraid of Hitler as the rest of us. He isn't anti-USSR in the way Margaret is, only disappointed. We wondered who would succeed if Churchill died: perhaps Bevin: but would the Army folk do anything for him? And would he stand it physically? I think normally Douglas, like me, feels profoundly unhappy underneath but quite cheerful on top so long as he is working; but now, ill and not working much (though he has the plan for a 'Tec book) he is gloomy all through. They are stopping him from using any Austrian or German refugees, however anti-Nazi, now, and the poor refugees (mostly eminent economists etc) write him hurt and miserable letters.

. . . At Tarbert there were several members of the choir to welcome us and give us tea; I went to deal with the stage lighting, the props they had provided, etc. Rosemary started making up. Sandy and Duncan went down to the harbour with Jack and girls to see the *Amy Harris*; Jack came back very worried, to say he and Duncan had given them the slip and he thought they had gone in to get a drink. I was furious, said just what I thought of them, in no unmeasured terms, to Denny M, whose sheep-skin I was pinning on. But they turned up, apparently o.k. I dressed Willie, tried to get the props on to the right side of the stage, dressed Lachie etc. Half the audience were in by now, saw the MacDonalds from Largie. Almost forgot to get made up myself, Val did it.

Oddly enough, we had a Campbell for our Chairman—he *would* call it a concert! and made a dreadfully bad speech. I saw a lot of Tarbert folk I knew but couldn't put a name to. Difficult to make up for a stage one doesn't know the lighting of! We began not too late, and the play went pretty well; I was aware of difficulties that probably the audience didn't get. There was a moment when Willie decided he ought to be on in a scene where he wasn't. My script fell into a tub of oil that was under the steps. I fell off with a loud crash; things were left at the wrong sides and Val had to run round and get them. But the pipes were found, not very good, but they did. Rob Ruadh's song was definitely bad. There was a lot of gagging but little prompting. The audience applauded spontaneously for Jemima's port-a-beul, Val's dance, Ishbel and Semple. I had my eye hard on Duncan, he said he must have a small drink half-way, I said all right; he did extremely well, especially in the epilogue. Then I made a short speech, emphasising that we could do this kind of thing all over Scotland, that the Nazis wanted to make people into machines, but we were refusing to be, we were individuals, this was part of democracy, etc. It went down well, also with my own people. Duncan was kissing me and saying I didn't let you down, did I? And I said no. Afterwards I took him down to see the Largie people, so glad and proud that he was sober (for the one drink had done nothing), and introduced Jemima too. She looked and acted like the beautiful, live girl that she is. Poor Denny M had been trembling during the last scene; I could see it in his knees and hands from where I was; and, as always, his gestures and everything were quite different from the rehearsal. But they were both excellent, all out to get it across.

Saturday 3 May 1941

. . . MacCormick, the sec of the SNP, had turned up; he very much wants to talk to Jack and Douglas about politics. But Douglas tired and Jack just grumpy and bored, and the girls not helpful! I get nervous and un-natural.

It was the cinema in the evening and, as it was a *Scarlet Pimpernel* film, I took over my watch, to exhibit as the S.P.'s authentic watch; it interested a lot of the grown-ups. We cleared about seven pounds. I went away as soon as everyone had come in and I had counted the takings, but found Jack and Douglas reading books in a gloomy or at least depressing silence, while poor MacCormick sat between them, not able to converse. I tried to start various conversations, but nothing happened and I was very tired anyhow. Then the others came back, also Betty, but still we had no political conversation of the kind which would have been valuable. And I got more and more tired and embarrassed, finally everyone went to bed, after altering clocks.

Sunday 14 May 1941

. . . Found Baillie Ramsay, up with a friend: took him round the garden. He said to MacCormick that he wasn't interested in politics, he didn't understand them. Went on to explain how much better things were for the working man than in his boyhood when he had worked a fourteen hour day at a tweed mill. But they hadn't gone fast enough. And why not pay the men on the Burroo twice as much and get them to work on the roads? And his brother had been bombed out of Clydeside and had wanted a house of the Duke's at Southend, but his brother was blind and had ideas (in an under-tone: he is all for Roosia!) and the Duke's Factor had put him off for a few days and had finally said that he had queer ideas and couldn't have the house, and was that right? Shouldn't the Duke's land be taken from him? And why was the Laggan not farmed all in one by the State with tractors, instead of being cut up into little fields? And so on. He also asked me if I was all right, and the petrol was cut down, but it would be a shame if I couldn't meet my husband who was working in London, and he would always see me straight, etc . . .

Again a difficult evening; at tea Jack and Douglas talking over everyone's heads about books that they liked, being hellishly snobbish, liking the poems of Thomas Aquinas, parts of Wordsworth, Gavin Douglas . . . Perhaps they do like them, but—! Again they wouldn't talk to MacCormick. Jack was reading collected Shaw (among other things), Douglas reading the Bible. Later, Douglas sang and made up quantities of small poems, some rather good. But it was tough on MacCormick, and made me feel acutely ashamed and uncomfortable. No doubt the SNP is a small body so far, but it has a lot of opinion behind it. And what right have they to look down on us anyway? . . .

Wednesday 7 May 1941
In the small hours, wave after wave of planes, rushing overhead, lower than in London, no wasp-wuzz but a flight of birds flattening one down. I kept on worrying about Margaret. So must Douglas have done. Bad nightmares. Mostly about Margaret and Humphrey.

Various farm and garden chores to do; more coupons have arrived. Wrote about Min of Information free films. But mostly Douglas fidgeting and me trying to make helpful remarks. Drove him in to Campbeltown, thinking I must be there in case they aren't on the plane. . . . Picked up the lawn mower. For a moment Douglas only saw Margaret and simply glared at her. Then they got in, Humphrey looking very well considering. They had four noisy nights, but she says most of the raids were on the outskirts, all places where I had friends now, and Greenock (which is full of Carradale boys) worst of all, mostly on fire. I suppose they've now knocked out most of Clydeside, Merseyside, Plymouth and much of the Bristol Channel. Glasgow wild with rumours; people saying all the windows in Sauchiehall Street smashed, whereas actually only about six were. She says that the people in Glasgow were—as I always say—extremely kind, everyone asking after Humphrey and doing small things for her. Her landlady, hearing she had a husband with diabetes, as well as the wee boy (for whom she had already provided an extra one) gave her six oranges. Douglas protests he won't take them all, so I've put in for a small one for Denny MacIntosh, who ought to be having them.

Thursday 8 May 1941
. . . Jack very depressed about going back; he really dislikes the extreme discomfort of his experiments, and also air raids. He is an exceptionally brave person, but I believe everyone except the really stupid is frightened of air raids. Pretending successfully not to be is a different thing. I was very sorry for him; yet hardly got below the mask, even so. Of course he and Margaret are a pretty damned bad mixture. But one saw how he must have a different philosophy from that of a safe person—even a person as little safe as my father, who, for his epoch, lived a fairly dangerous life. Mine seems so ridiculously and abnormally safe.

The level of drinking among the Carradale men was a source of continual distress to Naomi who saw it as a tremendous waste of energy and talent. Between 1941 and 1947, she used her poetry to express some of her feelings about this. The series of poems, *The Cleansing of the Knife* was addressed to 'Donnachadh Ban' and covered many of the events described in her diary during this period including the death of Jim MacKinven in the blitz, her farming, the fishing, Carradale gossip and one of her greatest friendships at this time.

On 10 May, she goes for a walk with Duncan.

Saturday 10 May 1941
. . . We started off towards Dippen, I feeling, as we crossed Semple's field, that I was throwing back over my shoulder the tiredness and strain and difficulty of these last few days. I tried to tell him of that, but not adequately, tried to tell him that this was my break, my holiday, my time to be care-free for a few hours.

We went up the pad on Dippen brae between the rhodies, I out of breath but happy, then across the road, where, he told me, they would be having a battle with the Campbeltown Home Guard on Sunday evening! He said that he and Duncan Semple had some kind of gun (I suggested a bren gun) but didn't know how to work it and anyhow there was no ammunition . . . In the dry heather there were small green butterflies with red streaks, very beautiful, and a black slug which, he said, was lucky on rough ground. But at the top of the hill we were only above Torrisdale Glen; he said he was cutting trees there; it was beautiful enough. The blond beech trees here and there among the dark pines were fair-haired like he was. Looking back there was our glen and the saw-mill and timber very clear and ugly; he wondered if it could be seen from the air by moonlight; I said why not, if anyone tries for it they may hit the manse! He laughed and said yes, Mrs MacKenzie had been round to ask me to camouflage it. I asked what they were planting for, was it for the next war but one? He said he wished they'd stop for the moment, till they knew where they were, what was four or five years in the life of a tree anyway? They would probably have to cut the wood behind my house, but he would leave it till the very last.

. . . Even the bogs were half dry; he was looking out for kinds of ground, for grass and rush which would point out fertility; he talked about his job, interestingly. But we had walked in a half circle and again we came out over the glen and the rain still fairly heavy. So we turned down the hillside for the shelter of the trees, a steep slope and I unhappy enough to be going back. The wood was mostly larch, very tall, straight trees, tufted high up with the light and lovely cloud of green. One was fallen; we sat down under it; we talked about America, he had had a chance of going there once—I was thinking it might have been better for him. Then I read him the poem about Jim. I think this body of poems I have written about Scotland are adding up into something pretty good, though the high-brows won't think so, and it is in a way hard to go on without encouragement from one's fellow writers. I get it from Neil Gunn though. But I want so much to be able to think about this long novel I have in mind; if we could have gone to the top of the ridge and watched the islands and had the long afternoon and evening, it might have cleared and settled my mind so that I could have thought of it again. But if I had said that, his mind would still have been fixed on Campbeltown, he might have felt uncomfortable for a time, but not enough to help me.

He was stroking and handling the fresh green of the larch, the bonniest green of all, the one that we forget all summer and autumn and winter, but that still remains in eternity. I wrote a poem about that once too . . .

Sunday 11 May 1941

. . . Worrying about London; everyone asks me if I have heard from Dick, but of course I haven't. And if anything had happened I easily mightn't for a long time. The evening news: a pity if Westminster Hall was smashed badly and I'd hate Big Ben to come down, but not much affected by Westminster Abbey. The Brit Mus doesn't sound much. But will they do it again tonight? Awful to think of the young men on both sides starting out, these lovely evenings, set for hell fire.

I'd had a very nice letter from Leonard Woolf, explaining that Virginia had killed herself because she was afraid of going mad. I do sympathise with that; one so often feels like that.

Had a long talk with Helen about Jack; I think she understands him. She says everyone is frightened of him, at any rate until they alter their attitude towards him, that it is largely that he is extremely kind but has no control of his minor manifestations of temper, so that, where most of us would control and still be smiling, he makes a frightful face, and that he is very shy and proud, like a little boy. I wonder if anyone really becomes adult? One always supposed the great Victorians did. But—? I think I am in parts. She also said that, as an air raid warden, she had acquired a good deal of contempt for the ordinary person who used their shelters; they made no attempt to amuse their children, for instance, nor to take responsibility themselves.

Begin to wonder whether after all I shouldn't have gone to Oxford . . . A picture of two people closely embraced in the park in *Picture Post*; Lachie brought it in to rag Lizzie who was a little embarrassed and said Yes, isn't it nice? But Sarah Blue just said Och, many a time have I been like that! This corresponds to Sandy saying how often he had had a squeeze with Sarah!

Monday 12 May 1941

. . . I understand that the Carradale Home Guard won! They had someone in the bed of the river who killed all Campbeltown as they came over (after killing the rest of Carradale, including Duncan Semple, who had killed a lot of people, but they wouldn't stop . . .) and was specially complimented by the officer at the end who said he deserved the George Cross! There was a large audience from both places, including a number of people who had come out by car from Campbeltown, also Campbeltown had brought its pipe band!

On 10 May, an extraordinary event occurred in Scotland. Rudolf Hess, Hitler's right hand man, flew a Messerschmitt to Scotland, landing close to the home of the Duke of Hamilton whom he hoped to approach with proposals for peace terms. Hess was picked up by the local Home Guard.

Tuesday 13 May 1941
The milkman says that Hess has come down in Glasgow with a sprained ankle by parachute! He says it was in the midnight news . . .

And after all it was! We all yelled with surprise when it really was true, and what a lovely story, the hay fork and the cup of tea and everything. Wonder what they'll do with him and how useful he can be made.

Thursday 15 May 1941
. . . Robbie says that a plane came down in Belfast; the pilot was killed but they hanged him on a lamp post all the same; Robbie slightly shocked. Lachie Paterson thinks Hess should be hanged.

. . . In the evening tried to write a bit, but everyone talking; and it's cold in my own room, besides I have everything down here. Wrote about half a story, as usual dealing with rape, revenge, forgiveness, emotions and so on; must try and write a story without emotions. Interesting anyhow to try an eighteenth century setting; find I have a number of new words, about the spelling of which I am uncertain, rather formal words like "aggressor".

Saturday 17 May 1941
. . . Later went over to the Hall, took tickets during the first film, one of these frightful Flanagan and Allens, which they all seem to like, and went in for the second, the Min of Inf one which I had asked for: *Men of the Lightship*. It was a magnificent bit of propaganda and photography. The audience talked all through it, as they do when they are excited, and there was a murmur of approval when someone in the film said The bastards! Several people screamed when the bombs dropped, and a number wept, including myself and various adult fishermen, Johnnie MacMillan for instance. But how much good they do, I don't know. It certainly encourages hate. Yet I'd like to have it shown in America! Young Gurrin came in half way. His wife had just had a son—and he said all Campbeltown knew before he did himself, and nobody told him because they thought he knew! He'd been to Lochgilphead to see her and was on his way back.

. . . Dick enjoying deeply being up here; talked over a lot of things. It does sound as if London was in a mess, including the poor old Temple. He says Law Reports will be very difficult to get hold of after the war—if anyone wants them! He has obviously had an extremely interesting time on Reconstruction, interviewing municipal authorities in all the bombed London boroughs, saying that some of them, especially Poplar, were frightfully keen on re-planning and decent housing, but all the inhabitants just want to go back to their own exact houses and neighbourhoods. The poorer the more so. Of course that's logical; they never had the possibility of imagining anything else. But it looks as if the City at least could be completely rebuilt.

The Carradale Dramatic Club was invited to perform at Largie Castle on the west coast of Kintyre.

Monday 26 May 1941

Mrs MacDonald rang up about 9.30 from Largie with various questions about the play. I thought the only thing was to go over and see for myself, so said I would walk over. Took the car as far as Auchnabreck; . . . A bit along the road a plane came over the brow of the hill and as I glanced automatically for possible places to hide a bird sprang from under my feet, a lark, I think. It had the most lovely grass nest inside a kind of cage of heather, and four very small nestlings in it; I hoped I hadn't disturbed it. Here and there were houses; the road ended at a ruined steading, with bracken over the garden patch; I went into the house and asked the people who might have been there to forgive us. There was no-one at all for miles and miles on those moors and glens, but now and then a dead sheep; it has been the worst lambing season for thirty years, what with the late snow and then the drought. Even the strong lambs that survived are dying.

Just by our march, at Narrachan, I saw someone waiting with two dogs and thought it was the Largie keeper; we said good morning, took one another for granted and walked on. I crossed Allt Narrachan barefoot; the water was almost up to my knees; then we went straight up, he never altering his pace, in the disconcerting way keepers have. My heart began to play tricks; when I began to feel literally sick with it, I lay down, wondering what was going to happen; as soon as I could speak again I told the keeper, and, after a time, when he realised that I just couldn't manage his pace, he began to be most considerate, stopped to show me things, to explain where rivers rose and so on.

There was a sulphur spring, and a grouse's nest with seven pheasant eggs in it—the pheasant must have laid in the same nest, but after the grouse, so the grouse hatched out her own and left the pheasant's. Reid (the keeper) said we should do some heather burning on our side of the Ducheran march; he says heather on this side should be burnt about every fifteen years and on the other (which is less soggy, so it grows quicker) every eight or nine. If you let it go longer, it is a while before anything comes, and maybe the heather itself is killed and nothing comes but the nardus grass. We talked about game and about people and about the future of Scotland, and how these small places the like of Tayinloan, will only do if there are more houses and some choice of work, some kind of other industry. He said he couldn't see how the government had plenty to spend on war, but couldn't spend the day's cost of it on houses and roads for Scotland.

... Mrs MacDonald, of course, comes from the same layer of society as my own. Here, we feel friendly towards the workers, get on well with them: much less with the middlemen or middle classes in general. We have a strong public sense, dating from the time when we really ran things (so we can be exploited by the real rulers), and, for instance, would never put our own convenience before what we conceive to be public welfare. I get on with her very well, yet I feel a deep, deep suspicion, the shadow of the clearances. I feel that, ultimately, we will not be on the same side, I will be a traitor to my class and my instincts, and she will find it surprising and shocking and will not understand at all ...

We went down to look at the wee hall; it will do all right, but I must get the chorus half on and half in front of the stage. We discussed lighting; I might be able to get two 12 volt lamps from one of the boats that would do from a car battery on the foot-lights; otherwise we should have oil lamps. Two cottages will do for our dressing: we shan't want much make-up. Mrs MacDonald will give us all supper at Largie afterwards; both she and I talked about the cast as though they were my people, my tenants, my children.

She left me up by the loch and I went on; my heart wasn't quiet yet, and I was a little nervous, and it looked grey enough ahead. At one point I began to wonder if I was right, I couldn't see a sheep fank that I had noticed on the way across, but that was only because I had kept on a level round the contours, instead of across them. It was wet that way, in fact the keeper had probably been wise to go up; but I just couldn't climb, that made my heart go at once. The water-shed was long and grey and the sheep stared at me. I saw the red bruachs above allt Narrachan a long way off, and found them frightening, a length of red earth precipice close over the river where I must ford it, by the deserted village of Narrachan. The wind was blowing in my face and I was wet through now; sometimes the bogs would make queer noises, and sometimes there were curlew; I said to myself that Naomi Haldane would not be frightened. I walked through the river in my shoes, getting no wetter than I was; even the hilt of my sgian was wet against my leg. The path was crumbly with rain; the birch boughs dripped on me; I drank at a small burn. It seemed a long enough stretch down the next glen, and, going up to the old empty house again, my legs were trembling with tiredness and my heart hammering; I began to feel a blister. But then I was on the old road again and the loneliness dropped behind me, and the terrible feeling of the clearances, and the hate I had on the sheep. Then we came to where I had once been, shooting, and soon in sight of Auchnabreck and I was pleased with myself for this walk, thinking I would speak of it lightly. I came down to the car, with a young collie barking and wreathing round my knees, and started it with my knife tip. I was too wet to stop at Brackley but came straight back and had a hot bath, and listened to the bad news at nine, wondering how long we would hold Crete and when it might be our own turn for invasion, wondering if Murdoch would be away from Cambridge.

Thursday 5 June 1941
. . . About a quarter to eleven we all went down to net with Hugh . . . also Lachie. I went in the boat to shoot the sole rope the first twice; we got nothing but dabs, very good to eat, though. Robbie said it was because the Home Guard had been firing at tins on the beach and frightened the fish—one boat had had to cut her lines and get away, the bullets were ricocheting every way. I said if we netted the mouth we would get mostly plenty; if they were at Torrisdale last week they would be here now. First he said he couldn't, then, after the second shot, when it was getting darker—and lovelier than ever with the moon out—he said he would. Dick and I and Matty waded out to the point, the others in the boat, Col Rendel delighted at seeing a new technical process. I believe I could manage a plash net myself now. We hauled in gently, throwing stones at the outside of the rope to get the fish in, and soon enough saw something jump and then a boiling in two or three places that showed we had the stuff all right this time.

Everyone was excited and pleased, running into the sea, Lachie and I telling one another urgently to keep the sole low—if one lifts it the fish may get out underneath. And there they were, gleaming and flapping, silver all over, not dark at one side like the dabs. We got them by the gills and took them right up to the high gravel, strong, arching beasts, hard with the sea muscle. We got fifteen sea trout, the largest 4 lbs, the next about 3, the rest ¾ to 1 lb, all good fish. We gave Robbie and Lachie a fair-sized fish each and two dabs, and gave Hugh a good big one and several dabs. It should help with the house-keeping. He was pleased, he had been rowing, said the oars were no poachers' oars, they needed muffling, even said he had enjoyed himself—no need to ask Lachie! Everyone ragging Dorothy for dragging the net too high and getting bits of seaweed into it.

It is the sport I like best in the world, but I would like it better still on someone else's river! We came back, with a basket full of fish and others I had strung with the string I brought with me, and made tea; I had been cold wading—the others wore gum-boots, I had bare legs and gym shoes—there weren't any gum-boots left my size—but now I was warm and tingling with the salt water. The house wasn't blacked out, but now, at nearly two in the morning, we blacked out the kitchen and one or two windows, though I didn't bother with my own room, getting undressed in the moonlight. There were three pairs out in the bay, and I thought I saw that one had dropped her winkie.

Val Mitchison has been attending Kilquanity School, a school run by John and Morag Aikenhead on A. S. Neill lines which was situated in Dumfries. Naomi visited her in June.

Tuesday 17 June 1941
Val sleeps in a room in the old bothy, which has been made quite nice, with a fifteen year old girl and sixteen year old boy, all very Dartington, not really, it is much less comfortable, they do their own housework and so on. The fifteen year old girl . . . actually was at Dartington, which she criticised as having become too fashionable and being full of the children of fascists. Her own elder brother is in America, partly to keep him out of the Army no doubt—there were some really beautiful photographs by him in the room. I thought the girl was nice and intelligent, and very grown-up; but the difficulty is that Val isn't in fact getting what I sent her to school for: companionship in her own age group and a normal life. This is as abnormal as

home. She has an almost adult vocabulary and knowledge of people, and she'll have a tough time; at her age she should be learning about *things*.

There seems to be a general woolly anti-war feeling, as though one could stop this bloody war by feeling against it. It is almost taken for granted that one should be a conchie. I really rather shocked Morag (the wife of John, the young headmaster) by saying that I couldn't quite see the C.O.'s position in this war, that one couldn't get out of things by just denying their existence. They don't seem to get the papers or to listen to the wireless; that may be just as well, but it means they're out of touch with ordinary life. I think most of the younger masters are C.O.'s and most of them are probably a bit odd in other ways; they tend to wear kilts with sandals, which aren't very appropriate somehow. Morag's brother Bill, who is a Carradale boy, was in the Merchant Navy but has somehow evaded being sent to another ship for five months, I'm not sure how. He seems nice, though, and a low-brow, so that I could talk to him easily.

Friday 18 June 1941
. . . Tried to talk to John Aikenhead about Val's work, while he was gardening but got nothing out of him; he seemed depressed. . . . Also I put my points about the need for a framework for the children, the need to learn to work and the fact that in all learning there comes a point when it is suddenly dull and you just have to do some apparently boring stuff—this usually before a startingly interesting time. Also children at that age can memorise easily, whereas it is hard work later on. I always tell Val to practice memorising last thing at night so that the unconscious can take over the job while she sleeps. John was very *piano* and accepted everything I said. I gather he is in a period of transition and much worried because two children were suddenly taken away by their parents because the girl was sleeping alone with several boys, one of them not white!

This boy, Ian Orchardson, is rather interesting and probably intelligent: grandson of the old painter, his mother is African, married to his father who has a plantation in Kenya, and a (good) witch. His father is trying to educate him to become a leader to his own people on his mother's side; the boy is obviously going to be very good at languages.

. . . Argyll showed me some of her [Val's] written work, which was much better than I thought; she is obviously getting on well with languages, finds Russian letters no difficulty, and is reading quite solid French. Her maths seem fine too; I told John she ought to learn to be less careless over spelling and writing in general. . . . Of course they make their own beds etc. But cooking, sewing and ironing are very useful these days. Also said she must get to bed in reasonable time.

. . . I went with Mary to the farm; the food is amazingly good, largely vegetarian but with cheese, eggs and lots of milk; they seem able to get dates and figs and various cereals. Excellent brown bread. Nuts, etc. Val loves it. The staff and various stray people were playing football with the farm[workers].

On 22 June, Germany invaded the Soviet Union. The Mitchison household, including their young guests, Cyril Gill and Francis Huxley, was in uproar. Later the same day, a bus full of sailors arrived. They were treated to the customary hospitality of Carradale House with food, drink and entertainment.

Sunday 22 June 1941
. . . Came in for 1 o'ck news. Rosemary and I were listening casually, but as we heard, I yelled for Murdoch to come too and they all came. As it went on I began to sob and shake with hysterics. I began to realise how I had been expecting another appeasement or worse. Now at last we are on the same side; this ache I have had all the war because of the Soviet Union, is now healed. Though goodness knows it doesn't make war any better or nobler a thing. Only something has been added. Molotov's speech was so oddly like everyone else's too! At one point Francis asked is this Molotov or the BBC? Cyril shook his head: Can't tell. The only thing one missed from Molotov was that God would assuredly support so righteous a cause. Yet I find myself almost praying that the Red Army will be all the things one has hoped. I suppose they may go three hundred miles through the Ukraine, which I remember as being extremely empty, but I don't see them going much further.

After the news we all made the obvious remarks: Which side will the Poles be on? Will the *Daily Worker* come out For King and Country? Denny and Ruth are at Oxford this week-end, which is rather funny! Wonder what the CP will do.

I went to tell Betty [Mackenzie, the tenant at Mains] who hasn't got a radio; her first remark: Oh!—David will get his Commission. But I doubt if this will mean that CP members will get a better show in the army! She and I and Angus and Dai all talked at Angus' door, all excited; Dai said Now the French will rise. Angus made some disparaging remark about the French, but Dai said There will be a revolution surely. It wasn't the French people it was only their leaders. You'll see. Betty said We'd better summon McCallum (our Tory MP) and ask him what he thinks. Dai said He's got a soft job, he got himself elected to get out of the Army. Margaret MacGregor only thought how "he" had broken his promise again, and the poor people. But most are excited.

Earlier Rosemary had been writing to a friend who is very unhappy; I suggested Mass-Obs. Of course, one realises that Mass-Obs is a kind of God-Figure—one confesses, one is taken an interest in, encouraged. Will Mass-Obs supersede psychiatry? I always recommend it myself.

. . . called to everyone to come in for Churchill's speech. Fifteen of the sailors, all the intelligent ones, and the NCOs, came in, also Betty and Matty and the little girls (oh yes, and we found that one of them has a dirty head, picked up at school!). Everyone listened carefully with occasional murmured asides from the more frivolous minded, like me—when Churchill said he'd told Stalin, and one felt naughty Jo not to listen to Nursie; I also felt it was pretty tactless in its general reference to Communism, though perhaps sound for American audiences, and that Churchill was obviously thinking of pre-war Russia, the Russia he knew, with its villages and ikons, and that it didn't fit in with the Collectives, or even the Russia I knew myself.

. . . The sailors, such of them as were interested at all, were excited and pleased. We all began asking what they'd play next Sunday, would it be the International? Betty MacKenzie was excited and thrilled, what with the USSR and the sailors, kept on jumping and clinging. Several sailors were humming the Red Flag; I said that if anyone wanted to borrow books, they could do so and return them to the Bus Office. The mathematician borrowed Hogben, and another boy borrowed some science. Then they were collected, very kindly, by the NCO with whom they seemed on very good terms. One of them had been playing the fool solidly all day, very well, but with incredible energy; some of them and Rosemary had played convicts in the wild garden; two of them had played racing croquet balls with their noses! At last they were all collected, and I picked them a few more flowers; we said goodbye; I said next time we'd hoist the red flag and sing it for them. A rather silent Yorkshireman said That'll suit most of us. All shook hands and said thankyou, very friendlily and nicely. They were far nicer and easier to get on with and more intelligent than I should ever have expected from the dances; I believe they're a different lot, though. None of these had been to a Carradale dance.

Friday 11 July 1941

... About 11.30, Denny M said goodnight and went down to the gun-room and borrowed a pair of waders—Dick's! And I slipped up and changed into a thick skirt and jersey, bare legs and rubber shoes. I had already cut all the outside buttons off my Burberry, as they might catch. Denny M and I met in the business room, and were kneeling over the suitcase, looking at the net, when Rosemary came in! She was extremely tactful but of course knew!—not that it matters. Then I paid out the net and Denny hung it over his shoulders, till he looked like a nineteenth century picture of a Yarmouth fisherman; we went out by the wee door, not that it was at all necessary, but it kept up the game. We were down on the beach at midnight, and the rain cleared off, but a bit of a jabble on the sea, and no sign at all of the boat. We redded the net, Denny complaining how short she was, and then sat on it, waiting and talking in the soft night. After half an hour he saw the boat, long before I could; he has amazingly good sight for distance though not for colour. I never can make out if he is slightly colour blind or simply untrained. She came in and we took the net down: they'd had to lie out, at the whiting grounds, for long enough, in case Robbie was looking. We waded in and on board; Dougie was there, shy and tough looking in his old coat and beret, saying gently Hullo Mrs Mitchison. I said we would try the east end of the Bay and got into the bows, after a few protests from Denny M that the weather end would be better. They acquiesced and Duncan [Semple] rowed across and Denny M gave precise directions. Dougie jumped on to the rocks, holding the end of the rope; the bow mustn't touch the rock or the noise frightens the fish—the vibration rather. Then Duncan backed out and we paid the net out, but it was a bit fankled, in spite of our careful redding (but it was dry of course), and didn't go in nicely. We rowed round and in the shallow water Denny M slipped out, holding the other rope and began shaking it, to get fish to go into the net, while we plashed with the oars; we had both slipped out into the water, but it deepened suddenly, and I went in well over my knees—I never said though! Then we hauled in, but there was nothing there. They were all whispering about Torrisdale, how Neillie Brown, the keeper, had gone to bed, and the other watcher—Dougie's uncle!—in bed too. Robbie would be in bed too; I said I knew he often watched till three in the morning. But the Torrisdale idea was gaining. Denny looked at me and said The Skipper says we're not to go. But we'd got nothing this shot and they wanted to so much and finally I said all right, we'll go.

. . . We went on across the Bay, Duncan rowing mostly and then Dougie, and I in the bows, feeling shy, not wanting to butt in on the men. Denny M said later that Duncan asked if I was in bad trim, as I wasn't speaking, and he had said no, this was how I was. And as we made for the point, Denny M setting the course, speaking of the rocks by their Gaelic names that are on no map, I began to feel a lovely sense of acceptance: the sparkles flashed out all the time from under our bows, and the men spoke in low voices, and I leant over the friendly sea; there was a jabble in places, but this was such a small and buoyant and unassuming boat, and no sea would hurt us. . . . Suddenly Duncan said to me that he thought he would go in and fetch his car and go round to Torrisdale and be on the beach to catch the end of the net, or, if Neil was there, to warn us; what did I think? And he called me, very deliberately Naomi, and that was the first time. And I felt very happy and said I'm in your hands, and we put the boat about and rowed her in to the Bay. Denny M could see Robbie's pipe at the boat shed, but we were well east of that, and Duncan slipped over into the water, and waded ashore and the three of us made for Torrisdale, Denny rowing now. I said would I not take a turn, but they wouldn't let me. They were talking about fishing and people and incidents I didn't know of, though sometimes they would explain, and one got the sense of this other world going on alongside the laird's world and far more real, full of things directly perceived, seen, smelt, accepted.

Still the sparkles slipped and streaked from under our bows and there was a sweet soft land-wind, smelling of bracken and corn and young heather, and Denny M had put his coat over my knees, so I was scarcely cold, and this conscious happiness was on me, this trust. I said that there could be nothing wrong with a thing that was so lovely, and they laughed a little and agreed, and soon enough we were round the point, first at South Dippen that is our own, and then beyond that on to Torrisdale . . .

We lay on our oars a few yards from the shore, in shadow, whispering, smelling sea weed and flowers. Then we heard steps and kept very quiet, wondering if it was Duncan or the keeper. The others had said that no one could catch me, if I was to stay in the boat; it was the one on land who took the most risk. Of course if Dougie was caught, Robbie, whose shed he has, would probably put him out! But it was Duncan; we said nothing, but threw him the end of the rope; she paid out nicely now, Denny M had redded her properly, but oh man, the short she is! We took her round quietly, headed the boat in and plashed, and then hauled. But there was nothing. They tried again, further along the beach, Denny M giving all directions, standing in the stern, his wet boots glistening a little, his head against the grey of the night clouds. It was shallower here, where the sea-trout lie, rubbing themselves; this time as we plashed, we saw a boil, and knew there would be something in it. Denny hauled in, with Dougie keeping the net taut by an occasional stroke, and I leaning over his shoulder to watch. Here was a good-sized fish, and oh the pleasure we all got from it! We got a second about three or four lbs—a bit further along. We knocked it on the head but it wriggled and splashed, for the punt was leaking quite a bit. Then we thought we'd try the mouth of the burn; Duncan held the rope on one side, and we brought it across and grounded the boat; we all got out, and I held the end while the others went up the burn a few yards and threw stones. This was the most dangerous; it was just by the road—there was a milk-can standing on the bridge and for a moment Duncan thought it was a man. I thought that if anyone came I would run into the sea and swim. But nobody interrupted and we got nothing.

We had two more shots, a bit further along; we nearly got a fish in one, but he escaped; he was a big one and had lain very still. This was the only time in the evening that one of those men swore and then it was Denny M and only in Gaelic and not very seriously; otherwise there was no rough or cross word, and I don't think that was merely because I was there. . . . We put the boat ashore and hauled her up in a wee white cove; we were hearing the fishing boats coming into the burn for the week end, the sound of the diesels that carries for a mile or maybe two across the water, and there was a light in the sky that was more than the late moon, and a freshness in the air. I kept on thinking suddenly that this cove was on a desert island, that there were strange beasts and adventures inland; but it was our own bonny bracken and ferns and trees, and a road leading up to the main road, curving between rocks and fern Oh see you not yon bonny road that winds about the ferny brae. Duncan said The smugglers will have come here often. We walked up and on to the main road, Denny M and Dougie with the net between them, and so to Duncan's car. Yet I could have wished that road longer. I was so happy, and even my sea-soaked feet were warm. Duncan put the net in his meal barn, over the rafters; Denny would put on a bit more, to lengthen it. They were all saying when would I come again? I felt I didn't have to say that they weren't to do it without me! (though they may . . .) I said this was a thing one mustn't get into the habit of, it was like whisky that way, and they laughed and agreed. I wouldn't take a fish; Duncan and Dougie did. Duncan said he'd encountered some "domestic opposition" and if he went back with something worth while, then it would be all right. I felt a bit uncomfortable about that; I don't want to worry either Jean Semple or Lilla.

It was half past three now; I was hungry but I had a bit of chocolate that Peter had given me; I hadn't energy to make a hot drink. But I hung up my mac, and the tweed hat—Dick's—which was just like the hats we'd all had. And then I went to bed without washing or brushing my teeth, but so happy still.

Thursday 7 August 1941

I do feel like hell; it is partly being tired, partly that I feel so stupid; I can't concentrate, I forget facts, I can't read a serious book. In the *Time* Current Affairs Test I only got 56, whereas Avrion, who doesn't know the amount of American politics that I do, or should, got 64; I ought to have got 70. I made elementary blunders about this war. I don't know anything properly. If I'm no good I may as well do manual work and wear myself out, it doesn't matter; I wish I knew if this was age or something physical or the beginning of some kind of mental decay or what. I so much want someone to be awfully nice to me for a long time. Oh someone that I love, stand up and crown me. And I get like screaming when all these girls talk at once. How can one write when one feels like that? I can remember now the things Denny M said to me yesterday about writing but what the hell; he is stupider than I am, it doesn't matter what he says. It's no fun being merely one-eyed in the country of the blind. Damn. I have dropped a stone and a half in probably six months. My muscles are good, my hands torn and hardened . . .

Sunday 24 August 1941

. . . In the afternoon talked about nationalism and about the kind of books I want to write, about the language I want to use for them, about the tradition of writing, and so on. I feel nervous about it; there is something deep down, I feel defensive and passionate, as I do about being a woman. Not quite reasonable. I feel I don't care about being in the same tradition as Shakespeare and Beethoven if only I can do something for my own people in Scotland. I would like of course, just for once, to be a best seller. I would like to have cheap editions. Oh had I the wings of a Pelican or Penguin . . . But it doesn't matter. I want what Yeats wanted. I want the small group. I want to write history for two or three dozen people who may or mayn't read what I write, for the small, tiny group who said I knew more about Pindar than anyone but Wilamowitz, I want to write like a bit of history in *The Blood of the Martyrs*, which probably nobody has noticed, but it is first class stuff. And then I want to write for people here, for Denny M and Duncan and Angus and Lilla and Jemima and Lachie, for Alec and Anna, for Willie and Johnnie—to make them confident and happy. But I don't want to write for the *New Statesman* boys, for the international culture of cities. I want a capital for Scotland, but not an international one with the jazz standards, the commercialism, the Judo-American stuff . . .

Wednesday 27 August 1941

. . . Then Denny M came over . . . He had notes for his article, but only "the bones of it". I was to "put it into grammar". I found out how he proposed to shape the article, and reminded him of an opening sentence he had used the other day. Gradually I got him going, usually making him talk and then taking the best phrases and putting them down, a process of selection. Making him put in the personal part, which immediately made it real. Half way he began drawing the kind of boats they used to have, on the blotting paper; he told me how his father's boat had been sold because they thought that he (at 15, poor kid) couldn't manage her (he now thought he would have been able). The other brothers had been drowned or killed in accidents. That was just before 1914, and of course if they'd held on, they'd all have been out of the wood. We got about 700 words done; when he came to read it he was astonished at "the good it was". He kept saying "Am I bothering you, my lass?" and I kept thinking it was worth being an accomplished writer oneself in order to be able to do this, that it was real "contact with the masses" and all that. He had read mine and liked "the pure Scots" in the writing of it; I have to strike a balance between what he, for instance, likes, and what is bothering for Murdoch with his tradition of Shakespeare to Virginia Woolf. Then we had coffee and the pleasing news that Laval had been shot, and we thought it would be fun to dance; for some reason all the young—and Eric —decided it would be even more fun to dress up, so they got out all the Slovak and other things and dressed up. By and bye Av went over and collected Lachie and the two Alecs; we danced to the gramophone for a couple of hours, country dances and odd waltzes and things, a good eightsome. A nice flower jar was broken, which is a pity as we have very few left—the Woolworth ones survive! . . . We gave them beer, and it was almost the end of the small cask. I have written for another, but—? The alternative is tea, and that means sugar. And rather more washing up . . .

Saturday 30 August 1941
At last it was fine. It looked like holding, the wind was round to the north and the glass rising. I did various household and garden chores, then went down to the field, to find Lachie scything the bad patches that the cows had got at and that had been laid by the rain too, and Denny M binding. Jane [Cole] and Rosemary came out, then later the others. Then I asked Denny M to take the scythe . . . and finish the bad patch while Lachie went for Jo. It was hard binding, as the oats were in a wild muddle. The long and soft stemmed corn that I'd put the ammonium sulphate onto, was worse tangled and laid than the other and iller to sort. I doubt if it pays in this rainy part of the world, though there was a better yield and much more straw. Eric [Strauss] was being awfully busy and rather incompetent, but ordering people about, especially the three small boys. He said joking but half in earnest "There ought to be a proper foreman on this job!"—he to be foreman of course. I felt a fierce anger at this; it was my corn. I said lightly that everything was going well and I almost said there was to be no foreman in any field of mine . . .

The reaper was on to the other half; Jane and I went over to bind, then the others. Denny M was binding beautifully, economically, with a light binding of a few straws, very tight. Later piling the sheaves, I always knew his binding. Denny and Murdoch bound slowly and conscientiously; the boys were bad. Bobbie was a bit of a nuisance. Ruth was enjoying it, looking lovely and wild and blàthshùileach.* I got a mouse and she ran over to look, then her Denny came too; I thought how awful it would be to have a daughter-in-law who didn't like mice. She found another herself, little dark, soft harvest mice, her colour, the colour of Denny's brown trousers . . .

I felt very happy; it was lovely to be getting it in at last, to see the stocks up all over the field. It looked lovely too, the pale gold . . . I felt consciously and immediately happy; I had been working, I would be working again, but my muscles were standing it; I could see the new muscle in my bare arms and legs (only the muscle of my strained right thumb was sore, from pushing in the ties). I was wearing only a shirt and shorts and sandals, and a cotton square over my head. And there was no fear of rain. Denny M had brought me a bit of chocolate; Angus and Lachie looked at us gaily, coming back to work for me on a Saturday afternoon, not minding; while they were harnessing Jo, Denny M kissed me quickly on the edge of the harvest field.

Monday 1 September 1941
I, having spent about an hour house-keeping and coping with Bella and our lack of staff, got frightfully fed up and howled. Then one damn thing after another, and everyone asking me, till ten minutes to one, when I was able to escape into the library and start writing the new bit of the epilogue. At lunch time I came out like a winkle out of a shell, but knowing I had to cope with feeding people. Was promptly squashed by everyone about the play and the epilogue; it all seems to be a bad art form. To hell with art forms. Denny and Ruth, however, defended me. But I was nearly crying all the time. I went off afterwards and finished it. Dick and Jimmie went fishing. So I suddenly said I was fed up and would go and get a deer. I really didn't know where to get enough for two protein meals a day, without starting on the tinned stores, which I don't want to do except maybe a tin of sardines now and again. Anyway I took the big car and Murdoch's gun and some buckshot and string and a suit-case to put the plash net into, and went over to Denny's. Then I found I had taken the wrong suit-case, the good one, but when I opened it, there was Avrion's missing dressing-gown! I found Jackie, Val and Tony, all at Denny's, and all rather surprised to see me arrive with a suit-case. Lilla knew of course, and we put up a great mystification, in real West Coast style. Then Denny M came along saying "I'll guarantee you'll

* Warm- or tender-eyed.

get a deer". I wasn't that sure, but anyway it was nice to be doing one thing instead of a hundred, and he petting me in old phrases: "You're dead tired, ma lassie" as indeed I was. He took the gun and I followed him up through the thick bracken and over our burnt braeside behind Portrigh; already I was less tense, and the heather smell, even on this dull day, was beginning to get through me. It rained a little, then cleared off, though it was misty and a bonny kind of grey blue between us and anything else. I sat down in the deep sweet heather, and began to learn my part, while he gave me some toffee and went on over the crest of the hill, to where he used to find deer in the old days, for indeed, it's lucky to go out with a poacher! Almost at once I heard a shot and ran over, pulling the sgian out of my stocking (I'd found its sheath in the small car—I'd left it there when I was using the knife to start the car!). The deer was dead in the bracken, its eyes clouded over, but the pulse still in its neck; he had shot it in one go off in the head. I gave him the knife and he stuck it into the big vein; we lifted the deer's body to make the blood flow quicker. He was so happy; it was a queer, fine thing, to be standing there, two hundred feet above the sea, with no one at all about and the deer dead at our feet and himself with the sgian and the yellow stone in its hilt. There was a great appropriateness about it, a touch of the most obvious and Victorian romance. On our way across the end of the bay we had passed a visitor and Denny had hidden the gun under his coat in one movement, and then had laughed: "Amn't I the silly fellow, there's no need now!" Then we thought we must do the gralloch, and we hadn't brought a spade, so we dug up the turf with the sgian and our four hands. He wasn't sure how to do it; before, he had always just taken the back legs off the deer, and taken them away, the way the poachers mostly always do. Once he had killed a deer on Grianan, because there was a man who had been daring him to, and then he did and took the man there, and the man was frightened and said he would have nothing to do with it, wouldn't help him at all.

Then we slit open the deer's stomach; it was a hind and there had been a fawn with it, but a big one, not suckling, so it would be all right. We saw several others, too. We cut nervously, anxious not to go too far; I knew things a bit from old dissections, including the Latin names, which seemed a little out of place. Various mixed guts came heaving out; we cut through the breast bone and diaphragm and the air came wheezing out; we turned the deer over, it was hot inside, I hadn't realised how much hotter than blood heat the guts are; we pulled and pulled and all the packing came unpacked. Denny got the end of the gut loose, and I cut the renal-portal vein—luckily avoided the gall bladder. But it was a bit of a mess. We hastily pulled and got most of it out and into the hole, and I swabbed out the rest with grass and left the deer turned over to clean itself. We were blood to our elbows now and all over everything, especially the sgian; I kept on wondering how one managed after a murder.

We sat down on the heather and talked, partly as usual, about our boat, only he is afraid of what may happen in the time—year and a half—two years?—before he can get it. I gather Dougie is very keen to come. Partly about D's adventures, about being poor, so poor he couldn't have a penny to spend on a newspaper and always watching the post for the threatening letters, and everyone being bad to him, as they always are if one is poor, and how he would do anything at all now not to be poor; it just couldn't be thought of, to be poor like that again. And his eyes narrow and darken and he looks away from me, and I say that if ever there are bad times again in Carradale, at least I can share whatever I have with the rest of you; for here in a small community it is as simple as that. And he shakes his head and says if there were more like you, and then he talks about Dick, saying he would like to be like him, how is it he is so good, so unselfish. "If I were in his position I would be a pure Conservative." And then he says no, he would try to be the same, now. Then he talks about the Galbraiths, and Lilla, "my one", how they were together since they were at school, and she is so "mild", all the years they have been together "I have seen her growing like a flower". Then he spoke of his early sexual experiences . . . He was one of the main wage earners of the family, poor kid, and they couldn't risk his wages going on an affiliation order . . . or that he should get married. None of them knew anything about birth control (nor do they still). . . . One could see the picture of the young fishermen, adolescents, burning for what they wanted, shy and clumsy, and for all that as beautiful as sea-trout under their thick clothes.

He went on talking, lying back in the heather beside me, his wild black hair against the blossom, and his face twisting with laughter or remembered pain and anxiety. He said he had never before sat by a "lassie in trousers", and then went on about a lassie who had come aboard the boat on one of the islands, and she'd had wee tight things under hers. As he speaks of these lassies, you feel that what is prized is a certain kindness, whether it goes all the way or not, and also a certain integrity of action. I shall know some day. But oh it was peaceful up there, doing one thing at a time instead of being impinged upon by a dozen, and the heather under one's back, and the poacher beside one . . .

Saturday 27 September 1941
. . . Went into Campbeltown to pick up Tom Harrisson and Dos Passos [the American writer], found Huie's shut so couldn't get the saw mended. The plane late—poor visibility. Dos Passos very nice, shy, I think feeling slightly guilty as a non-belligerent in the sort of Munich stage, towards a belligerent; I expect most nice Americans feel a little bit like that. He is so gentle though, as indeed a good writer should be. Tom trotting him round—if he thinks Tom is the typical Englishman! Tom frightfully sleepy but with tremendous vitality as ever breaking through like a last year's crop. The others went off to catch the afternoon plane, I took Dos Passos down to the village, saw the MacKinvens, had tea with Denny M and Lilla, who were most hospitable; Denny M had distempered the shed. Dos Passos thought they were like Spaniards . . .

Sunday 28 September 1941
. . . Bella's finger bad, got the doctor to come and lance it. Helped with vegetables and so did Janet [Simpson Smith]; I felt increasingly what a nice wife she would be for Archie. It cleared a bit, and was lovely in the afternoon. We had inquired quite a lot and come to the conclusion that the locals don't really mind about Sunday fishing, so Graeme and Archie got five finnock. . . . Later walked a bit with Dos Passos, and picked blackberries; he says he wants to take on his old family farm in Virginia and farm properly, he is sick of cities and not being neighbourly. I do think he is so nice and gentle. We talked a bit about writing; he is diffident, increasingly interested in history. Nice to everyone.

. . . had a violent argument with Tom about fishing, in which my Denny defended t'other Denny and the Carradale fishermen in what I have to admit is their rather narrow and capitalist outlook! Tom and I shouted at one another, he said they could be more scientific, I said how, where is the research being done? After cross-questioning him and getting nothing definite I wrote to the Plymouth Marine Biological Station, Easterbrook, and the Development Commission. I wonder if the research people have done any single thing which could be put into practice. We had a fine argie-bargie, anyway! I don't see how any govt control of fishing could work, and I doubt the ability of the fleet to set up a Co-operative organisation. I believe I could do it myself, but not if I am also writing books and peeling vegetables and filling up forms and dealing with ration books and typing stuff for Dick!—and having people to stay.

On a second visit south that year, Naomi visited Lois in Lynmouth where the staff and pupils of Badminton School were now billeted.

Saturday 11 October 1941
Went up to the Hotel where the school is and saw Miss Baker, discussed Lois' future, what school she should take at Oxford etc. Miss B very keen she should go straight on, not be deflected by war-work. Says that a lot of her girls are marrying very young, at nineteen or twenty, to equally young husbands; she is bothered about it. Saying when are we going to send an Expeditionary Force to the continent to help the USSR and is it true that there are those in high places who don't want to help. Said also how much she missed the school expeditions to Geneva. School catering not too difficult; they have made a lot of jam.

Then picked up Lois, went over the school, saw her dorm in the lower building and ate mulberries from the school tree. . . . Went for a walk up to Watersmeet, talking about life, poetry, etc.

On to Denny and Ruth, now living in Watford and still studying at UCH.

Tuesday 14 October 1941
. . . We had dinner and talked about the war; it seems possible it may last five or six years which is almost too awful to think of. I can't imagine that there will be much civilisation left. They were among the students who sent a letter asking for more help to Russia—it was in *The Times* and various reputable places. The Dean of UCH appears to be angry! How frightful the BMA is, trying to restrict the number of medical students, presumably to keep up its own fees, this while there are plenty of (less rich) districts much under doctored. Of course they may want to kill off the civilian population. But I don't think it's that, it's just money. Mass-Obs: can't something be done to check the BMA? The doctors seem to aim at becoming a Corporation as in a Corporate state.

It seemed such a shame that Denny and Ruth should have to start like this, ploughing their way through years of war. Yet perhaps it's at least better for them to do it together. We went to a news flick, there was one very nice old Mickey, *Hawaiian Holiday* with Goofy at his best, and a horrible Pop-Eye, goodness, I do think Pop-Eye is ugly and nasty. Then the Gaumont British news, with the commentator, "Leslie Mitchell"—and why the hell should they take a good man's name?—doing his stuff. They had some extremely pathetic pictures of the wounded Germans going on to the hospital ship and back, which might have stood on their own, and been good propaganda, but this bloody little twirp with his BBC ironics, simply must disgust any decent person and I suppose there are a few left. Also they had a horrible real war film of a British plane with four lovely new guns shelling a German ship, diving on to it. All one missed were close-ups of the faces in the shelled and unanswering ship! As far as I was concerned, the news film made me feel violently and unreasonably pacifist, made me feel this war can't possibly be worth while if it's turning us all into this kind of hell's denizen. Dick very gloomy, said people must be getting even nastier in other countries. Then there was an absolutely frightful picture of some "All-girl orchestra" in technicolour, crooning. I recollected sympathetically the words of Goering—was it?—when I hear the word culture I draw my revolver. If this is culture. What the hell are we fighting for anyway? How willingly I would see the producers, musical directors etc, of Quickies, put into concentration camps.

At Oxford to see her mother, Maya, and her friends Elizabeth Pakenham and Christine Hope. After Oxford, Naomi went on to see Avrion at his new school, Leighton Park, on 25 October before returning to Scotland on 31st.

Thursday 16 October 1941
. . . In the evening to see Elizabeth, still rather ill with remains of gastric flu, and nobody to look after the baby. Says she is becoming a shrew, she spends so much time shouting at her children and cursing them for being untidy etc. Yet they are a particularly intelligent and attractive lot, as she knows well. She was mending clothes, sewing on buttons etc, all evening, hardly gets time to read. It's the first time I've ever seen her so down. We'd had the evening papers with the bad news; she said she wasn't going to believe the USSR could be beaten. But she was afraid she was getting rather tired of war. Everyone now

seems to expect it to go on for three or four years. Both she and Christine commenting on Churchill's increasing unreasonableness and *Führerlichkeit*.★ I quote Acton. Elizabeth passionately anti-Roosevelt and anti-American, always with a laugh and a point of irony, but still real. Says they're the prize hypocrites.

On to Lady Agnew's where the Nashes were; she had a picture of his hanging there. I gossiped about painters, Wyndham Lewis etc, and old days in general. Some of his pictures damaged in Tooth's bombing. He said all pictures were hung too high, you wanted to be able to dive into them. The Agnews fairly cheerful. I asked everyone what they thought about Murdoch whether he ought to go into the Army or was he right to continue his scientific education and be exempted as a scientist; Elizabeth said keep out of the Army somehow. Christine wasn't sure, said she was afraid he might feel guilty afterwards (this is my feeling rather). Janet Agnew said she thought he ought to go.

Sunday 9 November 1941
. . . Afternoon, the sailors came, a very nice lot, easy to entertain and make friends. There were three socialists, one the sec of a London Party, a real left-winger, knew Jack. Dorothy and Mrs Muego came and were very good with them, though Dorothy wouldn't dance on a Sunday! A few of them wanted some good music, but most of them can't bear it, they only want jazz: the highbrows complain bitterly that when the Forces programme puts on anything decent someone always goes and turns it off. Several wanted to look at pictures and things; one boy sat down by the book-shelf of poetry and read solidly through book after book of Eliot, Auden etc. I've no idea what he thought of them, as he was no talker: quite friendly but just didn't like talking! I gave them hare, a rabbit pie, bread and marg, bread and paste, currant loaf, buns, salad, apple fool and some small raw apples, all of which they ate except the lettuce which they hardly touched this time.

Two of them complained (*Mass-Obs please note*) that there were so very few serious books distributed to the Navy; they are sick of just novels, they want biography, travel, history, some of them want science, even religion or philosophy, current affairs. They buy Penguins but can't get them easily at Campbeltown; they are so stuck that they sometimes buy trash. They would like something to educate them.

★ Apparently not a German word but NM probably means 'Führer-likeness'.

I brought out a dozen or so Penguins, and duplicates of various kinds, for them to take back, also Dick's *First Workers' Government.**
One of them borrowed my *Moral Basis of Politics*, saying he didn't like novels, this was the sort of thing he liked.

Val had brought a small orange back from school; she and Rosemary and I ate it, feeling frightfully nostalgic and talking about fruit we had eaten, she about fruit at school, Val and I about fruit in London, always cases of oranges, big bunches of bananas and all the foreign fruits, the plums and apricots and passion fruit and lichees, and London teas with the cream cakes Jessie used to make, and lots of crumpets. I can still smell orange on my fingers, it makes the blister sting.

To Edinburgh looking at evidence for the book.

Wednesday 12 November 1941
. . . To Edinburgh, walked up to Archie's through Charlotte Square where some of my folk have lived for generations. As he wasn't back yet, walked along George Street and Princes Street. A bonny, bonny town. A capital, half dead. But with the dignity, the assurance, the slight coldness, of Washington, say, or Paris.

Aunt Edith in for tea, and Uncle Willie, whizzing off—at 75—to catch a train. We talked about food. Aunt Edith can be counted on to see the gloomy side of things. After tea I went over to the Office, we got out the big deed-box and I took out all the early Haldane stuff, not all, but what I wanted. Later I went through it and took notes. Funny to have respectable tea with a silver tea-pot and silly little cups and plates, and later dinner with lots of silver, a glass of sherry, Mary waiting on us, looking as alarming as ever; only the helpings are much smaller! Afterwards Aunt Edith and I talked about farming, the evacs at Cloan (they have given up almost all the house to the Barnardo children, as well as the whole of Foswell), the war. Again, the gloomy and anxious side of things came out. Old Miss Lemon, the classicist, was in, very cheery, pleasantly occupied in being rude to Oxford dons who have been sniffy about Edinburgh classics!

After Aunt Edith went to bed, talked to Archie about life. He has written some more of the book, exceedingly good description, I think. But was in a period of gloom.

* A quasi-utopian account of the future by Dick Mitchison, published by Gollancz in 1934.

Thursday 13 November 1941

... Going along Princes Street and up the Mount to St Giles, felt a queer kind of pride and anger; the lion flag was flying on some building, I could have kissed it. Walked into Parliament Hall, with its bloody awful stained glass—all the pictures are put away—and thought of James VI's remark when young "There is ane hole in this Parliament" and suddenly felt the most passionate and disconcerting longing to be a Member of the first Scots Parliament under the New Order, or maybe the Supreme Soviet of Scotland, working with the others all over Europe. Tried hard to squash myself. Accidentally got into the Signet Library instead of the National. However the Librarian received me with open arms. He is a nice, sentimental man, a bit of a Jacobite, knows his eighteenth century, brought me piles of contemporary stuff. I settled down with Macintosh of Borlum's *Enclosure and Fallowing* written from prison, from some place not half a mile from where I was sitting, written without malice or anger or anything but generous acceptance of events, the work of a good Fabian and oh such a damned nice man and so near one in time. By and bye I found myself sitting crying over my books in the Signet Library, because he was so nice and I could never tell him so, never give him back kindness, only two hundred years away in time, one could get at what he was and what he wanted. If only one could tell him one was on his side, one was trying to do the same kind of thing with the countryside, I at least, was trying to be the same kind of laird he had in mind. That I too loved Scotland, and, like himself, knew that Scotland needed changing and was determined to do it.

They lent me some books from the Signet that I mightn't be able to borrow elsewhere—I don't know if they're supposed to. No nonsense about filling up forms! Later I read in the National Library too, being equally well received by the Librarian there, Meikle, who was immersed in documents, but came out to get me things, to show me how I could get books for myself, and to help me with economic stuff. What other library—a National Library on the same scale as the Bod [Bodleian Library in Oxford] or anything—would just let one root round? Meikle is, I think, a good Radical, not a bit Jacobite, in fact I had to explain that what I was after was economics not romance. But Meikle saw me as part of Scottish history, descendant and representative of the Haldanes and indeed of all the great families whose blood is mixed in mine—for indeed there is scarcely one of them that isn't represented, Highland and Lowland. And I felt in turn the pride and responsibility, immediately, that I had to write the hell of a good book, that I had to explain something very important, that it was laid on me. I felt this once before in my life, when I had taken my notes on the death of Wallisch—and where is Walcher and where is the girl who wept?—for all I know they have been given back to the Nazis by Vichy—and gone back through the dark and whispering streets of Leoben, the whisper *verhaftet, verhaftet*, and I knew it was laid on me to write the story for all socialists for all time, *es lebe die Sozial demokratie und Freiheit,*★ and now I must do this for Scotland. Oh well, it'll mean a lot of hard work this time.

On 6 December, the Japanese bombed Pearl Harbor in Hawaii. The next day the USA and Britain declared war on Japan and on 11 December, Germany and Italy declared war on the USA.

Friday 7 December 1941
. . . And now the news about Japan and America. I wonder how it feels out there. I only hope the Americans are prepared to jump on the Japs as effectively as they've done. I suppose it must be a relief in China.

Saturday 8 December 1941
One is listening to the news again. I suppose they'll get the Burma Road. At any rate it'll bring the States in very effectively. But it sounds pretty awful. It's extraordinary that the States let themselves be caught like that. They must have known. I suppose an enormous number of lovely things will be smashed in Japan, as well as a vast number of singularly innocent people who have had a bad government wished on them.

It had been a harsh year and the war news was persistently grim. On 10 December the Japanese had sunk two of the most prized ships of the British navy, the *Prince of Wales* and the *Repulse*. The death toll was immense. On the home front the demand for women and men for the forces and the munitions' industries was acute. The call-up was extended to men from 18 to 51 years old; individual justifications had to be made to reserve 'key' workers; on 2 December, it was announced that unmarried women between 20 and 30 were to be called up. In Carradale Naomi had recorded in her diary the feeling expressed by many of the local fishermen and forestry workers that they were

★ Long Live Social Democracy and Freedom. 'Verhaftet' means arrested.

not 'doing enough'. Rosemary, Naomi's assistant, had also been investigating the possibility of joing the WRENS. Eagerness to support the Soviet Union through 'Aid to Russia' campaigns was widespread. Meanwhile, the traditional celebrations continued. Preparations for Christmas at Carradale House were under way. As usual the house was crammed with the regular guests from London and on New Year's Eve, 'the Navy' was also entertained again. Jemima was engaged to be married. Naomi has quarrelled with Denny M over the role of women in marriage and they had stopped speaking to each other.

Monday 22 December 1941
. . . Ian MacLaren, the plumber, as usual most helpful, helped me to put up the two great wreaths of greenery in the library, which really looks lovely. Duncan was shy, had had one drink—probably to nerve him to coming—but perfectly sober. We didn't have more than twenty to thirty people; Peter Buchanan, who is gentle and musical, Johnnie MacLean and sometimes Peter, played the melodeon and Dougie played the pipes. Jemima sang, so did Willie, so did Ian MacLaren. We danced almost entirely country dances; the Petronella and Flowers of Edinburgh went well, but the floor was too slippy for Strip the Willow; we had two eightsomes and a Scotch reel; the Circassian Circle was a wild muddle till Duncan Semple started dancing it "the old fashioned way" which appeared to be just swopping partners all round! We had a set of quadrilles where he danced with incredible violence, fortunately I was dancing with Dougie and opposite Peter Buchanan, who were comparatively gentle, though even so I was off my feet. Johnnie likes playing better than dancing; I put on a gramophone record so as to let him dance, but that rather hurt his feelings! We played Sardines and Murder (where, very typically, Willie, not having the murder card, committed the murder—I rigged the detectives, so that Dick should be one!). They were a great success, though everyone was terrified of going about the house in the dark; the only people who hunted properly were Ian MacLaren and me. A good deal of hand-holding!

We had tea in the middle, buns and sandwiches made with sardines from one of my oldest tins, which I thought I should use. Dick gave a few at the end whisky. We had soft drinks too, as there was a bottle of lemon and barley. Murdoch and Val danced, the former quite well and looking fine in his kilt. He also made friends with Alastair Lynn and Christine; I do so want to establish good contacts with the young. Kathleen and Effie both went early, I think most of the girls simply want to dance with particular boys, and, failing them, are bored, don't want to attempt new contacts.

Jemima collected her wedding veil; she is awfully pleased with her wedding present from Denny, who sent her a set of brushes and apparently a very nice letter! I gave photos to her and Dorothy.

Lilla was looking tired and depressed; we both tried to cheer her up, but I'm afraid she is a bit gloomy about this quarrel between me and Denny; she brought me over a note from him. I don't think he sees my point very much, however it will no doubt clear itself up. I think it all means that my feminism is deeper in me than, say, nationalism or socialism: it is more irrational, harder to argue about, nearer the hurting core. I can write about it, from angles, and have, in *We Have Been Warned*, *The Home* and others, but unless people have the same experience, it doesn't get across to them. Denny thinks he sticks up for women, but of course it isn't the same thing, nor can it be until the economic side is cleared up. I sometimes think that I could work my heart out for people here, but yet they wouldn't really think as much of me as of Dick, because they know it isn't me who has the money.

At the end of the party they sang "Auld Lang Syne" and "She's a jolly good fellow", for Dorothy and me. Dorothy was weeping slightly, and I felt quite sentimental myself. I gave her a photo, also to Jemima. I felt most sentimental about the "tannenbaum", though, when the candles were lit. We had crackers and paper streamers —pre-war!—and they all loved them, and blow-outs, equally pre-war. It was very much of a children's party, really. At Blackwood's church they sang "Stille nacht"—and I sang it in German, but of course inaudibly, so that was all right.

Rosemary, rather doubtful, drove Peter back—Jemima and Johnnie had gone earlier, as they were both tired. I was a little worried, but thought Peter would stop short of rape; most of them aren't really tough, only boringly persistent.

Christmas Day 1941
The wretched children were still not asleep at 1 o'ck but giggling and bouncing, and had made a barricade of clothes, into which we finally inserted the stockings. The rest of us were awfully tactful about it! But Av and Val woke about 6 (Val had left a note in the kitchen Wake me as early as possible) and crept into my room with my stocking, whispering noisily.

I tried to sleep, finally got up, gave them Murdoch's and Tony's stockings to go in silently with, put on a dressing gown and we all sat on Dick's bed while he and I undid our stockings exclaiming with delight! A lot of people had given me pencils, various people had given one another chocolate bars.

The children were thrilled with their stockings, and Avrion with his main present, oil paints, palette, canvas in a roll and one stretcher—he can make others: brushes. He says they are very difficult to get. Val had tools. Lois had been given money, which she had spent on books. She and Murdoch came in in dressing gowns, and we were all late in breakfasting. Rosemary somewhat cheered by hers.

After breakfast we unpacked our parcels, various book tokens, handkerchiefs etc. Sweets from Christine and from Eric, some from Nurse for A and V, book tokens for the children, the Topolski book from Tom Harrisson. We all ate sweets. It rained, but I went out into the garden and worked on the ramblers for half an hour. I also took the maids theirs—I gave them each £1 in an envelope—with various appropriate greetings, also anyone else we saw, but the men were all working.

I'd asked Denny M and Lilla to dinner, but they hadn't answered and when it was 1.15 and they didn't come, I thought they weren't going to and that he was cross still. So we started. I'd got a turkey from the Loch Gair hotel, god knows what it will cost. I'm keeping the plum pudding till Sunday but we had half the maids'. We had chablis and a sweet white wine mostly. Then I saw Denny M and Lilla coming, and when it became clear that Denny was in his braws, I thought it was all right. They brought us presents, a silver brooch for me, a Celtic ship, which they said was Kishmul's Galley, another brooch for Rosemary, a pot of shaving cream for Dick (he ragged Lilla at giving him this after he—at my instigation—had kissed her the other night, and she, not having thought of it, blushed and giggled). Denny M and I greeted one another in a rather sidelong way and kept on giving one another verbal prods. . . . Neither of them had ever had turkey before, and they were excited about it, kept on talking about how nice it was.

Wednesday 31 December 1941 New Year's Eve
. . . At midnight Dick brought in his drink and ladled it out from the punch bowl; most of the women preferred the cassis. Then Dick gave his toast: To victory next year and to a just and honourable peace. Then we went through the rite of drinking and shaking hands;

everyone shook hands, with everyone else; there was a lot of kissing, and old Mr Downie shook hands very often with almost everyone. Red Rob had left, rather tiddly, after a last dance with me, as they had people coming in; Sandy was beginning to talk Gaelic. Old Mr Downie sang "Taties and Herring" and the Valparaiso girls' song, and Archie sang "Four and Nine" and "Billy Boy". Jemima sang, and Willie, several of them together sang "Fire on Moscow"; Mrs Nicholson—whom I didn't know as a singer—sang a Gaelic one and "Loch Lomond"; I was standing by little Dick who held my hand hard, singing "I'll be in Moscow before you".

From time to time I went and got more food; I cut up my Scotch bun, and handed it round, but couldn't find Bella's cake, though Peter MacLean and I went to look for it; both MacLeans were perfectly sober and all the nicer for it, of course. Peter told Rosemary he meant to sleep with her and had brought a special pair of silk pyjamas; I said there was at least one WREN in the same room and what did he propose doing about that? I'm never sure how serious he is; I had a St Bernard waltz with him which was the most highly-sexed dance I've ever had; for either one was clasped close in the inevitably close dancing, the two steps back and three forward, one's cheek at one's partner's neck, and the smell of his coat which was a farmer's coat not a fisherman's, smelling not of nets and wind and sea but of the warm dark of byres, or else one is swung out and turned in the twirl, only to be re-gathered into the tight dance embrace. . . . I was wearing an old white velvet dress, dating from some twelve or fourteen years ago, long, with lace in the low neck. They liked it. I mostly danced country dances with Dougie Campbell; Christine looked so pretty, and has such a real dignity of her own. Flo MacAlister who came with Jemima, stayed the night too; she is nice and intelligent, had very much liked the film about Women in Russia. Looked at books between times. We had the new photos arranged, Lenin on the mantel-piece; Stalin's photo kept on falling on Taggie's wife, and we all ragged her (the baby is due in April).

They wanted Val to do the sword dance; she didn't want to, but finally did, very well, I thought; we had no swords, but we had the newly sharped scoochers, pretty difficult to dance over, and rather impressive.

. . . Gradually people drifted away, between one and three; I think they'd all enjoyed themselves a lot. The Navy were sleeping in all available beds, Johnnie and Peter over at Mains, Jemima and Flo here.

At one point some of them went upstairs to my room to listen to Dougie playing the pipes. Then some others sang the "International" in the dining-room. The Navy had a lot of whisky but we didn't give much to anyone else.

1942

In 1942, CONFIDENCE in Churchill's leadership was at its lowest. The war at sea was still going badly and, during the early months of the year, the British suffered a series of ignominious defeats: the fall of Rangoon was swiftly followed by the fall of Singapore in February. Churchill still hoped for success in North Africa but on 21 June Rommel overran the British garrison at Tobruk. The turning point for the Allied troops in North Africa was not to come until the battle of El Alamein at which Montgomery finally won a decisive victory against Rommel in November 1942.

In Britain, huge rallies calling for the opening of a Second Front in Europe had taken place but Churchill resisted the pressure, preferring to concentrate his attack from the West on bombing raids. In May 1942, the first RAF 1,000 bomber raid was made on Cologne. Raids on other German cities followed.

The Russians retreated to Stalingrad leaving a trail of destruction ('scorched earth') behind them so that the advancing German troops could not sustain themselves on Soviet soil. The battle for Stalingrad was to continue from September 1942 until the German surrender on 2 February 1943.

Life on the home front in Britain remained difficult. A wide range of consumer goods and foodstuffs was in very short supply; great emphasis was placed on the production of food at home ('Digging for Victory'). Naomi devoted most of her time to farming: ploughing up land on the Carradale estate which had not previously been thought suitable for arable cultivation. She kept a small herd of Galloway cattle and later diversified into milking cows and into sheep. Fuel was restricted for priority uses. Naomi was able to obtain petrol only for agricultural purposes.

Her practical experience with farming and her growing familiarity with local conditions provided Naomi with a useful basis for her political and creative work which was becoming increasingly focused on Scottish affairs. She contributed in various ways to postwar reconstruction research by, for example, talking to Dick and writing to Douglas Cole on the Nuffield Reconstruction Survey and by making her views known to the newly formed Scottish Council for Industry, set up by Tom Johnston, the Secretary of State for Scotland.

In September, Naomi attended the first meeting of the Scottish Convention. The Convention had emerged from a split at the Annual Conference of the Scottish National Party earlier in the year. William Power, supported by Naomi's friend, John MacCormick (formerly leader of the SNP), had been narrowly defeated by the anti-war faction led by Douglas Young. It was a division which had been threatening since at least 1937 not only over policy on the war but also on electoral strategy. The Scottish Convention attracted considerable support from both moderate members of the SNP and from the ranks of the Labour and Liberal parties and trade unionists.

The hall had come into its own. It was used regularly by the villagers for meetings and social events. On 2 January, a big ceilidh was organised, beginning with a series of short speeches chaired by Baillie Ramsay.

Friday 2 January 1942
... Everyone excited about the ceilidh and dance.

We put on our tartan ribbons; Val looked lovely in an old white embroidered dress of Lois'. She wore the tartan ribbon floating. Rosemary had the one I gave her.

... Val and I and the two Mcyers and Dick came in, the others waiting for a bit. Dougie, all in his pipe band clothes, was playing; Mr Blackwood spoke, in English and in Gaelic. We sang the An Commun* gathering song. Then Baillie Ramsay was in the chair, on the platform. He smiled at me, he was enjoying himself. He said that he knew the Carradale river and glen well and loved it, and that some of them would remember a day 35 years back; he had never thought after that, to come back and cast a fly on Carradale water again, nor to preside at a concert here (all this referring to the day he was caught poaching). But times were changed. And everyone clapped. It was extraordinarily nicely done. Then he called for us all to sing "A Gude New Year to Yin and A". Then the songs began, mostly Gaelic songs, with the audience joining in; the Hall was packed, more than I've ever seen it. People were standing all round. It was very hot. Then someone told funny stories, then Val was called on to dance—I'd got the swords from Largie, and Grant played for her. I was standing near the door, by Dougie, then; there was a song, and in the middle of it I saw Denny Mac leap on to the stage and then Willie and several of them. First I thought Baillie Ramsay's chair had fallen over; then it seemed more than that. I went up to the front; Murdoch was saying it was an epileptic fit, and he would be all right. I couldn't see his face at all, there was such a crowd, and I didn't want to make it worse. I

* An Commun was the society which promoted Gaelic Culture.

stopped someone giving him whisky. I called down the Hall that someone was to take a car over to Cameron's to get him and someone else could go to the House and get Denny. Nurse MacAlister came up. He didn't seem to be recovering and the heat was awful; someone went to the First Aid post and got a stretcher. I kept on saying it wasn't serious, to the audience; I asked if he'd ever had epilepsy but nobody knew. I hadn't seen it for the first few minutes, myself.

I was by the door; they carried him out on the stretcher; I asked Nurse MacAlister how he was; she said she could feel no pulse. His hand was dropping off the edge of the stretcher; I picked it up and held it across him while they carried him to Angus' house. It was too dark to see his face and there were a lot of cars parked and blocking the gateway. A number of people went in, but I thought it would do no good, as the nurse was there, and stayed out. Denny and Ruth came over and went in; they said he was heavily cyanosed and it must be a cerebral haemorrhage, might be a stroke. Then Cameron came; after a time he rushed out to his car, to fetch something, perhaps coronin. For some time I stayed, everyone getting frightfully worried, I trying to cheer them up, saying we must wait for the doctor; I thought it was probably a stroke. It was cold and wet, and I was in a thin dress. I got them to go on singing, but the heart was out of the singers especially the Campbeltown ones. By and bye I went round to the other door and saw Angus and asked how he was. Angus said "He's gone". I said stupidly "Do you mean he's dead?" Angus said Aye, they have tried the mirror and everything. Then he said Dr Cameron didn't want anyone told till the ambulance came from Campbeltown; they had phoned for it. Especially he didn't want Annie to come in; he locked the other door. I went back disconsolately to the Hall; there was singing going on, but people were standing in the porch, the door half open in spite of the black-out. I stood there for a time; people asked me how he was, and I didn't know what to say. I think some of them guessed. Dick came out, wanting to know. Denny and I went over to the road with him, and I told him; he seemed unable to believe it and then burst into tears.

We went back towards Angus' house; Dick went over to the Hall, to arrange with Blackwood, who had taken on, as to what should be done. I went in to where his sister and niece and brother were sitting, and shook hands and talked with them. I knew the brother well by reputation, a Clydeside communist who had been burnt by a metal slip and lost his sight. For a long time he and I, Angus joining us later, sat and talked politics; he was taking it very well, saying that their father had died much the same way but after weeks of helplessness. We all agreed this was a good way to die; I was thinking that about the last thing he had seen was my lovely Val dancing in the white dress and tartan scarf and a red ribbon in her dark hair. We talked about the Clyde, about MacGovern and Gallacher and John MacLean.* They brought through the stretcher, with the big man, his chin bound up with string, his face cyanosed but interested and un-frightened, and they passed it out through the window, Peter MacLean, who should have been MC at the dance, carrying. The family went back, and some to Cour to tell his mother; . . . I was pretty tired and cried on Angus' shoulder for a bit.

Wednesday 21 January 1942
Wild storm, snow everywhere. I slept in, would have slept longer but Bella had to see me about housekeeping. Stayed in bed half morning and read Eric Gill's *Autobiography* . . .†

Curiously unaware of certain things old Gill was! I agree with so much, it's what I'm after myself. Smashing the idea that art is an expression of the artist's self and all that balls, that it is service. After all what is this book of mine going to be but service to Scotland, or rather, to the dumb Scots, the ones who need to be given pride and assurance and kindness, that's why I read it with such care to Denny Mac, why his opinion matters to me why indeed I need it in order to get on. He's the prototype, the image, one I've got to bring alive. But would old Gill admit that a woman can make a work of art at all? He doesn't. All his art adventures are between young men. The women are *there* certainly, very important, but in a world of their own, the world of conversation, of the house and farm and all; I see the point. I have that world. I know it matters. It matters like hell, that's why I think my farming and all that is important, I'm not just a potato factory. But also I'm an artist, I'm aware. I'm an adventurer. Like him, too, I know that discipline is necessary, though I don't accept his variety of discipline, probably because I am more intelligent than he was—not a better artist, but just more intellectual, a better I.Q., the hell of an intellectual heredity. I can think past him. He just hasn't

* Three Clydeside socialists active in radical politics during the 20s and 30s.

† Eric Gill is an artist best known for his sculpture, type design and his fine engravings and woodcuts many of which are explicitly erotic. Gill died at the age of 58 in 1940 shortly before the publication of his autobiography.

faced certain things, especially science. He has run away. You can't do that.

But he talks about "his" women, his family, his three daughters. I wonder what they really thought of it, or if they were just swept away by him, as one undoubtedly might be, would be if one wasn't very tough. And he doesn't know about them. He says "I do not gather that women have, in general, much of an eye for the beauty of their lovers' bodies . . . They are not inflamed by images . . . they do not make or go to or see or buy pictures of men as men do pictures of women." The hell he thinks that. The important word is "buy". Women haven't had the money and, until a few more can buy, the rest will be ashamed. They can be made more uncomfortable by censure than me. I remember awfully badly wanting to buy Gill's own wood engraving of Mellors in *Lady Chatterley's Lover* for exactly these reasons. He was a naked man, with all the Gill emphasis on the penis. But at the time I hadn't the money. It was five guineas. I never seemed to have any money. I was always lending it to people or getting extra things for the children or something; Goodness knows I had more, earned and unearned, than most women. Also I had a conscience about spending it on myself and this would obviously have been *for* myself. The only thing I haven't had a conscience about buying for myself is books. Which accounts for the general overflow of books.

And as to being inflamed by images—! The interstices of my days are full of erotic images. Quite often, of course, I use them as current to turn the mills of the imagination. I am 44 and should know what I'm doing by now. I can think clearly and unresentfully of my lovers in the past, certainly of their naked bodies. I should suppose that most women thought rather more in terms of touch and less in terms of vision than men (or conceivably a writer thinks more in such terms than a sculptor). I think also a lot in terms of smell. I can remember the smell of the neck of a man whom I haven't seen since we said goodbye in 1934—I was reminded of him just now through seeing his name as a lecturer. Here the interstices of work and thought are filled with the erotic images of the men I see and admire and work with: not, alas, their naked images, as they mostly wear three layers of jerseys, but their laughter, their eyes and mouths, touch of their lips and fingers, smell of them most of all. So long as I think of them without resentment and anger and possessiveness I know there's nothing wrong. I hope they think of me with the same vividness and love, the same admission that it's sexual and the same absence of guilt. The latter is the difficulty. So long as the convention is to think of these things guiltily, then people will make a mess of them. I don't think it wrong in any man that I love to have erotic images of other women. But if the other women think it is, if they think that we must only imagine in couples, then there's the devil to pay. They go back to Mark "Whosoever looketh on a woman to lust after her hath committed adultery with her already in his heart. If thy right eye offend thee, pluck it out . . ." Of course, that means you "lust", not just take the surface meaning, as interpreted by Banu Israel and by generations of owners, of possessors, of those for whom a wife was a tool, a thing of their own, a breeder, for whom love between man and woman was a wrong thing except in the regularised and commercial relationships, for whom that [relationship] was threatened by the stranger. If you "coveted" your neighbour's wife (and Denny put down coveting for C when we had Sins as one of our "Categories" the other night) you obviously wanted to own her. That's the wrong thing. That's the catch every time. Ownership. If I "covet" X or Y or Z here at Carradale, as indeed I do, it's not because I want to own them or to get anything out of them or to exploit them or their families in any way; I just simply like them; I like their shapes, I like their eyes, their smiles, the way they have of speaking or laughing; I want, as it were, not just a slip, not a tease, but the whole thing. Yet I know that if I were to take it, it would be misinterpreted, probably by them, certainly by anyone connected with them. I don't suppose they would go as far as to think out the implications of their condemnation, they wouldn't say to themselves, we condemn her because she is taking something that belongs to someone else; they would just condemn me plain, say I was a whore and leave it at that. And because I am doing work here, trying to give people other ideas of human relationships, starting with the simplest form of it, my own relations, first towards my family, then towards my friends, I mustn't jeopardise that. If they do condemn me in one thing they will condemn me in everything. And I couldn't blame them considering their historical conditioning and this god-awful church that thinks of sex as sin.

It is much more important that I should be able to change people's minds about one another in this other way, to try to show them non-possessive, generous human relations in other ways. If I can do that, the other thing will follow in time, in a hundred years, say. It is always a bore being ahead of one's time, and coming up here I move back fifty years from, say, London or Birmingham (though equally I move to a world where they still *can* understand generous relationships, where it hasn't all been killed by industrialism). Again, if I were to have love affairs, that would countenance other people in having them who might quite well not be disciplined about it at all, might allow them to wreck families, or might easily let the possessive motive creep in. There is of course much more of that in a society where the women have no money of their own and only get it from men, and their only saleable asset is their bodies. I hope it may help them a bit, being wage earners, forestry girls and so on.

Well let's hope nobody reads this who won't try to understand it . . .

Saturday 31 January 1942
. . . after tea I went down to Lilla's; it was the first time I had ever been formally invited to any house but the Semples', though of course I'm always dropping in on people. Lilla had invited me in a shy, casual kind of way . . . Denny M was there, looking tired—they'd been after the clams all day and trying for herring every night as well, the last night they had put in at Brodick (the first harbour they went to was tidal and they were afraid of being caught) but then came an Easter [wind] and they had to skeedaddle round the island again before they'd had two hours' sleep. But for all that he was clean and trim and pretty well—he said afterwards he'd no tummy aches at all. Then the Nurse came, then Willie and his Chrissie and Margaret. It was close enough in the wee room, just room for the lot of us, and tea and scones, and the stove hot. But the other people are still in their house, so they are needing to stay in the hut. I thought it was rather a triumph, and for me an honour; it must have been easily the first time that anyone from the Big House came there, like that . . . It is hard to reproduce the quality of the long evening we spent, ceilidhing. Of course I felt a little like an explorer who has at last been made a member of a secret society among the bongo-bongos, the same kind of pride: and I was listening to the stories, trying to remember them, but realising that most of the fun was in the method of telling. But also I was just enjoying myself, as I don't usually at parties, and wondering why; it was partly the constant talk about the fishing, a skilled and very fascinating job; it was like hearing research workers, say, talk; I was expected to understand it all, too. I did realise that fishing, even more than mining, say, calls for a sort of individual craft skill and courage that makes it impossible ever to run it as any kind of factory. There was some very

nice singing, nobody talked about the war, we played silly games and asked riddles, and laughed; I contributed a Belloc poem and a couple of smutty limericks which went down very well (they weren't my worst ones, of course!). There was no aesthetic, scarcely any metaphysical and little political discussion; nor was the conversation brilliant in an urban way. But things were said with great wit and amusingness, Denny M giving me some clams (the usual jokes about clams which are locally supposed to have an aphrodisiac effect—I'm not sure they aren't right about it, if you eat enough!) and crabs called crubans, and asking me what was the proper name for another kind of crab—I ask him what like. "Devilish cross" he says! Or Mrs Meenan, on a Campbeltown burn: "That's no a river, it's just a smell!" The vocabulary was not that of London or even of Glasgow, but it is a full and lively one on many subjects . . .

Naomi's friendship with Denny M continued to deepen. During 1942, they worked together on articles about the herring fishing, combining Naomi's skill with words and her access to the publishing world with Denny's wide experience of the local community. After the war a publication under both their names appeared entitled *Men And Herring* (Serif Books, 1949).

Sunday 1 February 1942
. . . I'd had a letter from the London Scots' Self Govt Committee* about Denny M's fishing chapter, had sent him down a message to bring his notes. We went over that with their comments which had been much like Tom Harrisson's, so all we'd done before would go on. I got in from his words, what struck me as a very moving passage about co-operation. I felt much prouder of it than I usually do of my own things . . . we talked about our boat and the Outer Islands in summer, the smell of flowers as you came in and the birds and how the six of us would be alone in the middle of a smooth sea, and it warm, and I would be able to write there—obviously he does envisage my going with them not for a single day or night but living in the focsle. Maybe I could sometimes come as cook, even; I haven't the strength for the nets, but I could do the odd jobs. And we thought what fun it would be at Mallaig or Castle Bay, to ask some of the other boys from other boats, aboard; and I would make an omelette or something nice for them. We know and the "wee fellow", Dougie [Campbell] that is

* The London Scots' Self-Government Committee was an organisation of predominantly London-based journalists and writers committed to the fight for Scottish Home Rule.

so desperate keen for it, wearying till the time comes for it, that it mayn't happen; yet I think it's a tolerably innocent dream to have. I said that I didn't think we'd ever have a right Fisherman's Co-operative, with the real co-operation and an ending of the small capitalism of the boat owners, till after there had been bad times. And I would see my crew through the bad times, one could do anything if one was cheery about it, and we'd be together; and then we could be the first crew into the Co-operative with a real feeling of socialism.

And Denny M suddenly said he would never forget me, never, neither in this world nor the next and he began to say that sometimes he thought this one was all there was to it and there was no hell nor heaven. I said no, one got these things in life mostly, but, though I didn't believe in personal immortality, there were maybe other kinds that we couldn't well understand and in fact we didn't behave as if this were all, we weren't comfortable if we just ate and drank and were merry . . .

Naomi spent most of February in England. In London she made her customary round of old friends, among them Zita Gielgud (back from France where her husband Lewis had been working with the Red Cross), the novelist, Storm Jameson, and her old family doctor, Dr Pirret.

Thursday–Saturday 5–7 February 1942
. . . Saw a number of people: Zita with stories of people escaping from Germany, saying the workers were very decent to socialists from other countries, tried to help the Poles etc, also bothered at not becoming pregnant, but fairly happy as most people connected with the land are. Storm Jameson extremely gloomy, owing to having dealt with refugees, especially Jews, since 1937 about, keeping alive people who would be better dead. Unable to see a tolerable new world. Eager for my news, just because I'm leading a good life and can put it across to her a bit. Has a gastric ulcer, very grateful for eggs, so was Dr Pirret. A fine story of the bourgeois of Tours going out and defending their town, led by the Bishop. Tours smashed, the bridge and hotel at Saumur, all the Loire country. I try to cheer her up.

On 8th February, Naomi travelled by train to Reading to visit Avrion, now established at the Quaker school, Leighton Park.

Sunday 8 February 1942

[Av] . . . seems very cheerful, balanced and happy. Has been starting Greek again, just to read. Spoke of a friend of his whose parents had both been killed in an air raid "but he seems quite normal all the same". They are making puppets, also all thinking frightfully urgently about social problems. They get into groups and do that. And the Junior meeting seems much more interested in politics than in religion. They seem to be feeding him well.

On to Oxford which is much as usual, the house awfully cold. My mother always talking about people whom perhaps I once knew but whom I've completely forgotten. Most of the billetees there. We heard Stafford's speech;* I think they were all impressed. When whatever idiocy the BBC put on afterwards came on, one of the young men, a complete Tory, said Shame to do that after a good speech! Afterwards I read my mother part of my book, but had a sore throat and feeling very tired. She likes to sit up very late. She has had a lot of things sent her from Canada and America, small parcels of odd food; some delicious, like guava jelly. But presumably that will stop.

Thursday 12 February 1942

. . . Went to the National Council of Social Service, talked over village development with various people; they were rather thrilled, because I was doing something not just talking about it. We talked of the possibilities of village councils, quite apart from present local government bodies, meetings, education, music and so on. They said they'd put me in touch with Edinburgh. I'd like to get on to their Scottish Council, it would be a fine excuse to go to Edinburgh, too.

Then went to *Horizon*, saw Connolly,† asked him about the possibilities of a Scottish number but he says no good; he can't get the extra paper; had I seen what he wrote about Edinburgh. I said yes, and he talked about the "Scotch", not the Scots! He obviously hasn't grasped it at all. He suggested I should write an article. But I don't

* Stafford Cripps (with whom Naomi was acquainted through Labour Party circles) had only just come back from Moscow where he had been the British Ambassador since 1940. As a result of a number of spirited attacks on Churchill's government and especially on its management of war production, Cripps had earned himself a significant position in the public regard. It was widely considered that he was the only serious rival to Churchill's leadership at that time.

† Cyril Connolly was the editor of *Horizon*, a literary magazine founded in 1940 which was dedicated to maintaining an aesthetic and intellectual forum for writers in spite of the less than poetic demands of the war.

quite know what he'd like. I felt very shy again, and was quite unable to ask him if he'd read or what he thought of my poems I'd sent him!

The calamitous war events were in everyone's minds throughout early 1942. From the Far East came the news that Rangoon and then Singapore had surrendered to the Japanese. Closer to home, Britain experienced a disastrous humiliation: the German battleships, *Scharnhorst* and *Gneisenau*, had sailed defiantly out of Brest and up the Channel towards Norway in preparation for a possible allied invasion in that region. The British were taken completely by surprise and suffered heavy aircraft losses in the ensuing battle. The incident re-awakened fears of German invasion.

. . . To the Soviet Embassy. Agnes [Maisky, wife of the Soviet Ambassador in London] deeply patriotic, hating, I think, to be out of Russia now, looking on everything from that one point of view. Asking what is thought by us in the north about Russia. I feel she is so nice and kind but a wee bit stupid, like most one-track people; happier so, doubtless. I think they take a simple view. Ivan came in, I asked him if he was still reading *The Decline and Fall*—he was rather shocked, thought it unseemly of me with the British Empire the way it is, somehow felt I ought to be patriotic as he was. Said the important thing was winning the war, not what was to happen afterwards. All very well for a Russian—!

Tea at my club with Noel, who has just been doing a broadcast for America. Pretty gloomy, thinking that if Churchill doesn't produce a victory soon there'll be trouble. But not expecting one himself: doubtful if a non-totalitarian (in the widest sense) country can fight a totalitarian war.

Dick seemed astonished, as other people are, that the *Scharnhorst* and *Gneisenau* had got away, that they could get out of Brest first, and then that this should have happened, kept on buying papers in the hope of something having happened after all. One thinks of all the pilots killed in the Brest bombings and all for this! And our loss of 42 planes . . .

Sunday 15 February 1942
A nice day, but for the news: The Sunday papers all more plaintive than I've seen them yet. We had a late breakfast with Murdoch, walked out to Grantchester and had a sandwich lunch, discussed the war, planning M's own prospects as a Signaller, his many friends, what will happen to money after the war, ethics of inflation etc. Called on various people in Newnham, nobody in; but it's new for males and

females to call in on one another so easily. Went to Francis' room and played Mozart; I read Lorca's poems. To tea with the Marshalls, Stevie Smith there, much as ever: am not so good at talking to intellectuals.

Several people to a rather scrappy dinner at the Arts, including a young soldier who turned up. The right film hadn't come so the film programme was mostly MOI [Ministry of Information] stuff, the Disney Savings cartoon, not very good, various nice gentlemanly, forward-looking, rather misleading MOI things, one from America called *Bomber* which provoked everyone to laughter. I think we're all bored with films of noble factories, we'd like more statistics. The best a short from Russia: *Incident at a Post Office*. One on *Oil from Canada*, a Grierson, which was lamentably out of date: Brooke-Popham [British Air Marshal in Far East] met with hoots of mockery. I went out for *Men of the Lightship*; it's very good but so painful, and I've seen it already . . .

. . . We missed Churchill, which was always something. A rumour that he was resigning! Sir John Pratt furious with him and the gang. Said he felt so bad, after sending people out to Malay himself. A lot of young at M's rooms, mostly talking about undergraduate affairs, having editorial conferences and so on. Beautiful girls with long graceful manes of hair, not permed or messed about, but well brushed, intelligent too. Tony as usual, needing to be ragged. Murdoch seems to know dozens of people. Mostly going, both boys and girls, to war jobs this summer. I wish one could know them. I wish there were tokens to tell, The fortunate fellows that now one can ever discern, And then one might talk with them friendly and wish them farewell, And watch them depart on the road that they will not return. It was all so hellishly like last time.

Monday 16 February 1942
. . . Back to London and Hendon, crowded journey, Margaret [Cole] away taking poor Lily, who used to "come in and help" to hospital —she has had a mis; there seem to be so many these days. Dick feeling angry with the Fabian Society, Douglas very sweet but Margaret rather snappy; I think really everyone on edge with the news. It was a bit uncomfortable. Tony [Pirie] came in later. I wrote a lot of letters. Tony really feeling *à la lanterne* with various people and reporting conversations overheard of ordinary people saying Churchill had just said nothing at all in a lot of fine words. Also a bus driver in the HG saying the bus people weren't allowed to take their rifles back—too

red! Is that possible, let alone probable? God knows. Dick, having tried vainly to buy a box of matches from a tobacconist, was then *given* a box by the proprietor of the shop . . . We all sooner or later talked about Singapore, wondering what we'd hear next, the fall of Tobruk perhaps. Wondering what the Japanese do with their prisoners; it was a bit grim in China, that way. But here? One feels a curious astonishment, however much one had thought it probable . . .

Wednesday 18 February 1942
. . . Tony drove me down to Harpenden; she is as usual cheerfully despairing about the war. I wonder how much she regrets having sent John [her son] to America.

Went to Jack's room at the lab and he talked about his latest genetics: a thing on anti-gens between mother and unborn child—in practice one in 400 babies die of this now, and could easily be saved. The first time anything quite as clear has turned up. We walked back, had tea: Jack awfully conscientious about food. He seems to be going to do another series of pressure experiments, of a much fiercer kind, quite soon; I hope he won't kill himself. He didn't talk politics, nor of Charlotte [his estranged wife], said he'd been writing some verse. We played Halma and he walked back with me to Piries; I hadn't my torch and he scorns such things. It was very dark and slippery with ice, but we each pretended we could manage perfectly! He was extremely sweet and amiable . . .

After visiting her friend Joan Rendel, Naomi accompanied Dick to Cambridge to see Murdoch again.

Saturday 21 February 1942
Murdoch to breakfast; they give one condensed milk with porridge, I simply hate it. Don't mind most war food, but can't bear this. He said he'd had an offer from his tutor of having his name put forward for (and getting) a Carnegie scholarship to America for two years, to finish his medical course there. He had refused, partly because he thinks he doesn't want to go on with medicine, partly because he feels he oughtn't to be out of this country or to shirk joining up. I think he's quite right yet Dick and I were both sorely tempted to say what a good idea it was. The only thing that might delay his call-up was that one of the Professors apparently wants a few scientists to do an urgent job in the summer in East Anglia (and S England generally) on agriculture.

Asked if it was harvesting he apparently said no, and there won't be any harvest unless this is done. Colorado beetle? Murdoch so very sweet and charming, and apparently cheerful.

Wednesday 25 February 1942
... fixed up to see Dai Grenfell* at the Ministry of Mines; MacLean told me he was on the Forestry Commission, the only Labour Member. It is very odd, I do find that people not only know my name but seem very willing to see me, I get treated almost like a grown man! I begin to feel quite important. Dangerous ...

... To Harrods to get my hair washed; pretended to the girl that I was a genuine herring fisher! I love pretending to people in shops or trains. But one shouldn't do it too much. Tried to get my watch mended, but the main spring has gone and they just laughed. Wondered if they had a cheap watch for Av's birthday, but nothing under £8! Tried to get a leather belt for my coat but no use. No black velvet ribbon, no strong braid for the coat. No rubber rings for bottling?—if I can't get them!

Then to Westminster to see Dai Grenfell. Got off the bus and ran almost straight into Stafford. I said Hullo! He swung off his hat, very gay, saying Hullo! You here for long? I said No, I'm down for a bit trying to get decentralised, and Congratulations! I didn't want to keep him but was glad he looked so happy. It was really rather a thrill meeting like that, when I'd seen him often having such a wretched time at Conferences and things.

At the Ministry of Mines, everyone very amiable. Dai came forward rather shyly, saying You'll remember me from Vienna? (That was in the counter-revolution in '34) I said Yes, that's why I've come to bother you. I then said You're the only socialist on the Forestry Commission, and I think there are various things wrong with it. I then explained that we needed devolution, that we could manage our own forests with only planning from the centre, that the foresters ought to have more power and a chance to rise. That the District Officers, though I had no quarrel with them, were Old School Tie men. He agreed with everything and when I explained what Forest industries I wanted, and also forestry crofts, he said that was just what he thought. I explained that the Forestry were bad landlords, that they didn't do a

* David Grenfell had been one of Naomi's companions in Vienna in 1934; originally a Welsh miner, he was by 1942 Secretary of Mines and a member of the Forestry Commission.

thing about the farms they took over. He said it was the same in Wales. He told me the Inverness District man was a good socialist, I should get in touch with him. I then told him about the waste of slabs and saw-dust, and suggested he should have a boat sent from Glasgow to fetch them away. He took notes, and indeed, did the same about all my suggestions. I told him the kind of community I had in mind, about the various industries, the siting of factories, the making of a live community. He was most friendly, put an arm round my shoulders, in the Labour Party way, said would I be writing a book about it. I said I was too busy. I do hope something will come of it.

Naomi returned north, taking in another visit to Val at Kilquanity School in Dumfries on the way.

Wednesday 4 March 1942

. . . The Glasgow train, late and, as usual dirty and over-crowded and stinking with cigarette smoke. No non-smoking carriages, of course, at least not thirds, and even so, people always smoke in them now if they feel like it. I suppose it's a necessary drug to most people.

Most of the passengers were soldiers, some reading 2d. "books" of a semi pornographic kind, again. One party with a nice, cheerful ATS girl with them. She seemed at first to be being rather uncomfortably much ragged by them, but I think it was really quite friendly, and they all liked it. The 1st class ladies waiting room at Dumfries largely pencilled with semi-obscene drawings and rhymes, with much use of the words fuck and tool. I wondered if they had been done by males or females.

Got to Glasgow in a mild blizzard. No taxis. Put luggage in cloak room and ultimately got a car to take me to Anna's; difficult to see the right stop but everyone very helpful. Anna's room beautifully warm, the snow dripped off my hair. We talked about friends and relations, her school work—she is now with the seniors, teaching maths. Very short of staff, and large classes, hampered also by having missed time earlier on. I gave her my bacon which she was delighted with, used my own butter. She says soap is difficult for anyone living alone; she used to wash out her stockings every day, so did most of the girls. Meant one could do with fewer. She'd had gastric flu and only half a pint of milk in two days.

Thursday 5 March 1942

... To tea with Dorothy and her psychologist,—Miss MacIntosh, a very tough looking lady in a *Well of Loneliness* hat. She gave us tea: very good, with strawberry jam and delicious cake, at the Cadoro, where she seems to be well known and had a private room. We argued about speech, she being in favour of English speech saying it was good for people to make the effort towards the "superior" universal language. We hammered away at it ...

Then Dorothy and I talked a lot; she says that since she came back, she has been to dances and cinemas and skating a lot, doesn't see any harm in it now, in fact has shed many of her "Christian" prejudices. But sticks to Christianity; a socialist friend of hers has just been baptised in a Baptist church, took a debate on "is Christianity worth while?" in an East End debating society; nearly equal votes. Dorothy herself more socialist, more Nationalist, keen to teach her children good Scots stuff. I have been asked to speak by the Socialist Teachers' Society, but she'd never heard of it, it may be a clique.

Then by myself to the Cosmo; a lovely, and rather moving, early Russian film, *Shchors*, so much better than the present ones! Also *March of Time*, a good *Silly Symphony*, *Tale of Two Cities*, and *Song of the Clyde*, a really lovely documentary, only marred by an English commentator; a lot of photos of Glasgow, everyone talked and laughed and pointed things out – the attraction of the familiar! I started clapping afterwards, and lots joined in.

Back – very slippery – to Anna's, ate toast and tea, and talked again. She's been working hard at the station canteen, says Glasgow is still a very bad place for "the boys" to land up in, little to do, especially on Sunday, not enough places to sleep ... During the holidays Anna drives taxis and lorries for the family business—the remaining brother will probably be called up—at Tighnabruaich made 30/- in tips last holidays, partly driving commercials to the farm houses, once an Education Inspector!—cross with old friends who don't tip her! We talk little of the news but feel rather gloomy. I have one of my more unpleasant defeatist dreams in which more and more countries come in against us.

The thing that strikes me again, as always, is the extreme kindness of the ordinary Glasgow person, the folk on the buses or anywhere; they may be soft too, but they are so friendly.

The 1941–2 winter was especially long and cold. When Naomi reached
Tarbert, the roads were completely blocked by snow. There were no buses,
and Lachie and Rosemary had failed in their attempt to meet her by car.

Saturday 7 March 1942
. . . Unfortunately I'd left my heavy shoes in London to be soled, but I
got a pair of black boys' shoes in Tarbert, and had them nailed. Betty
Campbell lent me coupons. I had of course to leave all my gear,
hoping it would come on by bus. They were very nice to me at the
hotel.

Half way along the west road we were caught up by the Islay bus,
which theoretically wasn't going further than the pier, but which
actually took us into Redhouse, so we started our main climb almost
fresh. The men, Johnnie and his brother-in-law who is a smith in
Northumberland, were carrying suit-cases. The drifts began almost at
once, we picked our way through or round following the grass edges,
the men going ahead. It was rather breath-taking. At Spion Kop the
snow was so deep we had to creep along the fences, holding on as best
we could and treading on the tops of the heather. There was a covey of
about thirty grouse here, talking to one another in a queerly human
way. All across, the drifts were bad where there was any shelter, but it
was thawing and where the wind blew, it was clear in places. The sun
shone glittering and dazzling as I remembered it in Norway, winter
sporting; sometimes we cut across the fields where it wasn't so deep as
on the roads. We kept on falling in, and the snow bit between one's
knees. We meant to try and get a car at Clonnaig and I thought of
stopping at the Clonnaig inn, but when we got there, and smelt the
living room where the window can't have been open since last
summer, and realised the inadequacy of the sanitation I thought I'd
rather walk. So we went on.

It was extremely beautiful. Arran was all shades of creamy green
and blue, the Sound smooth and green, the snow wreaths and drifts
lying like long breakers. The snow dripping and slithering from the
birch branches, that were in constant motion, the burns running but
half iced. People came out from farm houses, with news of Lachie and
Rosemary who had turned back last night. We could follow their
wheel tracks, easier to walk in; they would bid us "take a cup tea in our
hand", for it was cold. If one is going to have this kind of adventure,
Highlanders are the right ones to have it with. They were so gay,
always saying how far we'd gone, how well we were doing, and so on;

we all made jokes and talked "shortening the way". But it was pretty tiring . . . There was a final, enormous drift at Crossaig, then the road got comparatively clear. We got to Cour, where I was taken to see "the remains of Mr MacDonald" and said the right thing. I do hate the slight smell of a corpse, though. Then Durham of Cour, who had been very nice to them, took me back to Carradale in his car and I walked in on a somewhat surprised household, felt quite bruised at being kissed one on each side by Bella and Maggie!

Tuesday 10 March 1942
. . . Went to the Leys' for lunch.* Discussed the Labour Party and their very dull new pamphlet in words of one syllable. She and Bob talked of the general dissatisfaction with the aerodrome workers; the shop stewards are mostly CP, rather a nuisance (Bob is a left-winger, but believes in hard work!). However the shop stewards complained about the Fleet Air Arm coming into their canteen for tea, cigarettes and chocolate, but apparently when Bob went into it, the men themselves weren't complaining, indeed said they well knew they wouldn't have any tea but for the fleet. Many of the men are very unskilled, wouldn't normally eat chocolate, which is now provided for them!

The eldest Leys boy, who is an apprentice on the Clyde, doing night classes as well gets 24/- a week, the younger boy, Gordon, is a messenger and clerk at the aerodrome, gets £4/10/-. Nora collecting steadily for Russia, says nobody refuses now. And shops that used to be nasty to her because she had "advanced views" are now most friendly and want to talk!

Dick, Murdoch and the younger children had returned to Carradale for Easter; the Cole children had also come up.

Saturday 11 April 1942
. . . a submarine in the Bay signalled to us. Murdoch answered in morse. Rosemary thought it was her young man but when they got out it was Stephen Spring Rice. He came back and ate and drank largely. He was extremely gay, in the uncorked, violent way that submariners seem to be when they get out. It must lead to a curious life, a good deal of drink, no reading, but they play Ludo, called Ukkers. Talk of killing on a large scale, but he explained how much more he disliked having shot down a plane and seen the crew

* Nora and Bob Leys were a Labour Party couple who lived in Campbeltown.

struggling to get out, than torpedoing a complete ship, which was just a satisfying noise. But what *is* to happen to them afterwards? . . . Avrion talking to Stephen about subs, amazingly well informed; knows far more than most people about military and technical history. Stephen says that in action they put clips on the outside of the escape chamber (thus making it useless) as otherwise it gets blown off by depth charges. This happened to them once, they had to surface and only got away by luck. Apparently physics has made less progress than physiology here. I wonder if Jack knows.

Murdoch, Rosemary, Jane [Cole] and Av took him out to the sub in the small boat and went on board; it was a dark night and they upset slightly coming back. However it must have been very interesting . . .

. . . The fishermen are having a meeting to discuss what they will say to the Herring Committee. Gilbert 'Tosh talked to Dick about it, Dick may be going. I feel a little hurt that, after I have thought about it so much and written this report, there should be no question of asking me. It makes one inclined to say, very well, if you are going to treat me as a poor weak woman, then a poor weak woman I shall be and you can bloody well do all the work and I will trick you and cheat you and bleed you as women have done in the past. However I suppose it's transitional.

Thursday 16 April 1942

. . . In the evening to Campbeltown with Davie Oman to this lecture on When Invasion Comes. It was given by the officer in command of this military sub-area, an English gentleman, and all that, who was in command of the Highland Area. He began by some preliminaries about the Boche and the Hun who has had world conquest in his veins since the beginning of history, said invasion was inevitable, the Germans would want the aerodromes on the west coast, there were some fine ones on islands. I imagined them landing on Tiree! Then blood-curdling invasion details, how all Germans were treacherous, had no idea of "fair play", the paratroops on Crete were all doped and so turned bright green when dead . . . After this I decided this lecture was hardly for my intelligence group. But I waited for practical things; he explained that he wanted to keep the civilian population occupied as otherwise it would be so boring for them to stay put during an invasion and they might panic. He suggested they might observe things and send in reports, become stretcher bearers, clear debris from roads, help ARP etc. None of it seemed to apply. There were to be

Invasion Committees (each to include one lady, jolly good idea . . .),
one in Campbeltown. They could have copies of his lecture notes.

At the end he didn't even ask for questions; I rather furiously got up
and said I represented the Carradale Farmers and we wanted to know
what we should do about crops, stores etc. Should we burn them? Oh
no, he said, I wouldn't do that if I were you. After all, we'll get these
fellows out in ten days and it doesn't matter what they do in the mean
time. I said what about cattle, did we or didn't we want to inconveni-
ence the invader? He said we shouldn't do anything. Should the
Village Hall burn 40 gallons of petrol? Oh no, it wasn't worth while.
Should the Head Forester burn the saw-mill? Oh no, he shouldn't do
that, should he? So much for scorched earth. I don't think anyone else
thought much of it. Commander Moir smiled sweetly and said it was a
little bit old-fashioned. Donald Jackson and Hugh (I didn't know they
were coming) agreed it was complete balls. Davie Oman was utterly
unimpressed, and felt this was the kind of thing the English did. I tried
feebly to say that all soldiers weren't quite as bad. But I wonder if they
realise what an effect bastards like this produce.

The farm work was now very demanding. All the family were expected to
help. Often the local fishermen (Denny M and Dougie most often) helped
too. It was usually Val, the youngest Mitchison, now an accomplished cook,
who prepared the teas to fortify the workers.

Saturday 18 April 1942
. . . It was a lovely afternoon with enough breeze in it to take off the
heat, though we all worked with our coats off. There is something that
makes one oddly happy to be working with one's friends. The sower
comes striding over, and the corn sprays out like thin gold but the dust
blows clear away, blowing up while the corn falls. You steady the
bucket with your knees and fill it from the sack full of lovely clean
grain, cool and dusty, the insides of your hands are smooth with dust;
you lift the heavy bucket and tip it into the fiddle, rustling down
against your friend's body. The harrow comes jingling over, the other
friend holding the reins, the two big horses hot and steady. There is
the overwhelming smell of the oats, and, under it, like the drone of the
pipes, the smell of the earth, and the two live smells, the clean and
sweating men and the working horses, and sometimes the smell of
bruised young growth, or the passing smell of an old turnip broken by
the harrows. Folk go by on the road and speak to you, and gradually
the field gets done.

We didn't use all the grain; I hope we have sowed thick enough. It looked all right. Denny M and I sowed round the riggs, broadcasting, which is the nicest thing of all to do and then waited while Dougie finished harrowing. We lay on the ground smelling it, talking about herrings and politics, and then cut some rhodies at the gate . . .

Jemima was married in April. Naomi was closely involved in the wedding preparations and, as a token of affection, had lent Jemima her own lace wedding veil. Special wedding clothes, indeed any new clothes at all, were now difficult to come by. The clothes ration had recently been reduced and by the summer of 1942, the Minister of Trade had introduced the new Austerity Regulations forbidding the use of trimmings and circumscribing clothing designs.

Sunday–Tuesday 26–28 April 1942
. . . We made the church look lovely, with pale coloured rhodies, larch, daffodils and forsythia, in the earthenware jam-jars. We had to carry the water up from the smithy. I began taking over the darker rhodies to the Hall. Then I went to the bus to find the relations who were to stay with me, an uncle of the bridegroom, a costing clerk at Shanks in Barrhead (and a very nice, intelligent man as I found later, a good liberal) and several females, one the wife of a science master, and a little girl. Oh yes, one thing on Sunday had been making up the beds and getting the rooms ready, soap and all that. I took them round the garden, then went over to the Hall again, where I found the caterers laying the tables. They had got horrible little glass vases with a few daffodils in each, and when I substituted rhodies they took them off and we had a bit of a row, though, as they were Jemima's people, I didn't want to be too fierce. I was now taking benzedrine, but it didn't have much effect beyond making my heart beat hard and making me lose my temper easily. I at least got a silver bowl of my own with rhodies, for the bride's table, and put the others all round.
. . . The church was pretty full, largely with forestry girls, all in their best. I was left rather isolated in the middle of a pew, with people I didn't know, and my heart hammering from the benzedrine. I thought about fuel rationing. Denny M came in, with his kilt and velvet coat, looking like a king but remote. Duncan was in front of me, very serious, bowing his head to the prayers, wanting to be married to Mary himself. I knew lots of people, but I was apart. Jemima came in, with her father; she looked beautiful, and the rich folds of my lace veil made the white satin and the pink and blue net of

the bridesmaids look flimsy and cheap. But perhaps nobody else thought that. The lace went well with her own eyes and hair and cheeks, that were genuine too. My photographer, the Fleet Air Arm lad that I had collected for them, was there . . .

Back at the hall . . .

. . . we were told to take our seats, with partners. I felt very shy suddenly, and sat next Christine. The Campbell family were all nice to me. There was a mass of food, cold jugged hare or something, cakes, chocolate biscuits, sherry, madeira, whisky, tea, cream buns of a kind, wedding cake but rather less than usual. Mr Baker said grace, proposed the bride and bridegroom and did chairman; there must have been nearly 100 there. One of the senior ladies was in tears because her husband was drunk already and interrupting.

I did my bit, rather well, made them laugh, didn't say a thing about pheasants! Then the tables were cleared for the dancing. Most of us went out and stood by the Hall in the late sunlight. Everything looked very beautiful; I was glad my corn was in . . .

Tuesday 19 May 1942
. . . Wrote various letters. Oh yes!—and I had a letter from Ruth, saying she is pregnant. . . . It will put her back in her exams a bit, as it is due just at the time of the Final, but perhaps not too much. And it will mean then that she'll have to work twice as hard as anyone else, but that's what women can do. She said she was afraid I'd be jealous, as of course, I am. But god knows I've spent half my life being jealous and suppressing it (I mean suppressing it in myself, not merely its manifestations). She wrote a nice letter, obviously damn pleased only worried because it will be Christmas and the baby won't get two lots of presents! Hasn't told anyone else, feels her sister will be jealous as she wants one so much. I felt excited at first, wanting to shout about it. If only I could manage one myself too. It would be so very nice to have someone to be with one at times like this. But it's got to be my own. I think it's an asset for a woman doctor to have children. And what with the birth rate and all I'm sure it's a good thing. Poor little bull calf. I think Denny will be awfully pleased too. At this stage of the war it's one in the eye for Hitler.

Thursday 21 May 1942

Fine but not too hot. Went out at nine and found the fertiliser was there, much relieved. We spent all morning mixing it, trying to get it out at about 3½ cwt per acre with 42 lbs of grass seeds. It was rather hard work, mixing with the shovels, then getting it into sacks. Everything is so *heavy*. I was awfully pleased yesterday at getting a form saying I could have oilskins coupon-free as an agriculturalist!

In the afternoon sowing out; we managed about three acres, but it is pretty tough; with this heavy fertiliser one can't cast nearly so far, at least I can't, not really much more than nine or ten feet, and it kept on blowing back into one's eyes and stinging. It was bright sun too, and caught one's face—I had a hanky right over my hair. Suddenly at my feet quite bare on the earth, there was a peewit's nest with four lovely blotched eggs, like tops with the thin ends down together. It was extraordinarily moving, somehow. I called to Lachie and asked him to lead the horses round it, I began to think about a poem about it. We worked on rather late; I like sowing from a sack better than a pail, at least with this stuff.

Later I wrote the poem, and began an article for the *English Digest* for which I shall be paid some small sum. Jemima came in and we talked a lot; I think she found the honeymoon very satisfactory; she said she thought she knew him, but he was so much nicer and more considerate and gentler than she had thought anyone could be; she's a bit gloomy at being back. Wonders what he'll do when the war's over, says they're all saying what are we fighting *for*? This starts again now; in periods of acute danger, as the air-raid times, people didn't ask this so much, but now they do . . .

Friday 29 May 1942

. . . Walked round with Dick in the afternoon. Felt ill and depressed, all the more so as I have to fill in three govt forms, one for petrol, one for ditto for motor mower, one about the farm. No letters I want. Wish Murdoch weren't going into the army. Dick says it will be over next year; I say it will never be over. We've all got so into the habit of it; that's the way total war is. And equally I feel ashamed not to be more in it, not to have been in London during the proper blitz. Wish they'd go for Edinburgh next week while I'm there. Though I would be awfully frightened. Feel as if nothing I did was any good . . .

Monday 1 June 1942

. . . At Campbeltown, found the plane would start five hours late, owing to an ambulance call. Campbeltown in the rain not very attractive: we sat in the Royal which is nearly finished rebuilding after the bombing, I read Wells' latest, rather peevish, remembered all the things I'd forgotten to bring. Talked to the Co-op about ration books. It was a bit of a bore, to be stuck like that with nothing to do when I spent a fine Sunday typing out a report! and have been so overworked. I was so looking forward to a flick—almost any flick—in Glasgow. And dinner that I hadn't thought out. But we got to Glasgow with only just time for a snatched meal before their train. Shan't see Dick now for two months.

A WREN in the plane, we got talking; she was doing write-ups; I told her who I was and she said Not really!—and then told me everything, her fiancé, a pacifist who joined the RAF, killed on Christmas Day, herself trying to uphold pacifist standards of decency while doing this work, the toughening of everything, how much she liked flying now, and wanted to write one *good* book, her ambition now narrowed to one . . . These poor young, if only one could help them.

Met Dorothy at the station, we went back and talked till midnight, her mother producing delicious scones. She trying to combine socialism and Christianity. Told me how she has two boys in her east-side class who know all about Stalin, how she teaches them poetry, how she illustrated a talk on the walk to Emmaus with a Carradale ghost story, how she voted for affiliation with the trades council.

After leaving Glasgow, Naomi moved on to Edinburgh to visit her Haldane cousin, Archie, now married to Janet Simpson Smith.

Tuesday 2 June 1942

. . . Edinburgh seems so exquisitely civilised, tempting one to spending, a capital; where Glasgow is half savage, somehow warm, but you wouldn't be surprised if a fight started at any moment. It wouldn't here. These very wide streets, where one can go across unhustled by traffic, and the green squares, the house, even, where I was born, high and splendid in grey stone, depending on unskilled labour. But I do like Edinburgh. It's all condensed too. Jan and I walked right out of the respectable part, looking for a pipe maker, where I bought books of music for Dougie. The Lament he wants is pibroch all right. I wonder if he'll do it. I also got gramophone records and left the china to be mended. Archie and I are kennt folk here. Lovely dresses and things too—but not utility ones! Jan, though, wore one this evening, very nice.

Also we had ordinary pre-war meals with silver on the table and Turnbull, rather like clockwork, waiting. It made me laugh but was rather nice. We talked a lot.

Wednesday 3 June 1942

Spent most of the morning with the Forestry. A nice Deputy Commissioner Gosling, . . . was upset with me for calling them bad landlords, said it was all the war, and so on; that they were at the mercy of the Treasury. I said then why don't you make money by growing and selling trees and absorbing the nurserymen? We discussed forestry crofts, housing – I think they'll house their folk in Carradale – and communication with a village or forest district through a council, I thought he was on the right side though I couldn't agree that a University education was almost a necessity for the "officer class".

Queer going through this lovely town, which I am hoping won't be bombed, full of one's own class, a capital, and suddenly feeling this bubbling secret excitement because one is on the other side, when one sees the brass plate with Forestry Commission, one is part of it, either for or against, but in league with the roe-deer, the fairies, the foresters, against the keepers, the lunchers, the respectable. I have never felt this kind of thing, this sudden wave of sympathy with someone far off, except when I have been in love . . .

Friday 5 June 1942

. . . had a wire from Murdoch yesterday: Possibility of general war research job alternative to army intelligence required rather than scientific knowledge civilian at home military abroad further details Sunday what do you think. It seemed to me a good idea, and I also rang up Dick; it might lead to something afterwards, is anyhow likely to be much more interesting than plain army. But of course one's thinking all the time about their safety. Not that one can guarantee that. Either way. I think there will be some definite military development, whether a second front or something of the kind, within a few weeks, days perhaps. If only this Libyan news was better. I think it's pretty bad really . . .

At the end of the week, Naomi made her way north to the old Haldane family houses of Cloan and Foswell in the Ochils to stay with her Uncle Willie (Sir William Haldane) and her Aunt Edith. The purpose of the trip was to look at their tractor to see if it would be of use in Carradale.

Thursday–Saturday 18–20 June 1942
By lorry to Arrochar, noting the very good Forestry planting on Rest and be Thankful, with a mixture of conifers and some birch; I hadn't been there for years. Also watching crops—it makes everything so much more interesting, being a farmer . . . On to Gleneagles by two trains, wanted to walk back via Gleneagles, arriving late, but it would have been awkward for dinner, so they insisted on fetching me: felt annoyed at that and suddenly realised I was sounding on the phone just like Jack. I believe all Haldanes pretty good at dealing with large catastrophes, but very bad about minor irritations.

Cloan is now mostly lived in by twenty Barnardo children and a number of nurses—there are forty at Foswell, which they have to themselves. Aunt E and Uncle W and Miss Mackenzie (and at the moment a sister-in-law of Willie's) live in the back part, using the dining room as a combined sitting room and dining room, doing most of the housework themselves, which Aunt E is rather old for. They also have old Nurse and Agnes living there in the old nursery rooms, doing no work of course and making trouble! Are planning to put in more lavatories for the Barnardos. Seem to be on good terms, perhaps because they don't mix much. Uncle Willie has Uncle Richard's sitting room, still smelling exactly the same of bindings and papers and wood. We went up there after dinner—they stick to proper meals with silver and a polished mahogany table, though they do it them-selves—and Baird, who'd met me, came in and we discussed the tractor, which I had looked at. It was unprepossessing to look at, so was Baird but I liked them both. We had a lot of talk about farm gear, what I should need, what I ought to do; he explained to me about tractor ploughing, but obviously thought I was a bad farmer. He comes from the Mearns which is the best farm land in Scotland, knows everything, runs a great deal at Cloan and Foswell, and is very fond of Uncle Willie; for instance he told me that Uncle W was always running out of cigarettes so he, Baird, always kept an odd box of the kind he liked. He had made their own tip cart and is a good mechanic. One difficulty is that ploughing words are different here; he says fearns instead of hints. I'd decided to buy the tractor if I could work it the next day, and he said he'd get me a plough, trailer, cultivator, road rings to go over the spiked wheels (it has rubber wheels but only road ones not field ones, and one doesn't want to use them much), also a pair of saddle harrows for me to use with the horse. Told me I must try and get a 150 gallon container for paraffin, or two, as one gets money off it if one gets two hundred gallons at a time; also another harrow, perhaps two, as the tractor will take up to five.

Afterwards I asked Uncle Willie about keeping farm accounts. He showed me his, which are very elaborate. I saw, though, that he only made a little on the two farms, Cloan and Foswell, but he said he thought farming was a good thing: good to struggle with nature, not with other people. He liked to think he was growing porridge, eggs and bacon, milk and butter, sugar (beets) and shirts (flax). In fact he has the same sort of feelings about it that I have. But he is getting rather old and not up to hard work. And he doesn't really know much about, for instance, tractors.

The next morning—and why do I sleep so much better away from here?—I walked over to Gleneagles, looking at flowers and the shape of the Ochils: went into the chapel, looked at my folks' memorial stone, decided there would be just room for me under my father, but, as a bit of swank, I would have no long epitaph: only N.M. Spring Queen. Or, if this book is very good, better than *Corn King and Spring Queen*—Spring Queen and Kirstie.* Still, perhaps I shall be blown up.

Back in Carradale.

Sunday 21 June 1942
. . . In the afternoon picked up Dougie and walked over the hill with him to see his father and mother at the white house at port-na-scartain. He showed me the site of the old road and the ruins, and talked about people and crofts, and sometimes held my hand. It is all fixed up about his going to live in Denny M's hut and he was extremely grateful and affectionate. His father is 80, crippled with rheumatism, his mother pretty old too; the sister was there and later the brother who is a policeman in Campbeltown came in with his small boy, saying I know you well though you don't know me (and explaining how they didn't charge me yon time I left my car not immobilised and it got stolen).

* 'Kirstie' was the heroine in Naomi's novel *The Bull Calves*. *The Corn King and the Spring Queen* was Naomi's most famous novel to date, first published in 1931 and republished by Virago in 1983.

The father started telling stories, going back to the Peninsular wars, mostly about his own relations and the Campbell fairy which was either here at the house or at Saddell House, and which was at daggers drawn with the brounie at Largie, so that a cousin of his who married the niece of the man at Cara House (where the brounie was as much as at Largie—Cara is definitely haunted) had his bed almost shaken from under him by the brounie. We had a tea of honour, with date, tomato and orange sandwiches—the orange brought from Glasgow by Dougie's sister, and a cake. I had said I was only coming for a short time, as I'd meant to cook tea here, but obviously I had to stay. The old man told me the Gaelic names of all my fields and what had been in them for years. He told me about his grandfather evicted from one of the Auch-na-savil crofts "where it was said you could get the full of a bowl of meal and an unthreshed sheaf from any one of them all year round", apparently for being a Haldanite, a Baptist converted by my great-great-grandfather. About his uncle, the piper and poet, who would make poems that could take the skin off you, so you wouldn't show your face for six months after; but they were all in his chest that was robbed after he died, along with a gold riding-crop that was given him for piping at Largie, a bar of mottled soap and the makings of a beautiful shot silk dress that he had got for a girl that jilted him. They talked a lot about piping, about the ivory and the silver mounted pipes that were made by Roderick Ban Macintyre and the sweet tone they had and I said how much I'd like to hear them. Perhaps I will one day.

The Cloan tractor was sent by train to Arrochar where Naomi and Alec collected it in a lorry owned by a local man, Duncan Campbell.

Monday–Wednesday 6–8 July 1942
. . . At Arrochar a long wait, tried to write my book but couldn't. Read Bowie's *Future of Scotland*. Climbed into the truck and looked at the tractor and the lovely new plough. At last Duncan Alec Campbell turned up with his lorry; he unloaded and then we had an awful time getting the tractor on . . . we had to undo the tractor and wind it off the truck; I was afraid it would go through the floor of the lorry but it didn't. We got on the oil drums, and left Alec, whose lorry had been ditched and was late, to take such of the rest of the gear as he could. We talked quite a lot on the way back; he was well read, we talked about various things he had done, places, his geese, the future of Carradale and so on. He gave various people lifts and always offered them a

cigarette—also me. I liked him a lot, had never talked to him before. He said his father was a younger brother of Dugald Ban, Dougie's father; I never knew he and Dougie were cousins. Alec is a second cousin for that matter! We got in about eight and got the tractor off on to the bank by the saw-mill. With great trepidation but feeling I simply must, I drove it down off the bank; it then stuck, having no petrol, and there were so many folk about that he couldn't give me a drop from the lorry. He had been extremely intelligent about it, giving me time and muscle; I tried to get him to take ten bob, but he wouldn't, said "Take it as a neighbourly act". I said I would, and it was very nice having such good neighbours and would he let me know if there was ever anything I could do for him.

We put the gear—for the other lorry had turned up with the trailer and the plough—into the Mains, and fetched the tractor; I let Lachie drive it a bit. I thought our crops looked pretty good. It had been awfully interesting watching other fields as one went by from Arrochar and in the train, seeing the difference between fields that had been drilled or broadcast, what was being done about hay and potatoes, etc, the field at Sparisaig that had potatoes in it but hadn't been weeded, and it looks now as if there would be no crop at all, whereas mine which I weeded, is not too bad. Lachie had got the front potatoes and the ones in Mains set up, was doing the meadow . . .

. . . The next morning was wet but we went to the potatoes later; the boys from the camp joined us and when Lachie had put the grubber through the drills they looked better, were easier to get up. He has set up the cricket field, the bit of Mains and the first few drills in the meadow.

Then Murdoch and I went over and got some paraffin from Duncan to start the tractor; I wanted to try her out with wrack. The girls went down to the beach to collect it. Lachie and Murdoch and I with some trouble got the tractor started. I didn't want to take it on to the beach but the others all thought it was firm enough, and none of them could really manage the wheel-barrows up from the sand. I took her down and at first it worked, then, with a full load on the trailer, she stuck a few feet from the edge of the old track, and dug herself in. It was wretched, I do hate getting into a mess with a thing, we unhooked the trailer, but it made no difference. Finally and raging, I got all the men—Taggie is here on leave—and we dug her out, and get her up, leaving the seaweed in a dump. I felt all the time that everyone would say this came of a woman driving, and I said to Angus and Lachie that they were not to say so, and indeed, I don't think they really think it, they are pretty sympathetic; it was the hell of a job as the gears are very stiff, and one gets bumped on rough ground. I was awfully tired in the evening, when a few turned up to dance, including Duncan and Mary . . .

Naomi had been taking care of young Betty Gibson since the beginning of the war. But her father wanted her back and so it had to be.

Monday 20 July 1942

. . . I had an interview with Mr Gibson yesterday; it was long and painful and full of silences when I didn't lose my temper, but only with difficulty. He seems to think there's nothing else for it; his sister-in-law isn't going to go on keeping house. He had to have Betty back to look after him. He doesn't want to stand in her way but I didn't see what could be said. I don't think he has much imagination. I tried to get him to see Betty's point of view, not to speak of my own, but nothing happened. Then I had a talk to Betty this morning; she is very unhappy but doesn't see what else can be done. I urged her to go on working, to make something of her foundations here, not just to feel bitter and let it off on having a gay time: to work, perhaps to tackle another language, to make a life for herself. But I didn't want to pull her too hard, I wanted to make her feel it would be interesting and worth while; I asked her to write to me once a week. I said he'd promised to let her come back sometimes; she said she would have come back whether he let or not. Said she wasn't going to break her heart over any of her boys [boyfriends in the village], she'd fought with most of them.

Friday 31 July 1942

A lovely day, with a mild breeze. We picked fruit in the morning, put up the rest of the hay in the afternoon; there is now just the stuff round the house. People just turning up for fruit all the time, and all with some kind of special plea, children or invalids or something. Meanwhile I try and get on with the early local orders.

Murdoch back, and a satisfactory interview, will probably go into Tank operational research. Probably getting a fortnight first. He has had his hair rather firmly cut, so as to give a better idea to the Board!

Sunday 2 August 1942

. . . Dick so pleased to be back, has had a lot of legal work, but worried about the Nuffield survey, whether it will go on, whether anything will be accepted by the civil servants and so on. Douglas seems pleased with my thing even when I send him odd paragraphs to stick in. Tony [Murdoch's friend] worried as to what to do, though it's very much *my* future. It's this University assumption that one gets a really good job in London, that gets me down. He may be going to the Hogarth [Press] as [John] Lehmann's secretary. I said can you do the ordinary secretarial things, typing and shorthand. He said No, he has two women to do that. I couldn't help thinking what the "two women" might think of this undergraduate strolling in and taking over. It isn't as if he really had much judgement about poetry, he only likes his friends' stuff. But probably I'm not fair. Only it makes me very critical of the Universities.

I was very tired going to bed, had an awful dream that the Germans had invaded south England, were taking one town after another, Bath, Oxford, and the BBC making soothing noises, and now they were within a few miles of London (where I was in the dream) and I felt despairingly that we *must* stand, it mustn't be Paris over again, but if we did we'd all be killed . . .

Saturday 8 August 1942

. . . The whole evening, though, was entangled with my brother and Helen. She was terribly upset, intent on what he wanted. I became fairly clear about what had puzzled me before. The relationship was certainly not just that of a colleague. It then became extremely important that I should make no mistakes with my sister-in-law this time. I must succeed in being deeply kind to one who was suspicious of all kindness, prickly, distrustful, in some ways terribly objective though now appearing weak, largely owing to her own physical condition: a person of great courage and intelligence, not one to be aware of delicate personal relationships, of this Carradale thing and so on. Someone always desperate for her come-back, her defence. I mustn't ever let her come-back hurt me: it must always be turned by love, but love of a practical, unsentimental kind, love expressed almost entirely through action. I kissed her once, but only at a point where I knew what I had done was what I wanted by other methods, when I was sure she would not feel the need for a come-back. Nor did I do it in any way in order to weaken her.

We talked a great deal and I discovered Jack's curious structure of himself and his family, himself essentially as a Burdon Sanderson, not as a Haldane, real hate of my mother, not on the grounds that she over-loved him and "owned" him, but because he thinks she tried to make him conventional. Apparently when they went to stay he told Helen she was awful, and that Helen must answer back and not "pull her punches". To Helen's surprise, my poor mother turned out to be quite amiable and intelligent. Naturally she was puzzled. The main stated case against me is that, during the last war, I let his mice die—as though I could help it, with none of the food the mice were used to, and myself a rather unskilled mouse tender. I said that my mother had desperately wanted to become a doctor, was very much of a feminist. All startling to Helen. But god knows what Jack's book on my father will be like. A complete myth . . .*

Sunday 9 August 1942
. . . Spent the time till eleven making contacts, getting the plane seats (MacGeachy persuaded someone to give up his seat, I think this was objectively justifiable), packing Jack's and Helen's things, identifying a plant for her, finding a bottle for the newts and gammarus she'd got, writing labels and calming her down.

Then she went off by Tarbert, he by plane. I lay down, feeling pretty achey, tired out. Thought I would go on writing my book. A phone call from Glasgow, saying that one of the boy scouts (who are camping here) had a mother who hadn't heard about him and was anxious, finally drove me into hysterics.

In the afternoon I listened to Murdoch's records of Beethoven and finished Part One of my book. Then I typed it out. Then we had the cinema show and I took half the gate money and appealed for the Nat Life Boat Ass, using our new mike, as I am sick of appearing on the platform; it made funny noises. Then I went back and typed my chapter. Listened to the news, felt pretty cynical about the BBC and the Indian Government saying Congress are betraying China and Russia—as though we hadn't done that ourselves already.†

* This book was never completed. The completed parts went missing in India where JBSH spent the latter part of his life.

† Naomi refers here to news from India. During 1942, the Indian nationalist leader, Gandhi, launched the 'Quit India' campaign for Indian independence from British rule. He was imprisoned by the British, together with other members of the Indian National Congress, until May 1944.

A note from [George] Orwell at the BBC about taking part in a BBC debate for an Indian audience next month. Such a job to get south, but the first time they've asked me to speak myself. Rose, Val and Av cooked a wonderfully good and decorative tea.

Julian Trevelyan (who had known Naomi in London) was an artist, a member of the Euston School of painters. He had been involved with various other artists in the early days of Mass-Observation. During the war, he worked on camouflage in the army.

Monday 7 September 1942
. . . Julian Trevelyan was coming over from Inverary where he is doing almost nothing yet can never get away for a day's leave. Mr Lynn at Grogport rang up in a state of excitement to say that there had been an accident on the road, a friend of mine. Discovered it was the small boy Ian, Val's friend. It sounded as if he were at Clonnaig and I was preparing to go for him, with the doctor, but thought I'd better see what the bus had to say. The bus stopped and after a few minutes I discovered that he was in it; the poor kid was lying on a stretcher on the floor, looking pretty bad, wet through of course. Fortunately Julian had been looking after him. We got him out on a stretcher made of a ladder and took him back. The new doctor who seems to be a very dithering, slow-moving kind of man, came along; he doesn't appear to have any bad internal injuries, but they can't be sure yet.

Monday 8 September 1942
It seems fairly definite that he just had concussion and bruises. Nurse stayed the night. Poor kid, he was awfully restless and wretched. It was very upsetting, one felt he was rather special. I sent his father a wire. It was awfully nice having Julian Trevelyan to stay, talking about sane things like painting. In the morning he went off by forestry lorry . . .

Naomi planned to attend the first meeting of the Scottish Convention in Glasgow on 12 September with Denny M and Dougie Campbell.

Friday 11 September 1942
As the boy's temp was almost normal in the morning I thought I could go, but after a wild rush and the doctor coming and dithering again, I went out to the gate, found after a bit that the bus had gone past! Dick said he would race in after it . . . Dougie was much relieved to see me. It was a fierce bus journey as there were so many drunk or half drunk

English sailors passing bottles about and making noises meant to be songs. D and I had lunch at the cafe in Tarbert and walked down to the boat. I had some bits of Dick's rods to mend, and kept on trying not to get them broken again! But the boat was quiet and not desperately crowded, and we talked. He told me about his time on the Clyde, about the ship-yard and the solid feel of the men in the Union that they were going to get the bosses down. About being skipper or engineer in the Clyde ferry boat, working for the Clyde trust and how the Clyde banks were all owned by a group of shipping people instead of by the Corporation, say. How he tried to get the others at the saw-mill to join a Union but they weren't interested. Then he told me about the fishing on the Kyles where he had been as a lad, pointing out the places, and then about a lad he knew, in the police but a hard case, a drinker, who had joined the Argylls, was taken prisoner with his brother after Dunkirk. He and two others, speaking Gaelic all the time, decide to make a bolt for it at the next place where the French country people had left out a bucket of water to drink. He could have done it the second day but wanted to see that his wounded brother was all right, so waited till the fourth day. Then in the scramble, they broke away and ran up a close and hid in a shrubbery. A French woman had seen them, and, when all was quiet, brought them each a suit of peasant clothes, raked up from among the neighbours. Then they started south for Spain. Once in a wrecked village they found a bicycle shop and put together three bicycles, but these were taken from them by the Germans after four hours. They rested in pig sties and barns, they hitch-hiked 250 miles on a German lorry, and sang all the time, but never using a word of English. They got cigarettes from Germans. They crossed the Pyrenees; they were nearly led into a concentration camp by a Spaniard. They swam the Ebro and this chap went back to rescue one of his friends who had cramp. They were re-captured by the Germans who tried all their interpreters on them, then opened a map of the world for them to say. The chap pointed to Vladivostok. As Russia was not yet in the war, they were let go. At last they got to Lisbon and so back.

A crowded train journey to Glasgow, but somehow nice being with Dougie, listening to everyone talking, mostly naval ratings and girls wise-cracking, . . . And at Glasgow Denny M was waiting for us. We went to tea at the Corn Exchange and I put through a call to find out how Ian was and whether I should get an extra nurse. While I was away, some Americans had sent a message by the waitress to Denny

M asking him to get up and come over to them so that they could see his kilt. Denny M was trembling and clean affronted, but wouldn't let me go and tick off the Americans. I explained that they hadn't meant it like that, but the harm was done. They sent over two glasses of beer; Denny M and Dougie drank them, but weren't in the least appeased. It has probably left them both feeling anti-American.

Saturday 12 September 1942
. . . we went off to Convention. There were about forty people there, mostly oldish. Power and MacCormick spoke, very vaguely, about Unity of Purpose and so on, getting in everyone. They asked for discussion. So I got up, whispered to by my two, and said was it possible to plan without certain primary assumptions, for instance nationalisation of land? And would that be agreed to by people of all parties? . . . Or did they propose to do things bit by bit—things that were agreed upon generally? That might be sound policy, for, if sufficient small things were done, it might be found that big things were changed by it (Quantity alters quality). Then various other people spoke, about education, freights, roads etc. About democracy and local committees. Then a national committee was proposed. I didn't know most of the names—except my own! I had been wondering whether to go in or not, but now had to decide. I won't do anything unless I can really be in on it thoroughly.

We all had tea and talked round about; I talked to several people, including nice old Mrs MacLeod of Skiabost, and some of the Highland Development Council people. There were very few young people, except teachers, but I'm afraid that's inevitable just now. MacCormick is good. I proposed a vote of thanks to Power. It was funny, I was obviously one of the most important people there, it mattered what I said; but that may just have meant that the whole thing was pretty small scale . . .

Sunday 13 September 1942
. . . I saw a notice of a CP meeting at the Regal, with Jack speaking. I thought I must try and see him . . . One was supposed to get in by ticket but I said I'm Naomi Mitchison and barged in. Then found Jack wasn't there, not well enough to travel; but Allenson, the *Daily Worker* man, was very nice, gave me some news of him, said he was trying to look after him, but it was very difficult. A mad Communist rushed up and gave me a poem to give to Jack. Allenson had all the charm of the

working class CP leaders, Pollitt, Campbell and so on. Whereas the intellectuals have no charm. I went in to the meeting but the acoustics were bad; it was large and enthusiastic but not wild. A lot of fairly sensible speaking by delegates, mostly very keen and loyal to the DW [*Daily Worker*] but not always very intelligent.

. . . Came back with Denny M and hung about, waiting for the Convention people. MacDonald came, looking very respectable; but he is a socialist, and probably quite a good fox. Later John MacCormick came, back from a meeting at Girvan. We couldn't get a meal at the hotel, as it was after eight, so wandered off looking for one, finally got one at the St Enoch's Hotel—Denny M paying! It was very expensive. We had a long talk and I agreed to come into the council and to write a memorandum and to start a Kintyre committee of Convention and a few other things. Neither John MacC nor I really know what we may be able to do, nor whether we should make a general plan for Scotland or attempt to get through a number of smaller reforms; we agree we must back Tom Johnston. There is absolutely no anti-English feeling. But we must run ourselves. We discussed the formation of local committees and holding meetings. He says the meetings can always be paid for by a collection at the door; the ones that have been held already have been very good. His membership is still in hundreds rather than thousands, but from thirty to fifty applications a week come in. We thought about the people on the Council; some are Glasgow, professional and a few working class —J.M. has contacts with the shop stewards, and is correspondingly cross with the respectable unions. In the small towns the people are mostly professional, sometimes business, sometimes town councillors, the sort of people who would hardly call themselves socialist, but hate monopolies which are forcing them down, and would rather have revolution than go on as they are. People who wouldn't have gone left after the last war, but now would. Yet of course we really need the working class support. Denny M and I both emphasised the way the more prosperous working classes are accumulating money which they can't spend and becoming kind of wee capitalists, unwilling to take risks. Can they be squashed out between the conscious workers and the professionals—the "workers by hand and brain"? We don't know if Convention will work but we think it is worth trying . . .

Carradale

Monday 14 September 1942

. . . I talked to Chrissie Campbell about women getting out of the house, organising things and so on, as well as not being slaves, keeping their minds alive, reading: she said it was so difficult, you got so that you didn't want to move out. She didn't feel she could get other women to do anything—I talked about collecting sphagnum moss etc—but when I spoke of the possibility of communal meals at the Hall, she brightened up, she said what a good idea they could take turns cooking and washing up. I wish it could be done now, but don't see how it could be in the tiny kitchen. Dougie thought it would be fine too. I also talked of the silliness of being too house proud and generally lectured around, but Chrissie is sensible enough to see. I don't know which others would be.

Dougie wanted to know about Convention, went off to ask Denny M what he thought. I explained they must keep me straight, keep my feet on the ground, above all tell me what to do so that they wouldn't be betrayed by their leaders again. But he said How? And then You know us, and then You are our guiding star. And then he stood on one foot and said This Convention—it will not cut into the Labour? (They call the Labour Movement this so often.) I said well maybe, but is the Labour Party really what you want? Is it really the party that stands for equality of opportunity, for the workers by hand and brain? Isn't it the party of the trade union leaders, who don't really want to alter things, who see themselves as part of organised society? And he said yes. And then I explained about Convention, that what matters is our loyalty to one another, the way we stick together. And I could never be really friends except with a socialist, but would he and Denny M have been able to be as fond of me as they were, could we three have stood together for always, as we are doing, if I had not been a Scot? And I said how going to see his sister wasn't like the old Labour Party things, it was more; we were like intersecting circles, and there were bits which would never touch, yet, because we were Scots, there was a bigger area of intersection. But I know so well that the miserable Labour Party has gathered up all this lovely and noble loyalty, and has it still, and is wasting it. And I hate Transport House, and all its ways. I still try to defend Stafford, but I don't see what his game is . . .

Wednesday 30 September 1942

. . . In the afternoon we worked awfully hard in the middle field, turning and tidying up all the sheaves, moving down the bindings, and re-binding some. Lachie, Rosemary, Angus and I worked; we were hot in the sun, but it hardly dried out the sheaves; our arms were scratched and we were always getting straws into our faces. One has to take these miserable drooping stinking wet sheaves by the scruff of the neck, one in each hand and bang their heads together before they will stand, and they are very heavy, and the binder has done them in the wrong place, much too low down, so they are top heavy as well. Talk of winning the harvest, it's battling all the time . . .

Staying with Dorothy Melville and her parents in Glasgow.

Sunday 4 October 1942
Dorothy brought me breakfast in bed, which was nice. When I came down, her parents were just off to church, and she and I stopped to cook the dinner and talk. I wrote some notes for my speech in the afternoon. We talked about women cooking and washing up day after day; it seemed a new idea to her that it wasn't what one was there for, that it wasn't simply the noblest thing in life to cherish a tired man at the day's end. I suggested that bringing up children, even, was best done by a woman who kept alive, who was in touch with other adult minds, had time to read serious books and who was in the world, and in contact with its problems, as the home woman couldn't ever be. But it was new to her!

Afterwards I talked quite a bit to her father, who is sceptical of Convention. He is Labour, was in the UDC last war, but is very disillusioned about everything. He asked me if I really knew how the working classes lived; I said yes, I thought I did now; I'd had these years in the Labour movement: I'd lived plenty in such houses. He seemed pleased. They talked a lot about Ian, the boy, who is back from America with a commission, has done very well; is tall and handsome and clean living, never says a bad word, though he doesn't go to church now. He's in the RAF. I wonder how anxious they are about him really.

After dinner Dorothy and I went in to Glasgow to the meeting of the Socialist Teachers, about a hundred, in a small room, pretty packed: perhaps more. I gather more of an audience than they usually have! I made them a good speech, for about an hour, lammed into them, made them laugh, suggested all kinds of things. There were questions and discussion, in the course of which Oliver Brown (very decorative in his kilt—I hadn't seen him before) squashed one of the

Councillors who said that schools were really pretty good. I gather the primary schools are much the worst, including infant classes of fifty. When I talked about corruption, everyone laughed; it seems to be well known. No good socialist I know in Glasgow has much use for the "Labour" Councillors, We'd meant to go to the Fabian Society lecture on education, but young Kenneth Roberton, Sir Hugh's son, turned up and asked me over to tea there; I said yes, but with Dorothy . . . We went to a big, sunny living-room, not quite in my taste, but somehow jolly and comfortable and with the feeling of being lived in and having lots of people always turning up. Of course good taste itself as compared with most houses I see. Lady Roberton was baking and her very nice daughter-in-law and a German refugee boy kept on bringing in plates of scones and anchovy toast, and treacle cake and jam tarts and two kinds of jam and apples. It was an awfully good tea, and the Robertons kind and friendly and nice to Dorothy; we all talked hard, and ragged one another, and discussed music and politics and people and education. The young ones saw us back to our tram route afterwards.

In September German troops reached Stalingrad; the Russians struggled bitterly, still hoping for support from Britain and the US on the Western Front. Despite demands to open a Second Front, Churchill's attention was still on the North African campaign. An abortive attempt to land troops at Dieppe on August 19 had resulted in the tragic deaths of mostly Canadian servicemen.

Wednesday 14 October 1942
. . . People talking on and off about Stalingrad, full of admiration of course but—I don't think anyone was taken in by Churchill's speech; they say it's to conciliate people because of the girls being taken to England.★ It won't. We aren't such fools as we look in Scotland.

With the heavy bombing over, Denny and Ruth returned to River Court. Murdoch has joined them after leaving Cambridge.

Sunday–Friday 18–30 October 1942
So queer to be back in London, in River Court but Denny and Ruth in

★ The demand for more labour power led the Minister of Labour, Ernest Bevin, to authorise the transfer of young 'mobile' women from Scotland, Wales and the North of England to areas where they were needed in industry. Many Scottish women were transported to Birmingham.

my room, using it more or less as a sitting room, Murdoch having turned Dick's room into a very nice bed-sitting-room (he and Dick nest wherever they go, I just perch, ready to fly again), Dick and I in the boys' room . . . Meals in the dining-room—Sandy's fish—with the old, nice china, but kitchen cutlery, the drawing room too big and cold to use. Shopping with Ruth in the small shops along King Street, but she is still working at hospital most days, though very large. She's well and both of them looking forward to it very much, knowing a lot about it. I feeling very queer and jealous, but both of them so sweet to me.

Val has joined Lois at Badminton School, still at its wartime home in Lynmouth.

Tuesday 3 November 1942
Another day with the girls. We went up the very fine East Lynn valley, up to the town where we bought six cream or very near cream buns, for the rest of the sweet rations—the girls are rather dissuaded from getting them but mostly try to. The place is full of food and fruit drinks and oranges which I'm sure don't all go to the children. I saw Miss Baker [headmistress] who was very nice, as usual, thought very well of Val, hoped she wouldn't become completely part of the machine; apparently the school have the impression that she has completely adapted. Miss B not very keen on Lois going into the ATS, says they waste their good people so badly. Also said she was so sick of the Archbishop preaching about the changes, and all the well-meaning people perhaps the Communist Party were right after all; she was watching the old order entrenching itself in Govt offices and things and could see no way out but revolution. She has always seemed to be a good Liberal to the girls so it must have been a nice change talking to me . . .

Thursday–Sunday 5–8 November 1942
An awfully busy time, seeing people, trying to type the chapters I'd written, shopping, getting this thing done for the varicose vein and the strep and staph inoculation as well, so that I felt pretty rotten on Thursday, stayed in bed. All sorts of Carradale things following me, the nurse not yet arrived! Queer undercurrents of jealousy of Murdoch and his job by Denny and Ruth, still students and working so hard. On Saturday I got their rations for them, . . . stood in cheerful queues,

got sent a hare which I gutted and skinned, and cooked on Sunday, I thought rather well but thought too much pepper, also cooked them potato scones, but difficult with the gas oven. Everyone trying to be economical over light and fuel, keeping stuff for the Gibsons' rabbits, etc. After dealing with the hare we went to the party at the Soviet Embassy, just dodged being photographed with Eden as he came in. The Maiskys so cheery, quantities of generals and admirals, the lady sniper, looking like a good cook and a thoroughly nice woman, diplomats—the street crowded with cars—but not many of the old gang except the Pritts, Huxleys—I had a letter from Aldous and Julian [Huxley] so happy to see it—old Neil MacLean and a few others. The minor diplomats and Americans have finished the vodka! One felt it was like old times but different. Low [David Low, the cartoonist] said he was afraid it was no longer a lost cause and he wouldn't be able to go on going. But Agnes asked me at once was I going to have a baby: you feel there's something about someone who knows what your heart is really on. Told her about Ruth. Everyone approves of Ruth doing this. She has interviewed someone with a baby to share (from a *New Statesman* advt)—the woman was quite black but seems rather nice. A possible arrangement . . .

During November, the war news began to improve. Churchill had appointed General Montgomery to command the Eighth Army in North Africa. On October 23, Montgomery defeated Rommel at El Alamein. On 4 November, it was announced that Rommel's troops were in retreat and on 8 November, in an operation called 'Torch' commanded by the US General Eisenhower, the allies landed in Morocco and Algeria.

. . . this Sunday John Holloway turned up with the news. One was just beginning to believe in the Libyan one, and now this is really exciting. All the part of Africa I know too. Suppose they can pull it off and wipe up Rommel and then invade Italy or Greece? . . . a tremendous change in atmosphere everywhere.

Murdoch and Denny talk tactics and strategy a lot; Murdoch and John Holloway and Robin talking army stuff, as cryptic and boring as scientists, full of initials and technical terms. We discussed Aldous' philosophic and religious views on Friday, but this Sunday I was too busy cooking. Still, it's a change being with people who can discuss abstract subjects. Only I feel queerly out of it here, still tangled with the farm and all that. I discuss agriculture with people whenever possible—Sir John Russell★ and the Soviet Party! Jack asked me to dine with him next Thursday "Half an hour beyond Waterloo station".

Monday–Wednesday 9–11 November 1942
... I managed to get some brown knickers and sox. Then to Dr Harding who gave me another go of stuff for the varicose vein, pretty sore. Gave me a general examination, said my heart was o.k., and that I had extremely good muscles for a multi-para. I said my worst symptom was losing my temper. She says this is common at the menopause. Said what about, I said feminism and Scotland, the things I *feel* about. At that she began to tell me about herself, how people were still nasty to her and wouldn't understand her working, felt it was a pity, held it against her that she couldn't manage week-ends, that she had to miss engagements because of baby cases, etc ... She was awfully anxious to know if Denny was really nice to Ruth. I said I thought so ...

To my club where I had tea with Elmina† who looks ill. She seems to have had hell getting out of Germany, thinks her parents are under house arrest. Edla has sold all her pictures to buy food. Her nice young first cousin was shot in Crete as a hostage, among a number of young intellectuals. Her husband who is a first class engineer isn't being employed here (though I think he will be). To crown it all they were put into a detention camp and not allowed to write letters for a week when they came into this country!—though they had some kind of diplomatic pass and everything. These are people of the highest possible standing in their own country with a lot of friends.

I hear that Herbert Morrison won't let in any of the 2,000 Jewish children from France. One feels ashamed of being in the same political party as Bevin and Morrison.

Most people wearing poppies. Lots of crosses planted by Westminster Abbey.

Saturday 14 November 1942
... Oxford not quite as desperately crowded. In the afternoon read part of my book to Maya and Denny and Ruth, but constant interruptions, which, combined with my cold—! Maya ... looks very frail and is obviously suffering from various things, but works four or five

★ Agriculturalist and former Director of Rothamsted Experimental Station.
† Elmina and Edla are Greek cousins of N.M.

hours a day at the garden and feeding these beastly rabbits. No fire in hall and very rarely in drawing-room, dining room turned into general living room. Still a lot of Naval billetees. The lights so dismal as to be bad for our eyes, I think.

In the evening we went round to Elizabeth's—Frank very sympathetic to Scottish nationalism. They have made one of the smaller rooms, with a good gas fire, into sitting room, eat in the kitchen . . .

Saturday 21 November 1942
In the morning to the Trevelyans, and for old sake's sake and *solidaritat* to Graham, the newsagent, who was gloomy and says the local Labour Party aren't doing anything. We haven't paid a sub yet . . .

We went on, after a very crowded, uncomfortable journey, to a Bloomsbury party, which was most disconcerting because there were all my friends looking old and haggard, so that I hardly recognised them, while young, godlike creatures bounced round, whom one had last seen in their cradles. A grey-haired man, reminded me of old Garnett, and suddenly he said he was David . . .

Tuesday 24 November 1942
To the Scottish Education Dept, and had a long talk with them about what needed doing (and finished my article for Convention). They have no policy; I feel we must make one. I am full of ideas about it. The necessity of getting in the older women who have finished with child-bearing. Normally there is this second go of life in a woman, which is wasted. She is energetic, though with much sexual disturbance and emotions, and is liable either to feel completely frustrated or to interfere with her children, if she doesn't get a job. So many she-undergraduates with good degrees will get married (they are more attractive to intelligent men than the uneducated ones) and knocked out of work for ten years or so. But they mustn't be wasted for the community. . . .

In Carradale again, visiting Jean Semple on the neighbouring farm.

Monday 30 November 1942
. . . Over in the evening to Dippen, a dark night, and I was rather frightened going by myself along the lower drive and past Sally's Walk. I had a long talk to Jean about all kinds of things, including her own life, which is hard and circumscribed, yet probably not at all a bad

one, as she takes it seriously and steadily and is determined to make something good of it. The children intelligent, good relations with the farm servants, all on an equalitarian footing, and a fine farm. Then Duncan [her husband] came back from the Hall, we had coffee and three kinds of cakes she'd been baking. I read them "The Knife" [N's poem]. It had a curious effect because Jean began to cry and Duncan said 'It's marvellous how you put into words so that one can understand then the things I have at the back of my mind.' Who could ask better praise than that? I said I thought that was the function of the poet. I said the thing wasn't finished and I didn't know if it ever would be, and Duncan said It *will* be finished. He said It doesn't matter how it's finished so long as it is. And I agreed. Then he began to talk about co-operation, why it had failed, and why it needn't, how we could educate ourselves and make a social sense, and about the other farmers. . . . Yet if my poem makes people suddenly want to make agricultural co-operatives work, well damn it all, that's what one's for. Then he said he wished I would go on with my book even if I did less on the farm, and said he would find me a couple of harrows. Told me to plough the stubble first where I would have turnips or potatoes and must get a tilth. Said I should keep the sheep till near late December, as the price went up every fortnight. He also showed me a thing in the *Herald* about a Crofters' Supply Agency, a kind of co-operative—but the "crofters" are MacDonald of Largie, Stirling of Fairburn, Miss MacLean of Ardgour, etc! . . .

On 1 December, Sir William Beveridge published his long-awaited report on social insurance and welfare schemes. His Plan covered family allowances, the health services, old age pensions, unemployment and sickness benefits and was to become the foundation for the postwar welfare state.

Saturday 5 December 1942
. . . I went down to the village to collect my rent from Johnnie; he said he'd been going to come up with it. He was very cheerful and friendly and I had tea with them. The children have measles—there is quite an epidemic here, but mild. He hadn't read the Beveridge report yet, none of the fishermen read anything except at week-ends. I urged him to. He said he didn't believe in Churchill at all; I asked him who he thought could be a leader. He said Eden and Cripps; a good many of them think that Cripps has been pushed out, the same kind of way that they know of people being victimised for their views, and they feel

sympathetic. He said he didn't think Scotland could stand up to raids the way England had done, the English were wonderful; I said I thought the east coast could! . . . I am doing a Scottish Convention questionnaire on the BBC. They all agree there is not enough time for Scottish programmes, most of them complain that they are too late at night, and also that they repeat the same Gaelic songs over and over.

I told Johnnie they ought to have a meeting of the Association about building fishing boats (the government thing) and asked him to bring it up. He said that there had been a proposal (as I knew) to keep £1 per boat back for the boys who were away, as other fleets have done, but not everyone would agree to it, and it was dropped . . .

. . . After I came back, Denny M and Dougie turned up, Denny M gloomy, saying the Beveridge scheme was no good, it was only a try-on, a camouflage by the head ones, it wasn't for Scotland anyway; he was just being stupid. Then Mrs Pollok of Ronachan turned up to discuss a land-girl, as I am thinking of getting one. She said they were rather a toss-up and none had any training worth speaking about. Then she began talking about politics and Scottish Convention. She was at the last meeting. She is very much struck by the Beveridge report, thinks it is all quite right; wonders now whether Scotland ought to have separate finance, *if* England is going to put Beveridge through.

Saturday–Monday 12–14 December 1942
At Glasgow to speak at a public meeting organised by the Convention on education.

. . . Looked through my notes and wrote a bit of book, then with Kilgour to our Executive; we met in the Central, there not being anywhere else; I started by saying I thought we ought to be all truthful with one another; if Convention is to get anywhere it must be a kind of discipline. They agreed; I asked various questions, including about our relations with the London Scots Self Gov committee. We can't be too ambitious; the numbers have only gone up slowly, still under a thousand. Dr MacDonald too optimistic about publications etc. I asked what was our attitude to Beveridge. We had quite an argument, as Hogg, my chairman, is a businessman and sees things in terms of work, not "doles", got into the position of saying that machinery should be prohibited if it put people out of work. However we are supposed both to be honest and try not to quarrel, so we managed not to; he was rather nice, apart from this.

To the Cosmo, where we all met, including the 15 year old schoolboy whom Kilgour had found, a teacher and a girl student, also the nice manager of the Cosmo. I had rather a shock when Hogg said we were all to speak for ten minutes; nobody had been warned, and the teacher and I both spoke much too long, but I at least, cut down a lot on my notes, crowded my stuff, didn't give myself time to make my points, and never got the audience properly roused—it would have taken ten minutes to do that. The others were good, especially the schoolboy. I noticed one of last summer's scouts in the front row.

When it came to questions a number of people got up and blithered, about religion, sex, the Soviet Union, the sins of various councillors, the fact that their own children weren't doing well . . . they tried to give us life histories. A few were intelligent and helpful; some we answered as they ended, others waited for my summing up. I did that quite well, and got the audience, but again didn't have enough time. There were 3–400 people. Main points: Scottish education too crammed and academic, strain of exams, too large classes, more school councils etc, and education for citizenship. I put in a lot more, especially about the badness of education committees and need of running the thing by experts . . .

Carradale. Denny and Ruth's little girl has been born but they decide not to come to Carradale for Christmas. Murdoch too was unable to join the rest of the family.

Wednesday 23 December 1942
. . . Later Dick and I walked down to the beach; there was a seal bobbing about in the surf—a high tide. Then we got branches of all kinds of evergreens, and what holly there was, and pernettia, and then the girls and I made swags, and hung some of them. Yesterday I'd seen a newly cut Scotch fir in Blackhill wood, thought I'd just take it for myself—they've no right to steal the trees, it wasn't even a blown one, I'd give a tree to anyone, but they must have the politeness to ask. It will do well for framing, and Rosemary began to cut it, but it slipped against her wrist, broke the strap of her watch. In the evening a Hall committee meeting, the last of the old committee; we discussed various small things and Dick said he'd rather not be chairman next

year if they could think of anyone else; he and I went out and watched the bowls, but they all decided to have him . . .

We had a funny evening with all the children talking at once; Val seems to like her new school quite a lot! As soon as one starts on anything so do they all and we shout and laugh. If only Murdoch were coming. I don't even know where he is. An extraordinarily nice letter from Ruth! Amazingly sympathetic; it's odd, but she does manage to say the most healing things. The children talking about Christmas, packing things, I think they've now sent off everything.

Christmas Day (Friday) 1942
Woken early by Val bringing me my stocking; we all undid stockings and raced round one another's rooms. The children had given me all sorts of things, Val had made me slippers, Lois had given me six coupons! Rosemary came back from her dance, which had been a bit of an orgy, as they had collected most of the drink in Campbeltown, but quite fun. She brought a great whack of mistletoe which we hung up. I gave the maids £2 each—twice last year—and got much kissed, we undid parcels after breakfast . . . Someone I've completely forgotten, who fished here in summer, sent me a huge cake from Glasgow, various people sent hankies the nicest from Margaret, a wood engraving from Agnes [Miller Parker] but her work has become so fine it is more like a steel engraving than a wood one.

Lilla, Peter and Ellen came to dinner, we had a goose from the Lochgair hotel instead of the usual turkey; it was very good. The maids had a chicken; we each had a pudding, and I had kept some ginger. Lachie was ploughing and Duncan [Semple] came over to see how he was doing. . . . He went down and I followed after carving the goose; he was setting the plough a bit differently so as to get the skimmer lower; I hadn't understood what it was for. But he says Lachie is doing well, only that he should make his breaks with the horses not the tractor, so as to get them straighter. He also said I should get two new pairs of socs—one for ley and one for stubble, that they sometimes didn't last more than a couple of days of tractor ploughing. I didn't know that . . .

Then the children began to come for their Christmas party; we lit the candles, and brought them in. There were about 18, mostly small ones, including small Anne Jackson. I had a book for each, mostly Penguins and Puffins, and a whistle or blow-out, relics of pre-war or immediately post war. Goodness knows what I'll have next year.

They were all thrilled with the tree, which did look lovely. We played musical bumps and blind man's buff, but they tended to segregate rather firmly into boys and girls. We had made jellies with some rather peculiar jelly guaranteed to contain nothing, and some tinned fruit, but they didn't like it much, or the milk shake which I think is so good. We also had buns and biscuits with chocolate spread. We had the tree in the musical box from Munich turning round and tinkling.

Murdoch had written a post card, he is at Dover, had a good weekend in London with Anne [his girlfriend].

The children went on playing, finally left about 6.30. I tried to teach Cathie the schottiche. I was feeling pleased as we all were, at Darlan's assassination★ . . .

We had supper and went over to the Hall. There were finally about thirty-five people there, but none of the fishermen; Johnnie's wife had said he was very keen to be there, but she didn't know if he'd be back. They can't risk losing six or seven hundred pounds! Hugh, Angus and Lachie were there, but not, I think, from any employer feeling, also Donald, Duncan, Duncan M and Mary, Reppke, Ian Sellars and Jenny, various Patersons etc. Dick had been preparing this all day, and made a very good job of it. He spoke for an hour and a half, and I think held everyone's interest. He explained it in some detail, but it's difficult to remember figures at all. It would have been better with a blackboard. There were quite a lot of questions. Tom Mouth (Paterson), asking about pensions, Duncan about farm workers, Reppke, Donald, myself, an insurance man, etc. Donald getting very left over things now. Dick suggested things the fishermen should do, and old Mr Cook said they ought to take it up. Willie was in the Chair. It was all very informal, and worth doing. Some came back to the house afterwards to go on asking questions. . . .

. . . On the way out I drew Donald Jackson's attention to the mistletoe—whereat he seized me, took me right off my feet and gave me no end of a kissing. I had no idea he would be so strong though of course he's a farmer's son . . .

★ Darlan was a French Admiral and a firm advocate of the Vichy collaboration with Hitler. When Hitler occupied southern France, he finally turned to the Allies for support and, much to the disgust of many people in Britain, he was allowed to retain his authority. Shortly afterwards, in North Africa, he was mysteriously assassinated.

Around this time, Naomi began to develop her friendship with Rosalind (Rowy) Wrong, a young historian who was later to marry Murdoch Mitchison. Rowy became a frequent visitor to Carradale House.

Wednesday 30 December 1942
Still this awful cold, and my head feeling like a beehive. Val did tea. Rosalind Wrong and I had a very interesting discussion about ancient history and patterns of life; she calls herself a "Church and State Tory" but is obviously a "person of good will". I suppose this is the reaction against the left to which one expected all the young to belong, automatically. I feel she is no way an enemy and is very intelligent. All those Party labels are getting no end mixed up. She knows a satisfying amount about the middle ages . . .

Thursday 31 December 1942
Slightly better but a bit wuzzy after a big dose of dial last night. Read Storm Jameson's last book, rather good. After that when I came down, arrangements about the party, sandwiches, furniture moving, records, tidying, re-dressing the tree. Paterson sent me a cake as a present; I have had two from Glasgow as presents, very useful. . . . Dick fixed up with Duncan Munro about the tree that fell on Sunday, gave the men ten bob each and Duncan himself, after much protest, £1 and a branch of rhododendron. The praecox is all in flower.

Various people from the *Nemesis* [submarine in bay] turned up, but not Dorothy and her friends whom I half expected . . . Val's swords for the dance stuck somewhere in Campbeltown! Craig says he'll find them and send them back with Park. No buses tomorrow.

We got the party arrangements more or less done, the extra loaves and so on. I washed my hair, but hadn't yet got changed when Denny M turned up—I hadn't known the boats were in . . . Then, when I had put on my old white velvet dress, the rest came, though not nearly as many as I expected or as had accepted, even, but it was an awful night, wet and stormy. As it was they finished masses of sandwiches, buns, parkins, cake and currant bread, orange and lemon squash, milk shake but oddly, not quite all the whisky! However Denny M, Rob and Sandy all had their own bottles. Rob and Sandy arrived drunk, Denny M was dead sober all the time, Jimmie Downie was extremely drunk and amorous . . .

. . . with the others, alcohol had a definitely good effect; Lachie for instance, had got confidence, was gay, full of ideas, and kissed me without inhibitions at midnight. Ian MacLaren, who brought me a silver brooch, got rather class-conscious, kept on taking Bernice and Anne into corners and saying he was only a poor uneducated plumber, which was fun for everyone. . . . We danced a mixture, extra mixed because Anne had muddled the records, but some country dances, a good set of quadrilles, Rory O'More, Dashing White Sergeant; at midnight we all gathered; it didn't seem the moment for anything solemn but Dick told an extremely good funny story, bringing all the main characters in, starting with a herring, then they all sang "A Gude New Year" and "Auld Lang Syne", then we all went round, shaking hands and kissing one another . . .

After New Year four of the young cooks came round first footing; we offered them whisky which they wouldn't take, but did take milk shake and cake, and came in and danced. Rob had a great difficulty about going home because he couldn't first-foot himself, and his hair the colour it is! He also quarrelled with Robbie Campbell about some old poaching offence and I kept on trying to make the peace saying what's a salmon among friends, and he kept on saying the bugger, the old bugger.

We lit the Christmas tree again, as I have enough candles for next Christmas, and after that perhaps—and had enough streamers to throw about. They all liked the tree.

Meanwhile Denny M had fallen heavily for Rosalind Wrong. He really has an unerring instinct for girls, he can tell their points, like Duncan Semple can a cow's, and he can see when they are "kind of solid". And with that he will always and invariably stop when a lassie says stop. But what with him and Rosalind, Ian MacLaren and Anne or Bernice, and small Ian asleep on the sofa, one hardly knew where to go! Alastair and the two Lynn girls were both there, very friendly and nice, and the new District Nurse came out of it extremely well—when the chairman of one's nursing association staggers up to one asking to have his pulse felt—! The Navy enjoyed themselves very much, especially the custom of kissing at the New Year . . .

. . . It was funny how a quite drunk man, who can't stand, can yet dance a schottiche. But we didn't have many of the really nice country dances because there weren't enough people to do them. It is still the waltzes of various kinds that people like best. One lovely thing was that Rosalind had found a lot of flowering rhododendron, the praecox, so we had great bunches of it everywhere. We had about one long shelf of Christmas cards. *Forward* has a letter which I must answer about nationalism and education.

1943

ON 2 FEBRUARY 1943, the Germans were overwhelmingly defeated by the Russians at Stalingrad. Although the war was to continue for a further two years, it seemed like the beginning of the end. As the Germans were driven out of Russia, a massive wave of pro-Soviet solidarity swept through Britain, expressed through 'Red Army Day' and 'Aid to Russia' weeks. Less enthusiasm was shown to the thousands of American soldiers who had been pouring into Britain since January 1942. Naomi did not have very much direct contact with American troops although she frequently entertained parties of British sailors from the nearby submarine depot. It was to members of de Gaulle's Free French Forces that she extended the most sustained hospitality and care. In March, Pierre and Gilbert arrived at Carradale House and later Paul, Guy, Georges and Yves. Naomi gave them all pseudonyms in her diary for security reasons. Several of them had been in prison in Vichy France.

When she had time off from running the household, Naomi returned to research on her book, *The Bull Calves*. It was, however, difficult to devote as much time to her writing as she wished. She had been elected President of the local branch of the National Farmers' Union and was preoccupied with the problems of farming, particularly with bureaucratic battles over getting her cattle recognised as an attested herd. She had been allocated a Land Girl, and in January Maisie Black arrived at Carradale House to help with the farm work, particularly the milking. The Women's Land Army, which had been re-formed in 1939, organised teams of young women, many of them inexperienced in farming, to work on the land and to assist farmers in place of the men who had been called up.

Postwar reconstruction was a major topic of conversation. It was fuelled by the publication of the Beveridge Report in December 1942. Dick Mitchison was still employed with Douglas Cole in the Nuffield Survey and was well-placed to make submissions on the fishing industry from his discussions with the Carradale fishermen. Naomi's chief interest, apart from agricultural policy, was educational reform.

For the elder Mitchison boys, life was changing fast: Denny and Ruth both qualified as doctors during 1943 and Denny expected to be called up to the RAMC. They were sharing River Court with another medical couple,

Michael and Sybil, who also had a baby. Ruth planned to return to work as soon as they could organise adequate care for the babies. Murdoch was now engaged in war weapons research with the army.

Friday 1 January 1943
. . . In the evening was the ceilidh and dance. I wondered how many folk there thought of the bad luck of the last two New Year ceilidhs. I did, but of course said nothing about it. It was very full; the chairman was Neil Grant, secretary of An Commun. He made what I thought a bad speech, archaising, talking about the necessity of Gaelic and preservation of culture until I felt completely hostile! We *must not* archaise. The new Scotland may not be what any of us visualise, it may have a new set of values, it may go through a phase of hatred of ancient history, as the USSR did; we must not worry about that, it doesn't matter. The history will still be there. There was a little good singing, especially a red-haired Campbell from Campbeltown, who had a real sense of a song, but not a big voice—there was an excellent accordionist. Neil Grant sang an Oran Mor, which I liked enormously, though I don't know how many else did . . .
. . . I had a pleasant and useful talk to Grant about Convention, Scotland etc. He is really an old dear, well-meaning. When I was talking to Alec he said what balls it was, that everyone should concentrate on social change, not on keeping anything—the Gaelic should all be swept away—but I said that people like Grant couldn't do that, it wasn't part of their ability . . .

Saturday 9 January 1943
. . . Had a long talk, my first these holidays, with Avrion. Started with discussing truth, which he agreed was a good thing but not the most important. I asked him what was—he said Charity, adding Love. I said the difficulty was tolerance had been over-stressed as a virtue; he agreed saying active goodwill was necessary. He is very pro-Quaker, but not a deist. He said J.C. didn't believe in God; I said well, he kept on talking about his Father in heaven. We agreed that a lot of it was done to impress the fishermen, and that he had to do something like rising from the dead to impress them. Av said it was a pity he hadn't just told the truth and that he supposed that there had been various people who had done so, without miracles, and had been forgotten. Christianity could only be any use if you talked away the last fifteen centuries or more. People came down to talk at school services but

"none of them were Christians". But it looked as if something was happening in Europe. He also spoke of a debate on happiness at school, where one boy had read a good paper, he was a Czech whose parents had been killed; we discussed what effect it might have to have a sufficient number of foot-loose people such as that growing up. Another boy had spoken about bourgeois morality, the sort of stuff, said Av, that he had outgrown a year ago.

He talked of death and I explained that I found it now interesting and not frightening; he said he would rather not think about it till he was thirty. Also about the "good life", especially the Quaker kind, and how dull it seemed, and I said I didn't think it was when one got inside . . .

Sunday 10 January 1943

. . . The Beveridge thing most interesting; I rang up Johnnie and asked him to get hold of some of the others and come over this evening. It's very difficult to understand, all the same.

Johnnie, Rob, Sandy and Gilbert 'Tosh turned up, Denny M still in bed with flu. We had a long discussion. They didn't know much about the Beveridge report to start with. Apparently most of the boats now are insured so part of Dick's security proposals had to be re-written. They all want unemployment pay of some kind, but see the insuperable difficulty of deciding about it. Most of them make up their stamp books when they stop fishing in March; they are worried at the much larger payment involved under the Bev scheme, especially for the skipper . . .

. . . A lot of bad feeling about the threat to close Campbeltown and Tarbert and force the boats to go to Ayr. Thomson, one of the arbitrators, is always on the side of the buyers. The buyers say they don't want to waste petrol and tyres. The fishermen say there is a fish-carrier laid up in Tarbert and why not use that to take the herring to Ayr? It is very hard on the small boats as it is.

They were all very much interested, keen to get something done. I hope they will make Dick into some kind of official of the Fishermen's Association; it would be easier for him to work for them. Sandy, who had a Canadian fur hat, given to one of his sons by a Canadian steward (in exchange for whisky?), was unusually sensible.

Dick went back and worked on the letter till the small hours. I was pretty miserable, as I seem to have seen very little of him and there was a lot I wanted to discuss before he left . . .

Friday 15 January 1943
A fine day, and a pure Galloway bull calf born; we went over and petted it and tried to get its mother to let us look in her ears for the marks, but she was wild and swung about, so finally we had to drive her into the byre, with the calf; she went quite gently, and has obviously been handled. We found she was Rambler Rose, and the calf by Monarch, so we have called it Timoshenko [after the Russian General]. It is a lovely little beast and I think we might keep it to replace Monarch. It has a curly coat like a Labrador. I went to Dippen to borrow the forceps for marking it, but then found I didn't know how they should be marked. I have a TT number, but don't know the herd book arrangement.

When the girl comes I'll bring the bull into the mutton shed and take the cows down to the point. I think the new land-girl, when she comes, can do that . . .

Wednesday 20 January 1943
. . . All the day I was thinking about Stephen [Spring Rice] whose submarine is nine days overdue. Odd how it's always the flower of the flock. I just can't write to Margy. Enid wrote to me about George, saying how awful it was not to be able to protect one's young. Nobody ought to fight till they're forty. Till they're old enough not to die wanting their mothers . . .

Monday 25 January 1943
. . . Maisie Black [the new Land Girl] turned up, not obviously prepossessing but nice and sensible. I only hope she will be strong enough. Bella . . . doesn't seem to think she should have meals with me. However! I took her round and explained things, we made a bit of the compost heap. She seems a bit educated and keen on reading and so on, one sister is an industrial chemist, worked at evening schools after she left school, and so on. She seems delighted to have come here. Likely to be generally helpful. I think she is socially conscious too, though I didn't talk politics. We discussed education a bit.

Thursday–Saturday 28–30 January 1943
To Glasgow by plane; . . . spoke at women students' union lunch, rather difficult as audience coming in and out on way to lectures. Everything obviously being done by minority mostly communist and nationalist. Sat with girls making paper flowers and giggling and

talking politics: very friendly and a kind of relief. Met Education
sub-committee at Cranston's, Baillie MacNicol a nice old tough, left
of Labour, Kilgour, Agnes Thomson. Later a WEA man. Discussed
what we were going to do: make a report on the HCG of progressive
opinion about education. Made a list of heads. Decided who to co-opt.

Later went to an Executive [of the Scottish Convention], about a
dozen people, mostly Glasgow professional. A curious atmosphere,
rather bawdy, far more so than any southern highbrows. But oddly
earnest, people trying to be truthful with one another. I find it difficult
to express because what is happening, if there is anything, hasn't
emerged enough to be described. We decided about our meetings in
Edinburgh and Glasgow and what we were all going to say, and how
the thing was to be worked up. Decided to have the psalm "Israel shall
save" as the Convention signature tune (though I doubt if any of the
Executive are churchgoers) and to get it properly sung. Decided to
keep the old words though John MacCormick had written others.
They have taken big Halls in Feb. I suggest Mass-Obs gets some of its
Edinburgh or Glasgow people to comment separately. I got the
feeling that we were somehow reasonable and in a way disciplined.
Not just looking for places, for individual power. Yet gay some way. I
never felt like this about any political thing before, I never felt so
whole hearted about even the King's Norton Labour Party. It seems
more my kind of show yet I hardly know why. Difficult that we have
to be "conventionalists"—teasing one another on that, someone
whistling Kirriemuir. They are tough in a way that I recognise, that
appears to me right. Or what? . . .

Sunday 31 January 1943
Awfully tired. Couldn't sleep, kept on thinking about crises, also
about Margy. I don't get her and Stephen out of my mind at all. Dick
talking about Carradale after the war and things that could be done.
But I think there will be revolution and everything utterly different.
Sometimes I want that violently, other times I only want a lovely
holiday and everything done for me by pre-war maids!

Although Allied successes in North Africa had improved morale at home, the
British were still suffering heavy losses at sea. Gradually, towards May 1943,
with the introduction of radar techniques, the balance started to shift. It was
too late, however, for young Stephen Spring Rice, the son of Naomi's friend
Margery. Naomi eventually heard that his submarine had been torpedoed.

1 February 1943
Lunch with Lewis now a Col, and Zita. Talk about North Africa. Old
Friends etc. I prowled down to the London Library, much shocked at a
hammer and sickle in Asprey's window. Got Dick's choc ration from
Charbonnel and Walker. At London Library met Aylmer [a cousin]
and gossiped about the family. To Fabian Society, and had tea with
Margaret. We got a wedding present for Beveridge—two tea
cosies . . . I said I was sure there'd be some in the millinery department of the Army and Navy. A lot of Beveridgiana going about!
Back in a very crowded underground but I went on writing my
book.

At Oxford with Elizabeth Pakenham. As Beveridge's personal assistant,
Frank Pakenham had been closely involved in the preparation of the Report.

Thursday 4 February 1943
. . . Elizabeth tough and cheerful, iron-nerved, with five children
under eleven and only one woman to help; all having flu and middle
ear trouble. Says everything is grand, but she doesn't think she can
manage more than another year. Says she was afraid she was getting
cancer of the brain . . . but now thinks it's all right. I think Oxford is an
extra hard place to live in. Frank very cheerful; we argued about
Catholicism and Beveridge. He wants Dick to speak and do some
writing; I tried to fix up things with Dick later. Very good for Dick to
get back into politics, to feel he was doing something worth while. He
says there are Beveridge groups springing up all over the place "Three
psycho-analysts in Northampton" or some dotty gang like that and he
tried to get them speakers. Meanwhile Bev thinking he's going into
Parliament and becoming almost too megalo-maniac . . .
 . . . The Navy billetees [at Naomi's mother's house] very shocked
about N. Africa, as everyone is, but they, dangerously, put it all down
to the Americans and use it to foment anti-American feeling which
some of them have violently, my mother always had, but the Right
have it on nationalist grounds and because of American arrogance, and
the Left have it because they don't like Wall Street and American
foreign policy . . .

Naomi had been unwell with symptoms she suspected might be early
menopausal, and part of the purpose of her visit to London was to have some
medical tests. Margaret Lloyd had worked with Naomi at the North

Kensington Birth Control Clinic in the thirties and they had remained good friends.

The calls for the opening of a Second Front against Hitler had been intensified since Stalingrad. On the party political front, the truce between the large parties had left the way clear for the proliferation of smaller parties and independent candidates. One party, Common Wealth, founded by Sir Richard Acland and J. B. Priestley in July 1942, was achieving notable electoral successes. Tom Wintringham, former commander of the British Contingent of the International Brigade during the Spanish Civil War and a mainstay of Home Guard training, stood for Common Wealth at the North Midlothian bye-election in February and came comfortably close to winning a previously safe Conservative seat. The Common Wealth party urged the immediate implementation of the Beveridge Plan and was committed to a policy of 'common ownership' of land and industrial resources.

Jennie Lee stood at Bristol Central as 'Independent Labour' and although she was not elected, she caused a considerable stir in Labour Party circles.

Thursday 11 February 1943
The microscopic analysis is o.k. which is quite a relief, not that anyone ever breathed the word cancer! Feel all right only very rheumatic and difficult to sleep in the central heated room with heavy black-out. Saw Margaret Lloyd, who feels very red. Also in the evening Jane [Cole]. Both of them said they knew there must be a Second Front, but neither of them felt that they could shout for it, knowing what it would be in lives. "After all," said Jane, "it isn't us." Then talked about Stephen; they were to some extent in love . . .

. . . A very nice letter from Jean Semple, says she met Tom Wintringham in Edinburgh. Margaret although very sympathetic with CP hopes T.W. and Jennie [Lee] will get in. Not much chance though. Brailsford turned up, we talked about India mostly. God what a mess. I got up and took a small walk in the garden, which was nice. Also finished another chapter and some notes.

Thursday 18 February 1943
. . . Rosemary turned up, fairly well and full of news and talk. Saying how unpopular the Americans were in the south, the Aussies nothing to it. I said why particularly? She said oh, rape. I think we both felt a certain slight gratification as the Americans having been the ones to be beaten in N. Africa. One feels they deserve hell for wishing Eisenhower on to us, though God knows one doesn't want anything but victory! The Russian news at least continuously heartening. One feels com-

pletely fed up with Anderson and above all Kingsley Wood over the Beveridge report. But of course it's just what we all expected from the government . . .

On 18 February, the leader of the Scottish Convention, John MacCormick, came to speak at a meeting in Campbeltown. He was a man in his late thirties, a brilliant orator and one of the important figures in the Scottish Home Rule movement. He had been the first chairman of the Scottish National Party in 1928 and then the Secretary until 1942 when he left to form the Scottish Convention.

. . . Into Campbeltown. Lilla and Denny M in the bus, much to my relief. Also several other friends, whom erroneously, I thought might be going to the meeting. They were going to the flicks. We hung about in the committee room of the Town Hall, I feeling more and more nervous; then John MacCormick turned up. Finally we went up, and after giving them ten minutes after the time, started the meeting. There were between fifty and sixty people, so the hall was only a quarter full. No Navy, and few fishermen, but Mr Blackwood and various friends, and Willie Galbraith from Carradale. I opened badly, starting from cold. John spoke well and sensibly. Denny M spoke very well for a few minutes, asking fishermen of all parties "even the good old Communists" to come in. He didn't sound nervous, but his hands were twisting my bag to bits almost!

I did the latter part of the meeting all right, though informally; it was a dreich sort of audience and the Town Hall is a beastly room. So dirty. We had quite a good discussion, partly from old SNP men, partly from Labour folk, like Bob Leys. At the end they were all buying literature. We hurried to get the bus. It was crowded. Rather drunk, very cheerful. Old friend just behind me, rather drunk. I felt they were a damned ungrateful lot and deserved to be run by a lot of bloody Tories.

. . . John and I sat up till two in the morning talking about Convention and Scotland. I read him "The Knife" and he too became terribly excited, said it was magnificent, he had only had this experience once before, when someone was reading some old Scots poetry—and then he began to speak of adventures in his SNP and ILP days, and how he had seen a ghost between a meeting and a wedding and of the Sgiannachs* and their violent hospitality and of whatever the thing is in the Highlands.

* In Gaelic, Sgiathanach or men from Skye.

Naomi had been corresponding with Neil Gunn since the publication of his book *Second Sight* in 1940. Gunn had been active on Tom Johnston's various advisory committees on post war reconstruction for Scotland. Although sympathetic to the Convention, Gunn had been wary of joining it. The Mitchison/Gunn correspondence covered their shared political and literary interests especially Gunn's *Silver Darlings* (published in 1941) and Naomi's work-in-progress, *The Bull Calves*.

The meeting at the Convention seems to have been the first time they actually met.

Wednesday–Friday 24–26 February 1943
. . . Well then, meeting Neil Gunn in Glasgow, a tall, loose-limbed chap with grand bones, a kind of half squint, might have been Irish, might have been a fisherman, a bit like Willie Galbraith but with sense and ability. But probably as lazy—and maybe as fond of a glass, though he would take it with discretion. In no time at all we were walking hand in hand, laughing, he lifted me from a moving tram and kept his arms round me for that much longer than he need have. We talked mostly about Convention, the Beveridge report, committees, fishing, the film of his book, Alba our mother and the signs of the times. Yet there was an undercurrent through it all; he was saying he was going to the films that evening to see something special, but he came to the meeting. Yet, as we were going into the Usher Hall and the dusk on Edinburgh and the amethyst shadow deepening below the castle, he said Why are you going to this meeting? And I couldn't think at all, but I went. And when I got to the small room at the back where the other speakers were, and feeling nervous enough, there was Betty Mackenzie and by her a lad in battledress and it was a moment before I saw it was Stewart Watson, come up from Berwick on twelve hours' leave, and then I knew why I had come.

We trooped on to the platform, and everyone else seemed easy and confident except myself—and perhaps John MacCormick. Lady Glen Coats [member of Liberal Party] was being very much a practised speaker, and the Minister of course wouldn't worry. I felt half sick . . .

I was on fourth, after the collection and Lady G.C. who was pretty awful. There were about five hundred there, though the papers next day said more. It was an elderly audience mostly but I kept looking towards Neil. John made a good speech but didn't explain enough about what Convention is. The Minister was really talking about the church and I felt rubbed up the wrong way. I shoved the mikes away and pitched my voice low, for I know I could carry to the back of this Hall. I began to talk about ordinary people, and I think I spoke well and with passion and poetry, because I felt two or three times that tension in the audience, and I felt like a chewed rag at the end myself, and then we had "God save" and "Scotts wha hae" backed by the organs. Then I was talking to the Rendels and Uncle Willie and plenty more and Stewart looking at me with soft Highland eyes, and I kissed him. He had to get a train, but said would I send him papers.

Well then, most of the Convention folk went into the Rutland Hotel and everyone had drinks excepting myself, and Uncle Willie had gone back, so I said to Neil will you see me back—there had been a suggestion that William Power would come too, but I said Neil had better come back for him, and indeed Neil knew well enough that I was on for some devilment and away with us into the black-out and one another's arms, and I feeling all the time as though we were coming back from a Carradale dance and this Highlander the same as any of the rest of them. And the great pleasure we had to be kissing one another in the respectable midst of Edinburgh, and speaking of poaching and the companionship under the stars, and the fortunate thing that I had come back to Scotland! Yet all the time I was thinking also of Stewart Watson, the young Clydeside revolutionary and maybe more of a man and a leader than Neil. If he gets through this war . . .

Wednesday 3 March 1943
Mostly working at the fence round the hen run, tying on fish net, while Angus and Maisie finished the hen house. A snell east wind, after the warmth of the last two days. Rosemary got awfully cold. I don't know what to do about the house, I can hardly put on the heating just for her.

Jemima has had a baby girl, everyone says how disappointed she'll be, I wrote and told her how much her Dick would like it.

Two Free French who were in a N. African concentration camp coming to stay for three weeks, one of them had been condemned to death. I had offered to take a couple. They don't speak any English, it will be good for my French . . .

Monday 8 March 1943
The French turned up by the early bus, having got to Campbeltown yesterday. They started by being rather shy, but by the end of the day

were perfectly happy. Pierre speaks no English at all, Gilbert speaks and understands a little. Rosemary's French is very limited, . . . mine most fluent but highly inaccurate and occasionally I forget the most ordinary words. Gilbert is a low-brow, an extrovert, only wants feeding and looking after—he rushed off to shoot rabbits, I stopped him from shooting blackbirds! He also likes jazz music and all that. Pierre, who escaped twice from German prison camps (they were both in a variety of camps in North Africa), and was condemned to death by Vichy, is the hell of a highbrow, lived in the same house with Picabia and Dali, and so on; he is much more difficult, is gentle I think, but full of volcanoes. His folk at Toulon. Once he said if only his mother knew he was here. He particularly is wild about the beauty of the place, says it is so different from anything he had ever heard about the cold and fogs of Scotland, but I explained to him that there were fairies and so on. I took him over to the hall to play bowls; they were all very nice to him. We talked politics a lot too . . .

. . . We had a long discussion in the evening; Pierre showed me his dossier (photographed) and condemnation to death. Told me a lot about his experiences, some pretty mediaeval prisons, considerable torture, of the stripping naked in cold night and electric shock variety. A kind of cinema story with heroism and danger (once he was caught after not having drunk any water for four days, couldn't stand it any longer). Actually condemned after the American landing. Finally rescued because he had been discovered by a pro-Ally general, also condemned to death but fished out. His *avocat*, a man of the greatest courage, *un bon type*, sheltered him and others. I kept on interpreting. Gilbert talking of his adventures; both had tried various things to get to the prison hospital, easier to escape: G had pretended to be very weak, having refrained from eating and taken aspirin, was then given injections to give him an appetite but nothing to eat! Blessings of science. G kept on going off into fits of giggles at the prospect of shooting his judges *comme des lapins*, after the war. Pierre also much occupied with *revanche*. Thousands of French, and god knows, millions of Greeks, Poles, Norwegians, Dutch, etc, all feeling the same, what right have we from our comparatively bombproof pulpit to tell them off? They've got to be given something instead of revenge to fill the hole in the heart. I put my arm around Pierre's shoulder and said Take away power from such people but do not kill them. He said why not? I said because you won't want to. In a year one forgets. He said one must not forget. I said various semi-Christian things. I begin to wonder if one hasn't got either to be a Christian or else a historian, to avoid this revenge business ...

Tuesday 16 March 1943
... I had a surprising letter from Dick Acland [leader of the Common Wealth Party] asking me what happened to Christianity after the beginnings, having read my *Blood of the Martyrs*. I took down the Cambridge Ancient, which I think is my favourite book to look up something, almost wishing for an ivory tower.

Wrote letters but my own book some way stuck, perhaps because of being worried about "The Knife". Dr Somervell came and was really very good with these two; he hardly speaks any French so I had to explain everything; Pierre said he wanted injections of insulin; I couldn't think why, but Dr Somervell seemed to know that a small amount was good for putting on weight; he says he has dropped eight kilos. Somervell went over him fairly carefully, doesn't like his lung sound much, asked me to bring them both round to be weighed tomorrow. I was really horrified when I saw how thin Pierre's arms were, all the muscle gone; both of them a bit scarred about the body. Then Dr Somervell said didn't I think ten units of insulin rather much, I said hastily, knowing nothing about it, yes, I thought he should start on five and before dinner rather than before breakfast. And that I would give P some lumps of sugar to take about with him in case of a black-out, for insulin poisoning is the devil.

This evening they are dancing again, Maisie with them, I'm glad to say; it's nice for her and I'm sure they won't seduce her. Gilbert was looking at Gill's nudes saying all the time that there was this or that wrong, being a complete low-brow. I told him he ought to have photos.

The wretches went and shot two thrushes and a water-hen this afternoon; they brought them in and I threw a book at them and told them it was a *tuerie inutile* and they'd better bury them. The creature was so lovely with its green legs and red bill. I suppose people shoot anything in France.

Friday 19 March 1943
... I meant to go early to bed but went in to see the young and became engaged in an immense conversation about sex, which went on till two and was most illuminating, though, for my part, I found it rather shocking. The two men were completely practical, and somehow so

detailed, talking of love or of young women with the kind of concentrated attention and interest with which young Communists talk about politics. Betty [MacKenzie] didn't understand but Rosemary lapped it up and seemed also to find it in the same way interesting in detail and for *itself*. Now, I find love, or sex, interesting, but as part of something else: of society, of one's life and work, above all of general tenderness and *agape*. By itself it's no better than sugar alone with no other ingredients. Naturally if you take it by itself in this way, you find it a bit sick-making.

There was every kind of national misunderstanding cropping up, which I tried to soften. They had seen Piccadilly and various "dansings". They found themselves rather disgusted with the lack of finesse about everything, also with the difficulty of getting a room in a hotel where one could wash—and the slight amount of greater safety in a *maison tolérée*. I said it wasn't safe, but still it may be slightly safer than most large cities at the moment. But they think that everyone embracing in corners or in Hyde Park are going the limit, whereas they aren't in England; I tried to explain that but unfortunately my vocabulary rather ran out.

They said everyone here was dirty because there were no bidets and women didn't wash. I then got on my high horse as a North Ken B.C. clinic director and explained that douching removed necessary internal secretions and no modern gynaecologists approved of it! They also said how awful it was to have no means of washing in rooms after *accouplement*, and I said that obviously they had never really loved anyone, because when one did people went to sleep in one another's arms and to hell with washing. Then they asked if there were many girls of twenty-one who were virgins. Rosemary and I said that in the middle and upper classes almost all and in the working classes a good many. They thought we were joking. I added that a great many young men were in the same condition. That they thought even sillier. I told them about my own sons and their friends. Then Pierre and I got involved in long discussions about life and love, in which he was being "realist" and I "romantic" but he saying it wasn't possible for couples to have adventures after marriage: it was different for him, being "célibataire". I found myself a good deal shocked by this: if you are going to have sexual "purity" of any kind you bloody well ought to have it always. He seemed to think jealousy was inevitable; I said no, it could be made to turn other wheels; it was wrong. His general thesis was Human nature is like that, just like people say about wars. He seemed to think pretty highly of the family, but in an oddly abstract way. Meanwhile Gilbert, Rosemary and Betty were talking about fucking, if I may so express it, and about the smell that women in this country always have, because they don't wash enough during their periods. His head in Betty's lap—so that if he *really* dislikes B.O.!

Gilbert explained how fed-up he was with the English women who led you up the garden path and just at last moment said "Cheerio". I said I disliked that too, but it was a matter of *moeurs* and people here thought all that was part of the sport. Even the men found it amusing. Yet it did seem to me that there was this curious generalisation "les femmes". The man is individualised. Whereas women are just The Flesh. Not that this is entirely a French characteristic.

Monday 22 March 1943
. . . I went over to Dippen in the evening with my book, but stopped at nine as we all felt there really might be news from North Africa. Earlier I had helped to deliver a calf. When we went into the byre the calf's forefeet were sticking out, rather horribly, like some pale parasite; the heifer was in pain, mooing violently and disturbing the others. Two further along were fidgeting as though going to calf. Duncan [Semple] slipped into his overalls, and put a rope round one foot, then another round the other. He and Jean and I pulled, pulling hard when she contracted. The nose began to appear, the dark blind muzzle close down to the hoofs, we tried to loosen the stretched skin; Duncan put both feet against her, she was lying down now, and tugged with all his strength. Then the head came, he said he thought by the feet it was a bull. And then the shoulders and suddenly the whole thing shot out, a wet sprawl of eyes and legs, followed by a gush of blood. It lay limp on the floor of the byre and Duncan turned it over; it was a bull, would be sold next week or perhaps eaten by the thresher team. He took it away to the pens in a sack. The mother didn't heed, though the cow next her was interested. It was so astonishingly sudden, this new living thing in the world . . .

Thursday 25 March 1943
. . . Everyone was a bit flustered about the bombing of Glasgow, not that it seems to have been bad; everyone knew by the morning . . . We had another long, late talk in the evening, beginning with what it would be like if the Allies marched into Paris, and the general killing that would take place, and the smash of France, all the coast towns and

industrial towns just bombed to bits. Yet more chance there of a new socialist order of things: France as a soviet republic. We discussed Scotland and nationalism, but I found it incredibly hard to translate what I wanted to say into French, hard enough in English, but to get the shades of meaning, above all with the wireless dripping this frightful light music and jazz and stuff . . .

The news none too good, except that Russia holds. Dick thinks better of Churchill than I did. But Tunisia—! I wonder what Von Arnim* is like now, I used to think he was rather nice. . . . I keep on trying to correct Pierre's anti-German feeling into anti-Nazi feeling. But of course one feels acutely that we haven't suffered here. He has to be petted about France a hundred times more than I have to be about Scotland . . .

Friday 2 April 1943
They told me suddenly at breakfast that it was this Saturday they are going. I was rather upset as I'd thought it was the Saturday after, however they are probably at the stage where they won't get right till they have started work. I wish they could have had another few days, but there it is. Gilbert wants to see an eye specialist. I'd arranged for them to see Gimlet at Grogport, however probably he'd rather see a Frenchman. I tried to argue with them but there it was.

I felt all day like I do at the end of the holidays. One feels they are so defenceless, and besides I don't know if I shall ever see them again. I don't think I would have got as fond of any folk I wasn't so sorry for. I'm getting the addresses of their brothers in prison to write to, and they will send along friends in summer. I told them not to think of paying for the doctor. Then I gave Pierre the fair-isle jersey of mine he has been wearing. He blushed rather and then jumped up and kissed me, I feeling I mustn't be soppy. I explained that he mustn't think it was a tie, or that I was trying to get any rights over his mind or heart, that it was a token of solidarity and faith. I think he was rather moved, but god knows, he may be laughing at me, almost certainly will *sometimes*—not that it matters, indeed he probably ought to some times so long as he doesn't always—for after all the west Highlands aren't in it for lying compared with these ones. Yet what can I do but act according to my faith? It could be that my jersey would shake him out of a mood of cruelty or complete cynicism. It is odd, feeling so unhappy about their going! . . .

* German General.

Wednesday– Thursday 7–8 April 1943
Two days' threshing at Rhonadale. Av and I went, as I thought Angus wouldn't be able to stand the dust. We started from the house at 8.30. The first day there was a violent wind, constantly blowing and whirling the glittering chaff, striking one's eyes and nostrils with spicules, straw blowing, tarpaulins, whole sheaves, Duncan's trailer blown over into Rhonadale marsh, twisting itself free from the tractor. Through this the large humming thresher went on, counter-driving with its belts, simple mechanism, tying us all down to work its time. We worked in the steading at Rhonadale, the square of house and farm building. In the morning Av and I were mostly pitching up to Willie Hogg who was making the long blocks of straw in the dutch barn; I found that pitching up one of these great rough sheaves of straw was all I could do, strained my shoulders, I thought my heart. In the afternoon I took over from Lachie at the tail of the tractor, pulling out the bundles; he was nearly blind and so was I at the day's end.

We were thirteen at dinner in Rhonadale kitchen, waited on by Mairi and her sister who is back on leave. We were all too tired and blown about to talk. We had good vegetable soup and stewed brown veal—one of Duncan's calves. Milk to drink, I was sitting by Duncan [Semple] and he gave me the top of the milk. The others had mild ale at dinner and tea afterwards. Scones and pancakes with delicious pale farm butter and jam. It was like a Flemish last supper, the men rough and lined, only Av young and oddly innocent looking. Duncan occasionally said something and I made a few feeble jokes, teasing Duncan Williamson, the red headed handsome tinker. The tractor men were friendly and nice, one from Campbeltown. There were Hughie and MacBain from Paterson's and a shy, quite young Mac-Kinnon boy; the older MacKinnon, in a bright blue jersey, came later. We all agreed that we felt the worse for double summer time; it's awfully hard on farmers, and one feels it's so much earlier in one's bones. One has to start—a dairy farmer must because of his milk round—yet one breaks off early when the sun is still high and one can't comfortably go home and sit by a fire.

We had tea at five, milk for me, and "pieces"* and pancakes. Then we went on till a bit after six. Got a lift back on Duncan's trailer on top of the full sacks of corn, comfortable and somehow romantic, sweeping under the young larch.

* Thick sandwiches.

. . . last night there was a Hall Management Committee. They brought up the question about the amplifier and my letter asking for Sunday opening. I didn't expect to get it past but thought they might be a little less reactionary. However they all were against me. Peter MacKinven proposed opening the Hall for "religious instruction", a lecture, by someone, perhaps him, or a missionary! Duncan Semple said that they might have that in the church, the Session would approve. Then there was some backbiting about the churches . . . They mentioned the failure of Dorothy's bible study class. Of course it isn't what the children want. I tried to be awfully reasonable at first, then got more and more annoyed with them for being so bloody stupid. So bloody narrow. Finally I said I thought they were all being selfish, none of them were considering what the young people really wanted and needed, how they needed to be creative, not destructive, the sort of boys I was after wouldn't want to be lectured to, they'd want to do something. That was why I thought a debating society would be some good. Jessie Ban then went for me because they'd talk politics and politics weren't for Sunday. I said I thought they ought to learn how to speak, learn the elements of democratic organisation and then they wouldn't sit like dumb fish at the Fishermen's meetings when they grew up. At this Gilbert said (he is very Sabbatarian) that it was like the Hitler Youth. I said Nonsense, and from that moment I was seeing red. Gilbert then said that some boys had asked him would the Hall be opened on a Sunday. How did they know the question was to be brought up? I jumped up and said I was acting for the same reasons that had led my great grandfather to come to heathen Kintyre and to speak against the respectable, and if they accused me of breach of confidence, I would tell them that I had tried to find out what the boys wanted before writing the letter and had asked the boys, if my proposal was accepted, to back anything that was done and show they would help, and then I suddenly burst into tears and walked out. God knows what they or anyone in the Hall thought, and I don't care. I hope it will shake them to know they hurt me. I'm going to try and be tough. I hated them all, I hated Carradale. I knew they couldn't have hurt me if they had been indifferent. They only did because I loved them and wanted to help. Then Denny M and Dougie came in and I bit them, and they said nothing but tried to be kind. Then Denny M said something funny about dealing with people and wanting to be "Half-square" with them. I began to laugh. Then they petted me a good deal, and Denny M disowned his cousin Gilbert. I went on feeling pretty sore all the same; I said I had never refused to help any of them, and I was now half inclined to say why should anyone like me with a world reputation, have to submit to being bullied by a lot of villagers? I half wished I hadn't lost my temper and half felt serve them bloody well right, and that it might shake some of them up to know they'd hurt me. I shall try and rub it in to Angus. I didn't get a chance with Duncan today because we were so busy. But I was extra polite to the lorry men, who are staying with me now . . .

Friday 9 April 1943
. . . The children came tumbling off the bus in a heap, Lois and two friends one of whom hasn't been here, Val, Jane [Cole] and Humphrey [Cole]. We all talked hard, splashing against one another like waves . . . They all seem very quick and intelligent and knowledgeable after Carradale, very willing to help, too. All have quite a lot of school work too. Lois still very keen to join the ATS.

Sunday 18 April 1943
To Campbeltown, to fetch Denny, Ruth and baby, and to do various jobs. I took in the empties, got some cider, some of the rations, a pail, clothes pegs, things from chemist's shop, meat on emergency cards (one can never get extra here), lovely Cadbury's Dessert on sweet rations, buns, tried to get a spare battery for the electric fencer. Ruth looks very tired and thin, half weaning Petronella, Denny not too well either. Both had notes when they got back saying they'd passed, Denny now a doctor, Ruth about where he was in October. He is told he must sign a register before Monday, which is too silly, we concocted a telegram.

An awful conversation about the things that were bound to happen yet in the war—epidemics, death and disaster—I get so tense I could scream. Anything to get it over sooner; yet I *can't* "rejoice" at bombing Berlin, sinking troop carrier and so on.

In November 1942, regular raids on Berlin had begun and in May 1943, the RAF attacked the Ruhr dams.

Friday 30 April–Tuesday 4 May 1943
I got so depressed I couldn't even write my diary. It was Dorothy Melville, who had been over at Dippen and so on, seeing people. I feel now she may have got it wrong, but what she said was that they were

saying why on earth was I playing at farming, I was doing harm to the land, which someone else could make a good job of, and so on. They admire me as a writer but think otherwise I'm just butting in. That just doesn't square with people's actions, but I think there is that much in it, and it may be at least half true, and if it is, then everyone is laughing at me, even my own men. I felt like chucking the whole thing, but yet I couldn't. I've taken on commitments of various kinds. But I was prickly and black with hate and misery and the feeling that I had been betrayed.

It didn't help that the fishermen had a meeting about the pier and had got Brodie, the Glasgow engineer, down. He was staying with us—it was I who had first got hold of him for them when I heard vaguely that he had the old harbour plans. They asked him and Dick and Ian Stewart and Provost MacNair and the County Engineer (whom I would particularly have liked to meet) but not me, to see the harbour and so on. I gather Brodie himself was a little shocked and told them they should have asked me . . .

. . . On Saturday I was so unhappy that I went into the garden and shot a bullfinch. They have been taking all the apple buds and are perfect devils, but all the same I hate shooting them. It was singing while it ate the buds, and then I shot and it came tumbling down in a small cloud of falling blossom like something in one's heart.

I felt I hated my own men, I didn't want to go on farming with them. But one can't just stop. I felt I was anyway doing the whole thing badly, and then there was this garden opening on Wednesday and all the *canaille* of the village coming to look at the house. And I couldn't go on with my book because it was all about these folk and they had betrayed me, and I couldn't any more think or write in their tongue. The only thing that cheered me at all was that Denny M had rung up from Glasgow to ask how the harbour thing had gone . . .

Paul, another member of the Free French Forces, has arrived in Carradale.

. . . Dick very busy being hospitable to the Frenchman [Paul], who is very nervous and talks all the time, but is awfully nice, all the same. He says some odd things for a CP organiser, for instance that he wishes Trotsky were alive, if he had been, there wouldn't have been this war, the Comintern didn't see things right. That made me blink! All his folk, Alsatian by origin, have land and factories and things in North Africa, are all sympathetic, for instance he can always commandeer one of their many cars for a meeting, or if he has friends hidden at his house he can always get a few turkeys or wild boars or what-not from a brother. His mother brought up two wild boars with a bottle . . . they feed the pigs on peaches . . . all the family have lots of horses and guns, are boxing champions . . . he has nine nephews and nieces, seven brothers. He was speaking of the radio after the fall of France, the big double salon, and the bedrooms beyond it, and each brother listening with his door open, and then gradually all stealing into the salon and turning it up louder, and all weeping, but each of them thinking beforehand that the others mustn't be upset—and the underground organisation, the De Gaullistes, some CP and some not, the tact necessary for dealing with Americans who would have been horrified if they had thought him communist. And so on.

Dick gave him brandy and cigars, I gave him milk. He is down a stone and a half. I took him to the doctor's to be weighed on Monday after the others had gone. I think he is more friendly than the other two, deep inside, he has hope and if you have hope and faith you can afford to be sympathetic, to think of other people, I expect he will be slightly edible! But the language thing is a strain. Even Dick, who is very good, was a bit rusty. The children all tried hard to talk French and got on a bit. Av was fooling and extremely funny, even to the chap who didn't understand it all . . .

Wednesday 19 May 1943
. . . It was rather nice painting [the greenhouse]; I am getting better at it and when I get fed up I go and lean against the ventilator of the low house and smell the hot wind coming up out of it off the peach trees, like a wonderful drink. I kept on wondering whether a German woman, doing the same job, might feel it was marvellous to be doing the same as the Führer had done. I am having my usual squabbles with Mr Downie about vegetables. I did a risotto for supper with lots of herbs in it, which was good, also chocolate biscuits, potato scones and a salad, mostly water cress and slipped in the mud and nearly sprained my ankle getting it. I used some of my remaining olive oil on it, too.

Paul suddenly explained about a girl, now in the ATS, to whom he had been more or less engaged . . . Anyhow he seems to be staying on and I wrote and asked if she could come for a weekend; she probably can't. I showed Paul my letter in which I explained that he was like a son of the house and he became very emotional. We have got past the stage of shouting at one another and he is now just very affectionate.

The doctor diagnosed that Rosemary was suffering from an internal cyst and an ambulance was called out to take her to hospital in Glasgow. Naomi went with her.

Wednesday–Saturday 26–29 May 1943

. . . We drove through and past midnight, the blackest time being on the Rest. It began to lighten on Lomondside and the mountains beyond with patches of low mist on them. R a bit fidgetty, I cold and wanting to sleep. We got to the hospital at four where a sleepy house surgeon and two or three more or less cross nurses took us in hand. After several people had asked R her name, age and religion and prodded her, and inquired after her state of cleanliness and had left her about on a stretcher, and I trailing after along corridors and in lifts, carrying various packages and feeling like something the cat had brought in, I made up my mind that the Voluntary Hospital system must GO. She was then put into a room and left, luckily still under the influence of morphia. I was told to go in for a minute, was then turned out; I sat outside and after a bit asked rather sternly if there was any reason why I shouldn't go in. After that I sat with her and tried to keep her calm and cheerful . . .

About seven, one of the real surgeons turned up, so I went off, saying I'd come back, feeling very cross and tired, asked my way from the porter who said take a car going west. I said how would I know which west was and the sun not to be seen. Then a policeman took me over to the bus stop and several times asked if I was sure I had the money, he would gladly pay my fare . . .

. . . In the afternoon I went twice to the hospital, rang up Dr Hunter, Dr Mackenzie etc, sent wires and letters to Rosemary's folk, got her stamps and things and generally tried to be useful, was pretty tired by the end. Went to a Convention Executive, where we argued and abused one another for two and a half hours but none of us lost our tempers nor got hurt with one another. Discussed organisation and nominations for the National Executive. I said I'd stand as vice-chairman if I had to. We discussed who were any use and whether it was a good thing to have people as far to the right as Liberals and so on. John proposed Denny Mac for the national committee. The education committee met, and incidentally scrapped my pamphlet which is a nuisance, rather, as I did work on it at times when I was frightfully busy and would much rather not have. However, as a matter of principle, I accepted it as a decision. I wish I could get up more often ...

Saturday 5 June 1943
Wet in the morning, fine in the afternoon and lovely down on the beach. Margaret [Lloyd] and I walked and talked. Paul wrote his article and insisted on reading it aloud; alas, he uses the most awful clichés all the time. I may be able to translate it into something, but—! ... Margaret and I still talking hard. I do so like having someone of my own, as it were, to talk to. I usually have to listen to people, and I have my human moments of wanting to talk about myself—instead of just putting it into this diary.

Sunday 6 June 1943
... In the afternoon Ian [MacLaren] turned up, we sat by the fire and discussed books and politics, later joined by Hugh. Ian wanted to try Joyce, but having looked at *Finnegan's Wake*, turned it down. Finally borrowed Eliot and some Auden (whom he had never heard of I read some aloud). He had been reading Lawrence, said what interested him was to see the author behind the poem. Then we talked about how the Conservatives were pulling themselves together and already forgetting their promises of 1940. He said I don't like revolutions, but I see no other way out of it. Then he attacked Hugh about the badness of education, and said the schools should all be improved—as a plumber he knows the Carradale school well! I asked him how his own job was from the social point of view and he said he liked it very well, it was always interesting, only his apprentices sometimes didn't know how to write their own names, he had to lam them sometimes. I said that was no way to deal with the young. But all the same I don't think he lams them hard! Then I groused to him a bit about Carradale, and we discussed Convention and what could be done.

Tuesday 15 June 1943
... In the afternoon we got the sheep into the tank and began shearing. I did seventeen. Several had the beginnings of maggots. Very horrid. We rubbed on dip and then removed the dead maggots with knife blades. There were a lot of ticks too. But the fleeces were lovely inside, a bit warm and rough. When the sheep were half sheared they looked like ideas coming into words. I kept on thinking about

that and about Spencer's picture, and the new images for my book and whether anyone would want real wool after the war . . .

. . . At 6.30 there was the harbour committee. Dick in the chair, McCallum, the MP, Peter John Campbell and Provost MacNair on the platform, and the rest of us on two rows of chairs. They would address us as "Lady and Gentlemen" which was annoying. Actually it was all quite useless; nothing happened, except that McCallum was very affable and said he'd help all he could—not that he can, but he wants votes. Peter John just blithered. He explained how he had wanted the harbour for twenty-five years while he was factor getting thirty shillings a week—but of course MacKenzie didn't want it! He said how he looked forward to Carradale becoming "a proper seaside town" with lots of bungalows all along the Bay. Here Duncan Semple whispered to me that he liked Carradale better as it is. Dick said that of course he wanted to see everybody properly housed, but wasn't it the duty of the Council to "house the working classes"? Peter John said they had done that, had built "a beautiful city—sixteen houses"! Provost MacNair rather unfairly blamed us for not sending the petitions in yet; most of them are done, but he had told Red Rob not to send them in till July. Afterwards the McCallums and Peter John came back and drank coffee and whisky. Dick tackled Peter John about County Libraries. Peter John said what was the good, they only read westerns and anyway, books only put ideas into people's heads. Provost MacNair who is rather proud of the miserable Campbeltown Library, got quite angry . . .

Thursday 17 June 1943
. . . I talked a lot to Guy [a new French soldier] who is extremely full of hate and wants to destroy all the Boches. I try to point out that historically nothing ever comes of revenge but at the same time, he's bound to feel like that—for I don't want him to feel embarrassed at talking to me. He's got to be able to talk, get all that into the open. He stood his two years of prison extremely well, I think. Far better than Gilbert. He also said that women in the army lost all their feminine charm and added that he was awfully shocked at the way women in London would sleep with four different men in one evening. I can't think where the French find these ladies! He added that I mustn't think *he* behaved like an American. They do hate the wretched *Amériques*. I keep trying to put in some pro-American propaganda but not much use. The French make up their minds and that's that. Though all the

same I think I may have got at Paul more than he would for the moment admit.

Tuesday 22 June 1943
. . . Much to my surprise the BBC have accepted my education script and want me in Glasgow on the 15th. I am thrilled, as I have never been allowed to broadcast before. I am practically a virgin! And there are various things I want to say in the script. And it will be nice to get an excuse to go to Glasgow. Only I can't get a plane that day which is a nuisance, they are all full of tired businessmen going to play golf on Islay . . .

Thursday 24 June 1943
Midsummer Day Fairly fine. We finished off the turnips, Lachie hoeing quite efficiently, I getting mud to the eyes. Then we drove the cattle up from the Bay into the meadow. I am pretty sure that one of the quey calves is a pure-bred, in which case we got the mother's ear markings wrong. They are awfully pretty calves. Old Monarch dashed through the fence to get a bite of potato tops which was very naughty of him. But he is a friendly old thing on the whole. It was lovely driving them along between the blue sea and the green bracken, everything all rain washed and brilliant . . .

. . . I had a long long talk to Guy, in fact I was nearly asleep at the end, all about politics and people and his various odd friends among the French and what might happen and his father. He is a nice, intelligent, brave boy and I do hope he survives. He has a great admiration for some of the old aristocracy—who have, I suppose, been winnowed out a good deal. In his part they have little holdings and take their own stuff into market and only go to Paris for a fortnight once every two years, but everyone looks up to them and loves them and they have great influence. Whereas the bourgeoisie are hell. This is the point of view of a thinking socialist, possibly near Communist.

Monday–Thursday 28 June–1 July 1943
. . . Very, very hot, we bathed a couple of times but when I'm by myself I never do. I am even slightly blistered with sun-bathing, go about in shorts and shirt but heavy shoes because of Jo [the horse]. I am dealing with him, hope I do all the right things, he is very friendly and sensible, better with me than with Maisie. He had one rather awful

time plunging about in the mower and broke a fence, but it was the flies. I am always being bitten by clegs, then the other flies come for the blood . . .

Constant small chores to do, people to see etc, and get very very tired. Usually wake with a headache, longing to get one good long night. Sleeping badly but daren't take dial in case I get a hangover. Feel at night as though I were going to faint . . .

. . . Quantities of people wanting to come in summer, no help to be had in the house. Feel like a distracted boarding-house keeper. Wonder whether to use all saved sugar this year or keep some to next . . .

Rosemary was discharged from hospital and returned to Carradale on 9 July, A third Frenchman, Jean, has arrived to join Paul and Guy.

Friday 9 July 1943

. . . A curious evening. Jean started talking about Commando training and parachute jumping. It was partly a show-off, so as to make the French girl and me say ooh, *les hommes*! I didn't. I tried to take it all as a circus though sympathetically, because I think it's dangerous if women start admiring men for being brutal, taking risks and generally living in an unintellectual and insensitive way. But even allowing for exaggeration, the commando training sounds pretty tough. The parachute jumping sounds really beastly; obviously they find it hell and always have their hearts in their mouths.

I asked if they were volunteers and was told not exactly, they had to volunteer for the honour of France. If anyone just couldn't, he had to take back his still folded parachute to the girl who had made it. I said I thought that was awfully unfair, especially to the girl; they didn't look at it that way. It sounded to me as if Judo would be a great help for any of these things. They are all bothered about the suppression of the "Marseillaise", though perhaps not so much as I am myself . . .

On her visit to Edinburgh to do a broadcast for the BBC, Naomi tried to find a replacement for Maisie Black, the Land Girl, who was about to leave Carradale.

Tuesday–Saturday 13–17 July 1943

. . . There wasn't a room at the Bath Hotel so I stayed with Miss Guthrie, we sat up frightfully late discussing Convention, rather gloomily, and I frantically sleepy. Next morning before my train I got a woolly vest and knickers (on Thursday a pair of sox), all I shall need this year. Then went to Edinburgh, got my books from the Signet, and read and made notes . . . The HQ [of the Women's Land Army] in George Square, the most exquisite part of Edinburgh, where I would love to live. It seems to me that people like me who want high-grade living, with all its pains as well as its pleasures ought to be able to have the eighteenth century sharp contrast between Capital and Country (though in either they can *work*). And we can't all crowd into London (which by the mere crowding becomes less a capital) so the more capitals the better. I would simply love to live half here and half in Edinburgh *if* Edinburgh was truly a capital, if I went there to sit in a Scots Parliament, or as delegate from the Kintyre Convention or Soviet.

. . . Then the BBC. I was awfully nervous and they rehearsed me for a good hour; I gather I was all right at the end, better than any rehearsal, but it was so difficult to remember all the points they told me and I felt a bit claustrophobic in the windowless room with the hard little mike in front of me. The people were all nice, at least I didn't like the director or whoever the senior was. I gather it was a triumph for Scotland to get any of their people on to the front page of the *Radio Times*. I said I thought some of the Carradale people would be marvellous at telling stories, hoping to get them taken. I kept on thinking of Carradale listening to me!

The Mitchisons allowed their land to be used for camping. The most frequent visitors were members of the YCL (Young Communist League) from Glasgow. Lois, Av and Val had returned for their summer holiday and the usual guests were also arriving: Jack and Helen, Eric Strauss, the Coles and Bernice Holt Smith, Lois' friends, the Angel sisters, Rowy Wrong, and Dick's friend, Tish Rokeling.

Sunday 18 July 1943
. . . Went over to the YCL camp in the morning, talked to them about town and country, what could be done, etc. We had an interesting discussion. One of them very keen on classical music, had started a class, now they were all going to concerts. A very nice lot, but with tremendous prolet accents, I think they're rather poor. I told them to go slow with the village and it would be better propaganda.

Later three more bicyclists, friends of theirs, turned up and asked if they could camp. I sent them over, they were rather fierce at first, but when one was a little nice to them, they thawed, produced sweet smiles and good manners. Finally two girl campers turned up, having walked from Tarbert, half dead. I gave them boiled eggs (they said they never got them) strawberries (same) and tea, put them to sleep in the library, as we have so few sheets. They too had almost unintelligible accents, would obviously have been like all other slum dwellers, but they had heard about me. It is rather disconcerting; they are *so* warm and trusting when you are nice to them; they suddenly let the whole burden of mistrust slip, they put the whole thing into your hands, as though you were their mother. It makes you feel (quite wrongly) that everything could be solved by people being reasonably kind.

Sunday 1 August 1943
Dick and I talked about things in bed for a long time though largely practical matters, arrangements about children etc. Murdoch's possible movements . . . He may be going to a special job which, though not as dangerous as Commandos, is quite sufficiently so. I do wish I could see him. . . .

Monday 2 August 1943
. . . my new land girl [Lena] turned up; being an Irish Catholic, she was shy of wearing dungarees; However she said one hopeful thing, that she wanted to be a nurse, but had found it boring because she got no lectures . . . She seemed quite competent [at milking] and Linda stayed still, but she has never washed a cow by herself, still less worked a steriliser. I showed her the byre things. After that Val and I picked fruit. We got three and a half lbs red jam gooseberries and two and a half red currants for our own jam. After tea we picked them over, and Bella made the jam, Bella very cross about the land girl, especially when I said she was to have a cup of tea to start with and breakfast after milking which is only sense . . .

Sunday 29 August 1943
. . . I felt awfully tired, so started properly reading Jung's *The Integration of Consciousness*, which I'd looked at before. I have had it in the house for several years but only just felt it borne in upon me to read it. Almost at once I came on the clue which showed me where my book was to go next, the moral plot, I mean, Kirstie and William as animus and anima, the projection by intelligent people who half know what

they're doing. I went half to sleep, getting this into images of a kind, then had cider for lunch, felt drunk and elated and talked, I think, with considerable brilliance and semantic quality, to the others, very largely about the difference it would make if there were not four airts or compass points but five, and so no complete opposite to anything . . .

For the past two months, the allies had been engaged in Italy. They had invaded Sicily on 9 July, and on July 25, Marshal Badoglio had replaced Benito Mussolini. Soon signs of a peace settlement were in evidence and Italy finally surrendered on 3 September.

Wednesday 3 September 1943
. . . Ian MacLaren rang up . . . I forgot it was six, but Rosemary went to speak to him and dashed back, saying he was listening at the same time and said Italy had capitulated. I turned on the radio but it took some time and we'd missed it and it wasn't in the summary. Sarah hadn't heard, but Hugh confirmed it. We were awfully excited, and told everyone . . .

. . . I felt frightfully pleased at tea and got out a pot of raspberry jam. We had the venison steak, but various people took enormous helpings, before the shooters who had got two hares, came in, and I was jumped on for not "as usual" providing enough. It is so bloody difficult catering, and I felt upset and hated them all, sitting round drinking, I just couldn't join or be pleased any longer. It's all very unreasonable, but they are all having holidays and I'm not. I feel like a hotel manager. I shall always be sympathetic with them after this.

Then the various dancers turned up. We did a couple of dances and then went in for the news. Everyone crowded round the rather faint radio; there was a general feeling, I think, of slight scorn of the Italians, and several people saying "a stab in the back" when it came to their remarks about the Germans. Only Bernice was wholeheartedly glad. I kept on thinking the German line would probably run south of the Lombardy plain, by Florence and Assisi and places like that. We also felt a kind of mixture of irritation and scorn against the Americans and Eisenhower, but hoped that all atrocities would be put down to them. We felt they would probably manage to push down the tower of Pisa and so on . . .

We none of us recognised the second national anthem but supposed it to be American. The dancers went back after the Italian news. I stayed for the Russian and the playing of the "International". I was so glad they had played it after all. I went back and told Dougie they had played it; we were dancing a waltz, he kept on squeezing me tight with happiness and solidarity. I said Now we can really begin to plan, and to think of after the war. He said Aye, it will be our fight . . .

Monday 13 September 1943
. . . A lot left, Humphrey and Margaret, the two nice Angels, who are just sufficiently American not ever to be English school girls, Dick for a few days, Rowy and Murdoch. If only I could be sure when Murdoch would come back. I shall, I suppose, water his cactuses and all that. His empty room still smells of him. Rowy will come back; we had a long, running, political argument. We believe in so many of the same fundamentals, but she calls herself a Tory, because she has read so much history and believes in a structure of society which she calls the State, and also in the individual and feels that both may be overthrown by her (wrong) concept of revolution. We argued endlessly last night about the individual and society, Av occasionally crashing the argument, Val coming into it and wandering off on to the individual and creation.

When people come it is partly pleasure and partly the feeling of more work to be done. When they go it is partly misery and partly the feeling that now one will have to tidy . . .

Wednesday–Friday 22–24 September 1943
Glasgow . . . I had a long talk to Philip Dundas [a distant cousin who farms in Kintyre] in the Hotel; he is inclining to a woolly form of socialism, means awfully well, may get depressed because people don't respond at once, hopes to run Kildalloig as a co-operative, is starting Ayrshires. We talked about morals, politics, cows etc. Then went out to John MacCormick's flat up some very sinister stairs but modern and comfortable when one got there, a very nice wife, plain and pregnant and full of kindness and awareness and good sense, two small boys. He was helping to produce the *Express*, didn't get in till late.

. . . The next day back on the boat, very crowded, various people I know, including Mrs Ferguson who says that when she has herring in the café the naval officers all like it but the ratings don't.

I talked to the old man with the xylophone or dulcimer or whatever it is who used to accompany Mrs Kennedy Fraser.* I always ask him for some special Gaelic song but he hardly ever remembers it but usually gives me something else. His face always works while he's playing in an almost mad way. I think his instrument is pretty awful but it gives him such pleasure to be taken seriously.

I also wrote a bit of my next chapter. At Tarbert, a bus was induced to go to Carradale. Several of the fishermen got in, including Denny M and Willie, to whom I showed the answer the Fish Division have sent to Scottish Convention about Carradale being a landing port. They suggested answers. Denny had some herring for me. They'd had a fair week, but some boats had had badly torn nets, and one went on to the rocks and was nearly lost.

Thursday 7 October 1943
A miraculously lovely day, still and half warm and full of the clearest colours. We spent the morning chasing the sheep on the point. But only got two. We saw deer, all the goats, a lot of seals, some dark and some very light, sunning themselves on the rocks, and I saw rock pigeons in two clefts near the cruban. I went right round by the shore, very rough going but incredibly beautiful. The point was all soggy with water, one was constantly plunging into holes. I wrote a bit of a poem too. Finally we got the sheep away. Scott [sheep dog] wasn't much good, but Lachie says he hasn't been out enough, is too "keen". We tied ropes to the sheep's horns, and played them along into the field like salmon.

Then the boys went to Dippen and I did up a hellish great parcel of things the girls wanted, took it down and went to see Lilla; I found her terribly depressed and worried, but was, I think, successful in cheering her up. She said Denny M wrote her nice letters but when they were together he was kind of cross with her for being tired and feeling ill; I said that was exactly like Dick and came of his over-worrying about her, that men couldn't bear women being ill because it made them feel guilty, and that one must trust to the nice letters because they were what they really thought when they weren't just biting because they couldn't help it. I think most long-married women should occasionally be able to miscall their husbands to some other woman who is sufficiently fond of the husband for it to be all en famille and understood . . . I think I reassured her about Denny M anyway. Then

* Singer and collector of Scottish folk songs.

we told one another some of our dreams. She talked to me about Ellen, saying that Denny M says she has the right ideas; I said I think that's only Denny M saying "yes" to a lassie just once more. If Denny M goes religious that will be just too bad! But I don't think he will. She wondered whether she ought to feel like Ellen, I said there was no ought about it, but different things suited different people and different epochs, and I told her the parable of the raft that I use so much. She must get hold of whatever bit of it appears to be under her own hand.

Sunday 17 October 1943
. . . Duncan and Mary [his fiancée] came in after tea, wanting to know if I had heard from Neil Gunn again, Duncan speaking with the utmost enthusiasm of the *Silver Darlings*. We talked about books, education and so on. Duncan got hold of Jameson which always fascinates them, and started looking up words, then proverbs in the later Lowland Scots glossary I have, I was saying that I only noticed words if they were different from the east coast ones.

Then Dougie came in—but Denny M not as Lilla isn't too well. When Duncan and Mary left, Jane and I teased Dougie—we were all talking about the Home Guard, Duncan and Dougie both feeling rather bored with it now—and then talked about poetry, I said them a lot, and then about working conditions and Unions and what people really want. Dougie had always had good conditions with the Clyde Navigation Trust, he spoke of them, and then of how much he had really enjoyed steering his ferry boat and seeing the Clyde always so busy, but had the others in the stokehold enjoyed it? He also said he wouldn't stay a minute longer with the Ministry of Supply when the war was over, it was pure slavery. I said what nonsense, you're always knocking off, and Duncan only goes for you when some of his bosses go for him. Dougie then instanced specific grievances (not having oil-skins because they are under shelter, though they handle wet trees, for instance). Said nobody wanted to go on there, they'd sooner work for the Forestry, I said Yes, Ian Macrae's bosses aren't always chasing him; you in the saw-mill are making essential war things, pit props for mines mostly. He said aye, and we would do it for the miners but it is for the Duke of Hamilton. He said we would work if it was Russia. I said you'd bloody well have to, so would I. Then he said nobody hears your men complaining. I said that's because everything's always breaking down and then nobody can work, and it's all very well you lying about on the grass talking to Jane, but it isn't always like that.

But the more we talked the more it seemed to me that partly he wanted shorter hours and more pay and a really long week-end especially for miners and dockers, but mostly to be treated decently. He wouldn't really mind having a boss if the boss would treat him like a man and not like a hand. I was reminded of Neil saying what a fine chap Cook the outfitter was to work for—when Italy capitulated he gave the girls £5 all round. He wanted security, Beveridge as it were, and then holidays with pay, a long week-end, and this decent treatment. Then he spoke of two friends of his on the Clyde Navigation Trust who were up for two months each for stealing syrup—I'd seen it in the papers. He was passionate about it, saying They werena thiefs, Nou, no, they werena! They had been sharing with the four policemen, another one had happened to catch them, and they had meant to take the stuff home, not to sell it (as with poaching, the only dishonourable thing is to sell!) One of them was going on his holidays to Islay, and here the poor chaps were, with long service and all, and each of them up for two months! It seemed an awful shame, looked at like that. Doudou [Dougie] also said, with some surprise, that although there had been any amount of oranges lying about always, he had never taken any.

Friday 22 October 1943
... Young Dick and Alec came over in the evening to talk about re-forming the Argyll DLP. Dick thought he might get to the meeting too. I said I'd fix an interview for Alex, but suggested that if they re-started I myself wouldn't be in it. I might join Common Wealth or maybe the CP. Alec said he could see nothing wrong with Common Wealth. We talked about Beveridge and about planning. Dick said how much he'd like to plan Kintyre. He also said he didn't think women should have the vote till thirty ...

London

Tuesday–Saturday 26–31 October 1943
... Next day I went and read at the London Library, lunched with Dick. He is giving me a dress for my birthday it is ages since I had one. We went round looking but I can't get into anything as they all have these narrow skirts. Nobody will make under three months. As a last resort went to Busvine, whom he knows over politics, got a dress which will be great fun. God knows what it will cost but anyhow I'm

not paying! They had enough stuff to put gathers into the skirt, it is a kind of navy with highly coloured sleeves and trimmings, I look very nice, I have got to the age when it pays, occasionally, to *dress*. They were very intelligent, much amused with my arm muscles . . . I dined with Archie and Jan . . . They are going back to Edinburgh anyhow as Uncle W can't manage the whole business. Graeme hoping for complete control of West European electricity. Nice to be as thorough an expert as that. When I got back I rang up Paul; he told me that Guy had been killed in Russia. He was the one I loved best of them all. It's always like that. I hope there are more of his kind, for France's sake.

. . . In the afternoon read at London Lib, had tea with Lewis [Gielgud] who was less tired, said the War Office had been consistently wrong about Russia week by week—I was reminding him of two years ago when they said Russia would be knocked out in two months and I said she wouldn't. We said, as several people have, that possibly they would end the war before ever we get our Second Front going, and might help us to clear the Americans out of Europe. He says he thinks all Europe will be nominally Communist in five years except possibly ourselves and the Scans. I say all the more reason for a separate Scotland. Everyone feeling anti-American though individually they are so nice, although a bit un-grown-up. After crossing Piccadilly Circus in safety I said to Jack I felt like the Grecian Urn. The black ones are much more popular! . . .

Lynmouth

Sunday–Monday 7–8 November 1943
An awfully nice week-end, only I kept on writing my book, which is at the most exciting stage where it is like reading something only very slowly, because I don't know what is going to happen till I have written it. I only know just before I write it what it will be. Meanwhile we went for walks, masses of girls came to tea, we played games, I was doing a lot of organising, talked to parents, ate apples and sweets and orangeade and so on. On Monday in a fit of enthusiasm a lot of us danced reels and things in the road—and Lois took a collection for the cottage hospital . . . I read "The Knife" to the Literary Society. On Sunday I had supper with VIa who were awfully nice, Vita Gollancz particularly intelligent. They talked about what books they were going to get, and lots of things. Not so much politics as Winchester,

say, but a lot of general awareness. Also a certain amount of energy goes on clothes etc and that side of things. Especially now . . .

Rudi Messel invited Naomi to stay at his farm in November. Messel was an old friend who had worked with the Mitchisons at King's Norton. He was a left wing journalist and writer and had financed the pre-war publication *Fact*.

Tuesday–Wednesday 9–11 November 1943
Three good days with Rudi, no longer at Ford but at a smaller farm house, gaily painted, with a lot of his old furniture, and books and some nice modern pictures, masses of dogs . . . Lovely farm buildings, not very elaborate but what's needed on a farm. Red Devon cattle, sheep, mangels all in, potatoes being dug. He was as sweet as ever, rather grey haired but no less good-looking and his hair still crisp and wavy and using the same scent. It was all rather nostalgic, but I wrote my book hard, only being lured into potato gathering one day—a poor crop in numbers but a sufficient amount of huge ones. Also herding the sheep which was rather fun, they are much tamer than ours. I think he is succeeding in producing a community and a form of good life. They were all acting Hamlet. Farm meal times and so on and the house definitely a farm; the men all call him sir and me Naomi. I wrote two chapters of my book and slept well, wish I could have stayed a week.

Saturday–Monday 13–15 November 1943
. . . I got the feeling that London morale is worse than the tail of the blitz, worse even than last time, a lot of bad work with the Americans, and general depressions about possibilities of real change. Went to see the London plan, everyone there pointing out their own street and what was to happen to it. Don't see what can be done without a revolutionary change, . . . More anti-Churchill feeling and general hope among the left that the Russians will win the war in time to chase the Americans out of Piccadilly . . .

During November there was sad family news. Jan who was married to Naomi's cousin Archie had a miscarriage; from Cloan came the news that Aunt Edith had died. Naomi decided against attending the funeral.

Friday–Wednesday 19–24 November 1943

. . . Eric asking me, almost point blank, if I think that there is another world of some kind; he has to treat his patients orthodoxly, saying their apparitions are from their own mind and so on, but he half thinks they may be real or rather external. I say I don't know and don't see any possibility of making certain which are from within and which from without, the way bits of one's anima can be detached and take on strange shapes.

One begins to feel no need to bother about anti-semitism, as the Americans have completely taken the place of the Jews—stories about rape, etc. It will end by making one quite pro-American. Nobody has a good word for them and the ones one sees about look mostly pretty awful. Ruth takes the orthodox CP point of view about Mosley;★ I say it's rather nonsense, and some day one of them will be kept in and not let out for illness; not that I mind in the least if Mosley does die in gaol, it's only a wee matter of being consistent. A lot of local feeling about it at the Doves. But I'm bored with the CP. They support the government on all the wrong things . . .

Murdoch seems to have put through something, by way of his boss, that has saved the Min of Supply a very large sum. He is now going to drive tanks at Lulworth. It is awful, all this saying goodbye, I can't bear it . . .

Carradale.

Friday 26 November 1943

. . . Oh god I do hate coming back. I wrote three and a half chapters in four weeks, while I was away, now shall get stuck again. Convention wanting me to edit the education pamphlet. If I could have a competent secretary for a fortnight. Jesus, it is bloody to be able to do things but not have the time or the material i.e. a secretary, but to have to do something I can't do well like farming and which is incapable of being done really well by anyone—farming bad land. I wish I'd gone to some more flicks and plays, such a lot I would love to see.

I wonder if London is going to be shelled. Or gassed. These bloody Germans burning the Naples library. I hope to god they've put away the stuff in Berlin though . . .

★ Oswald Mosley, leader of the British Union of Fascists, had been interned under Defence Regulation 18B in 1940. In November 1943, he was released by the Home Secretary, Herbert Morrison, on health grounds. Morrison's decision was met with a storm of controversy.

The Allies were still battling against the Germans in Italy driving them very slowly northwards.

Sunday 5 December 1943
I stayed in bed late and did little all day but still remain devilish tired. I have a sort of buzz in my head all the time; I suppose it must be disregarded, as my blood pressure is o.k. But it is an unpleasant companion. I have still got a bit of a cough too. I cleared up a lot of letters in the morning, almost all the immediate ones. In the afternoon went to see the Jacksons, who seem much pleased with their baby. If mine had lived she would be very companionable by now. I finished a draft of the BBC script but I don't think it's good. I don't seem able to go on with the chapter I was writing when I left London. Virtue has gone out of me. I stopped at the mill on my way back from the Jacksons, talked to old Shaw and Dougie and the engineer. Dougie said he would come over this evening but hasn't. I expect someone turned up and he couldn't. But I wish someone could have. I read *To the Finland Station*. All the time I kept feeling two things; the personal side of it, Jenny Marx and that awful succession of children and probably never a spot of chloroform, her bleeding breast and there is no surface pain that I know of so bad as a sore nipple: and then, was Marx right? Can one analyse society, can one foretell what is going to happen? If I could only concentrate, get past this buzz in my head, get down to the facts, the documents, if they exist, could I know what was going to happen? Could I be competent to be a revolutionary leader? Or would I lead them all astray? Sometimes I feel I've damn little to lose but my chains. I'm not doing at all what I want. If I can't break something soon I will break myself. And the Second Front hanging over one, and this bloody Churchill gloating over suffering like a great mediaeval devil . . .

Saturday 11 December 1943
. . . I was feeling a bit gloomy, and then Dougie suggested I'd come down to tea with them, so I did and they were awfully pleased to see me, and who was sitting there but Denny M just back from Glasgow, Lilla having gone on to Dunoon. It was great fun, we all had sausages and tea and got quickly warm in the wee room and talked and laughed and then Dougie and Denny and I walked out into the bright moonlight, back to the Hall; it was bright enough for no difficulty in walking and yet it had the quality of night and intimacy, and I said I

wish we were all three walking to Campbeltown, I wish we were walking further to some strange town where none of us have been, and suddenly I stopped because I had an acute sense of this having happened before or of it going to happen in the future . . .

Thursday 16 December 1943
My two [Georges and Yves] French very nice, younger and more innocent than the others, both in artillery with less of the violence and un-social character of the pilots. Both speak some English, both politically left and both keen Gaullists and extremely anti-American. I try to put the case for the "good" American, but the answer is a shrug of the shoulders . . .

Tuesday 21 December 1943
I was reading some of Kathleen Raine's poems. When I first looked at them they seemed hopelessly difficult and obscure, but on second or third reading one begins to get them and some are lovely. Though I wonder if people ought to be so obscure, so putting off. It means you aren't writing except for a limited audience, those who will try again. Even so I don't get all of them and doubt if it is worth making the tremendous effort which might be necessary to do so; one should perhaps put that effort into research or political work . . .

Friday 24 December 1943
The cattle had been at the potato pits again, so we had to take in all one pit, with Monarch and his beastly wives all standing round mooing at us. It is beastly grovelling among dung and trodden earth for wet potatoes. Duncan came over and he and Robbie and the French went off with Dick to get the deer, there were several about the Bay. Then Lois, Av and I harnessed Jo and took him down to get wrack; it was rather full of leaves but we got a couple of carts in; at one point a shot was rather close and Jo bolted down the beach, luckily with a laden cart so he didn't go far! They got two and we took them back. Duncan took one over.

Poor Georges has to go back—we had no luck over getting any extension of leave—but Yves, who has fallen heavily for Christine [Campbell] undecided. They are so specially young, these two . . .

Saturday—Christmas Day 1943

The first hour or so unpacking stockings—we had done them yesterday and stockings for the French, I gave them each a fountain pen from America, some choc and some stationery. I managed to produce quite good but rather utilitarian stockings for the others, mostly things I knew they wanted. We unpacked the various other parcels, one from my mother, Denny and Ruth and a book from Jane. Things Rosemary had sent for me to distribute. Then I found Yves had made up his mind to go too, so we saw them off; they were both awfully disappointed to be going. Then we hastily hung up the green garlands, finished decorating the tree and put the books and things for the children, labelled, on to trays.

Then my dinner guests, Lilla and Denny M, Peter and Ellen, turned up; we had chicken a very good ersatz Christmas pudding which Av and I had duly stirred (I suppose everyone stirring this year had about the same wish) and tinned pears. The maids and Joan had the same but for the pears. Dick gave them some Sauternes and they all enjoyed it very much . . .

. . . The buns and cookies came from the bakers and we jammed them; the French did tuck into the jam! Nice it will be when the time comes when one needn't worry but open masses of jam. Fortunately I have plenty of orange and lemon for the children. They began to come at 3.30, but we played games in the hall and drawing room till most had arrived and then lighted the tree and gave out the books . . . Dougie and co came and helped. We played masses of singing games, some of which I didn't know: Broken Bridge is falling down, my fair lady, breakfast, dinner, tea, supper, nupper, nup her! (not "London" bridge). Bluebell: Tip, tap on her shoulder, in and out the dusty (dirty? naughty?) bluebells. Who'll buy the milk cart: (sell father's featherbed, where will father sleep, etc, ending with pigs sleeping in the wash-house, where will mother wash, wash at the seaside, what if she gets drowned, send for the slow boat, slow boat is too slow, (all going round slowly), send for the quick boat, quick boat is too quick (all rushing round—and that apparently is all). Also I lost my lovely penny (?) in the music hall, then someone else pulled into the ring: red cheeks like roses, everyone rubbing their cheeks, then each of the two seize on one of the ring: this is the one that I love. Etc. I quite see how all these tunes get messed up, one person mis-hearing what another sings. Of course they all played the farmer's in his den, a painful game for the dog or the bone. They stayed till after seven, when Duncan

Semple came and herded them away. Obviously they enjoyed themselves very much, but I hadn't nearly enough crackers to go round, and had to give them as prizes for musical bumps.

I was so exhausted at the end that I had some gin and orange which went straight for my head. Dick meanwhile had a talk to Christine about her exams. I spent the rest of the evening in a state of exhaustion reading Compton Mackenzie's *Keep the Home Guard Turning* . . .

1944

THE EARLY PART of 1944 was dominated by the build-up for D-Day. On 6 June, 156,000 Allied troops landed on the French beaches; more followed in the subsequent weeks and the great push to force Hitler out of France began, culminating in the liberation of Paris in August. Ironically, Britain suffered another spate of air raids just when it seemed that the worst was over; in February, London was subjected to the 'Little Blitz' and from June onwards, to the horrific V1 and V2 flying bombs.

Naomi was taking on new responsibilities in Carradale. She helped to set up a debating society which met at the village hall; she played an important role in the local branch of the District Nursing Association. The very poor medical facilities available in the remoter parts of the Highlands and Islands had prompted the creation of a form of publically subsidised health care which pre-dated the National Health Service by several decades. The District Nursing Association was part of this scheme and, in Carradale, subscriptions (and fund-raising events) supplemented by public funds ensured that the village could employ the services of a fully trained District Nurse.

Naomi also began travelling further afield to give talks or lead discussions to members of the Forces. She specialised in postwar reconstruction themes, particularly those affecting Scotland such as the proposals for a hydro-electricity scheme for the Highlands. Adult education for the troops had been introduced earlier in the war and although ABCA (Army Bureau of Current Affairs) supplied its own lecturers, speakers from outside were also invited provided they confined their talks to 'non-political' issues.

Later in the year, Naomi was appointed to one of the early Rent Restriction Tribunals. A national system of rent tribunals was not established until Labour came into office in 1945 but there was already considerable concern about the housing situation which had been exacerbated by the complete halt to building work during the war. One of the recommendations of the Ridley Committee, which was set up in 1943 to examine the workings of the Rent Acts, was that "persons of experience in public affairs" should be appointed to tribunals to determine fair rents for unfurnished dwellings.

Despite the intensification of her public activities, Naomi continued to work on *The Bull Calves* which was now nearing completion. She no longer had the help and support of Rosemary whose illness in 1943 had left her unfit for farming work. In December 1943, Rosemary moved to London where she was directed into office work to continue her national service.

Lois and Av were preparing for their return to school after the Christmas holiday.

15 January 1944

. . . All this business of finding last minute things and so on. Questions what to get with limited coupons and all that. All very nerve-fraying. Finally Lois and I had a wild row, over nothing at all, and both screamed and behaved exactly alike except that Lois had a nose bleed which was one up to her. We both felt very miserable both at the time and after and gave one another chocolate and so on. Val had done exactly the same the day before. I think it's just a general tension and worry, partly war, partly family. I think we all feel that after the war we shall just throw away the whole bloody lot of things and never darn or mend or make do again. The whole thing is so bloody silly and one feels such a fool, with the sails of one's soul jibbing. I had to draw a lot of money for journeys, clothes etc, and that means asking for more and I simply hate that, although goodness knows Dick doesn't ever bite me. The wages bill is considerably up after the New Year adjustments. The house books are very small, but there are always small bills for material and repairs and so on . . .

. . . Then the children and I went over to the Hall for the meeting to start the debating society, there weren't many there but a few were young boys . . .

Decided to start on the 29th, me to be chairman, which I didn't want, but supposed I'd got to do. I have probably more idea of rules of procedure than the rest. But I know I'm not good at it . . . On the way back I cried all over Alec who said I was the only one that kept the damned place going. He came back and we discussed debating societies with much help from Lois and Av who have both done a lot and both been chairman much oftener than I have . . .

Wednesday–Saturday 19–22 January 1944

The usual long journey to Glasgow, though very lovely along the west side in sun after storm . . . Val, who has a theory that she never eats on journeys ate eight buns. We got in, found there was no sleeper for Sheila [Val's friend]. Went to the Grosvenor who hadn't a table, wouldn't promise one. As I'd said I'd meet Lois there I was rather worried, finally went to the head waiter and told him in French that I was a friend of free France—at which we got a table! It was then too late for me to get the train to Edinburgh, so, after seeing them both off I went to the Central rather disconsolately to phone Edinburgh and then get myself a bed for the night. There was a merchant navy captain just in, in a state of fury and indignation because he couldn't get a bed anywhere. Everyone was very sympathetic, blaming the Americans and trying to soothe him and moderate his language, finally a man phoned up what I knew was Scottish Airways at Renfrew and apparently got him a bed in a kind of club there; I heard him telling them over the phone to have drinks and a hot bath for him, and he said he would run him out. I suppose he was an official. Glasgow folk are awfully nice once you get past the first barrier . . .

. . . The next morning I went on early to Edinburgh; I felt very exhilarated, in spite of not having slept, at being back there, I kept on thinking what a bonny bonny city it was . . . I flounced into the BBC and said I wasn't going to cut my script. It all finally boiled down to their not wanting the two words "free German" together. So I rewrote it in rather stronger language! This they took and were interested in some of my poems, though thought it unlikely that the English would be interested in my Scots ones.

Naomi spent a few days in Edinburgh with Jan and Archie Haldane mostly working on her book at the National Library of Scotland. She returned on 22nd January to Carradale.

Saturday 29 January 1944
. . . saw a thing in the *Herald* about a lot of fucking capitalists saying the Clyde should no more be called Red but "True Blue" (applause). I wrote a letter to the *Herald*. If I was a Clyde worker I'd take that as an insult. Then to the Nursing Association meeting . . . Nobody would take on secretaryship, but Duncan took on Treasurer, nobody being willing. Chrissie Paterson said she had too much to do being chairman of the Lifeboat association! Everyone hopefully said they would co-opt somebody who would do it. Meanwhile I have to take it on, also pay nurse etc.

Then we had the debate; I had got Postie to move the table down from the platform so as to bring the meeting together; I made some remarks and read the rules of procedure and a few people put things into the hat. They varied from extremely difficult like "What are politics?" to frivolous like "Why is a man's shirt longer at the back than the front?" There were some young people there . . . I think a lot of Carradale went into Campbeltown to see the Rex cinema which has been burnt. I thought the standard of debate was remarkably low, little Dick was not too bad; the ball was kept rolling by him, Alec, Duncan, Reppke and Red Rob. Chrissie Paterson made a few remarks including a marvellous defence of the Empire saying India was only "dis-affected because of religion". You realised how she felt that she "held" India. Duncan and some others were incredibly reactionary about education, saying secondary education should be voluntary and most people should go to work early (more cheap labour for Duncan). I was really shocked and remarked from the Chair that the govt was pledged to raise the school leaving age. There was a bit of a wrangle at the end and various people explained to me that a "hat night" was a kind of brains trust, people answering questions. I said I thought it was a pity to start off that way. Anyhow the responsibility for the next debate—which will be purely political!—is off my shoulders. I think I was pretty bad as chairman though perhaps no worse than anybody else would have been. For a bit I got Red Rob to take the chair so that I could speak from the floor. Dougie spoke, I think for the first time in his life and very shyly; neither Denny nor Lilla did, but at least Denny didn't smoke all the time which was something. Dougie and co came back for a bit afterwards, which I was glad of because I was feeling a bit depressed . . .

Sunday– Tuesday 6–8 February 1944
On Sunday spoke on education and a whole host of other things at the Glasgow University settlement, a lot of awfully nice, hopeful, rather good-looking girls, very friendly and pleasant, all training for welfare, hospital almoners etc, thinking of going to America, full of bounce. Had a good discussion. Got a first sleeper so came south in great luxury. Amazing how one feels it's no time at all since one was last in the Underground. Only rather disgruntled with looking at myself carefully in the LMS mirror—I never do at home—and noticing the railway lines of wrinkles and general appearance of age . . .

Ruth was now pregnant for the second time. She and Denny were still living at River Court with Michael and Sybil. Between them they had hired a nanny to take care of their babies. Murdoch also used River Court as his London base. Mrs Gibson and her family continued to act as the caretakers for the Mitchisons.

Saturday–Monday 12–14 February 1944
. . . went to Kew in the afternoon with Denny and Ru. The houses were lovely, beautiful orchids, great pinky-brown cymbidiums, and lots of ordinary things in the greenhouse. I kept thinking what I could grow in Carradale. Denny and Dick kept talking about turning River Court into flats. Denny wants to take all the woodwork and so on away so as to be more labour-saving. I think that it's not much use having a period house if you are going to take off all its trimmings and the shell itself perhaps not so very durable. I went round to pay my Labour Party sub to the Turners who were very friendly and pleased to see me. I said we were thinking of turning River Court into flats. Mr Turner said You can't leave your library! I said we'd taken most of the books to Scotland. He said Oh I meant the book-shelves—as a joiner. He had always liked looking at them so much: a lovely bit of work . . . I am so bored with the Labour Party but the people are so nice. Dick seriously thinking of going back to King's Norton.

Jack and Helen came to supper, seem to have finished the Admiralty work, but being very mysterious about it. Both in good form. Denny has applied for one hospital but thinks of industrial medicine later, rehabilitation and so on. All his testimonials speak of his kindness and tact with patients.

On Monday morning I wrote quite a bit of stuff including a thing about education—I've done the introduction for the pamphlet. It is hell having no kind of secretarial help now. All sorts of farm muddles too.

Went up to Hendon to see Margaret (I'd sent a valentine to Douglas) who is a bit shaky still after pneumonia, read the last chapters of her novel. Dined with Christine, Dick and Murdoch, at Josef's; on the way summoned up courage to ask three Americans to stand on the right on a moving staircase! . . .

Thursday 17 February 1944
. . . tea with Joan [Rendel] at my club. Poor Joan with an acute feeling that she is incompetent, that she just *can't* cope with things, that she gets everything into a mess (except—a large exception of course) the children. Ruth who is really awfully competent, has the same feeling. So, my god, have I. It's just because these bloody domesticities are so

boring that one inevitably thinks of something else, and then forgets, like Alfred, the cakes in the oven. Meanwhile we all try to be enthusiastic and competent about saving fat and similar idiocies. But it's a bloody shame people like Joan having to. She is not able to write anything, I say never mind, you are storing it up. But—?

. . . We all dined at the Isola Bella, where Tony [Brown] fresh from the BBC Home Guard blew in, saying My dears, I nearly brought my sten gun! He also said, which he oughtn't to have, that the password for the H. G. to get ready before the Second Front was Bouncer and the final action stations was Bugbear! Someone with a good sense of humour must have thought of that.

Anne Richmond who is in the Min of Inf is training as a despatch rider, has done quite a lot but is rather upset at the number of girls who turn up with enormous scars on their faces for retraining after accidents. She says her chap is in the part of Japan which has been inspected by the Red Cross, which is something, I suppose. She is very firmly sticking to him which must be rather difficult sometimes, as she is extremely beautiful and attractive. It may in a way account for the despatch riding. I think everyone in the south anticipates a fairly serious time, and even the HG are being taken seriously . . .

After being comparatively free from air raids for nearly two years, London was once again subjected to air attack between late January and April 1944. There were thirteen heavy raids on London during this period which became known as the 'Little Blitz'. Other places were also affected but less seriously than London.

Friday–Sunday 18–20 February 1944
. . . We were just going to bed afterwards when the sirens sounded, and pretty soon it got noisy. Murdoch finds himself rather out of it in the top room, and the boys came down to our room in dressing gowns and discussed what every noise was; there was only about one bomb, but I noticed the automatic way Denny, who has seen more raids than the others, got behind a corner. They looked awfully vulnerable in their old dressing gowns. Dick wasn't bothered a bit, finally went to bed. Ru and Sybil stayed downstairs. We looked out and there was a big fire across the river . . .

. . . another raid. This time it was much noisier. I had started reading my chapter, which I finished typing after the sirens but before the banging. Ru brought Su down to the drawing room. Then we began to hear bombs, and Ru and Denny both got very nervous. We argued about where to go, Sybil came running down with Jan, to get under the curve of the stairs. We decided to go up to her room, which was warm, and neither top nor bottom—but we think another time we had better get under the beam in the dining room. Question how much difference shutters make to flying glass. While we were going upstairs, having picked ourselves off the drawing room floor, there was an even louder rattle and Joyce Gibson and her sister came running through into the dark hall—the blackout isn't too good there—and we all went up, the two mothers and babies got behind a wardrobe and the rest of us got on to the floor, Murdoch with his back to the space between the windows, polishing his army buttons. We all flattened ourselves out when we heard the bombs whistle and I kept on reassuring Joyce about her father and mother who finally turned up, Mrs rather scared having been very near a hit in King Street. Dick meanwhile went to the front door and looked. When it was over we went to the roof and saw the ring of fires all round, smelled the nearer ones. It was a lovely feeling when it was all over, all gay and comfortable like recovery from illness. We were all rather frightened except Dick who really wasn't.

Thursday–Friday 24–25 February 1944
... We went out to Jane Eyre [film] at the local place; when we came in they were doing a news flick of bombers which we didn't like. It explained what a good target the river was at Hamburg! I don't think it pleases any of us much to think of other places being bombed, and I think the general feeling, among the poor, anyhow, is that it is a kind of natural catastrophe; and if everyone all over Europe feels like that it will make for a possible international relationship after this. Mrs G really worried about all the people who had just had glass put in and so on—here we'd had the windows cleaned for the first time since 1939! The film went on and there is a place where lightning strikes a tree; that happened and the warning went on to the screen. Ru had decided beforehand to go and I had decided to go with her. Most people left, quickly but not panicking. Outside there were guns already. Denny came too and they started half running down the passage to the river that ends in old Hampshire Hog Lane. The searchlights were swooshing about and suddenly Ruth began to run all out, I called to them to go on, I would follow. Denny ran with her, anxious in case she stumbled. She is past three months pregnant. I ran slower; the guns were banging away when I got to the Mall, and for a moment I

saw the beams catch a plane. I went to the side door—I had already put carbons of some of my stuff in the shelter.* Not that it would be of any use for a direct hit. There was a sparking and starring of flashes above and light shrapnel. Ru was crossing to the shelter with Su and so was Sybil with Jan. Murdoch and Anne had stayed on but decided to get to Ravenscourt Park as she wanted to go home. Murdoch stayed in the shelter there. Anne rang up after the raid, to say the house next hers was on fire and an unexploded bomb at her back door, she had run up for her necklace and was spending the night at her Ministry. Dick was firewatching at the Temple. With us there was the hell of a lot of banging and at one moment everything bright as day with flares. We had buckets and tins and things but we share a stirrup pump with a neighbour who keeps it. The babies were both cross and yelled. I thought it was high time to get them away. Talked to Ru afterwards about Scotland. I thought they should both come but when I suggested it to Sybil she got awfully upset. I said I thought Jan would have more security from being there than she would lose from not having her mother. But Sybil wept. She is thinking of adopting another, and I thought three babies at Carradale and a doubtful nannie would be a bit difficult. She planned to go to Caterham which isn't much better than here, or to Guildford, wants to go on with her work. Ru also wants to take her house job next month. I said I would deal with the situation if Ru would stay at Carradale over the week when I shall be lecturing at Oban and places. Poor Denny awfully worried at not being in the army and not getting a hospital job yet.

Naomi returned to Carradale with Denny, Ruth, Su and their nanny.

Saturday 4 March 1944
. . . After tea Alec and young Dick came over, told me about the debate, at which apparently Mr Miller got up and said it was a "biological fact" that the white races were superior to the black, and that the white man's duty was to exterminate the coloured races. The debate seems to have gone to seed rather over the matter of missionaries; luckily I wasn't there or I'd have put my foot in it! Reppke also being obstinate about paying or rather not paying for the Hall—had

* The shelter was a room across the garden which had originally been designed as my work-room, below the very thick floor of the squash court and with thick walls. But it meant a run across the garden. N.M.

put up admission free on the notices. The rest of the committee
—which hadn't met—disagreeing.

Then Johnnie and his wife, Willie, Dougie, Chrissie and Margaret,
and Lilla came, but not Denny M as he was too tired. Dougie said he
had torn his net three nights running and he spent the day mending it.
Of course if it had been his own boat he probably wouldn't have
worried, but as it was Willie's—Dougie said they might come over on
Sunday. We danced almost all the old-fashioned dances . . . Denny and
Ru really enjoyed themselves and Nannie was induced to caper. Ru
looked about sixteen as usual, is getting worried as to how to appear
grown-up to her patients. It doesn't make any difference being
obviously pregnant either.

On 6 March, Naomi travelled to an RAF camp near Oban and from there to
the island of Tiree in the Inner Hebrides, north-east of Kintyre.

Sunday 6 March 1944
After a scurried morning chasing round after the drainers etc Denny
and I went off by the Tarbert bus. I left him there and came on by
Ardrishaig to Oban. The Education Officer wasn't at the bus stop but
a WRAF girl rushed up to me, saying she'd heard I was coming to
lecture—a Campbeltown lassie. It was an incredibly lovely day,
bright hot sun, and Oban bay looking like a picture postcard. They
put me into a comfortable looking Victorian hotel, with good food,
but I wandered round for half an hour, feeling incredibly leisured,
looking at shops. I bought three gramophone records of Hannah
dances, but as usual no cough lozenges.

In the evening I went to a gramophone record concert run by the
Education people, a Sgt introducing the records, all in a very good
dramatic setting, coloured lights and decorations by the art club. The
room was packed, about fifty people, all quite quiet and intent, all
ranks and all services. Outside magazines, maps etc, and all in a jolly
atmosphere with murals by their own art club. Lots of classes but
difficulty of continuity. The education officer was an ex-Glasgow
secondary schoolmaster. We discussed education. The records were
not very highbrow though quite enough so for me. Apparently much
less than usual . . .

Tuesday–Wednesday 7–8 March 1944
An early start in the morning for Tiree, moon almost full and the sea
still, the calmest sunrise, with a high eye-brow of pink cloud lines

above the faint mountains. I had to shake myself to remember I was not in the Aegean, and kept on expecting it to get warmer, which it didn't do. But all the time there was the feel of the Greek islands, the same barren beautiful hill shapes, like Samos or Paros, and everything, Mull and Morvern and beyond, delicately shading from mist blue of land to mist blue of sky. The boat on the other hand was one of MacBrayne's more uncomfortable efforts, nowhere to sit and awful food. A lot of the passengers were RAF but two farmers got on at Coll with a quey and began talking in half nasal and unpleasant Gaelic and half very foreign English about cattle dealing . . . had some discussion on the colour bar, which I mention in my lecture about the cotton states. An Amercan got up and said the blacks should be kept under and a Canadian got up and said they didn't have colour bars in Canada and why didn't the Yanks do it as well as they did? I had to remember that I wasn't a political speaker and must remain as neutral as possible, and tried to make it all as light as possible.

I gather there is some friction with the Americans even here. They all say that the discussion groups are a success, that they discuss things like bombing policy, and always post-war reconstruction. I thought the average face of the RAF was nice and intelligent, much more so than the Navy which look pretty stupid and wooden *en masse*. Also I felt discipline was easier here.

I had a letter from a Captain Russell asking if I would write a local letter for the Divisional newspaper of the Fifty-first—when they are off on the Second Front of course. And who else could I get. This apparently suggested by Mass-Obs—to whom my thanks! I felt very proud to be asked, wrote back suggesting some names. It is nice to be to some extent a prophet in one's own country.

Friday 10 March 1944
. . . Early afternoon talked to RN, men and women and a simply sweet, oldish Naval Captain, who talked like a kindly uncle to the audience, about international understanding and so on. He was very deaf, and had been to Russia, I tried hard to be nice to him. Then to Maritime Ackack, a small meeting, but intelligent people, I thought. Afterwards had high tea with Captain Ross, another officer and an RASC Lieut from Lancashire, all decided that what was wanted was Soviet Republic of Europe. All sniffy about Scottish nationalism which I tried to explain was compatible with this, especially the Lancashire man, who was also rather anti-French having been there

during the 1940 time and felt we had been betrayed by the ordinary people of France, the peasants etc.

Then I didn't know where the evening lecture was, nor did the Padre who was left in charge of the Education Office and is rather a mutt, but finally, after my insisting, a pencil note was found about the YWCA where it turned out to be. By this time the weather had broken and it was very cold. At the Y, which is run by two awfully nice women who are hoping to go out and do relief work in Greece, there were about a dozen or fifteen men and women. I duly talked and there was a lot of discussion, especially from "Ginger" Grant, the Campbeltown lassie, and an English boy called Charles. As usual we talked about hydro-electricity, the future of Europe and above all Russia. I think these small groups are really more important than the big ones and one doesn't have to fuss so much about being non-political. They always like the photos, I wish I had more . . .

Carradale again. Joan has replaced Lena as the Carradale estate Land Girl. Murdoch has returned on leave.

Friday 17 March 1944
I can't think of anything except something horrible I have had to do, getting the warble fly maggots out of the cattle, oh god it was filthy. The chap came to licence Timo [the bull], said he'd pass him but he wasn't very good, he thought I'd best sell him locally, gave me a lot of good advice, . . . then said he had warble flies and pressed an awful maggot out of his back, I was nearly sick. Duncan says not to worry too much, they all have them, but give them a dressing of sheep dip. He was very lousy too. I got in the two Ayrshires, we rubbed the dip into their backs, neither had any lice, but Linda had two warble maggots, I pressed them out, I couldn't make Joan do it. They pop out, it is a real nightmare, I couldn't bear one to touch me, nor could Joan. I tried to do Timo but he kicked like a sledge hammer, I expect all the Galloways have it. Oh dear, it is one of the many things I didn't know about . . .

Saturday 19 March 1944
. . . Philip [Dundas] rang up last night to say his sheep were lambing, were mine? I had meant to take them in on Friday but then this man came to see the bull and Lachie was trying hard to get some ploughing finished with the government tractor, so we didn't manage it. I

thought I'd better try this afternoon. Lachie was being sick—some kind of flu—but the family and I went with Scott, [sheepdog] but he wouldn't work for any of us.

We found most of the sheep, but there were three lambs. Murdoch and I were on the island trying to get the rest, and there was a sheep with an unborn and apparently dead lamb sticking out of it. I didn't know what to do, but tried to pull. The lamb was quite limp, and only one of its feet out, the other seemed to be stuck. There were no contractions going on and I thought it might have been like that for a long time. The others thought they could get the rest back. Earlier we had found one of them very exhausted but not apparently lambing . . . I stayed with the sheep and still nothing happened; it was very cold and rather wet and the sheep just lay about with this awful half born thing. I rubbed her belly and pulled again, and suddenly there was a kind of cry from the limp rag of a lamb and suddenly she was struggling with it and I pulled, getting my hands half into the womb, not of course sterile, and the dreadful stretched membrane. I was feeling awfully upset, talking to the sheep and suddenly the thing came and it was kind of half alive but as limp as a rag. The sheep dashed off, then came back, nibbled the cord, smelt at the lamb but didn't do much else. I didn't know what to do, and soon the lamb was completely dead, and the sheep went and stood at the very edge of a precipice and occasionally stamped.

By and bye Murdoch came back saying they had got the sheep through the gate on to the warren and then they had bolted back by the sea, and his only shoes had sprung a leak. Denny came back with a stretcher, but the sheep seemed all right. I was very worried all the same, thinking I had done the wrong thing. I was also very tired and bruised.

A second lecturing trip to speak to members of the ATS at Inverary.

Tuesday 21 March 1944
. . . I was early at Inverary, but had to think what to say at my lecture. Tried to get on with the book, but it is stiff going just now, and I couldn't, only the boys ask what's happening.

Quite a good lecture, though it appeared that they hadn't expected me till the week after! They were all very lively, full of questions. I talked about Scotland as it used to be with special reference to Inverary and the Duke. Finally they asked why there was no fried fish shop at

Inverary, I said it was the sort of thing the Duke wouldn't allow. They said it was a shame and that the Duke should be turned out of his castle and made to keep a fried fish shop himself. I said it was easy enough breaking the power of Dukes but they didn't want to fall into the hands of industrialists instead, then I remembered that lecturers were supposed to be non-political.

I liked the officer girl who was quite young and said she couldn't imagine what it would be like to be grown-up but not in the army. Said she hoped I didn't find it too informal. And that the girls all wanted to be married and have homes of their own rather than to have careers, that was what the army had done to them; when she told them it was possible they mightn't all get married, they tore her to pieces.

There was a snoring owl making an awful din behind the camp.

Tuesday 28 March 1944
I took the day off with the boys while Lachie and Joan limed in front and on the blackest, peatiest part of the meadow. Unfortunately the sheep which had been ill, and which seemed all right, died in the night. We ought not to have left it out but Lachie thought it was all right (and so did I). Still no signs of the others.

The boys and I walked up Rhonadale, talking, and in the afternoon sat by the sea; it was quite warm and lots of seals close in. Murdoch has been all round the garden with Hugh, planning and watching things. I do hate them going. I hate it so much that I almost wish they were gone so that the pain should be over ... They both talk immensely about details of planning, houses versus flats, private gardens against parks and so on. We also discussed fee-paying in Russian schools and Churchill's speech last night which we had listened to and thought was a grand speech if one could have believed a word of it, and of course we all wondered who he was getting at. One supposes that his reference to feint landings was a double-cross to puzzle the Germans and that probably it means there won't be.

Denny and Murdoch returned to their respective war jobs in the south, Denny leaving Ruth and Su behind in the comparative safety of Carradale. A French visitor has in the meantime arrived—Paul, the parachutist. Later in April, Jean, who had visited the previous year, returned to Carradale. Paul fell rather heavily in love with Dougie's young daughter, Christine, who took history lessons with Lois and French lessons with Naomi at Carradale House.

Sunday 2 April 1944

. . . Paul, who had been having a hectic bout of energy yesterday and had cut masses of rhodies, became intensely talkative, showed me his poems that he'd been writing and told me most of his life history, how his fiancée's mother had persuaded her to chuck him and she had become someone else's mistress and then, when he was on the run, tried to remarry them. Showed me his family photos, the father like a Yorkshire business man, the ironic, sweet face of his mother—they are obviously a very devoted family and of course he hears nothing of them—his small brother, the "Boche", an intelligent looking German girl who helped him to escape. I tried to draw internationalist morals here. Then he went on about the awfulness of the army and army brothels, and how terrible it was to be disillusioned, and then how I was his mother, he my motherless lamb—on the model of the stable lamb. Poor devils—But I take it the thing is worth doing though the hell of a sweat being sympathetic in a foreign language. Healing people is always exhausting.

Monday 3 April 1944

. . . I was tired and would like to have gone to bed early but Paul had written a poem which he wanted me to read and criticise—difficult in a foreign language—and then to talk about how he was feeling and the sense of general guilt. I said I thought that was universal, was the guilt of a past generation coming back on the innocent. He said he thought now he ought to have joined the internal resistance movement, he should have been in the maquis now. Then he talked about prison and how he had first started writing poems there, learning them by heart at night and scribbling them down on to odds and ends of paper in the lavs and so on. He said it was being so unhappy then and now being so happy, had got down to the same part of him. This was the first time he had been happy for three years, since the collapse. I did my best, I *tutoied* him, to make things seem more family, kissed him goodnight and so on. Lois and Av try and talk to him a bit. He's such a nice chap . . .

Tension was mounting over the Second Front. No one was quite sure when it would happen. People were watching out for signs: cancellation of leave for the forces, train services altered, rumours and so forth. The waiting made everyone slightly nervous and irritable at Carradale House.

Thursday–Tuesday 13–18 April 1944
. . . Dick dealing with income tax, worrying round with my farm accounts, making me feel miserably inefficient, discovering I have occasionally added things up wrong and so on. This gets me down badly, though at the end the farm losses don't look nearly so bad as they did because I have been accumulating stock and crops and value generally. This on the top of everyone bouncing round me, partly to tease me, partly affectionately, but always distracting me, making me have to attend to a hundred things at once, so that I get quite dizzy, and people from the village ringing up and one thing and another. I began to sleep badly, to have buzzings in my head, to be so wretchedly tired that I could hardly see straight, couldn't concentrate at all, was only doing things with the outside and semblance of myself.

Am supposed to be writing an article for the SMT to be in by Saturday about Kintyre . . . I am falling behind the children all the time.

And all the worrying about the Second Front.

Av's other school friend can't come because he is German (though with a brother in the army) and this is a funny area of some kind and he would have to go through Glasgow which is protected. Silly, I think. The other friend, Dugald Campbell of Tarbert, came over and was charming, we got him to stay on, he is a nice mixture of Tarbert and the good Quaker civilisation of Leighton Park.

Another visit to speak to members of HM Forces at Inverary.

Tuesday–Wednesday 18–19 April 1944
To Inverary by forestry lorry. Got off at the Navy camp but found that the schoolmaster who arranged it had gone on leave, nobody had been told and it was an impossible time! However the first officer was Miss Rasmussen who used to be a Gollancz manager and knew me of old and we talked hard about booksy days, then went off round the camp. I saw quite a bit of exercises and people working and got very much the feeling that things were about to happen. The old Mississippi river boats they have there look very odd.

In the evening talked to the ATS about democratic institutions and got quite a lot of response, girls saying why can't we vote and talking about education, children's councils at school etc. Said they'd start a wall newspaper. I said I'd help. Stayed the night in the Wrennery which was rather nice. I borrowed Miss R's typewriter and did half my article on Kintyre etc.

Next day came back by various lorries etc, but pouring rain and I got rather wet while I was walking between whiles. Finally a lift from a Navy car with two nice-looking young officers with Oxford accents. They thought that democracy was all nonsense—I said I'd been lecturing—and most people wanted a benevolent autocracy like the Navy. The English way of life was the only one, all foreigners should be made to conform. One of them said he would like to be given a German town of 10,000 people, he would treat them just like a ship and there would be no more Nazis. They went on to say that the Dunoon landladies wouldn't take in billetees and rooked them in various ways, that all the Scotch thought of was money, etc. The WREN who was driving them was a Dunoon woman, she answered frigidly and officially. I tried to be sweet and reasonable and not to take it all too seriously, remembering that "the Scotch have no sense of humour" but I did suggest alternative points of view. When I spoke of Scottish nationalism in a very mild way they hooted with laughter, still in their public school manner. Then they said that Sunday closing was hell. I said jokingly that all the English thought of was drinks. By and bye they stopped at the Bellochantuy pub to ask for eggs and perhaps to get a drink (they had been chivvying the girl to speed, though she was going at 50 and then stopped!). She then turned to me, dropped her mask and said Talk of drink! They treat me like dirt, you've no idea. She explained how she had been left sitting in the car—forbidden to leave it because it had confidential documents—with no food, while her passengers spent hours getting drunk, how she often had to do twenty-four hours at a time, and how these elegant young men were completely thoughtless. Then they came back and she shut up and became their butt again. It was all very shocking. I had said earlier that I wasn't sure that 100 percent of Navy liked being autocratically run. Now I knew.

It was a relief to get out at Campbeltown and talk about them to the man at Lipton's where—it was the only shop open—I got some points★. I don't know who he was, but he knew me and he was a Scot, feeling as a Scot. Then I had lunch at the Royal and read a small book about the wars of religion and came back by bus . . .

★ "Points" ration coupons could be used for a number of different commodities such as tinned food, etc.

Thursday–Saturday 20–22 April 1944

... All Saturday was taken up with the Nursing Association fête; actually the children and I had to do most of the preparations, arrange and make slide show, get flowers and so on. The "ladies of the committee" did the tea. Avrion and Jimmie made two ugly-wugglies, one in my bed, the other very realistically sitting on the lavatory seat. Once this became known, crowds went to see them, including Red Rob who rushed up from the village about 6 o'ck, by which time news of them had got round! The children of the village rushed all over the house in their usual unrestrained way, the ladies of the committee saying oh isn't it awful. The sideshows were a success, and they all enjoyed it. I auctioned the cakes instead of selling them and they went very well after I made a sufficient ass of myself. Two Navy people who had come up stayed on to tea and coffee, as it was very wet. Paul was in rather a state because Christine isn't being sufficiently nice to him. He expects more of her than someone with her lack of experience can produce. He wants this tenderness which an adult woman can produce while thinking about something else all the time. She is probably rather frightened too and perhaps bored with taking the weight and responsibility of him. The funny thing is that his intentions are strictly honourable. Meanwhile he wants me to look after him and Joan wants to talk and I want to see something of my own children and it's all bloody.

They [The Labour Party] rang up from Dundee asking me to stand at the next election. I just couldn't say no at once, it would be such fun, but of course I can't. Only I don't like having to resist temptation. And it's a winnable seat.

Wednesday 3 May 1944

... yesterday evening when Lois was beginning to think about packing we saw a parachute drop. From what Ellen had said I thought there was something up, but I phoned the policeman on chance, was told it was all right. I took my gun just on the off chance, and tried aiming at the parachutists. Obviously one could have killed perhaps two and then been killed oneself. All the village were rushing to the Bay and then one stick after another of parachutes dropped from quite low, opening as they came out, like jap flowers, so that you saw the man blown sideways in the slip stream and then dropping quite quickly, swinging, with their packs below them and spider's lines that they pulled up and down on. There was a nearly full moon and it looked marvellous. Having played at shooting them Lois and I went up and made tea and brought down the big kettle full and bread and marmalade and milk. They were awfully pleased and all came up and I refilled the kettle . . . There was a rather silly officer, but he was worried because one plane hadn't come (not an accident, some sort of muddle) and he hadn't got a map. Finally I lent him mine with slight misgivings. Meanwhile others were having tea in the kitchen. It was a wonderful night but got very cold and I with no stockings and the rheumatism creeping up my legs. However at last they went off and we went in and finished off the rum and gin of which there was a little left. I heard afterwards that the platoon's rum ration was in a haversack that was dropped! An American pilot managed to drop one into the sea and was thoroughly cursed. He had taken them over several times before they dropped and what was such hell was preparing to jump and then it not coming off. Nobody ever seems to get used to the actual jump.

Saturday 6 May 1944
. . . The debate in the evening. I moved for conscription, making a completely insincere speech, full of holes which nobody spotted. I pointed them out myself in summing up. Little Dick read Mr Miller's notes which were, in a queer way, rather scholarly, but quite off the point, and then the debate dithered along into pacifism. There were along about 15 people there, none of them young except Nonna who of course wasn't out. But the ones whom conscription might effect were playing football or just mucking round in the road as it was a fine day. No girls either . . .

Jimmie and Joan Rendel with their small daughter Jane and a new baby were staying with the Mitchisons during May. Lois has left to join the ATS in Glasgow.

. . . Jimmie and Joan and I discussed what hell it was having anaesthetic when young and quality of the nightmares afterwards. And how one still remembers the peculiar sound effects. I said how the furniture used to walk about. Jimmie said how his raised itself half way from the floor and then spun round till he screamed. It was the same quality. And everything one read was nightmarish. And we thought it would be pretty good hell to die in that state as most people do who die under modern conditions in hospitals and nursing homes and so on. And I kept on thinking about Geoff [Naomi's first-born son] who died after seven operations, probably in that state of hell. Only I couldn't speak of it.

Sunday 7 May 1944
I wrote that this morning and then landed up in a state of violent tears. Of course it is not the first time I have thought it. But one mustn't let the past savage one. It's got teeth all right. Sometimes I think I am going completely crackers. I spent all morning writing necessary letters and this diary . . . Jane and the baby with mild gastric flu, Joan worrying. I suppose one can stick all this for another year or so. Last night I tried to get the midnight news, but first got music, then the news in Welsh which seemed so peculiar, I thought it was quite crazy. Then Joan said they had started triple summer time and I completely believed her for a minute.

I talked to Joan a bit about Geoff and about my general state of nightmares and we walked round and picked crab-apple blossom. But most of the day I had to write letters and tidy things up generally. One keeps on turning on the news and it's still air bombing. Joan saying that one would never have thought at New Year that one would have to wait so long and would people afterwards ever know what "Second Front" meant to us emotionally, how much we wanted it. I said I wasn't sure if we wanted it or dreaded it most, but at least it was at the highest emotional pressure from both sides . . .

Saturday 13 May 1944
. . . I was showing Joan some of my diary, sitting in the sunshine in the grass with a blaze of colour from the azaleas and wild hyacinths and the very green grass, and a blaze of sweet smell from the Mexican orange. Jane was jealous, wanted her mother's attention. Joan was kind of half patient but it really is a difficult situation. Jane is too damned intelligent to be put off and realises relationships. Once this time she played on Joan so much that poor Joan broke down and wept. Jane is perfectly o.k. with me because she can't put it across me, but she likes to use her power when possible, just like all the politicians in the world! We read bits of the diary, always with half an ear for the babies. This hellish business of being a woman always with half an ear for babies or husbands or god knows what.

We went on looking at that diary in the evening, Joan and Jimmie reading the times when they'd been here. It was queer re-reading it. I was rather impressed. I felt for the first time that it was worth doing for itself, not just because it was a kind of thing to hold on to, a kind of standard for myself . . .

Sunday 14 May 1944
. . . I said to Joan how I wished something lovely would happen for which I wasn't responsible, for instance for the Son of God to be born and she said yes supposing Lachie came in and said he was in the stables. I suppose this is partly this awful ache about the Second Front, the thing one wants and fears so terribly, that is at the back of one's thought all the time, like a wave, a tidal wave coming in from the horizon blotting out everything. In ten years nobody will know, one won't know oneself, what the word meant emotionally, to all of us . . .

Wednesday 17 May 1944
. . . In the evening, Denny M came over and we had this talk that I had been wanting for long enough . . . now I take it we have arrived at a durable relationship which will last until as he says "I go to Brackley". I can now again look on him, as I think he is, as a good and sincere and sensitive and rather noble person, and, important for me and perhaps increasingly important in the next few years, as a symbol of the common people of Scotland, the ones whom I sometimes don't believe in at all but of whom there are enough to make them worth fighting for—as Jean said: *les purs*. Half way through he said, for the first time since I've known him, could he have a drink to make him speak easier, so we finished the madeira.

As Joan had warned me to be, I presented myself as basically strong and unshatterable, as indeed to some extent I am, and, having established that, allowed myself the luxury of crying on his shoulder. I was oddly happy, though with a gingerly feel at it as though I was not sure what the morrow would bring. . . .

Sunday 28 May 1944
Dick and I spent the morning walking round while he tried to explain the family financial situation to me and I kept on completely unable to understand it because I never feel that money is particularly real, and so much of it seemed to me to be just a question which side of a balance sheet you put a thing. Only I must have been rather irritating. It is difficult all the same, understanding without a pencil and paper . . .

Bella, the cook, has left Carradale House. Margaret Cole was staying.

Tuesday 30 May 1944

. . . Bella turned up in the afternoon looking devilishly ill. Says she has a job in Glasgow with two men and a gas stove. Sounds more appropriate. We gave her forty pounds, being six months' service. She was extremely pleased and excited and said she would love to come back and help anytime. We parted most amicably, though I hope it's my last kiss! . . .

It was really hot; Su is leaving off nappies. I put on a sun-bathing dress, wondering whether anyone as old as I am looks ridiculous in it. We got some green gooseberries and topped and tailed them, with Su helping, putting the gooseberries carefully down and picking them up again. In the evening Margaret and I, feeling pretty gloomy, thought some alcohol would be good for us. The govt madeira has no more kick than a sheep. I rather gather from Margaret that my long history note is probably all too vague and inaccurate. I feel I might do something with it, but not in odd times. It would need a week and reference books and above all no interruptions. As if I should ever get that. I went on to rum, which had rather more alcohol and induced a certain degree of euphoria. But I sometimes wish I had a less strong head.

Monday 5 June 1944

. . . I tidied a lot and went to see the milking, as I have neglected the farm rather. Joan must have proper overalls. I rang up the Land Army people about it, also they have never sent me the new rates. Neil Gunn has sent me his new book which looks lovely, so has Olaf Stapledon, so has Maisky. So I have some reading!

. . . Douglas has been offered a chair at the LSE—Cambridge has been offered and he has been asked to put in for Oxford. He can't complain now of being misunderstood! He won't go to Cambridge on principle, and only to Oxford if all his enemies are removed first. . . . Will perhaps take London.

At breakfast time on 6 June, the BBC announced that the Allied invasion of Europe had begun.

Tuesday 6 June 1944

Got the news from Angus as soon as I went over about 8.30. All the men talking about it, more or less, especially Fred Brownie who was a volunteer in the last war . . . We listened at 1, but no great excitement among the females. Hugh talking gloomily about how many would be killed. Earlier on Angus had said that as soon as the shelling stopped here we would know the thing was on, and there has been none for more than a week.

I went about all day in three layers of consciousness, partly fidgeting about this, and being so remote and out of it . . .

. . . Listened to the King's rather revolting broadcast, felt awfully ashamed of that kind of bilge. Listened to all the rest. Very exciting stuff by the correspondents.

An arrangement to see Denny M has fallen through.

. . . I mind more, of course, when I'm not feeling well enough to work at my book or anything of that sort and when as tonight, my eyes ache so that I don't even want to write letters. I think that the only thing I want, the only thing that would be a rest, would be to shut my eyes and lean on his shoulder. Surely an innocent thing if ever there was one. No doubt one shouldn't grouse when the Second Front is on and all that, but if I'm to be truthful—This is the second year. It hurts that young Dick never comes, though I suppose it is customary among the ignorant for a man to drop any female friends he had before his marriage. But he comes up often enough to the Hall! If he had really cared for politics, I suppose, he would have come. It hurts that Duncan Bàn doesn't come, yet it makes up for it that he is apparently cured or as near as makes no matter. I hardly expect the other Duncan to come, though it would be nice. I would have thought Alec might come but he doesn't. These are about the only ones I can talk to, have intellectual exchange with . . . Of course Denny M is the one I want to see most, with whom I can be completely at ease. And he is hurting me so much . . . To hell with Carradale and the soft speech of the twisting Highlands . . .

. . . Jemima and the baby came by the bus. I was ridiculously pleased to see her. Poor dear, she hasn't read a book for months, and is very worried about her family relationships; Johnnie and Margaret had said they would take on the farm, and the old man wanted to retire. . . . Jemima, who has tried to be generous and who has done all the work and so on, is now getting the thick end of the stick, though her father is nice . . . Jemima wants to go south and live with her husband. . . . The baby talks very well, can't walk, but that's obviously because Jemima can't let her crawl around on the damp stone of the

old kitchen floor. She seems generally intelligent and very friendly . . .
She is exquisitely kept. Poor Jemima made a rush for a bath! She talked
about politics, Scotland, the Second Front . . .

London was now facing a new bombardment. On 12 June, the first VIs
(known variously as pilotless planes and doodlebugs) hit the city. The VIs
were long range flying bombs which came roaring over in daylight, crashing
to earth often after a momentary silence when their fuel ran out. They caused
a considerable amount of damage and distress, particularly along the path to
the city centre, in Kent, Sussex and Croydon. Nearly 6,000 people were
killed and 16,000 injured. Although other areas of Britain were affected
occasionally, Scotland remained safe. The attack ended in August when the
Allied armies in France overran the launching sites at Calais on their way to
Antwerp. In September the V2 attack began. The V2s were deadlier because
they gave no warning of their approach.

Friday 16 June 1944

All day I was worrying a bit about the pilotless planes. One feels one
should be there, somewhere nearer than this anyway. Not that anyone
is very likely to get involved. But it must be beastly having them in the
day. I also keep on wondering how much ordinary people in Norman-
dy *want* to be liberated. I mean, having their farms burnt and cattle
killed and everything. I wish I really knew what they thought, not just
what the papers and radio say. One is kind of conditioned not to
believe anything from correspondents. Or would one be so excited?
No doubt I would want it myself, as it were, but would Duncan? Yes
probably. But would the MacLeans and MacKinnons?

On Midsummer Day, Naomi travelled by plane to Glasgow to meet Denny
M and attend a Scottish Convention meeting. They had to some extent sorted
out their misunderstanding.

Friday–Wednesday 23–28 June 1944

. . . We went to the Convention meeting, late, and I found that, as one
of the ones who hadn't managed to withdraw their names in time, I
was a vice-chairman again. It was very dull and Lady Glen Coats even
worse than usual. I saw Hector MacSporran among the press and
knew we should have at least one frightfully bad report! I think they all
were. Convention growing slowly but they did look a frightful lot of
people. So then Denny M and I went and had tea at the Corn Exchange
and went on chattering, and then we went down to a pub in south

Glasgow kept by one Jo Devlin . . . who is going to stay with Robbie this summer . . . who welcomed me and Denny with literally open arms. We went and looked at the beer engine whose construction I mastered, then I came up out of the cellars into the back of the bar, facing hundreds of surprised male faces including Hector MacSporran . . .

I said to Jo to ask him into the sanctum and swore him in not to tell anyone, for goodness knows what would be said of me, and indeed I was quite shy going in myself to my first Glasgow pub, but it was fairly nice, and Jo tough enough to turn anyone out. Jo who speaks colloquial southern French and has a son who is a medical student, told me a number of things including a very fine story of a man who wanted to get off with me on the boat but I was writing! We each bought a bottle of whisky and a bottle of cider (whisky for thirty shillings) and he gave me six tiny ivory elephants that fit into a red bean. I think he would have given me almost anything. He also filled to us a pint of gin—or very nearly—and we staggered out and on to the Highlanders' Institute where there was piping. Everyone was being turned back but Denny M wanted to go so much that I said firmly I was Mrs Mitchison of Carradale and walked in. We each had hellishly heavy bags, because of the bottles, but no doubt people are used to that!

. . . The next day I spent most of the morning in bed after a bad night, having thought I'd sleep without dope. Nice to find Denny M in the morning, the friendly feeling of being under the same roof. The MacKenzies [Colin and Betty. Colin was a doctor in Campbeltown] treating me like gold, too, both of them. In the afternoon Robert Britten and George Kilgour and I wrastled out the education pamphlet at Convention office. At one point I got so cross on the feminist question, that I pulled Kilgour's hair and swore at them both. Kilgour was sick! But he would have been anyhow. It was very funny. I get so annoyed with these Knoxian Scots. Dorothy came in and we all had tea. She very keen about Common Wealth and much liked Brailsford's book on Germany, had been talking it over with her wounded brother. Then I went on to a meeting at the Cosmo of doctors and trade unionists about the white paper. I decided to be a delegate of Scottish Convention and asked a question which was most inadequately answered. So were many of them, by the speaker, a nice little CP doctor but talking the most frightful nonsense sometimes . . .

Saturday 1 July 1944
. . . I'd not much more than finished cleaning up the dairy when it was
milking time again. Daisy was rather fidgetty, at least when I was
stripping. The new pail with a lid came which keeps the midges out of
the pail on the way back. We are feeding Avril whole milk for a bit to
buck her up. Quite heavy rain and no chance of getting at the hay. I
hope we shall get the turnips done tomorrow or rather Monday. The
potato drills need going through too.

I wonder how many women feel as I do when they're milking, the
teats in the palms of one's hands, over which one has power: one
drains them and they stiffen with the springing of the warm milk
which one shoots out. It may be unusual amongst the prolet dairy-
maids, considering the modesty of the average countryman and the
fact that they are shocked or frightened to have a woman's hand on
that part of them. However I always think it with Daisy who lets her
milk down freely, not so much with Linda, whose teats are smaller
and rougher. Butter making is nice too, though with a less obvious
sexual significance—I think it's all the same, the churning and getting
out the butter milk . . .

Wednesday 19 July 1944
Again the early start and I worked in the meadow, once we had got out
the tractor which started by bogging. I worked on, while Lachie
scythed again and sharpened the spare blades. It was rather tricky as
one didn't want to go along the line of the old drains, and one had to
slope one's cuts accordingly. It is awfully interesting working over a
field one has known intimately over a series of crops, seeing one's
mistakes of a year and more back—where Rosemary got into a
muddle sowing the grass seed and couldn't remember where she'd
ended, and was cross, so there was a bare patch. Where we should have
got the head rigg smooth and didn't. All a lesson. But it was lovely
working, everything so green and sweet and fresh . . .

Saturday 22 July 1944
. . . There is a simply grand feeling about finishing work. I'm pretty
sure I get the same feeling as any worker. And I was so pleased to have
got on so well and to have the lovely hay in. I talked about it at tea till
everyone laughed. We had all been bothered at lunch to hear that
Wallace had been kicked out as Vice-President of the USA and
horrible Truman chosen instead. I gave a short lecture on it!

Sunday 23 July 1944

Again the lovely feeling of leisure, not that there isn't plenty to do but it isn't quite the same pressure, you can take a bit more time and look round. I did various things in the house, got together the picnic, wrote letters and went on at the education pamphlet. I was still tired though. And practically all my sandals have one of the pair broken. The YCL came and picked fruit for themselves. Nan cooked. They [Denny M and Dougie] turned up in the middle of the afternoon, and we walked off up the hill at the back of the house to where there was a wee pad that Denny M knew from old days. But it was overgrown with brambles. We went on up through pine and birch and high bracken, up to our heads and over, and so to the dike. Sometimes Denny M sang, or talked and broke into singing. We went on over the dike into the heather. They kept on talking about serpents, and finally I found a looper caterpillar and pretended to them that it was a baby serpent which they believed for a minute, then when they realised it wasn't —"See it standing up, the soul!" Then we found a hollow out of sight of the village which one sees amazingly from almost everywhere and sat and ate gooseberries and talked, and I read them a chapter, and Dougie told some fairly smutty stories, rather like the kind one gets in the upper forms of girls' schools, but Denny M liked them very much . . . Then Denny M said we would plant three wee trees and they would grow there and be standing long after ourselves were dead and he scratched my initials on a shilling and drove it into a crack in the rock with a stone. It was extraordinarily peaceful to be up there with the two of them, so close in the hollow of fern and heather, a cup of sweetness with the half opened bells of the heather and the moss below. Once we heard a wild goose pass far overhead, and there were small mice and birds and things. We ate our picnic and Denny sang; we were all so close together under the rock that I could feel the sound vibrating directly from him into myself as though I too were singing . . .

Friday 28 July 1944

. . . The two new French turned up, a highbrow called Michel and a lowbrow called Albert. They seem very nice. We bathed rapidly after work and before I made tea. It was cold but rather nice and good for one. I made a risotto and washed and scalded a lot of dishes. The cook lassie can't come for a fortnight as she has an abscess, but Nan says she thinks we'll manage. A bomb fell on the old lead mills and brought down a lot of ceilings at River Court, also smashed window frames and the kitchen blackout, but nobody hurt—the room Murdoch usually has covered with glass, but the shutters held on the bottom room. The French say it is pretty awful, Jack says it is like being shelled . . .

Once again Carradale House was filled with visitors. Jack was staying, and Murdoch had returned on leave before being posted to Italy. Naomi was now being helped on the farm by Joy, a young veterinary student from Glasgow who had come to replace Joan.

Thursday 3 August 1944
I took the day kind of partly off, to be with Murdoch . . . he is going to Italy, which is a good idea, I think, and will no doubt not be exactly front line, but interesting and with interesting possibilities. Otherwise he might get whizzed off to the far east for years. Obviously he ought to do something. He may go on to investigate German factories before they smash them, or get involved in AMGOT.* I talked to him about the future. I just feel I can't go back. I have a mass of things I desperately *want* to do, whereas Dick really hasn't, is tired, but mentally, not physically like I am. We get on one another's nerves just now, at least I suppose I do on his as well as he on mine. I sometimes get so angry I have to go out of the room. He doesn't think my farming worth while, well it probably isn't in most senses, but he does think I ought to be about for his times and conveniences. . . . Probably this is quite unfair but I am writing in fury, and it isn't the first time I've been in the same state today . . .

Tuesday 15 August 1944
Murdoch went off by plane and one feels for an indefinite time. Of course an excellent thing and he must be looking forward to it, but these constant partings pull the heart out of one's breast. One has to be cheerful about it and goodness knows it's not like the far east. But one has to avoid asking too many questions. Every now and then I get a glimpse of what he's been doing.

We took the car into Campbeltown with veg and potatoes. After M left Dick and I had coffee and shortbread at the Hotel and Miss Matty wouldn't let us pay. They are really very nice. We did a few other

---

* Allied Military Government of Occupied Territories.

things but it was the beginning of Campbeltown Fair week and a lot of shops shut . . . We'd had an argument in the morning about myths and countries à propos of Neil Gunn's book. I think a proper classical education at a public school unfits people for certain kinds of receptiveness. They get shocked by some acceptances of what's a bit below the intellectual level of consciousness. Yet however much he and I argue we aren't in fundamental disagreement . . .

Ruth's second baby, Graeme, was born in late August in Glasgow. Lois and Naomi paid a visit to Ruth in hospital. In the meantime, Naomi has heard that the Coles' house in Hendon has been damaged by a doodlebug.

Wednesday–Wednesday 23–30 August 1944
. . . Today I heard from Andrée Scott that Pierre is killed, after great gallantry in the first battles of the landing. He was wounded and then bayoneted to death by the Vichy French. I suppose he had a death wish on him. I suppose he mightn't ever have been a happy or well balanced person in peace time after all that had happened. But I do hate this . . . I kept on thinking how little we really can know about the French, now even I can't really keep contact. And now Pierre gets killed. I remember his back and chest so well when I used to rub him and how I worked to try and get him to feel well and loved . . . It seems hard that the Americans should get all the most exciting part of the fighting, this sweep up into the old country, and it won't mean so much to them as to us. We beat them on the Marne, we beat them on the Aisne, we gave them hell at Neuve Chapelle and here we are again. And all that. They will be insufferable after this war.

I wonder about the Warsaw business, whether the Russkys are doing it on purpose. Goodness knows. I am having a pro-Soviet correspondence in the *Courier* . . .

The news from Europe was encouraging; the Americans were engaged in the west of France and the British under Montgomery were sweeping northwards. Paris was liberated on 25 August. The Russians had launched a massive offensive which brought them close to Poland at the same time as the citizens of Warsaw were rising up against the Germans. The Poles were mercilessly crushed on one of the most dreadful atrocities of the whole war. There was considerable unease felt by observers in England, including Naomi, at the Russian decision not to intervene and stop the massacre.

In Carradale, Naomi was now involved in the work of the local Rent Tribunal.

Thursday 31 August 1944

. . . My letter in the *Courier* and a sniffy bit about the rent tribunal. The paper is getting more and more Tory. I have a lot of papers about the work the Tribunal is to do which I must get into my head somehow. Trying to get wood for another clothes horse before the baby comes. And all this cooking and so on. Though Val takes a lot off me. I have bottled peaches in gin as I think the other isn't going to come off. Then Av wants to talk about philosophy and I find I have forgotten everything. I never read a serious book. I have even stopped wanting to write my own book. I am dropping out of the life of the mind. Meanwhile the news is very exciting but oddly remote. Sometimes a name starts everything. Today the name Le Tot. I wonder who of them are there still, whether the old lady is alive. "On the south side of the house there are green grapes" and all that. And then all the names from the last war. And I find myself arguing with Lachie and Angus for not destroying Germany, which they want to do, because of the atrocities, especially mining wounded men of the 51st Division, which I think made everyone crying mad. This was the Camerons mostly. I try and recall to Angus that it is not right for a socialist to think in a purely nationalist way, that we have our socialist comrades in Germany who must do the remaking, and I even try to persuade him that a Christian must forgive, but he never seems to apply his violent Christianity to this kind of thing!

I keep on wondering, myself, how the ordinary people in Germany are taking all this. One can't imagine that they can go on believing in victory.

I have been sending grapes to various people, including the Coles. It seems as if their house might become habitable, but it is a mess just now, and Humphrey, on whom the ceiling fell, is rather shaken.

Av is just plunging through various philosophy books, is now tackling Broad. He reads them only from a sociological point of view . . . I have had a lot of documents about the rent tribunal, a large packet of PAYE★ stuff and a new agricultural form. One of the lambs has been killed apparently by a dog. An awful pity as they were in such good order and I am sending some away on Tuesday.

★ PAYE (Pay As You Earn) had been introduced in April 1944. It was part of a system which made it compulsory for employers to make tax deductions from pay on a regular basis. Although it ensured that employees were not faced with unexpectedly large tax demands, it increased the accounting and paperwork for employers like Naomi who had several workers on her payroll.

Tuesday 19 September 1944

. . . All the afternoon tidying up etc in preparation for Tom Johnston*
and co. It really is hell getting the drawing room tidy, putting away all
the books, bits of sewing, papers, apples and nuts, half written letters,
Su's toys and bits, various coats and hats and pieces of string and tools
and screws and ink bottles and so on. I arranged a lot of flowers, a great
bowl of roses and a stalk of auratum lily—the only one—and a table of
food, cake and pies from Annie, cups and saucers borrowed from the
Hall as none of our own match. I'd also been helping Val to pack, and
cut her hair—I'd cut Av's already. She had made some nice chocolate
sponges. Finally T.J. appeared with a number of civil servants and a
young highbrow secretary, also our own various fishermen, Ian and
the Provost. I brought them in and poured out . . .

After a bit T.J. came and looked at my Scots history books, signed
my *History of the Working Classes* for me (I wondered if he would
disown it!) and then talked about Scotland, rather inspiringly, I
thought, about people coming back from Canada and America to find
ancestors, about part of our job being to trace them. I said we mustn't
make Scotland into an antique. And he said we would even do that to
buy her future. He talked about various of the great, showing off a bit,
but not badly. Then we went to the Hall. I was afraid there would be
the usual two dozen, but the place was packed. I was awfully pleased.
Dick had been wandering round all day thinking what to say, and got
it very well—Robert was in the chair. Dick talked about T.J.'s
socialist past (I wasn't sure how much he really liked it, but maybe he
did). T.J. had said very audibly to his secretary when he saw the crowd
"Will my Campbeltown speech do?" He made it very well, all the
same, rather eloquently sometimes, talking about Scotland and education and housing and security. I thought he would be nice to work
for. Then we got well on to the harbour. Men from Campbeltown and
Tarbert supported us, very well . . .

* Tom Johnston had been the original editor of the socialist journal *Forward* in
Glasgow and was the author of *History of the Working Classes in Scotland*. In 1939, after
having been a backbench Labour MP for ten years, he was appointed the Regional
Commissioner for Civil Defence in Scotland which gave him responsibility for,
among other things, the evacuation of children. It was as Secretary of State for
Scotland, however, which he became in February 1941, that he made his greatest
contribution to the revitalisation of the Scottish economy. He established a Council of
State and set up a number of committees of enquiry. The most notable achievement of
his term of office was the pushing through in 1943 of a bill to introduce a hydro-
electricity scheme to the north of Scotland.

Altogether it was a good show and T.J. and his entourage were obviously pleased and quite impressed. He had been talking about primary products of Scotland—oatmeal, herring and potatoes—so I chased Dougie over to get him a bunch of grapes to take away. He also promised me to come and lay the foundation stone of the harbour.

Everyone thought Dick was very good. Angus said to me as I went out: The boss was just grand. Donally, going back with Dougie, said: You will be knowing Dick Mitchison better than I do. Tell me in the Lord's name, have you ever known him speak better?

Friday 22 September 1944
Philip had rung up to suggest we should go to the ram show and sale at Lochgilphead with him, as he had some beasts there and I wanted to buy a Leicester. So we started fairly early, and it began to rain. It rained all day in Lochgilphead. I had stupidly not put on a woolly as well as my shirt and skirt under my mac. I had taken my half tidy mac and it seems not to be waterproof at all now, anyway to west coast weather. So most of the day, in spite of borrowing Dick's waistcoat half way, I was wet, cold and aching with rheumatism. Otherwise it was rather fun. Philip got a second for one of his blackface rams, which fetched 30. All the prices for good sheep were high and I had made up my mind not to go past ten for the Leicester, and it went to seventeen. Some of the less good rams only fetched three or four pounds and some of the ram lambs less than if they'd been graded. I never could tell the difference, except that the very good and very bad ones were fairly obvious. What seemed to me silly was that good solid lambs weren't bid for because they had a bit of black in the fleece or alternatively too much white in the face. I doubt if that sort of thing is directly inherited. In fact I don't think it was scientific at all.

The Duke's man was there bidding up on the good lots. There were a fine lot of Tangy sheep and Ballochgair did well too. Jock MacDonald bought Philip's best sheep, and Philip bought a good Tangy one.

I felt very shy, was recognised quite a bit, argued with some dear old farmers about double summer time which I had rashly defended in print in the *Scottish Farmer*. We ate sandwiches and drank coffee. Philip got more and more excited. It was all a very male show and obviously a good deal of bawdy talk being swopped round among the packed spectators and bidders. One or two children and land girls, but mostly these chunky looking farmers and shepherds . . .

Edinburgh.

Monday–Thursday 2–5 October 1944
. . . Archie and Jan very nice though Archie seems a bit worried as usual. Jan working at the Botanical gardens. We discussed the future in various aspects. Jan worried about Warsaw and what it all means, as one can't help being. In the train I read the Communist Party's policy manifesto. It seems rather pinko and Liberal and full of good resolutions and things which I should think almost everyone would agree ought to be done and lots about getting together and so on.

Oh yes, and I began writing some more of "The Knife", all about Tom Johnston's meeting really. I finished it in my bath. I always like the small warm clean bathroom at the flat and the fact that we have late dinner and silver and all that and Mary's excellent cooking! . . .

. . . I had asked Joy to lunch at Rogano—and Denny joined us! Joy was awfully nice, as ever, finding it difficult to keep up her end at the College as the male vet students seem to be like medicals only worse. We had a cheerful and delicious lunch and afterwards Joy and I finished some shopping. Denny M had said he would meet me later but of course disappeared, as he found someone and "had a yarn" with them. So I rather gloomily—and after leaving my diary in a phone box and then re-finding it—slumped into the Convention offices and found Jean and John [MacCormick] about to go to a Liberal Party rally, Jean looking very tidy with a hat and gloves and all. They asked me to come and I was rather reluctant because I had neither stockings nor hat, however I went and the Liberals were all over me . . . There were a number of Convention people there, mostly, to my knowledge, Labour or communist—though dis-satisfied ones. We all sat together and ate the good tea the Liberals provided. Dingle Foot made rather a good speech, accusing Labour and Tories of acting hand in glove on various matters and saying with some justice that the Liberals were the only ones with real foresight pre-war, which, remembering my own pacifist Labour past, I saw the point of. But the others were no good and most of the Liberals present were like so many empty boxes. I had quite a talk with Bannerman who is definitely standing for Argyll, and who appeared willing to make some compromises in a left direction if we would support him. Of course I was speaking quite unofficially. I had half meant to go and see the Labour Party people but I have no official position and I don't think I would like them and if the Carradale party don't play I'm not going to help them. If Alastair

[MacNeill Weir] insists on standing I must help him but I do hope he won't. There's no chance of getting out McCallum [MP for Argyll] if he splits the vote and he has far less chance than Bannerman. I also met Montrose but he is almost stone deaf which must be quite a help at Party rallies . . .

Since Bella's departure, Naomi has had difficulties finding help in the house. She solved the problem to some extent by offering a home to single women with babies who in return would help with cooking and housework. Rita arrived on 16 October; Belle was already established and May arrived on 23 October.

Monday 16 October 1944
. . . The new cook, Rita Flynn, turned up in the afternoon, with a terribly thin and old looking baby, only two lbs over its birth weight in seven months. But I think it has just not been properly looked after in the home where it was. She seems very sensible and competent.

Tuesday 17 October 1944
I feel as though Rita were likely to be good value. She asked the right kind of questions and got down to the cooking in the right way.
. . . Ruth is getting more and more doubtful about taking the babies back to London on the 11th; there are various rumours about V2 and so on and if one hasn't got to be there it seems silly to go. Nannie has definitely given notice which isn't much loss, but would make London that much more difficult. I don't really know about going myself. I'd like to go to the Labour Party conference in the beginning of December. It all a little depends on Denny's job. It is being good for her here, and she is getting rested and even managing to read a little, though it isn't easy to tackle anything stiff. I find that myself. I wrote a lot of letters and a thing for the Convention news-sheet, and then I tried to get going on my book but could only nibble a bit at the notes and stick things in and realise that an awful lot wants re-writing . . .

Sunday 22 October 1944
. . . This evening a nursing committee and we had little Nurse Kidd over and I hope were nice to her. Ian of course going on with his rather American ideas about putting the Association on a sound financial basis, which were suitably squashed by Rob and Duncan, who pointed out that this would have to be raised at the annual meeting.

And I told him various things he'd got to do about the car . . . They have decided to have a sale of work at which thank goodness I shan't be present, and a dance at New Year. I gave them coffee and some excellent cakes Rita had made, and Belle came in to say Nannie was having one of her bad turns, so Ru and I rushed out and found her having hysterics in the kitchen and drumming her heels on the floor. She has been much more cheerful the last few days with the prospect of going away, but . . . I thought the Nurse might as well come and be professional, so she did and got her to bed and we gave her brandy again. . . . Ru and I kept on laughing which wasn't very fair, but I don't think she noticed. She has been incredibly silly lately.

Monday 30 October 1944
. . . I am getting awfully tired of this diary. I never seem to write about what is really happening in my mind, and the various jealousies and resentments and fears that seem to get into me and the idiotic worries in the night, and thinking I've paid the tinks too much and wondering if I'm making the hell of a muddle of the farm or if I'm getting enough work out of people or if everyone is really laughing at me and if my various boy friends are really double crossing me. Or for that matter this plain god-awful feeling that one is getting old, that the only pleasures of the flesh left to one are eating and drinking—which I have never taken very seriously, that one regrets all lost opportunities, and oh god being fed-up with Carradale. Often in my dreams I get a horror of age, in the dream I am young and think no, it's all right and then I wake up and age and work and weariness on me. And it becomes of less and less use to consider past achievement when I can't get on with my writing. And one feels the war will go on and on and yet in a way one dreads peace and having to make up one's mind again about courses of action, and the feeling that one will never be able to have a holiday because there will be so much to do for ever to tidy up some of the mess of Europe and yet it will be no good . . .

Wednesday 1 November 1944
. . . My mother sent me some chocolate which reminded me it was my birthday, the first time I have completely forgotten it. Then Anson, the Labour Party organiser, turned up . . . He was rushing round organising, wouldn't hear of any kind of compromise or of trying to get the Tory out by supporting the Liberal. He will run Alastair [MacNeill Weir] and let M'Callum in. He said Liberals were as bad as

Tories which would come all right from a real revolutionary but not from a bloody sod of a party cog wheel like Anson. He wouldn't have any truck with Common Wealth, said the CP were purely emotional, that they had dwindled since D day etc. Had no use for Scottish self-government, himself a bloody geordie from Tyneside. Why the hell they put an Englishman into the Scottish office! I fetched in Hugh and Angus, later Alec. None of them were enthusiastic, especially with him saying that old Huie was in the chair for his Campbeltown meeting. He seems very proud of the fact that a Labour candidate is standing against Cripps in Bristol. I told him at one moment that he was talking the most utter balls, and I don't think he liked me, but no doubt wants my money. Asked if Dick would think of a Scottish seat. I said yes and added that he believed in self government, to which Anson said cheerfully that they would knock that nonsense out of him. If it wasn't for Dick I would leave the bloody party, but if he does want to stand I obviously mustn't get in his way, but really Anson is frightful. He tried to persuade them to re-start the Carradale branch. Nobody very enthusiastic. But if Alastair is standing I suppose we must back him. I think he's rather the limit not to have written to any of us . . .

Monday 6 November 1944
. . . We had an awful argument in the evening about "punishing war criminals". What I mind is the attitude of the CP, being so smug about showing everyone that Nazi-ism doesn't pay. They won't achieve that end unless the people to whom this salutary thing is to be shown, agree that the procedure is reasonable. Otherwise it's just revenge. And I can't help thinking of Hang the Kaiser. Revenge may be necessary but I don't like talking about trials and crime, as though this were anything like criminal law. I only hope it will happen soon enough to get counted as one more bloody awful bit of the war, not as anything "legal".

I have persuaded Belle to have her baby vaccinated—told her she was selfish not to, and lazy, both things being probably true. Also dissuaded May from getting a pram on hire purchase.

Wrote more post cards to some of the French, trying to establish contacts—old friends, I mean . . .

Naomi was part of a Scottish Convention deputation to Tom Johnston on 10 November.

Friday 10 November 1944
The deputation met at the Scot Con offices and talked over what it was to do. Gallacher of the Co-op knew the ropes and introduced us. T.J. very friendly and anxious to talk off the record, but won't do anything political during the coalition. Emphasised all the economic things he had done, and the machinery for progress which he had produced, the Grand Council etc. The difficulty is it may all be swept away by his successor and he doesn't seem to want to stand again which is an awful pity.

He told us a good deal about himself and I found it fascinating though it wasn't really what we wanted . . .

The trip which Naomi had planned south had to be postponed when Ruth suddenly became ill with a cold. Lois was on leave from the ATS. Naomi was eventually able to leave Carradale and, together with Lois, travel to Lynmouth to see Val at Badminton School. They met Margaret Miles, the history teacher who later became one of Naomi's closest friends.

Saturday–Sunday 18–19 November 1944
It was quite fun on Saturday, apart from the awful weather, running round Lynton and Lynmouth, shopping—I got a baby's bottle for Ruth to replace the one I cracked and went to the nice book shop and got some children's books for the tree etc, also lots of apples at various places, buns and so on. Val and later Watto were up most of the time. We went down after supper and had coffee with Miss Baker . . .

A wild gale in the night rattling the windows so I slept badly and have been tired all day. Val and Watto turned up, later Seed and another girl. We played snooker very badly, ping pong and adjectives and adverbs.

There is something rather sinister about this hotel with the howling wind and old ladies and plush sofas and lavatories out of order. I seem to get nightmares. My foot still aches a lot where Jo trod on it and altogether I feel miserable. Lois thinks of spending a night with Lou, wonders if Dick will mind if she only has a night in London; I say go and stay with Lou. It used to be such fun staying with other girls of one's own age and one never gets that again. Margaret Miles came over in the evening and we all drank rum and peppermint, a filthy drink I thought, but nice talking to Miles, who is going to Bristol to do teacher training under the MacNair scheme.* She'll be good.

* The MacNair Report was responsible for establishing a national programme of postwar teacher training.

Monday 20 November 1944
Left after paying a rather extortionate bill—especially for the meal taken by Val and Watto, five shillings for almost uneatable dinner, two shillings for tea mostly provided by us, etc. The bus to Barnstaple, the small train, Rudi at the station. We went in and had a drink of cider at the pub and drove back through the rain making silly jokes. When I got to the house and stepped over the threshold of the room I suddenly burst out crying because it was like coming home. Then we had dinner with Leslie, and sat talking away about ourselves and our friends and books and politics and farming and then we put the cows in the lovely shippon, and we put the bull in. It was so nice carrying hay and bruised oats, I was hardly envious of the great barns and all the stirks and the Christmas geese, only pleased they were doing well. And we went on talking and I had a lovely bath, and there was a fire in my room and we had tea in the kitchen with Edith and the children and it was chicken for tea, and Rudi went off to rehearse Macbeth and I am sitting by the fire, feeling happy and released, not even worried that it is only for twenty-four hours, feeling out of time, released, and my headache gone, and I think in a minute or two I will be writing my book again. I suppose Rudi and I love one another without either of us wanting anything from the other—anything other than trust and amity and kindness. And the whole house seems full of that.

Tuesday–Friday 21–24 November 1944
... The next three days in London which I find rather nerve-racking, much more so than if it was a place one was actually working in. I was more or less frightened almost all the time, except perhaps immediately after a bang when one felt at least that one hadn't been hit. There was one lot of horrible sirens at night ... I saw various people, Rosemary, as ever very tired and rather depressed, Jack and Helen in good form and absorbent of alcohol, awfully nice but like St Bernard puppies ...

I also interviewed Shepherd at the Labour Party about the Party's attitude towards Scotland, couldn't get a straight answer out of him at all; he is obviously worried by Tom Johnston's non-party methods and doesn't know what to do, can't understand that administration and legislation are two different things. And anyhow what the hell does parliament matter now. It was funny when the girl clerk asked my name and I told her and she and the other one caught one another's eyes and grinned as if to say now the fur will fly. And indeed it did ...

A bomb in Smith Square, a pity it got the wrong corner. An awful lot of bomb damage really and in new places.

Monday–Tuesday 27–28 November 1944
. . . I wrote a poem about being frightened and felt better, more objectified. I think it was partly wandering round those dark wet Bloomsbury streets and the ruins by UCL and the fact that Jack and Helen are both really frightened, Helen saying how earlier it has been periodicity that got her—would she ever wash her hair again . . . and so on. I wonder how many people are scared like that.

I drafted a letter for Scot Con to send to the Lab Party. I think I have only three or four chapters more of my book to do but a lot of work on notes.

Shopping has been rather disconcerting; there looks as if there was lots of stuff but there isn't really. Lovely hankies and things but one's points don't last. My mother seemed so short that I gave her two coupons. She can't after all exist without stockings as I can, and her usual shoes have elastic and are no longer to be had, and I think she is being very brave about it all.

London much less crowded than in Feb, quite few Americans. I notice that hairdos are simpler, more like mine sometimes—I shall tell the Carradale girls so! For the first time for ages I am in fashion with a hanky over my head, and very used to it as I often wore one in the old days when it wasn't fashionable. I got a grey-blue Liberty one, as I don't think the printed ones are my line. It's quite odd getting a thing for oneself. I went to get Val a frock. Some lovely ones at Harrods. But at a price!

Thursday 30 November 1944
. . . Then dined with Margaret Lloyd at the White Tower, joined by a Canadian who had been with Tito and was passionately keen about him and the whole Jugoslav set-up. Could talk of nothing else, speaking of the brotherhood and equality and all that, much as people did of the USSR in the first days. I suppose it's much the same. How to keep that feeling? A lot of people I knew were there and it was fun speaking with them, Joad, the Pritts, Rose Macaulay, Cecil Day Lewis. But I had to go off to Euston where the train didn't get in till nearly ten, and everyone waiting on the platform got very nervous. As usual and in spite of immense comfort I didn't sleep though got less

stiff than on a seat. I wish one could sleep the length of the train as in Pullmans.

On her return to Carradale, Naomi was summoned to a Rent Restriction Tribunal meeting at Lochgilphead.

Friday—Saturday 1–2 December 1944
. . . The Campbeltown chap a darling old socialist, used to come here in the Clarion Scout days. Two women, three men, besides me. The Clerk came over from Glasgow to be questioned by us all. The men took up legal and financial points, the women practical ones. The chairman was a very nice, sensible big farmer. Said he was feeding potatoes to his stock (this à propos of the Islay farmer who was fined for refusing to grow any more potatoes—everyone's sympathy with him, he was a good farmer) but they hadn't enough calcium. We all had dinner together, very pleasantly, and taking our responsibilities seriously, though no relevant cases so far. Dunoon and Inverary haven't come in. It is really very interesting, an act administered almost entirely by lay men and women with advice from civil servants.

Ruth and Denny dithering rather about whether to go back. Have finally decided to, Ruth feeling that if she goes to Oxford, Denny will go there and won't be left alone in London with rockets etc. Probably the risk of taking the children for ten days negligible, though I must say I wish she wouldn't. But I feel I'm an interested party and mustn't put too much pressure, whatever I think.

Su is charming and very tough. Graeme getting very friendly and sweet. I do wish they weren't going. But it is almost impossible for Denny to work here . . .

Naomi accompanied Denny and Ruth and their two small children south on 6 December. Although blackout restrictions had been partially lifted and the Home Guard disbanded, the V2s were a constant reminder that the war was still in progress.

Wednesday 6 December 1944
A rather hellish journey, the govt having taken all the first sleepers, however the children behaved quite tolerably and the boat wasn't too crowded. We started in sleet and hail storms, and certainly none of the other Kintyre farms looked any drier or further ahead than ours. The

Central Hotel staff were awfully nice, which makes me feel very ambivalent about it, as it is a bloody place . . . I was rather sorry for the poor WREN who was the fourth in the carriage. Everyone very nice to us, especially the she porters, who got all goofy about the babies. When we arrived, the cot was missing but we hope to find it. The small travelling cot that Denny made was very nice. Mrs Gill [Ruth's mother] came and the first news was that some great friends of theirs at Croydon had got a direct hit, all killed. Ru feeling rather nervous. We did all the re-registration, etc and I got the children's rations for this week.

Am very upset about this Greek business and think something should be done by the learned world to bring pressure before the debate tomorrow.* Wired Maurice. Rang up Violet Bonham Carter but it was the last day of Mark's embarkation leave. It is too fantastic that Churchill likes Tito because his romantic son likes him, but has the opposite policy towards Greece, presumably because he person- ally likes the king or something. We shall smash up a whole lot with indiscriminate bombing too if we don't look out.

I went to Nancy Pearn to discuss where I was with Constable. Unfortunately my contract says to submit the next two novels, however it's mutual agreement. She seems to think publishing in Scotland is a batty idea but I expected that. On my way a great rushing overhead and everyone looked up, prepared to duck, but there was no bang. I suppose it was just a plane. But for a few minutes afterwards people looked nervous. A lot of talk about the V2 by Selfridge. Lois says she is getting Christmas leave which will be very nice.

Saturday–Thursday 9–14 December 1944
. . . I went to the Labour Party conference which was dullish except for the Debate on Greece which was exciting, and everyone yelling and snarling and shouting like they did in the old days over Cripps. It isn't a clear cut division between soft hearts and hard heads, nor between right and left, because the left is partly ILP in origin and partly

---

* There were protests in the British press when news came through from Greece that after having driven the Germans out of Greece, British troops had been instructed to suppress the communist dominated Greek resistance movement (ELAS). At a heated debate in the House of Commons on 7 and 8 December, MPs voted to support the British government in this action. Churchill went out to Greece on Christmas Day 1944 and imposed a provisional government on the Greeks. It was part of an agreement worked out between Stalin and Churchill the previous Autumn on the political control of eastern Europe.

half CP and that means differences now. One gets a curious impression of cruelty and ignorance from the general thing, though no doubt any gathering of politicians in bulk would be the same. I saw Edith Summerskill, just on to the Executive to her great surprise, saying she had met James Walker in the House who had said to her "You keep off, we can manage our own women". I don't suppose he really did, but probably something of the sort. Laski was an irritating chairman, making wise-cracks and being sarcastic like a bad schoolmaster. Nye Bevan was far the most popular man there: obviously his parliamentary attacks on Churchill have been generally approved. He got far the best reception—and also got on to the Executive. Jennie [Lee] is back in the Party; she is worried about him, still looks pretty but is dyeing her hair rather obviously; she is a bogus lass, but I like her. And I'm awfully sorry for her. I saw a mass of old friends, especially King's Norton, and had tea with Harold Nash and talked of old times . . .

There wasn't the same split between DLPs and TUs as before, at least I don't think so, but considerable general impatience. It is a bit awkward for them that a Liberal, Beveridge, has said all the things and made all the detailed plans, that they haven't had the sense for. Nor does it help to say Beveridge is a traitor because he isn't Labour!

Dick said Beveridge was very good at the Oxford conference, which must have been fun. I didn't see any of the French, which I would have liked to do.

The Mitchisons have decided to sell River Court and have found a buyer. Dick intended to find himself a small flat as an alternative. Jack has offered Av a job as a lab assistant when he finishes school.

. . . This chap who wants the house is an architect himself, and suggested first that we should take a flat above his office off Eaton Square. It is very modern and full of plumbing and heating and rather nice, but not much cupboard space. He then suggested a small house he had modernised. He sent down various electricians and plumbers to look at River Court and is very enthusiastic. Dick asked ten thousand which seemed a fair price; we paid eight thousand and spent another couple on it, and it is a bit bashed. But I think the man would have gone to twelve . . . Still it is probably sound not to ask too much, as well as being honest. The Gibsons were rather worried but I said we wouldn't let them be turned out with nowhere to go. She was very nice, washed my things etc. The hospital aren't doing much for her leg.

Av and his friends went to the conference, also to the House of Commons and other places, and I met Zita [Crossman] at the conference. . . . I get regular letters from Murdoch which is very nice. Denny very worried about jobs, but finally thinks he is getting one as pathologist at Watford. He thought it would mean a house, and so it does but it is a tiny house and there is already an old lady in two rooms of it. However if she likes Su she may help to look after her, and if she doesn't she may move.

Carradale.

Tuesday 19 December 1944

. . . The news none too good; but one doesn't really know what's happening. And nothing at all from China which one would like to know about. Damned little from Greece. No result from my appeal for Yugoslavian relief in the *Courier*! I thought at least I'd get a few odd reels of cotton. But people here haven't much imagination. Of course it was much more to the point getting Lady Glen Coats to send quite a lot of cotton thread from Coats'. I gather Val's school also sent a lot of stuff for Cretan relief and Av has sent some for Yugoslavia.

I think I have finished Christmas presents and any cards I meant to send.

. . . Lois turned up late and cold and hungry but in very good spirits. She and Av went at it solidly; they get on extremely well now. They talked a lot about exams, swapping experiences. Also went on eating things almost indefinitely! . . .

Thursday 21 December 1944

. . . I am a good deal worried about Dick and the Labour Party and all; he wouldn't go to the conference. People asked me where he was and I kept saying he was in court or he would be along. Harold Nash talked a lot about him, saying he had wanted him to come back to K.N. [King's Norton] as candidate but he had seemed so depressed and it was no good having anyone in that mood. I see just how it is; I said to Harold it was the effect of Yorkshire doing the dirty on him. But it's no good always thinking of that. He wants to get into Parliament. I think because he would be very good at seeing through things, seeing the details, drafting things and all that, in fact a lawyer's job. I don't think he's good on committees really. But you can't will the end without willing the means, and if he wants a seat he must remind them of his existence, Tom would do his best, but he won't make an effort to see Tom. I can't do it for him. And god knows I'm ambitious too; I want to be Minister of Education for Scotland. I don't suppose I ever shall be, but I am taking steps about it. But it's hard if I'm also to put a lot of energy into shoving Dick. It's no use his just sitting and glooming about it, and makes me impatient, and that does no good either. He has never written his Fabian pamphlet on housing which would have been bought up eagerly and would have put his name before everyone. He says he is too busy but he isn't nearly as busy as I am and god knows I'd have done it. . . . I don't know how much this gloom is health; he is taking halibut oil capsules . . . Of course we are both getting old, but at least I have a big body of achievement to look back on . . . That's partly bad luck but partly it's waiting for something better to turn up and it never does unless one makes it, and partly doing a number of other pleasant and complicated things—or merely complicated ones—which people with money tend to do. This isn't quite fair because of course I have profited by his money to write instead of looking after house and children all the time, but I believe I would have done nearly as much on much less money, and just as well. I feel very guilty about it all and don't know what to do. If he could resign himself to less ambitions, to just being the right sort of person instead of being a *thing*—an MP—it might be better. But probably he needs a certain amount of success to function and he has a high standard of success. And it's hard to be married to a tough like me, I suppose.

Sunday—Christmas Eve 1944
An awful lot to do. We finished the swags and put them up and decorated the tree which we had brought in; and Av got a small silver fir for the musical box with lovely half shed cones. We packed the stockings with the usual giggles . . . We also went and looked in a pool for creatures, didn't find much, only a lot of mussels which we had for tea. There seemed to be a lot of catering and washing up and tidying all the time. Duncan M and Mary came in after dinner for coffee and we talked about education mostly. The tree looks lovely and everything is ready for the party. Annie has given me a cake. A thing fell on my toe while I was putting up branches. And I am very tired. The swags look lovely with a dozen different kinds of green in them, pine and spruce

and silver, juniper and cypress and golden cypress, macrocarpa, cedars of all kinds, ivy and the golden green or berried shrubs from the wild garden. The maquis. One keeps on hoping ELAS will win. I suppose it was like that in the Boer War. And yet it is all delaying the end of the thing.

Thursday 28 December 1944
. . . In the evening I went over to Dippen for a meeting of the branch of the NFU. A lovely moonlit night, so bright I could see all the colours in my kilt, and I passed Sally's Walk without a tremor. There was Tommy, Charlie MacKinlay, Johnnie MacKinnon, Duncan and me. Macheath wasn't there, nor either of the MacLeans nor Harry, and the Baker doesn't belong. We appointed office bearers, discussed all sorts of things, felt we couldn't very well start a Young Farmers' Club, or anything educational, till there was better transport, discussed the proposal for the Milk Marketing Board to take over retail milk trade, etc. Nobody behaved like a typical farmer, everyone talked about the common good, the health of the nation's children, clean milk, and the consumer being represented. Then we talked about why rushes, which don't have flying seeds, appear on a field so suddenly, about the golden eagle, about buzzards, and about deer—Charlie said it was only some of the deer which went for potatoes and all the ones his way were "good" deer . . .

Sunday 31 December 1944
I felt exceedingly depressed and rather tired all day. Though it was a lovely day. We went and talked to Philip the ram, and looked at the cattle. I then tried to make sense out of my farm accounts, and to value the stock etc for income tax which I always find so difficult. Dick talking about the prospect of standing for the County Council against this frightful man P. J. Campbell who does nothing but booze around but whom people will no doubt vote for. He is very depressed at not having a parliamentary seat and at having had this quarrel with Brighouse, though I think it would have come sooner or later. Nor is the war news, cheerfully though it is put, so very cheerful, really. However let's hope the Greek thing is settled for the moment. One sees what Churchill really wants.

Av is very upset because he is reading *Rats, Lice and History* and the author isn't a Marxist, whereas Av had got it into his head that all good scientists must be; and he likes having things in order . . .

... Val and I cooked, and in the evening we played categories and crossword fives and unravelling and pictures and titles, and just before twelve Denny M and Lilla, and Betty and Colin, and Willie, turned up. We drank to the New Year, mostly in lemonade, and all kissed one another except Av; Denny M had a bad cold still! Then some of the young turned up, Colin first-footing as he is dark. They sat about awkwardly and various people sang songs, but Denny's cold was too bad. Then the young went off to dance. I told them where the modern records were. I had carefully arranged all the other dance ones in their box after yesterday when they were all scattered about the place. But even when I came in an hour later they were all over, and next morning everything was out including most of the numbered pages of the box. I can't get new records and it's rather maddening to have all the old ones messed up. They could so easily have put them back. They also tore off the written index!

... There is a kind of saturnalia about it which is probably healthy, the fact that one comes to the Big House and plays hell with the furniture and gets waited on and so on; and equally there is a breaking of class and other barriers under the influence of alcohol. Some of the lads were really quite sober, especially Roy, who brought a bottle of lemonade as a New Year present. He is very much improved, will be a nice lad.

Rita went to bed early, being shy; I think though she will be in the good graces of the Carradale women for it.

A lot of people asked for news of Murdoch.

<h1 align="center">1945</h1>

MANY PEOPLE HAD hoped the war would be over by Christmas 1944 but it was to drag on until May 1945. The Red Army had begun a major offensive against the Germans on 12 January and reached the Oder, less than 40 miles from Berlin, on 3 February. From the West, the Allies battled forward despite appalling weather conditions until, by 13 March, they had taken over the whole of the west bank of the Rhine. Meanwhile Stalin, Churchill and Roosevelt met at Yalta to discuss the postwar settlement including the peace terms to be settled on a defeated Germany, the establishment of the United Nations Organisation and the entry of Russia into the war against Japan. The heavy bombing of German cities continued; a devastating attack on Dresden took place on the night of 13/14 February. Victory in Europe was finally declared on 8 May.

Naomi did not stop keeping her diary when the war in Europe ended. She covered the immediate postwar months when her husband Dick stood as the Labour Party candidate at Kettering in the General Election of July 1945. Dick was successfully elected. The last diary entry was written on 12 August soon after the news that the Americans had dropped two atomic bombs on the Japanese cities of Hiroshima and Nagasaki.

On New Year's Day, Naomi and Dick called upon their Carradale neighbours and tenants, stopping for New Year's drinks with some of the fishermen at Dougie Campbell's.

Monday 1 January 1945
. . . We discussed various village affairs and particularly Dick standing for the Council. Rob and one or two others said he would never get in, but I think that's partly a general and deepening feeling of gloom. This is partly with New Year itself—the feeling that another year is over and little to show for it, that one is making good resolutions and won't keep them (in fact that one must have an excuse to drown one's sorrow in whisky . . .) and partly, here, that the herring have been scarce all the year, that they may have been killed out by catching too many of the small ones, that already people are less well off than they were a

year ago, and that there were bad times after the last war. I think Scotland is feeling that more acutely than England because of the closing of west coast factories.

Friday 5 January 1945
The coupons from the Ministry of Health didn't come and I wasn't certain if they would, so I took the bus in for the Rent Tribunal. We met at the house, MacClement, Hardie the chairman, MacLeod the clerk, and me. We went over the house, which was quite well furnished. We all started with the intention of protecting the tenant but came away rather disliking the tenant and thinking the whole thing was probably a quarrel. The rent was thirty shillings a week for sitting-room, with bed, small bedroom, use of bathroom and kitchen —really 80 percent of the flat. It faced the sea, gas was halved and no quarrel about that. The furniture was rather horrible but solid and obviously both landlady and tenant liked it. The bathroom was pretty awful but obviously better than many. The landlady cleaned the landing and common stair. There was a child but I don't think he was much nuisance. We were all rather apologetic and tried to be friendly. Ian Stewart was representing the landlady and as we trooped in he teased us about the end of individualism. When the clerk told us the rent was thirty shillings we were rather dismayed; Hardie said "I would have been much happier if it had been three pounds!" We all felt this was our first case and we ought to encourage people to come. The landlady was very respectable, and kept on saying that she had never thought to come to this and she would never be able to hold her head up again. We went to the council chamber and I tried to reassure her and tell her this was merely an amicable way of adjusting things, and we farmers were always having land courts and so on. But I really felt next time we ought to have an official bottle of smelling salts! We sat down, Hardie firmly refusing to take the chairman's high chair; we wanted it to be informal. We asked varous questions, Ian told us about rents in other similar flats, by which it appeared that this was nothing out of the way. Hardie did most of the talking, I prompted him sometimes, MacClement was very deaf and always asking me what had been said. He got his papers muddled, whereas I not only managed to fill them up properly but even to do the requisite bits of mental arithmetic, such as taking 80 per cent of things! After they left we all agreed that it wasn't profiteering and indeed we were doubtful about the whole case and why it had been brought, but there was slight

pressure by MacLeod, the clerk, to bring it down, just so as to encourage people. I also felt a bit that Miss MacConnachie the landlady was one of the Campbeltown respectables and as such to be discouraged. But I didn't care for the tenant either—her husband was an officer or petty officer at Nimrod and didn't appear. They were leaving next week and we felt there was a bit of spite in bringing it up. However we got down to figures. We had rent and rates. We got the price of coal for heating and so on. We took a tenth of our estimated value of the furniture. This was partly the piano which (although nobody played it) put up the price. I didn't think they allowed quite enough for the landlady doing the cleaning and put that up. We allowed thirty-three and a third per cent profit which seems an awful lot but even so it didn't work out at nearly thirty shillings a week. I thought 28/- would be fair but MacClement moved 27/6 and that was generally accepted. We took a long time about it this time but no doubt we'll do it better next time . . .

Wednesday 10 January 1945
. . . I had discovered late last night when doing accounts that I had completely muddled the PAYE cheques. I had simply not got the right wages down to start with and on some of them I had copied figures of overtime. God knows why I had been so stupid except that I hate dealing with money in any form. I didn't tell Dick as I felt I couldn't face that amount of arithmetic and my own bloody silly mess-up. I got on to it with Humphrey after tea. He found even more muddles; it is really rather difficult adding small sums together over and over again. I found that Downie ought to have been paying a small sum and that Angus and Johnnie ought to have been paying more. I wasn't going to let them have to pay what was overdue, so I wrote a letter to the tax people and sent them a cheque from my own bank. I only hope they won't be cross, but I expect hundreds of people are doing the same. Must now tell the men . . .

Friday 19 January 1945
. . . I was writing to some more of the French in the evening when Denny M suddenly turned up; as usual all my annoyance and resentment melted like the snow itself when I saw him. He swears he never thinks with resentment of me, but that's likely enough as he has absolutely no sense of time. A wee chat which he minds on and which is yet a pleasure to him may have taken place yesterday or a year ago

and something is going to happen equally if it is tomorrow or a year hence. Whereas I am clock-bound. He was much better, the flu really gone, little fishing; he had been in the Bay last night and had seen my light . . .

Saturday 20 January 1945
. . . The Russian news very exciting, and they may be in Berlin before the Americans. I am getting increasingly frightened of going to London, which is silly; but, just because I am frightened, I must go. If I don't I shall regret it all my life. Besides one can't just give way to fear.

Sunday 21 January 1945
As it was Sunday I milked three quarters of an hour later, when it was light enough to see. There had been more snow. It was so lovely last night, with the moon, coming back from the cinema. I wrote a mass of letters including one to the *Courier* about housing. They say they aren't going to build any Carradale houses till five years after the war and then only 12! Perhaps I should have passed it to Dick (they haven't published his letter about school meals by the way—why not?) but I thought it was my turn. And it took me five minutes instead of five hours. Snow went on falling on and off but there's not much on the point so the sheep should be all right. I even wrote a bit of my book. Also sent on things for Ruth, etc. At last a letter from Murdoch who has been very busy and cold . . .

All the lies Churchill and the BBC told about ELAS gradually coming out. I keep on wishing I had accepted Dundee. However I don't suppose I'm as good as whoever they'll get . . .

Av seems to be enjoying himself and doing quite interesting work as lab boy. Helping Gip Wells for one thing, my old bottom-pinching friend. No mention of V2s.

Wednesday 24 January 1945
. . . The Scottish Reconstruction Committee★ sent me a paper they have been writing with a rather silly and abusive article by Hugh MacDiarmid which they asked me to answer. I am not going to get involved in controversies with him, so I wrote them a short letter

★ The Scottish Reconstruction Committee had been formed in 1943 by a merger of the London Scots' Self-Government Committee and the Labour Council for Scottish Self-Government. It was predominantly a left Labour body which campaigned for socialism and Home Rule for Scotland.

which I said they could print if they liked, not arguing, just giving a couple of sharp socks to the jaw. The man doesn't even mention Gunn, just his crop of horrible young pseudo-poets who seem to appear like a mildew at the moment. I wish him joy of them, and them of him.

On 26 January, Naomi travelled to London. On her first night back at River Court she received a telegram to say that Ian MacLaren, the Campbeltown plumber and one of her good friends, had died from meningitis. He had been out in very bad weather conditions on an urgent plumbing job and had got very badly chilled. He never recovered from his illness.

Saturday 17 February 1945
Spent the morning with furniture, labelling things for the flat or flats in the Temple, for Carradale and possibles for Sotheby's to look at. Also sifted out some complete junk that had better go ... I shall sell my obscene book of classical stuff to Zwemmer, I think. Don't know what to do with Gert's head of me—I don't want it a bit. We also did up some things for me to take to Carradale this time.

In the course of tidying I went through a certain amount of my old papers, notes, stories etc. A lot I had forgotten. Masses of notes for an enormous book on feminism that I never wrote. God knows what to do with them ...

Back in Scotland Naomi was invited to speak to a group of farmers at Largieside on the west coast of Kintyre.

Wednesday 21 February 1945
... Some fifty young farmers crowded in and all listened with apparent real interest while I talked about America and the USSR. I tried to be fairly objective and not to talk politics, but the questioners, mostly girls, tried to get me to take sides. We discussed how, if at all, a collective or co-operative would start in Kintyre, whether women here would have been as good guerrillas as the Russians, about land nationalisation, the Hydro Board etc. My chairman, a very nice girl, talked, and, after the meeting, one of the girls came and asked again about land nationalisation, said she had to take the side against it in a debate but couldn't think what there was to say ...

On 2 March, Naomi visited Edinburgh, chiefly to continue research for her book. She travelled on to Cloan with Jan Haldane to spend the weekend with her uncle and then returned to Edinburgh for a Scottish Convention meeting on education. She was working with, among others, William Gallacher (the Co-operative member not the Willie Gallacher of the CP) and the much respected scientist and social reformer, Sir John Boyd Orr, whose work on nutrition formed the basis for the wartime food rationing policies.

Friday–Tuesday 2–6 March 1945
It was really nice in Edinburgh and I felt as usual on top of the world and as though I could take on anything and in this spirit went bouncing off to St Andrew's House and interviewed Dunnet of the MOI about this book I want to write about T.J. and government by consent. They were all very friendly and I felt if I could sit down then and there I could have roughed something out. They said T.J. was about to start the Grand Council, gave me a lot of stuff and indeed I did a bit of work on it till I came back . . .

It was incredibly nostalgic going back to Cloan round the lovely flank of the Ochils; I had forgotten how they looked, and yet all the same I knew completely. I hadn't been to Auchterarder station for god knows how long. Jan drove us up and then she and I walked up the garden and a little way along the glen in the lovely light. There are young larches in the old pasture and in the rose garden the yew hedges have grown proper peacocks and thistles.

They opened a bottle of champagne for me which I drank most of, and were all so nice. I sat up late talking to Uncle Willie in Uncle Richard's old room which smells the same with the quotations from Hegel carved on the book shelves, but now there are farm books and accounts all about. The Barnardo children have a lot of the house including all the ghostiest rooms and the drawing room which now looks quite enormous, but it leaves a very nice reasonable size house for the rest of the family. I slept well as I always do away from home.

In the morning we went and saw the Aberdeen-Angus cattle, the old bull with most of his hair rubbed off and rather disgusting and the young bulls with wrinkled faces and bow legs like dachshunds, and beef coming right down the leg, beauties, and the calves and the fat stock in a lovely cattle shed and everything just right in the way of buildings though nothing fancy and I felt rather envious. But mostly I didn't want to come back and start work and responsibility and this awful feeling that I'm doing a job I'm bad at while there is a job I am extra good at waiting to be done. It was a nasty crowded train anyhow with everyone smoking, but up to time . . .

The National Committee of Convention was a bit of a wrangle, as Gallacher of the Co-op wanted us to come down against fee-paying schools and we wouldn't and he was rather shocked, because like most Labour folk he can only see things black and white. He made us a whole speech about it. I was sitting next Orr who was charming—is going to stand for the Scottish Universities—spoke of my father whom he revered. It was all rather tiring and I was regretting Cloan. We went back, discussed what to say at the education meeting and our memoranda to the Sec of State about the Bill, etc.

Thursday 5 April 1945
Dick went in with the car to meet Lois, Rowy etc, at Tarbert but was late, not for the first time, and they had already taken the bus round! I got very worried, it was the kind of day when everything I planned went wrong and I got a bad headache and a fit of acute misery. Stormy weather. Ian Sillars said something about Lois and the ATS to which I replied about the good thing it was for girls to leave home and be on their own a little. After a few remarks of, I suppose, a prickly kind, he said "We men like our women to be a little effeminate". It was in a way a merely comic remark, but annoyed me so much that I said to him that this was only true of remote and ignorant places such as Carradale and that he could no more speak of "we men" than I could of "we women" . . . Obviously he thinks of himself as a dominant male; he dances roughly, even if one is dancing with him in a reel, which spoils a dance completely for me, he hauls everyone round . . .

The Allies from the west and the Russians from the east were converging on Berlin. Articles and photographs revealing the nature and extent of Nazi atrocities were beginning to appear in the British press as the Allies reached the concentration camps. In the Far East, the Russian refusal to renew the non-aggression pact with Japan led swiftly to the Japanese surrender of Rangoon. But the news was not always so welcome: on 12 April, the US President Franklin D. Roosevelt died. He had been popular not only in his own country but also in Britain and his death came as a great blow to many people. His successor, Harry S. Truman, was much more of an unknown quantity.

The news that the Russians had reached Vienna stirred Naomi's memories of Vienna in 1934 when she visited the grave of the socialist leader, Koloman Wallisch, executed during the Dolfuss dictatorship.

. . . The wireless keeps on fading which is annoying just now. It does look as if London would be all right. But what the devil is going to happen in Italy for instance? No more news about the landing. Glad the USSR has broken with Japan. The only cheering thing—really —in the news is that apparently the Finnish elections *were* really free! I wonder if they or we or the Americans will smash Würzburg and Bamberg and Göttingen and all that. One tries to remember where the railway stations are in relation to the rest. Myself, I get pretty excited about Vienna—Wiener Neustadt where I visited a concentration camp in disguise, a red place all right, but are any of them left? Bruck an der Mur, Wallisch's own place but he has taken long enough to be revenged, *es war so schön im roten Wien.*★ But who is left? Will the Karl Marx Hof survive?

Friday 13 April 1945
Angus met me at 8.30 at the workshop saying bad news, I said what is it, he said Roosevelt's dead and told me the details. We talked of the possible implications, he asked what sort of man Truman was, and so on. We then talked about sowing but the weather is bad still and the ground cold and damp, would clog the seeder. I was wondering if this would mean another war and felt deeply depressed. Fred was depressed too, on his way down to work on the ditches. I came back, thought I'd see what everyone said. Rita Grant . . . Isn't it awful. He looked so ill when I saw him last—in the pictures, after Yalta, quite worn out. Rita Flynn . . . Yes, Joan told me he's dead. He must have had too much work. Humphrey . . . God! . . . God, this is frightful. Then after a few noises, a pity it wasn't Dewey last time. I say why, I think it's a kind of fate. Jean Semple . . . Isn't it sad. Such a good man and he never saw the end of his labours. A nice way for him but an awful shock for his people.

Then Margaret Cole . . . This is rather a blow . . . what the bloody hell will happen to the treaties . . . Then, after a little silence and a few remarks between us about Truman and the general situation: They (Americans) won't be able to do anything about it . . . why couldn't it have been Churchill! Me: Quite! Just what I was thinking. I'm not sure, even, why couldn't it have been Stalin! We went on to consider that both Churchill and Stalin were older than Roosevelt, and what a situation it would be if they both died before the peace, leaving Hitler

★ It was so lovely in Red Vienna.

and Mussolini alive. I said it shows God isn't on our side. Margaret said I don't think I can stand for a joke of those dimensions.

Joy . . . made little comment beyond "It's bad, isn't it?" I was working in the kitchen when Rowy came down; I came back to find her and Margaret discussing over coffee, heard Rowy saying Better Truman than Bricker. We discussed whether they would manage to take all power from Wallace, and whether he could have done much even if he had been vice-president, we tried to recall what we could of Truman, and wondered if this might split American politics into a right and left. Discussed how all parties depend a lot on one man except possibly the British Labour movement and still more the Co-operative movement.

I left them all to go up for Eric's tray. He . . . said Oh God . . . That's bad. Who becomes . . . ? Me: Truman. Eric: But he's nobody. Me: And they can't get rid of him till the end of the term.

When I came down they were still talking, saying this would teach the Americans what a bad constitution they have, wondering if it would mean a policy of muddle, in which case the business men would have their way economically. I said I wonder if this will bring any nearer the war in which we shall be exactly half way. And we began to talk about Stalin and who might succeed him, which nobody knows . . .

Saturday 14 April 1945
. . . I couldn't help being delighted about the Motherwell election,* and then about Orr getting in—I had done anything I could for him and it is about the first time any candidate I have been specially interested in has not been beaten. But most Carradale people seemed more interested in the fact that Scotland had taken a slashing at the football. Nor was anyone really interested in Roosevelt, or upset as I have been. Eric heard a record of himself over the BBC after the fall of Vienna. It sounded very odd and unlike him. Edda and Donald were pleased about Orr.

At the meeting Duncan asked about the County Council: Any way

---

* At the Motherwell bye-election Dr Robert McKintyre won the first parliamentary seat for the Scottish National Party. Dr McKintyre had taken over the leadership of the SNP from John MacCormick when the latter left to form the Scottish Convention. The seat was lost again to Labour in the 1945 General Election a few months later. Sir John Boyd Orr was also elected MP for the Scottish Universities in April.

to hurry them on? Ian answered I think the Motherwell Election will help.

Sunday 15 April 1945

. . . In the evening we were listening to Ed Murrow's broadcast [Ed Murrow was an American political commentator] on a concentration camp (the one, I think where Ossietzky was, and no doubt a lot of others one knew) and that made us talk and talk about what was wrong with the German soul, what could be done, and how such catastrophes could be avoided in the future . . . Eric has the great advantage of being a Catholic; in some ways it's far the most intelligent thing to be, they have so much experience of the soul. At one point Margaret asked whether we believed in any form of personal survival after death; Eric did, she and Joy didn't, Humphrey and I were doubtful. The others were practising sword dance in the library.

You feel the whole thing is exceedingly important and none of our rulers paying any attention to it, in fact thinking it is rather bats. When it is far more real than any of their decisions . . .

Monday 23 April 1945

. . . In the late afternoon I dashed back and drove my car-load over to Campbeltown where we duly had our blood transfusion taken. Obviously the organisers were having difficulties as half the people who said they were going to come didn't while others did come who weren't expected. The only unpleasant thing was horrible cups of sweet tea that we were made to have . . .

. . . My fellow blood transfusers talking about the prison camps. That really seems to have got under the skin of even Carradale. I keep on saying that when some of us talked about concentration camps three years before the war the people who talk about them now, wouldn't listen. One just can't quite imagine the quality of the hell it must be in Berlin. I suppose Hitler and Goering will either get themselves killed or commit suicide. I hope they won't be martyrs anyhow!

On April 28 it was announced that Mussolini had been shot; the German armies in Italy surrendered. Adolf Hitler committed suicide on 30 April but it was still several frustrating days before the Germans surrendered at Rheims on 7 May and the war in Europe was officially declared over.

Sunday 29 April 1945
. . . The 1 o'ck news looked very like the end coming. If they are given two days to surrender it may be May Day! And dear old Renner the Chancellor in Austria. I do hope they'll make a good show of it. I'm so glad they're getting food into Holland.

Wednesday 2 May 1945
. . . One feels Hitler's death is just rather pointless now. He should have died some time ago. I wonder how many people comfort themselves with thinking he's frizzling. The Italian news is grand, I wonder if they'll go on over the Brenner. I know this part of Austria where the fighting is, pretty well, the Voralberg pass, the Innthal, all so magic and lovely. I wonder what's happening in Denmark.

Saturday 5 May 1945
Again not V day. Dull and cold. Got through some letters etc. Clem [friend from London] came in the afternoon, oddly unchanged, though I felt I was. However he didn't seem to think so. Also Jemima and baby. I had arranged a party for her in the evening, and with an eye to Val and Lois. But it was very wet, only Denny M, Duncan and Mary, and Edda, turned up. We talked quite a bit as well as danced and Jemima and Lou sang. I've never heard Jemima better.

On 7 May, Naomi and her friend Clem with Val and young Rose Angel travelled to Glasgow where they stayed overnight before the journey to London. Everyone was waiting for the announcement that the war had ended.

Tuesday 8 May 1945
There had been no flags in Motherwell, but a few in Wishaw and two bonfires. Just before it got dark Tinto was beautiful. The children next us had flags and red white and blue ribbon in their hair, and some passengers were making ribbon knots. As we came into London we saw more flags and found it was actually V day from the porter. We had the big school box and would have needed a taxi to Paddington, but I managed to get it off at Euston. There was a lot of live-stock, chicks and so on . . . We left Euston about 7.30 and got to Hammersmith by Underground, most of the bunks had gone already and I wondered where people were sleeping. Still the odd feeling of London being safe! We got there just before nine, Dick having his bath. I

suddenly remembered I hadn't said anything definite to the men about a V day holiday, found a telegram wouldn't be delivered, so rang up. We had breakfast, Mrs G in very good form, saying again it was like heaven with no bombs. The Gibson girls with ribbon in their hair, and other girls coming in to take them off to the west end, all with ribbons.

We spent a couple of hours at the house, discussing what furniture was to go where: the Morgans [new owners of River Court] have already started moving things about and taken down a partition. Then we went off to Piccadilly Circus, where we met Av looking as untidy as ever. I bought a small USSR flag for Val; she was wearing a blue skirt, light blue blouse and red silk scarf and looked beautiful ... I ... wore my croix de Lorraine. She put hers in her hair. We had lunch at the Café [Royal] at 12.45. It wasn't very full or decorated, nor did the people look special in any way. But when we got out there was quite a crowd. The children had wanted to go to the Zoo but Pic Circ seemed better, so we wandered along slowly, looking on. A number of other people were doing the same thing, in fact almost everyone was tired and wanting to look rather than do. They were sitting when possible, lots of them on the steps of St Martin's. Most people were wearing bright coloured clothes, lots of them red white and blue in some form (I was wearing my kilt and a blouse, much too hot, as I found). Most women had lipstick and a kind of put on smile but all but the very young looked very tired when they stopped actually smiling.

Of course there were Americans and young ATS girls making whoopee, and indeed I have seldom seen so many ATS so much drunk on so little! A lot of hats were worn, and occasionally someone had put one on which looked really chic, though most were rather silly; hardly any but the elderly had real hats. The sellers didn't nearly get rid of all their flags and badges and things, but I thought other street sellers were doing a good trade. I bought a comb for Val. There were huge queues for ice cream so we never got any.

Dick wanted to book a place at the Ivy but it was shut; we tried to get ballet tickets but there was none. We walked down to the Temple where a few people were happily resting on the benches in the gardens. It was amazing how the half blitzed trees had sprouted again. In Chambers looked up trains for Oxford; we were walking back and then there was a muddle about whether Ru was coming to dine etc, and we went back to phone and were all rather hot and cross. My feet were aching by this time as I was wearing comparatively tidy shoes. Dick and I went back leaving Av and Val to wander round. They seem to have got into a slight international incident when some people got annoyed with the Americans.

At the house Mr and Mrs Gibson were sitting smiling on the lawn (he is a transport worker). I talked to her about coming to look after Dick when he moves to the Temple, which seems a good thing. She was delighted at the idea, and it would certainly be nice for him as she is so trustworthy and kind and likes all the family. He is very gloomy about leaving River Court, much more than I am.

We started back, after I'd had a bath and changed, about a quarter to six, but trains were few and far between and we were late getting to the Greek restaurant, the White Tower. Jack, Helen, Denny and Val were there and the place crowded. We had a very nice dinner and cider and coffee and talked about the universe, time, Marxist psychology, the Party Line over the Poles (Jack being much less aggressively Party than Denny!), the BBC, etc. Jack very amiable and friendly to Dick about Kettering, where there is quite a chance.

After dinner we walked down through Soho to Pic Circ again. There were a lot more drunks and broken bottles than earlier, and a few people crying or having hysterics or collapsing, and a lot of ambulances. But still most people were looking on; there was a man doing antics on one of the roofs but he didn't fall off. People were sitting all along the pavements, no general dancing. We wandered round, looking for a pub, as Jack was longing for beer. My feet were getting very sore indeed so that I could hardly think of anything else; I was also very tired after my journey. Americans (and perhaps others but one always blames the poor Yanks!) were throwing crackers which weren't altogether popular. Jack and I always jumped. Av had gone back to dine with Ruth; he wasn't really interested. Finally a bit after ten, Jack, Helen and Denny went off to a Northern station and Dick and Val and I queued up at Green Park. She really rather wanted to go back to the crowd, but we weren't sure about when the trains would stop running and there might have been a rough-house; the Americans were being fairly tough, and I wasn't keen on her staying, and she didn't seem to be *that* keen on it by herself. We got out at Hammersmith, which was flood-lit but by these filthy Neon lights that turn everything purple, so that the crowd looked pretty ghastly. There was broadcast music of a kind and we stopped to look on. Then I heard someone say we should have a reel, so I took his arm and said come on. But, as he said, it wasna easy without the music, and most of the music was rather drawly modern dance music. He was a nice drunk Glasgow sergeant and we danced a bit, reel fashion, much to Val's embarrassment I'm afraid, but it was fun and my feet were better after sitting in the train (which wasn't too crowded). Then I joined in one or two "snake dances". They were an elderly, very respectable crowd, no Americans. I said to Val to stay if she liked, but she didn't. A very drunk and rather repulsive lady tried to get off with Dick, who didn't like it, and we walked back towards the Town Hall across country. The Town Hall was flood lit and there was some dancing and a nice bonfire in the open space. Dick and I went into The Doves, hoping to find some neighbours, but Val made a dash, saying it was against the law for her to go to a pub, and finally went back to the Town Hall and says she joined a kind of war dance round the bonfire, and was next to two people who sang There'll always be an *Ireland* very loudly. In The Doves there was nobody we knew. People were singing but (just like everywhere else) with the minimum of tune. I think mostly There'll always be an England and Roll out the Barrel . . . Val came in just before midnight and we went on the roof and looked at the searchlights whirling round and reflected beautifully in the river. Then we listened to the midnight news and went to bed . . .

Naomi left London on 14 May for Edinburgh where she attended one of the reconstruction committees on postwar education. It was one of the many committees of enquiry set up by Tom Johnston before he retired as Secretary of State later that year. As usual Naomi stayed with her Haldane relations. Then back to Carradale.

Monday 14 May 1945
. . . Quite an interesting committee—sixteen people, mostly women but Mr Clyde is chairman. T.J. gave us a talk and we discussed what our remit covered and the overlap with the Juvenile Delinquency committee. I got the hang of the people and who was going to think what. Most people had some special qualifications or represented something except me. We discussed a questionnaire we wanted to send round to a number of institutions. Then I went off and had tea with the Inverness member who turned out to be one of the founders of the Highland Independent Party, after having been 25 years in the Labour Party and finally got so sick of Transport House that she left. Then I came back, talked farming with Uncle Willie who feels himself rather old, and finds in a way that he is already missing the sense of urgency and common purpose of the war and . . . can scarcely face the

added energy that is wanted for post war problems which he realises will be so much more difficult. It was a relief, all the same, to talk to someone who wasn't bitterly anti-German nor screaming for a "hard" peace. He was very tentative with me, obviously feeling that I, as one of the younger generation, must want a "hard" peace. And of course I don't. I think it's all nonsense, and I believe I would think the same if I had, personally, suffered more. I see the *New Statesman* hasn't published my letter. I suppose it wasn't sufficiently orthodox . . .

Wednesday 16 May 1945

. . . One doesn't seem to want to listen to the news now. And god knows, one now fails to see any road at all out of the mess we are in. I feel more and more depressed. However a long and delighted letter from Murdoch whose group has decided to "sever our connection with the 8th Army" and who has been rushing round in his jeep, has been to Venice and Ferrara, and has been liberating hill villages and having parties with all the girls and partisans dancing jigs with loaded sten guns. Has finally fetched up in a German HQ which had just been deserted by its inhabitants and where they get as many hot baths as they want.

Tuesday 22 May 1945

I am thinking of getting a pig or rather two, and hear that the best place to get them is from the Mental Hospital! But oh dear it is going to be awfully difficult to run the farm with this election coming on. I shall have to dash up and down to Kettering. That is, if Dick is successful, and the odds seem to be on. I feel a bit jealous about it too.

Thursday 24 May 1945

. . . Dick is more and more counting on getting Kettering, as Tom [Baxter] seems so certain and has asked him to do a thing for the papers which I went over with him. One has to plan as far ahead as possible but at the same time it's counting your chickens. I'm afraid he will be very disappointed if it doesn't come off. Shall know Saturday. I feel a bit jealous, but shouldn't, as I don't really want to get into Parliament, only to have the fun of the fight. I rang up Robert Britton yesterday about Convention and what we should do about questions for candidates. It really is awful losing T.J. . . .

Saturday 26 May 1945
All of a dither all evening before Dick rang up about Kettering, much the same as when one of the children is in for an exam. Finally he rang up, almost imposs to hear, however he has got it and Tom seems to be doing his stuff. Really the whole thing is Tom. I am now trying to tidy things up here and get everything in order so that I can get away. None of my clothes are suitable for a Labour candidate's wife though, and I suppose I shall have to get some stockings.

After Dick's adoption as the Labour candidate for Kettering, preparations for the election campaign began in earnest. Polling Day was to be 5 July. Naomi spent most of June commuting between Scotland and Northamptonshire. The Kettering constituency was known for its strong co-operative movement and the large Scottish community made up mostly of Clydesiders who had come in to work for Stewart and Lloyd's (steel works) at Corby. There were two other candidates, both ex-servicemen: Conservative John Profumo who had been Kettering's MP since 1940, and Mr Dempsey, an Independent Christian who was also a local County Councillor.

Saturday 2 June 1945
. . . We are staying at an awfully nice hotel at Kettering or just outside with frequent buses, but alas they can't keep us the whole time. Went to the first workers' meeting, met the rather nice agent, must remember to call him Cyril. Also some charming young Communists, full of vigour, one a Skye man. Most of Corby Scots. It gives one the feeling of being a nice town with a lot of civic consciousness, very good library—the party sec a . . . lively girl librarian. Pleasant green country perhaps needing slag. It is all going to be the hell of a job and they won't see why I can't be down here the whole time. I have advertised Mains in the Scotsman, failing finding anyone among our friends and that's going to be a job in itself. Furniture to be moved etc. I wish I had anyone at Carradale to delegate things to.

Monday 4 June 1945
. . . The meeting at Corby was good and Dick did it very well. I would have liked to speak too. But I expect I shall have to do women's meetings and that sort of thing. I don't really know about English education. In fact I don't know much about "women's subjects". And care less. Still, there you are. You've got to fit into what they think you ought to be . . .
    I think its all very uncertain. Lots of people aren't interested. Lots

aren't on the register. And I don't see how they are to be got at. The Christian Socialist will probably get some local Conservatives but more Labour. The sub agent for Kettering is an ancient Co-operator who doesn't believe in canvassing.

They obviously want me back as soon as possible. It is all going to be very difficult. They don't recognise that a wife has any job apart from her husband. Nor does Dick really recognise this farm. And never has recognised that writing is anything but a spare time occupation. I suppose the next generation will be better.

Naomi went to Oxford on 5 June to see her mother and her friends the Pakenhams. Frank was standing again as Labour candidate for Oxford City.

Tuesday 5 June 1945
. . . on to Oxford. The taxi driver I came up with seemed to think the Liberal might be a good thing for Labour. I went round in the evening to see Elizabeth who was being an electoral good wife, encouraging Frank, sitting by at meetings and not being allowed to make speeches except to women . . . and all that. Hard on her, after standing herself.

She has become an anglo-Cath which seems to me to be odd though I quite see the point, once you can swallow the first steps. If you are going to believe in a personal piety you may as well get all the advantages of a creed which has worked out rules for not making bad mistakes in your personal relationships. I think it must be very nice in many ways, especially if you are having a pretty tough life as she is.

Thursday 7 June 1945
. . . Very crowded train to Kettering but went First on my Glasgow ticket, so managed to write letters. Went straight, after changing at the Office, to a Co-op women's do. They were very friendly, politically conscious and some of them young. I didn't know I was to speak till they shoved me on to the platform, nor whether I was to make a Labour speech. I talked in general about Co-operation, was a bit soppy and feminine, then the chairman said I should have appealed for help as they were all Labour. At which I jumped up again and appealed, talked about canvassing etc, getting much more political and definite. Then they presented me with £10/2/6 which they'd collected and I made yet another speech! It was all very cheerful and I got them laughing and then Dick came in and they started singing He's a jolly good f. and I dragged him out into the middle and emptied my pocket, so it was

quite a good act. He made a much more political speech, saying different things, then we had buns etc. Anyhow established ourselves I think . . .

Carradale.

Sunday 17 June 1945
. . . I'm feeling generally a bit worried about the position here and more than a bit about the future. I am feeling increasingly tired and unable to cope with it. I don't look forward to a rather strenuous time immediately after the election, between fruit picking, hay and thinning the horrible turnips. I'm pretty sure none of the men work so well when I'm not there. But I don't yet see what's to be done about it . . .

Wednesday 20 June 1945
. . . Came on to Kettering and walked to the committee rooms. Then went with Dick on a loudspeaker tour of villages, quite fun as it had to be connected up to someone's light. Very friendly hearing but at last loudspeaker buggered by someone treading in it. I sat most of the time on the knee of Ted Wittering the CP busman, a very nice chap . . . We had the old Packard which is going well but lots of odd bits don't work. Ended in Burton Latimer in the British Legion Hall. Met a number of people, including the independent candidate, nice but barmy . . .

Thursday 21 June 1945
. . . I collected stuff for Mass-Obs but most fortunately an observer turned up and took that job over. Took down some stuff dictated, wrote some notes for myself, looked things up, telephoned. When Margaret [Cole] turned up she and I went over a Co-op clothing factory at a smart trot. The director very proud of it and it looked good on light, welfare etc. He was frightfully pleased at the king and queen having been round and showed us photos. The rooms where models displayed looked really very posh. Then gave poor Margaret tea —also Co-op! Then we did a Kettering meeting with a middle class audience. Margaret and me both all right, though I had the awkward business of holding up for the candidate who was twenty minutes late after four meetings, and Dick unfortunately growled and snarled and shouted where he should have talked facts and foreign policy. It was mostly being so rushed.

Then in our hurry he ran over a cat and killed it and we were all rather upset. The people at the house very angry. I thought he'd been going too fast. But we had to go to Corby at 50 mph and even so were an hour late, a packed meeting in a small hall which had already had two hours and was too tired to respond, a lot of men going off on late shifts. Again he shouted too much but it didn't matter here. I spoke for not more than two minutes. Mrs Ross in the chair let it turn into a kind of ceilidh at the end with raffles and things which are rather against the law though normal Co-op social events. I'm afraid she was breaking the election laws, but hope it won't be noticed. Rather worrying all the same and not our fault!

We were then very late and Margaret both tired and hungry. We drove back with the Mayor who is being awfully nice, especially as he might easily have been candidate. Nearly midnight when we got to the hotel but they had kept food for us. Margaret and I tried to explain to Dick about not snarling nor going all out *yet*. He is worrying about the cat. All very tired.

. . . Profumo's village meetings are mostly his own car-loads and flappers who get his autographs. When asked questions he runs away into the car. But he has got the small shop-keepers frightened. We had few questions yesterday except from the British Legion. If doubt if the *Express* is having much influence.

I then went over with Cyril to Northampton, passing Dick's meeting at Broughton and a lovely gypsy caravan listening. It was fun driving the Packard which slides up to 60 at a touch. A lovely road but not well cambered at some corners. We went through Northampton —another Division—and turned along the edge till we came into our own again at a housing estate. We plugged in by a pub, where a large audience were drinking just inside an open window. Common Wealth were there in force, and introduced me. There were also various Communists. Cyril made various contacts and Rainbow Jo and I talked. I'd never done an open-air mike speech before, but there was a thing to rest it on and I talked about controls and the bosses who do run monopolies. Someone said I made a "sturdy" speech. It is rather difficult when you don't get any response but I think people listen. I sold a lot of the Labour programme; there were a few questions but I always find it difficult to get the hang of them . . .

Clement Attlee, leader of the Labour Party, has announced his intention to visit Kettering in support of Dick. Other reinforcements arrived as Polling

Day drew nearer including Naomi's brother Jack, Douglas Cole, Denny M from Carradale and Lois and Av.

Wednesday 27 June 1945

Great excitement about Attlee and the weather! The hotel awfully nice, but all very complicated about putting people up.

Several Labour ladies and I rushed round several villages, mostly Tory strongholds where Profumo is having garden parties and there is a good deal of feudal feeling . . .

. . . We'd had an awful job fixing the mike, as there was a huge crowd in the playground and road, all wanting to hear, but I didn't think it was fixed yet. The hall was packed. So I started with no ideas for a speech at all, by saying I hadn't expected to speak and hadn't even brushed my hair—which was broadcast over the now working mike to Kettering!

I went on to talk about foreign policy as it was the only thing I could think about. Then Dick came and I thought thank goodness that's over, but had a note shoved under my nose saying go on, so I went on and was just developing another theme when I had another note saying stop. Well then, I thought that was that, but only one mike was working so I was fished out into the back playground to talk to a crowd there from a table, which I did and when Clem Attlee came, I fished him up to say a few words to those people, most of whom were there to see him. I went on talking to a few people about foreign policy till they drifted off, and then talked to Mrs Young, wife of the ex-agent and intelligent, but we couldn't hear Clem at all. But at one point an aged supporter rushed up to us saying "He's just answered that point I told you about! It's just as if I'd whispered to him!" He was so happy.

Then at the end I went out to take the Attlees back and found a queue of autograph hunters. They say it has been the same everywhere. I took them back and walked round the garden and fed them. Attlee spoke of America, the Kaiser works etc, and said he thought Beaverbrook, being a son of the manse, thought himself predestined to damnation and was allowing the powers of evil to work through him.

Friday 29 June 1945

We are trying to get the election addresses out—the service ones have gone—and also to publish an Election special. Profumo has a rather dud one. I kept on writing soppy bits for them. Then Jack turned up and I went round with him, first to Corby. Not a big audience but a picked one, a lot of managerial people, councillors etc. His speech was full of stuff but delivered like a mixture of lecture and battering ram. A few questions. Corby was distressed not to see Dick—it is a greedy place, so I offered to stay, and make them a speech, which I did, on foreign policy. Then Denny Mac was made to speak, which he did rather well, but saying in a most bogus way that if only he could have spoken in his own tongue he would have been able to say all he wanted, and ended with a few words of Gaelic—there were obviously a few people in the audience who understood more or less . . .

. . . Jack again spoke well to a bigger meeting at Desborough—the Corby one was outside and of course it rained. I found his stuff very convincing and got frightfully upset in case a Conservative govt were to get in. Then we picked up Dick and came back and fed him and took him to stay the night at the Kirbys' up the road.

Usually we have odd meals at the Greek restaurant who are very friendly and give us rolls etc, and took some photos of Dick. Denny sent me a prescrip for a very strong bromide mixture which practically knocked me out. But wonderful for sleeping. The chemist seemed to find it surprisingly strong . . .

Tuesday 3 July 1945
A small meeting at the Co-op, I spoke and then Lois, to the great pleasure of the old ladies. We think there can probably be no more Tory last minute surprises, but I am feeling bothered about the "Churchill" vote. Thought I would be best employed going round Kettering with a mike, speaking to the women. Lois went off to do Storefield . . . Then she and I (after Jean and I had scuttled into the main street for a bourgeois ice and milk shake, having got fed up with Co-op cups of tea) went off with Mr Spence and the mike in the small van.

We did six meetings, mostly in housing estates, and I hope I got the women roused up a bit.

The mike technique is quite interesting and I think I got it; I spoke about twenty minutes—debunking the Churchill govt, the Laski*

* When Churchill invited Attlee to accompany him to the Potsdam Conference to represent a unified Great Britain, Harold Laski caused a storm of controversy by saying that Attlee should go purely in the role of an observer. Laski, who was Professor of Political Science at the University of London and, at that time, Chairman of the Labour Party, was severely criticised for his position. Attlee did not take his advice.

thing and the savings thing, touched on controls and on construction, spoke of housing. Answered local things such as the rumour that the LP were abolishing pre-training units. Then went round talking to people at garden gates—such lovely little gardens full of roses!—and trying to answer questions, but usually failing as they were about pensions and things and I simply know nothing about poor law, especially in England. Only one place was at all hostile.

Wednesday–Saturday 4–7 July 1945
... I drove Dick round, keeping him to time, which was fairly easy because he had lost his voice rather, and at this stage there weren't any questions, or only such as could be answered Yes or No. Douglas turned up and I took him to the hotel and handed him over to young Angus, who drove him round. I thought Douglas would like him. I gather he spoke very well. The best meeting really was Rothwell, were we hadn't expected it. The Central Hall at Kettering not quite full but pretty solid. No heckling anywhere. Lois spoke at two meetings, I gather shortly but very well ...

I can hardly imagine what a win would be like. My election pattern is of loss. But we never felt this way at King's Norton. I don't know, though, what Dempsey got. Some of his electors wouldn't come with us as they wanted to be picked up personally! We met the Dempseys at Rothwell, an awfully nice girl, his daughter, but on the defensive. Everywhere there was a friendly feeling. At Little Rushton I asked one of the checkers who looked Labour where the committee room was. She explained we had ever such a nice committee room by the station and that she thought everyone had been fetched and we didn't need a car. Then another teller came out with a pot of tea for both and explained that she was the Tory! But all very friendly. The only bad place was Felmarsh where a Tory lady was sitting inside the school next to the village constable taking everyone's name "for the committee room". Dick turned her out, much to the delight of the village constable who made pleased signs to me behind her back.

We kept on running into the film unit, and had various photos taken. In fact it was all fun except that Dick hit his nail on the pump at Cottingham. But it didn't hurt for long. In a lot of places there was co-operation about cars. But in general the Tories had far more. I think they tried to concentrate on Broughton and probably did a good deal there. I think we are 60/40 at Kettering, but I'm not sure. The difficulty is Dempsey may have our 10 per cent. Rather more than that at Corby and Desborough, half and half at Rothwell with a lot for Dempsey. Against us at Burton Latimer and most of the villages, but I think for us in the Northampton outskirts. Unfortunately at least half our servicemen have no votes. Even on polling day women kept on turning up with letters from sons or husbands saying they'd filled in the proxy papers and giving them instructions. They'd had none. The town clerk's office were most helpful but could usually do nothing. At Geddington the oldest inhabitant was heart broken because this time he'd had no vote.

There was a long gap between Polling Day and the announcement of the results on 26 July because of the time it took to bring home the votes of all the servicemen and women still overseas.

The Mitchisons returned to Carradale. During the waiting period, the furniture from River Court was delivered to Carradale. Their London home was finally sold.

Sunday 8 July 1945
Awfully tired. And rather envious of Dick having a real holiday and being looked after. How I would like that. People here are sweet —Dougie and some of the YCL turned up last night—but I would like not to be the STRONG for a few days, just to be looked after. They're at me already for a lot of things. Dougie has got his release from the mill but hasn't found a boat; he wants to get a share in a small boat and try for the clams. A good idea I think. He was rather envious of Denny M going to Corby. Denny M told nobody till afterwards! But he isn't well again. The YCL said they will help with the turnips.

Wednesday 11 July 1945
. . . Then with no warning, the movers came with the Hammersmith stuff—a telegram arrived some time after they did. I wasn't expecting them for a week. I found first that they had taken off the brass hand rail and suddenly remembered that there had been a pink label accidentally tied to it. I wept with frustration and said I was so tired after the election. As soon as they knew I was Labour, the three men became charming, assured me that everything could be put right—they hadn't brought the big bed as the label had come off it, though I thought I had made it all clear to Mrs Gibson!

We got the things in and I was struck with a terrible misery. I didn't want them here. It was an invasion of ghosts. It was like seeing one's roots torn up and withering in the sun. The dining room is full of china and things. Everything wants washing before it is put away, but we can't do that with no water. Later I went through some of the drawers of my desk and turned out masses of stuff with Nan Carrick who is being very nice. But ghosts kept on leaping at me. There were letters from so many people who were once dear but who now have as little part of my life as though they were dead. Walter Greenwood. Thea and Ben. The Melenevskys. We tore and tore at the old letters for I know now that it is no good keeping things. I threw away masses of press cuttings and letters about books and plays. But sometimes come on something I feel I must keep. And all the things from the children . . .

Sunday 15 July 1945
Tired. In the morning picked fruit with the YCL girls who were very nice. It was sunny and we all felt fairly cheerful and talked about the election and Churchill in Glasgow where he seems really to have had rather a bad reception and how someone did some kind of barracking and he suddenly looked an old man. I thought the girls were definitely sorry for him, in spite of their political convictions, as indeed they should be. Though he who takes power shall perish by power. But he must have felt how ungrateful everyone was.

Monday 16 July 1945
. . . I spent most of the afternoon sorting papers again. I had crammed such masses into the various drawers and now I thought I must destroy them and much of my past life with them, for why should they or it be thought worthy of being kept? I chucked out all the press cuttings and most of the letters of praise from people, for if I was to survive it must be on my books as they stand, not for what anyone says or said. But there were runs of correspondence with people, like that American Philip Horowitz that I flirted with in Russia. And stuff about King's Norton and various political things. And any amount of projects and essays and poems and stuff half written and photographs and god knows what. Every now and then I found something I wanted to keep, like the poems about *The Conquered* that some anonymous and charming school child sent me. And then I came on the last letter from my aunt, who obviously knew she was dying when she wrote it, and suddenly I began to howl with general misery and wishing there was someone of an older generation to turn to. I wish

either Aunt Bay [Elizabeth Haldane] or my father had lived rather longer. Though maybe they were better out of the war. But it was so queer tearing up all those bits of one's life. And yet perhaps it's getting free of the wheel. But there were letters from so many of the great and good, and this vigorous intellectual life, and now I'm mucking around here with turnips and fishermen. Oh well.

Dick and Naomi returned to Kettering for the General Election results. The campaign had been filmed from start to finish. Dick was returned with an impressive majority. His victory was repeated throughout the country. Labour had triumphed.

Wednesday–Saturday 25–28 July 1945
. . . when we got to the hotel, Dick was fairly confident, from what had been seen by the locals when emptying out the ballot boxes yesterday. We had breakfast and went in. For the first half hour it looked about even and most people said it would be narrow. But soon we were going ahead. A lot of the service votes had gone to Dempsey, no doubt because he was the man they knew. Quite a lot of votes —several hundreds I think—were invalid because they hadn't been properly stamped. A few were spoiled. Gradually our people got more and more pleased and excited and the others gloomier. I became very sorry for them and tried to be nice to them. Profumo himself was being very decent, and so was his mother . . . Meanwhile the film people were clambering round with cables and lights. I helped them to move chairs. There was a bit of filming but I kept out of the way on the whole because after all it was Dick's film. Our people were glowing with happiness . . . It was raining and the returning officer (who *never* managed to get Dick's name right and was obviously very upset at the turn things had taken) said he would announce it officially at 12.30 . . .
. . . We then heard that Tiffany was in for the next constituency and our own majority of over six thousand made us hopeful of what might be happening all over. But it wasn't till 12 when we listened to the news that we began to realise it. There was a bowl of gladioli in the pub and I stuck two in my hair. We listened with delight at the names of the men who were out, especially Bracken and Amery and Grigg. I was slightly sorry about Harold Nicolson and very about Lady Bonham Carter and Mark and somewhat about Sinclair. Beveridge will do fully as well out of Parliament as in. But there were no Scottish results yet.

Meanwhile a lot of the others were having tea at the Club; Then it was the official declaration in pouring rain (and I had expected a heat wave and only brought a cotton frock!). Dick made a very good speech. Profumo who was very red and unhappy made a good one and made the gesture which was not really very tactful of giving Dick a sheet of House of Commons note paper. It was meant well. I was so sorry for some of his working class supporters who were there. He asked Dick to come over and have some things and cases handed over to him and asked me too. I thought I would go but as it turned out I didn't drive up. I had meant to do a lot of shopping but it was early closing day, and I didn't manage to.

We all had lunch at the Greeks, who are delighted. Then we listened to more results and began to realise that there was a Labour govt in. Almost all the country had gone left, including Paget whose father is a Tory land-owner in one of our villages. I began to remember the scene in my own book of the Labour government getting in and hoped that the succeeding chapters could be averted. I began to feel a weight of responsibility and a depression that was partly reaction, and partly tiredness . . .

Carradale.

Tuesday 31 July 1945

. . . Young Dick turned up in the evening when I was just going to bed—early. He wanted to talk about the election, all he had done and said and everyone else had, how he had spoken at a meeting in Tarbert, and Tom Johnston's old agent, who happened to be there, had been astonished to find socialists from Carradale. How the news had come through in the tea-room where he had left the door open, and how the YCL folk there had kept on saying "Christ!" and the other respectable people having coffee had clicked their tongues in distress. How Alec had come saying he had never dreamt he would live to see this day; he thought he would die still preaching it. I said well I'm afraid this isn't exactly socialism in our time yet. And he agreed that the first five years must be slow going, people must get used to it gradually. He said a lot of the girls here voted Labour, but that most of the Liberals had ratted and voted Tory in the end. Poor Reppke has lost a lot in bets!

We talked about our dance that we are going to have and decorating the Hall, and Dick agrees that we ought to have the St Andrew's Cross and Union Jack with the red flag. I think I'll suggest that Ruth might do prizes. We could have spot dances. I'm glad Dick agrees about collaring the Union Jack and all that. The Campbeltown people wouldn't let Colin MacKenzie have crossed red flag and white ensign (for Alastair) at the Campbeltown meeting. We also discussed the purging of the Campbeltown party and who is to stand for the Council if young Dick doesn't. He says he would like to, which at least means that I needn't.

Wednesday 1 August 1945

. . . Such a nice letter from Uncle Willie about the election and also the general estate position. He is a dear, especially to me. My mother is obviously so full of horror at the result of the election that she is speechless! Duncan [Munro] said he had voted Liberal, as he liked Bannerman, but now he would begin studying politics seriously, as it would be worth while; things might be done now. It was grand that Tom Johnston was a Forestry Commissioner and maybe the contractors wouldn't be let loose on the woods now. I think the Lab govt has quite a chance, as after all this time the people with money *can't* export it. Dick says some people have been speaking of the possibility of his getting the Solicitor Generalship, but I don't think it's likely.

On August 6, the Americans dropped the first atom bomb on the Japanese city of Hiroshima. They dropped a second one on Nagasaki two days later. The Japanese surrendered on 14 August (VJ Day). The reaction among Naomi's friends was relatively muted. Only Murdoch is recorded as having been horrified and repulsed. Joan and Jimmie Rendel who had come to stay at Carradale were 'on the whole happy' and like many other people relieved that the war was completely over.

Carradale House was once again filling up with summer guests. Dick had remained south for the opening of Parliament.

Wednesday 8 August 1945

. . . The Wilsons who are staying at Robbie's turned up in the evening; he is rather a don, with a real fear of communism and horror at the idea of the new bomb being shown to Russia. I said that it was quite hopeless and also wrong to keep any scientific discovery a secret; this was much too big for that. Found the next day that Dale had said much the same thing in *The Times*. I kept on thinking about it all during the day's work.

Friday 10 August 1945

. . . All the time one keeps on thinking of this bomb, and what it may make the future look like. A perpetual menace over everything but may be as salutary as hell fire was in its time. I wonder. The Soviet Union of course should have it. Probably the world is in for a period of communism. It will be unpleasant in some ways but it won't destroy other values nearly as badly as Nazi-ism. I intend that my children shall survive.

. . . We wonder if this really is VJ day or whether the mikado business will hold things up. One hopes they won't go dropping another bomb. We all read all we can in the papers and discuss it fruitlessly.

Sunday 12 August 1945

. . . We listened to the stuff about the atomic bombs and kept on wondering if the war was really over and whether the mikado was a menace, and whether, if he alone stood between his people and peace he shouldn't kill himself. I wonder whether the mikado himself is brought up to the bushido business or whether he is so sacred that it doesn't apply. Discussed censorship and freedom—Denny inevitably believing in censorship for the moment, until the withering away of the state, I as inevitably believing in freedom and being unwilling to commit *le trahison des clercs*. All the new splits in society showing. Can we possibly keep up with our physicists? Or with the interests that take their stuff? I was afraid it would be definitely peace before Monday morning in which case I wouldn't get my gasket! . . .

. . . the girls and I and Joan discussing this business of babies. It really is doing in both Joan and to a lesser extent Ruth. And the same thing has happened to me. I can no longer concentrate myself, feel I ought to be doing something else, at any rate I ought to be in half an hour. One is listening for the telephone or for a child. Even if I want to join in a conversation I feel myself impelled to distract myself, not to give full concentration, to read a book at the same time. I *can't* now think in a pointed way about *anything*. I can rather more easily concentrate when writing. But it is rare to have an hour undistracted. Because of this I know I can never be first class at anything. The mornings are slightly better, but are more occupied by other things. By the evening I am too tired to do anything. I cannot even read a serious book now. Ruth may escape because her job is itself more separate. For Joan and me—there, now I've had ten minutes in the kitchen dealing with a joint that has had the flies on it, one gets the maggots off with vinegar and then it's perfectly all right, but no town person can do it—for Joan and me, our lives are part of our work. The poetic ideas bud all the time, and either live or die. Joan was saying that constantly things and situations were shaping into poems or stories but they never got written down. I'm the same, but at least when I was young I learnt to work fast, to type at a professional rate, to write on scraps of paper *anywhere*, to be fairly ruthless. But not enough. We are both of us full of ideas and images and all the gestalt of writing and it may be pigeon-holed for ever; it may never be dealt with for the future as such things should be. What we might do is lost except in so far as we can pass it on to our children in our chromosomes. The fact that our children are voluntarily begotten makes it all the more difficult. We cannot just say they are something that has happened to us, an act of God or however it should be expressed. We deliberately took on this burden. Yet we didn't know beforehand how crippling it would be. Ruth thought she could combine her work as a doctor with having children. But she may yet be able to. I am more doubtful about Joan. She is almost deliberately sacrificing herself now.

Well, here is the end of the war, and the end of this diary, with some of the same people in the house as were here at the beginning. But all older and tired. I feel far more suspicious of the Carradale people than I did; I know them less capable of either thought or generosity. Yet I am considering standing for the County Council with all the worry and extra work that this will imply. I am more cut off from London yet miss it more. However I have done my job for and with Dick.

I know we are going to have hell trying to work the peace, trying to give people a worth-while-ness in their peace time lives comparable with the worth-while-ness of working together during the war. We shall probably fail. I think we are in for a civilisation based on communism with its new system of classes. It may be unpleasant and its immediate values are not those I care for. However I think if we accept it and work from within in the sphere of values (and bloody well see that we and our children are in the ruling class—technocrats and commissars) the new civilisation will have a pretty good chance. It means taking the long view. That, at near fifty, is hard. The short view is the County Council and all that implies.

This was the last instalment of diary which Naomi wrote for Mass-Observation. She stood successfully as a County Councillor for Argyllshire in December 1945. Her historical novel *The Bull Calves*, on which she had worked for most of the war, was published by Jonathan Cape early in 1947.

ALPHABETICAL LIST OF PEOPLE

Naomi mentions well over 250 people in her diary. I have tried below to list as many of them as I have been able to identify. Some people appear twice because it seemed useful to list them both by their first name and their surname (the surname is in capitals). No attempt has been made to provide up-to-date and comprehensive biographies; in general only information relevant to the diary and the wartime period has been included. People who appear only briefly and/or whose identity is self-evident have also been omitted. Despite Naomi's indispensable help, it was not always easy to disentangle all the names and I apologise in advance for any omissions and inaccuracies.

Alec MACMILLAN: Carradale fisherman, married to Annabella.
ANGEL, Rose: School friend of Lois Mitchison at Badminton.
Angela BLAKENEY BOOTH: Friend from London.
Angus MITCHELL: Carradale estate joiner, married to Annie.
Anna SIMPSON: Teacher evacuated to Carradale from Glasgow in 1939.
Annabella MACMILLAN: Alec's wife who does dressmaking for NM.
Anne COLE: Younger daughter of GDH and Margaret Cole; a medical student.
Annie DOWNIE: Kitchen maid at Carradale House.
Annie MARTINDALE: Wife of Eddie, the underkeeper at Carradale House.
Annie MITCHELL: Angus' wife.
Archie DOWNIE: Estate worker at Carradale.
Archie HALDANE: NM's cousin, son of her Uncle, Sir William Haldane; an historian.
Archie PATERSON: One of the family who owned the Carradale bakery.
Avril: A cow in NM's dairy herd.
Avrion MITCHISON: NM's youngest son.
BAKER, Mr: The minister of the Presbyterian Church of Scotland at Carradale.
Bella: Cook at Carradale House.
Belle: Maid at Carradale House.

Bernice HOLT SMITH: Lodger at the Coles' house in Hendon and research assistant to GDH Cole at the LSE.

Betty GIBSON: Glasgow girl evacuated to Carradale and under NM's care during the war.

Betty MACKENZIE: Nurse and wife of Campbeltown doctor, Colin.

Betty MACKENZIE: Tenant at Mains, the Carradale estate farm house; married to David in the Forces.

BEVERIDGE, Sir William: British economist who drew up the Beveridge Plan, 1942, which formed the basis of the present welfare state.

BLACKWOOD, Mr: Campbeltown United Free Church Minister.

BONHAM CARTER, Mark: Student friend of Murdoch Mitchison.

BOWRA, Maurice: Professor of Classics at Oxford and Warden of Wadham College.

BOYD ORR, Sir John: Professor of Agriculture at Aberdeen University from 1942 and author of *Feeding People in Wartime* which was the basis for the wartime rationing schemes. Elected as Independent MP for the Scottish Universities in 1945.

BRAILSFORD, Noel: Socialist journalist and author; worked with Kingsley Martin, editor of the *New Statesman* during the war.

BUCHANAN, Peter: Willie's brother in the Forces.

BUCHANAN, Willie: Undergardener at Carradale House.

CAMERON, Dr: Carradale doctor.

CAMPBELL, Mr & Mrs: Dougie's parents near Carradale.

CAMPBELL, Chrissie & Dougie: Carradale couple with a daughter, Christina; Dougie (or Doudou) worked at the saw-mill during the war.

CAMPBELL, Peter John: Argyll County Councillor.

Cathy: Small child evacuated from Glasgow in 1939.

Chrissie CAMPBELL: Dougie's wife.

Chrissie PATERSON: Red Robert's wife.

Christina CAMPBELL: Dougie & Chrissie's daughter.

Christine HOPE: A cousin of NM living in Oxford, married to Michael.

Chrystal: Carradale girl.

Clym: The Mitchisons' dog.

COLE, Anne: Younger daughter of GDH & Margaret Cole; a medical student.

COLE, GDH (Douglas): Economist and political writer. In February 1941, he became Chairman of the Nuffield College Reconstruction Survey which looked at planning for postwar Britain. In 1944, he was appointed Chichele Professor of Social and Political Theory at Oxford.

COLE, Humphrey: Youngest child of the Coles and friend of Avrion Mitchison.

COLE, Jane: Elder daughter of the Coles.

COLE, Margaret: Close friend of the Mitchisons; writer and politician, founder of the Society for Socialist Enquiry and Propaganda and Hon. Sec. of the Fabian Society.

Colin GALBRAITH: Young Dick's brother; a Carradale fisherman.

Colin MacKENZIE: Campbeltown doctor, married to Betty.

CRIPPS, Sir Stafford: Ambassador to the USSR 1940–42; Minister of Aircraft Production 1942–5. Friend of the Mitchisons through Labour Party circles.

Cyril FAULKNER: Labour Party agent at Kettering during the election campaign in 1945.

Cyril GILL: Brother of Ruth Gill who married Denny Mitchison.

Dai: Local Carradale fisherman.

Denny MacINTOSH: Carradale fisherman and close friend of NM; married to Lilla. Known as 'Denny M' or 'Denny Mac'.

Denny MITCHISON: NM's eldest son.

Dick GALBRAITH: Carradale fisherman and nephew of Denny M. Known as 'Young Dick'.

Dick MITCHISON: NM's husband; practising Barrister (KC). In 1940 he joined the Beveridge manpower survey and then worked with GDH Cole on the Nuffield Reconstruction Survey. In 1945 he was elected Labour MP for the Kettering Division of Northants which he held until 1964.

Dolly: A Campbeltown police woman, fiancée of Peter MacKinven.

Donald JACKSON: Headmaster at Carradale School.

Dorothy MELVILLE: A young teacher posted to Carradale with children evacuated from Glasgow.

Dougie CAMPBELL: Carradale fisherman, sometimes affectionately known as 'Doudou'. During the war works at the local saw-mill. Married to Chrissie.

Douglas COLE: See Cole, GDH.

Duncan MUNRO: Head Forester at Carradale.

Duncan SEMPLE: Farmer and landowner at Dippen, married to Jean.

DUNDAS, Philip: NM's cousin; farmer and landowner in Kintyre.

Eda MUEGO: Teacher evacuated to Carradale.

Eddie MARTINDALE: Underkeeper at Carradale House; married to Annie.

Edith HALDANE: NM's aunt at Cloan.

Effie FISHER: Carradale girl.

Eglè PRIBRAM: Young Jewish girl, a refugee from Austria, who stays at Carradale House.

Elaine GILL: Sister of Ruth Gill who marries Denny Mitchison.

Elizabeth JERMYN: Student of JBS Haldane and friend of Helen Spurway.

Elizabeth PAKENHAM: Friend of NM in Oxford; married to Frank.

Ellen MacKINVEN: Sister of Lilla and married to Peter.

Eric STRAUSS: Physician and psychotherapist based at St Bartholomew's Hospital in London.

FORSTER, EM: Author and London friend of NM.

Francis HUXLEY: Friend of Avrion Mitchison.

Frank PAKENHAM: See Pakenham, F.

Fred BROWNIE: Carradale farm worker.

GALBRAITHS: Carradale family including Sandy, father of John, Dick, Bob and Colin and brother of Willie, Lilla (MacIntosh), Ellen (MacKinven) and Jennie.

GIBSON, Mrs: Housekeeper at River Court, the Mitchisons' London home.

GIELGUD, Zita & Lewis: Old friends of NM from London. Lewis was the brother of the actor John Gielgud.

Gilbert: Member of the Free French Forces who stayed at Carradale House.

Gilbert 'TOSH (MACKINTOSH): A Carradale fisherman; Denny M's cousin.

GILL family: Mr & Mrs Gill have four children: Ruth who marries Denny Mitchison, Cyril, Elaine and Phyllis. Professor Gill is Ruth's uncle.

Graeme HALDANE: NM's cousin, elder son of Uncle Willie; an electrical engineer working in London with a home at Cloan.

Graeme MITCHISON: Denny & Ruth's son.

GUNN, Neil: Scottish writer; corresponded with NM about writing. Founded the Highland branch of the SNP with his friend John MacCormick.

HALDANE, Archie: NM's cousin in Edinburgh, younger son of her Uncle Willie; an historian.

HALDANE, Edith: NM's aunt at Cloan.

HALDANE, Graeme: NM's cousin, elder son of her Uncle Willie at Cloan and London; an electrical engineer.

HALDANE, JBS (Jack): NM's older brother. Professor of Biometry at London University, 1937–1957, and engaged in work at Rothamsted Experimental Station, Harpenden, during the war. He was also Chairman of the board of the *Daily Worker* and a prominent CP member.

HALDANE, Kathleen (Maya): NM's mother, living in Oxford.

HALDANE, Richard (Viscount Haldane of Cloan): NM's uncle, a statesman, lawyer and philosopher. Originally a prominent Liberal, he led the Labour Opposition in the House of Lords in the '20s. He died in 1928.

HALDANE, Sir William: NM's Uncle Willie; senior lawyer in his family firm, Writer to the Signet and Crown Agent for Scotland. During the war, he farmed at the family homes, Cloan and Foswell.

Hank EARLE: Student friend of Murdoch Mitchison; joined the Navy in 1940 and was killed in action the same year.

HARRISSON, Tom: Founder member of Mass-Observation and an old friend of NM.

Helen SPURWAY: Student of JBS Haldane. Married him in 1945.

HOPE, Christine: Cousin of NM living in Oxford with her children. Married to Michael in the Forces.

Hugh MACGREGOR: Gardener at Carradale House.

HUGHES, Emrys: Editor of the socialist journal *Forward* based in Glasgow. Becomes Labour MP for South Ayrshire in 1946.

Humphrey COLE: Youngest child of the Coles and friend of Avrion Mitchison.

Humphrey PEASE: Colleague of Tom Harrisson at Mass-Observation and an ornithologist.

HUNTER, Dr: Gynaecologist from Glasgow.

HUXLEY, Aldous: English author and childhood friend of NM. Leaves for America before the war.

HUXLEY, Francis: School friend of Avrion Mitchison.

Ian MACLAREN: Local plumber from Campbeltown.

Ian ORCHARDSON: School friend of Val Mitchison at Kilquanity.

Ian STEWART: Food Officer; becomes the new young Fiscal in Campbeltown during the war.

Ina GIBSON: Child evacuated from Glasgow; sister of Betty and Matthew.

Ishbel: Elderly Carradale resident from Uist who still spoke Gaelic.

Jack: See Haldane, JBS.

JACKSON, Donald: Headmaster at Carradale School.

James MACKINVEN: Carradale Billeting Officer; brother of Peter.

James MACMILLAN: Young son of Alec & Annabella and contemporary of Val Mitchison at Carradale school.

JAMESON, Storm: Novelist and London friend of NM.

Jane COLE: Elder daughter of the Coles.

Jane RENDEL: Baby daughter of Jimmie and Joan.

Jan (Janet) SIMPSON SMITH: Friend and later wife of NM's cousin Archie.

Jean: Cook for the evacuee children at Mains.

Jean SEMPLE: Wife of Duncan, Carradale farmer.

Jemima MACLEAN: Carradale girl who trains to be a nurse in Glasgow.

Jessie: Cook at the Mitchisons' London house.

Jennie: Sister of Lilla and Ellen.

JERMYN, Elizabeth: Student of JBS Haldane and friend of Helen Spurway.

Jim MACKINVEN: Carradale youth who dies in the Glasgow blitz; son of Ellen & Peter.

Jimmie RENDEL: Scientific colleague of JBS Haldane and husband of Joan, NM's friend.

Jo: Farm horse at Carradale.

Joan RENDEL: Writer and friend of NM. Married to Jimmie with a baby, Jane.

John RITCHIE: Proprietor of the Carradale Post Office.

Johnnie MACMILLAN: Carradale fisherman.

JOHNSON, Mr: Minister of Lorne Street Church, Campbeltown.

JOHNSTON, Tom: Labour MP for West Stirlingshire before the war; appointed Regional Commissioner for Scotland in 1939. In 1941 he was made Secretary of State for Scotland and was responsible for a number of reforms including the introduction of hydro-electricity to the Highlands.

Joy: A veterinary student on placement at NM's farm at Carradale.

KALMUS, Mr & Mrs: Jewish refugees from Austria. Mr Kalmus is a distinguished biologist working with JBS Haldane.

Kathleen: Carradale girl.

Lachie PATERSON: Carradale man.

Lachie (Lachlan) MACLEAN: Farm worker at Carradale House, originally from North Uist; married to Mary with a small son.

Leslie: Friend of Rudi Messel.

LEHMANN, John: Literary figure and editor of *New Verse*.

Lena: Landgirl who comes to work on the farm at Carradale.

LEWIS, Wyndham: Artist and friend of NM from London; painted several portraits of NM and her children. Emigrated to America before the war.

Lewis GIELGUD: Old friend of NM from London who worked with the Red Cross in Paris during the war.

LEYS, Bob & Nora: Labour Party couple in Campbeltown; Bob was a school teacher and Nora Secretary of the Argyll DLP.

Lilla MACINTOSH: Denny M's wife; runs the Harbour shop in Carradale.

Linda: A cow, one of NM's herd.

LITTLE, Mrs: A social worker who stays at Mains to care for the evacuated children.

Lizzie: Carradale girl.

LLOYD, Margaret: Old friend of NM from London; they met while working at the North Kensington Birth Control Clinic in the 1930s.

Lois MITCHISON: NM's elder daughter.

MACALISTER, Nurse: District Nurse employed in Carradale by the local branch of the District Nursing Association.

McCALLUM, Major: Conservative MP for Argyll.

MacCORMICK, John: Glasgow lawyer and Scottish Nationalist; founder and leader of the Scottish Convention.

MacCRAE, Ian: Carradale forester.

MacDONALD, Mrs: Landowner at Largie Castle.

MacGEACHY, Mr: Manager at Machrihanish Airport.

MacGREGOR, Hugh: Gardener at Carradale House.

MacGREGOR, Margaret: his wife.

MacGREGOR, John: Architect of the new village hall.

MacINTOSH, Denny & Lilla: NM's Carradale friends; Denny M is a fisherman and Lilla runs the Harbour shop.

MacKINVEN, Peter & Ellen: Local Carradale couple.

MacKINVEN, James: Billeting Officer during the reception of children from Glasgow; Peter's brother.

MacKINVEN, Jim: Carradale youth, son of Peter & Ellen.

MacLAREN, Ian: Campbeltown plumber.

MacLEAN, Mr & Mrs: Neighbouring farmers, son Peter and daughter Jemima.

MacKENZIE, Rev. Carradale Free Church minister who lives with his wife and sister at the Manse.

MacKENZIE, Betty & David: CP couple who rent Mains from the Mitchisons. David is in the Forces.

MacKenzie, Colin & Betty: Campbeltown couple. Colin is a local doctor and Betty is a nurse.

MacKillop, Mr: Campbeltown joiner.

MacMillan: Alec & Anna: Carradale couple with a small son, James. Alec is a fisherman.

MacNair, Provost: Provost of Campbeltown.

MacNeill Weir, Alastair: Labour Party activist, originally LP candidate at the 1940 Argyll bye-election but stood down as a result of the party truce.

MacTaggart, Mr: Glasgow acquaintance of NM.

Madge, Charles & Inez: London friends of NM. Charles was co-founder of Mass-Observation with Tom Harrisson.

Maggie Brown: Carradale resident who (with Sarah Blue) did the housework at Carradale House.

Mairi: Carradale girl who married Willie Buchanan.

Maisky, Agnes: Friend of NM in London and wife of Ivan Maisky, the Soviet Ambassador to Britain during the war.

Maisie Black: Landgirl who worked on the Carradale House farm.

Mamie: Carradale girl.

Margaret Cole: See Cole, M.

Margaret Lloyd: See Lloyd, M.

Margery Spring Rice: See Spring Rice, M.

Mark Bonham Carter: Student friend of Murdoch Mitchison.

Mary Galbraith: A teacher and Duncan Munro's fiancée.

Mary MacLean: Lachie's wife.

Matthew (Matty) Gibson: Evacuee child and brother of Betty.

Maurice Bowra: See Bowra, M.

May: Cook/maid at Carradale House 1944–5.

Maya: NM's mother, Kathleen Haldane who lived in Oxford.

Melville, Dorothy: A young teacher posted to Carradale with the Glasgow evacuees.

Melville, Mr & Mrs: Dorothy's parents in Glasgow.

Messel, Rudi: Friend of NM since the King's Norton bye-election in 1934; left wing journalist and writer who financed the publication *Fact* 1937–9. Farmed in Yeoford during the war.

Meyer, Mr & Mrs: Friends of the Mitchisons from Denmark.

Michael Blakeney Booth: Small son of Angela.

Michael: Young doctor who shared River Court with Ruth and Denny Mitchison. Married to Sybil.

Michael Hope: Husband of NM's cousin Christine in Oxford.

Milla Rosenthal: Austrian housekeeper at the Coles' house in Hendon.

Miles, Margaret: Val & Lois' history teacher at Badminton School.

Mitchison, Avrion (Av): NM's youngest son.

Mitchison, Denny: NM's eldest son.

Mitchison, Dick: NM's husband; practising barrister (KC). In 1940 he joined the Beveridge manpower survey and then worked with GDH Cole on the Nuffield Reconstruction Survey. In 1945 he was elected Labour MP for the Kettering Division of Northants which he held until 1964.

MITCHISON, Graeme: Denny & Ruth's son.

MITCHISON, Lois: NM's elder daughter.

MITCHISON, Murdoch: NM's second son.

MITCHISON, Petronella Susan (Su): Denny & Ruth's daughter.

MITCHISON, Valentine (Val): NM's younger daughter.

Molly: Taggie's wife.

Morag: Maid at Carradale House.

MUEGO, Eda: Teacher colleague of Dorothy Melville also evacuated to Carradale.

MUNRO, Duncan: The head forester at Carradale.

Murdoch MITCHISON: NM's second son.

MURE MacKENZIE, Agnes: Scottish historian; author of *Scotland in Modern Times 1720–1939*, published in 1941.

Neil RITCHIE: Carradale fisherman.

Nora LEYS: Secretary of the Argyll DLP; lives in Carradale with her husband, Bob, a teacher.

Nora PATERSON: Carradale resident.

OMAN, Colin: David Oman's son.

OMAN, David (Davie): The Carradale Harbour Master.

PAKENHAM, Frank & Elizabeth (now Lord & Lady Longford): Friends of NM in Oxford; Frank had stood as Labour candidate at the 1938 Oxford bye-election and was Personal Assistant to Sir William Beveridge 1941–4.

PARK, Isobel: Teacher from Glasgow evacuated to Carradale in 1939.

PATERSON, Mrs: Taggie's mother.

Peter BUCHANAN: Willie's brother.

Peter MacKINVEN: Carradale shopkeeper, married to Ellen.

Peter MacLEAN: Carradale farmer from Brackley, brother of Jemima.

Philip: A ram from the Carradale House farm.

Philip DUNDAS: Third or fourth cousin of NM; a farmer living south of Carradale in Kintyre.

Phyllis GILL: Ruth Gill's sister.

PIRIE, NS (Bill) & Antoinette (Tony): Friends of NM; Bill is a research biologist and Tony specialises in ophthalmology. They have a small son, John.

PIRRET, Dr: NM's family doctor and friend in London.

POWER, William: SNP candidate at the 1940 Argyll bye-election and later member of the Scottish Convention.

PRIBRAM, Mrs: Eglè's mother.

RAMSAY, Baillie: Local magistrate and friend of the Mitchisons in Carradale; owns a garage.

Red Robert PATERSON: Carradale fisherman.

RENDEL, Colonel: Father of Jimmie Rendel.

RENDEL, Joan & Jimmie: Friends of NM; Joan is a writer and Jimmie a colleague of JBS Haldane at Rothamsted. They have a baby girl, Jane.

REPPKE, Mr: Campbeltown fish buyer.

Rita FLYNN: Cook at Carradale House.

Rita GRANT: Housemaid at Carradale House.

RITCHIE, John: Proprietor of Carradale Post Office.

ROBERTON, Sir Hugh: Friend of NM in Glasgow; Conductor of the Glasgow Orpheus Choir and well known figure in Scotland.

Robin GANDY: Student friend of Denny Mitchison at Cambridge.

Rose ANGEL: Friend of Lois Mitchison from Badminton; stays at Carradale House together with her sister.

Rosemary JONES: Employed in 1940 at Carradale House as NM's secretary; transfers most of her energies to farm work later in the war.

ROSENTHAL, Milla & Peter: Austrian Jewish refugees who act as the Coles' housekeepers at Hendon during the war.

Rowy (Rosalind) WRONG: Historian and friend of NM; married Murdoch Mitchison in 1947.

Ruth GILL: Medical student and later doctor; married Denny Mitchison in 1940.

Sandy GALBRAITH: Carradale fisherman.

Sarah BLUE: Carradale resident who does the housework at Carradale House.

Scott: Sheepdog at Carradale.

Seed: School friend of Val Mitchison at Badminton.

SEMPLE, Duncan & Jean: Neighbours of NM; farming and landowning couple.

SIMPSON, Anna: Teacher evacuated from Glasgow to Carradale in 1939.

SIMPSON SMITH, Jan: Friend and later wife of Archie Haldane.

SMITH, Stevie: Writer and poet, friend of NM in London.

SPRING RICE, Margery: Writer and reformer; an active worker for women's health services and co-founder of the North Kensington Women's Welfare Clinic.

Stafford CRIPPS: See Cripps, Sir S.

Stephen SPRING RICE: Margery's son.

STEWART, Mr: Procurator Fiscal at Campbeltown. When he died, his position was taken by Ian, his son.

Storm JAMESON: Novelist and friend of NM in London.

STRAUSS, Eric: Distinguished physician and psychotherapist based at St Bartholomew's Hospital in London. Frequent guest at Carradale House.

Stuart: Student friend of Murdoch Mitchison.

Sybil: Young doctor who shares River Court with Denny and Ruth Mitchison; married to Michael.

Taggie PATERSON: Underkeeper at Carradale estate.

Tish ROKELING: Friend of Mitchison's and occasional guest at Carradale House.
Tom HARRISSON: See Harrisson, T.
Tom PATERSON: Carradale man.
Tony BROWN: Friend of Murdoch Mitchison at Cambridge.
Tony PIRIE: See Pirie, NS & A.
Uncle Richard: See Haldane, R.
Uncle Willie: See Haldane, W.
Val MITCHISON: NM's younger daughter.
Watto: Schoolfriend of Mitchison's at Badminton.
WEBB, Fr: Priest at Campbeltown Roman Catholic Church.
Willie BUCHANAN: Undergardener at Carradale House. Married Mairi.
Willie GALBRAITH: Carradale fisherman, brother of Sandy & Lilla.
Willie MACBRIDE: Carradale fisherman.
Wyndham LEWIS: See Lewis, W.

GLOSSARY

Atholl Brose: A mixture of whisky, honey and oatmeal.

Baillie: A municipal officer or local magistrate.

But an' Ben: A two-roomed cottage.

Ceilidh: A neighbourly party with singing and dancing.

Dreich: Slow, tedious, dreary.

Fiscal (Procurator Fiscal): Public prosecutor of a shire or other local district (in Scotland).

Oran Mor: A great song (literally translated from the Gaelic).

Port-a-beul: mouth music, nonsense words to a dance tune.

Provost: A head of a municipal corporation or burgh; equivalent of English mayor.

Sgian-dhu: Dirk or dagger usually worn in the top of the sock.

Winkie: the light dropped by a ring-net fishing boat to show where the net had been shot.

ACRONYMS

ARP	Air Raid Precautions
ATS	Auxiliary Territorial Service
BMA	British Medical Association
CO	Conscientious Objector
CPGB	Communist Party of Great Britain
CWS	Cooperative Wholesale Society
DLP	District Labour Party
HG	Home Guard
ILP	Independent Labour Party
LDV	Local Defence Volunteers
LMS	London Midland and Scottish Railways
LP	Labour Party
MOI	Ministry of Information
NAAFI	Navy, Army and Air Force Institute
NCO	Noncommissioned Officer
NM	Naomi Mitchison
NFU	National Farmers' Union
NS	New Statesman
RAF	Royal Air Force
RAMC	Royal Army Medical Corps
RASC	Royal Army Service Corps
RN	Royal Navy
SNP	Scottish National Party
TT	Tuberculin Tested
UCL	University College London
UCH	University College Hospital
UDC	Urban District Council
WAAF	Women's Auxiliary Air Force
WRNS	Women's Royal Naval Service (a member is called a 'wren')
WVS	Women's Voluntary Service
YCL	Young Communist League
YMCA	Young Women's Christian Association